SUCCESSFUL RESTAURANT MANAGEMENT

From Vision to Execution

Thomson Delmar Learning

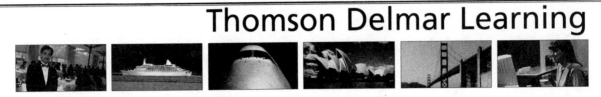

Hospitality, Travel and Tourism

Options.
Thomson Delmar Learning offers comprehensive and up-to-date teaching, learning and professional education resources to help you prepare for professional and support careers in hospitality, travel and tourism.

Careers.
Explore our hospitality, travel and tourism education specializations to find textbooks, laboratory manuals, software and online companions.

Service.
Customer service and satisfaction should be the highest priority for any successful business. If you have questions or comments regarding any of our products, or if you have a product proposal, please contact us at the address below.

Air Fares and Ticketing • Catering and Banquet Services • Conducting Tours Cruising • Customer Service • Dining Room and Banquet Management • E-Commerce and Information Technology • Food and Beverage Cost Control Front Office Operations and Management • Geography for the Travel Professional • Hospitality and Travel Marketing • Hospitality Sales • Hotel, Restaurant, and Travel Law • Hotel Operations • Human Resources Management Ice Sculpting • Internet for the Retail Travel Industry • Introduction to Travel and Tourism • Math Principles • Selling Cruises • Selling Tourism • Training Design

---

Thomson Delmar Learning
5 Maxwell Drive
Clifton Park, New York 12065-2919

For additional information, find us online at:
www.delmarlearning.com or
www.hospitality-tourism.delmar.com

THOMSON
DELMAR LEARNING

SUCCESSFUL RESTAURANT MANAGEMENT

From Vision to Execution

DONALD WADE

THOMSON

DELMAR LEARNING ™

Australia   Canada   Mexico   Singapore   Spain   United Kingdom   United States

THOMSON

DELMAR LEARNING

Successful Restaurant Management: From Vision to Execution
by Donald Wade

Vice President, Career Education Strategic Business Unit:
Dawn Gerrain

Director of Learning Solutions:
Sherry Dickinson

Acquisitions Editor:
Matthew Hart

Managing Editor:
Robert Serenka, Jr.

Assistant to the Director of Learning Solutions:
Anne Orgren

Editorial Assistant:
Patrick B. Horn

Director of Production:
Wendy A. Troeger

Production Editor:
Matthew J. Williams

Technology Project Manager:
Sandy Charette

Director of Marketing:
Wendy E. Mapstone

Channel Manager:
Kristin McNary

Cover Design:
Joe Villanova

Cover Images:
Getty Images, Inc.

For permission to use material from this text or product, contact us by
Tel   (800) 730-2214
Fax   (800) 730-2215
www.thomsonrights.com

Library of Congress Cataloging-in-Publication Data

Wade, Donald.
  Successful restaurant management: from vision to execution/Donald Wade.
       p. cm.
Includes bibliographical references and index.
ISBN 1-4018-1985-0 (alk. paper)
1. Restaurant management. I. Title.
TX911.3.M27.W33 2005
647.95068--dc22

                                        2005031991

NOTICE TO THE READER

■ This book is dedicated to my wife Erin who supported me during the writing of this book and the time that I devote to the restaurant business. ■

■ Special thanks to Monica Mahaffey for all of her hard work and patience during the editing process of the original manuscript. ■

Table of Contents

Preface

The restaurant business can be fun, exciting, and rewarding. It is a business where focusing on the many details is critical to success. The margins are small and can erode quickly if there is not a balance among the following elements:

1. Developing the management and staff—The restaurant business relies on quality individuals to achieve success. The management and staff must work together for customer satisfaction. Some employees are comfortable arriving at their job every day and simply going through the motions to meet the minimum production expectation. This attitude will not work in the restaurant business. Caring and passionate people drive success.

2. Producing sales—Generating top line sales is the first step to success in any business. Increasing the top line sales depends on keeping in touch with the market and the needs of the market then having the ability to act on those needs.

3. Controlling operational costs—No matter what sales volume is generated, controlling costs and producing a profit is the true measure of a successful business.

Balance among these elements means that one is not sacrificed for another. For example, to develop managers and staff, the restaurateur must commit to investing in developing their skills. This investment may drive up labor cost slightly, but it is necessary to ensure futoure growth of the individual and therefore the company.

Understanding how to be proactive to changing customer needs is one factor that separates the successful ventures from the *failed ventures*. It is impossible to understand consumer needs if the consumer is not being personally "engaged."

Plan logically, using time-proven business methods. Be methodical and know the market and market segments. Become educated about the industry and seek professional help when and where needed. There is no reason to "reinvent the wheel."

This is a comprehensive book that includes initial planning, implementation, and operations. It covers menu development and design; site selection; concept development; marketing; employee hiring, training, and development; sales techniques; cost control systems; financial analysis; and tips for success.

This textbook also includes basic, generic forms for compiling a business plan; daily and weekly checklists, administrative responsibilities, operational guidelines, and much more.

Remember that delivering quality food is not the only measure of success in the restaurant business. A restaurant must be inviting, and once the customer walks inside, the restaurant and the people operating it must make a statement as to what the business strives to offer the public. The food quality, atmosphere, music, energy level, service quality, cleanliness, attention to detail, and value all add up to a great restaurant experience.

When a patron goes to a restaurant, that person consciously chooses where to spend his or her hard-earned money. Whether it is lunch or dinner, people consider certain criteria when making their choice. Depending on the individual, the reason for their specific restaurant selection might be:

1. Convenience,
2. Personal recommendation,
3. Menu selection or type of cuisine,
4. Entertainment value,
5. Value (price to quality perception),
6. Relaxation,
7. Need for pampering, or
8. Simple hunger.

If the restaurant can not deliver what is expected, the customer will not soon return and may even prevent other potential customers from frequenting the establishment.

The restaurant business holds a unique place in the hospitality industry. It demands that the restaurant staff works hard so other people can relax. People in the restaurant business are working when most other people are relaxing and enjoying themselves. A restaurant worker's day off usually falls in the middle of the week. Still, those that choose the path of this wonderful business enjoy it immensely. Once involved, they are easily and quickly caught up in the *excitement*.

It is important to note that the hospitality industry is 20 percent technical knowledge of the culinary and business side and 80 percent knowledge of how to interact with, motivate, and build rapport with people. Pleasing the customer, motivating the staff, developing the management team, and working with salespeople are all part of a day in the hectic life of a restaurateur.

Through this book we hope to teach the techniques to accomplish all of these duties and promote the enjoyment of this wonderful, crazy business.

Cheers!

Supplemental Materials

The following supplements are available to accompany this textbook:

Instructor's Manual (print version) containing chapter overviews, restaurant development assignments, answers to chapter review questions, definitions of the key terms from the chapter reviews, suggested quiz questions, and recommended assignments.

Online Instructor's Manual containing PDF files of each chapter in the instructor's manual, and PowerPoint slides to accompany each chapter. To access, go to www.hospitality-tourism.delmar.com, and click on "Instructor Center."

Online Student Companion containing useful web links and Microsoft Excel spreadsheets correlating to illustrations in this text. To access, go to www.hospitality-tourism.delmar.com, and click on "Online Resources."

Acknowledgments

Monica Mahaffey – Editing this work.

Reviewers

Robert Bennett
Delaware County Community College

Leslie Furr
Georgia Southern University

Lisa Kennon
University of North Texas

Charles Martin
Spokane Community College

Jay Demers
Eastern Maine Community College

Douglas Miller
Utah Valley State College

About the Author

DON WADE is a restaurant consultant, author, and owner. He has worked in the restaurant industry for more than twenty years and is credited with opening more than thirty restaurants for corporations, for individuals, and personally. Don has held various positions with corporate restaurant chains from General Manager to Director of Operations.

Don has also written articles for Sante Magazine and Foodservice.com and is presently working as a consultant on several projects including seminars and workshops focusing on: Owning the Dining Experience (The Real Key to Delivering Outstanding Customer Service); The Importance of Planning and Budgets; Menu Design and Engineering (Building Sales and Loyalty through Menu Management); Management Basics; and Advanced Management and Leadership Skills.

Don's operational background includes:

- Consultant on several projects including opening units and troubled units;
- Owner of the Cide House Restaurant at Orchard Creek Golf Club;
- General manager of John Harvard's Brew House and offered a regional position in Atlanta;
- Director of Operations, Mozzarella Cafe.

Introduction to the Restaurant Business

The restaurant business is a business, not a hobby or an activity taken up because it seems exciting. It is a business that takes tremendous passion, effort, dedication, sacrifice and patience. It takes the same enthusiasm to serve guests in a restaurant that a person has for entertaining guests in their own home.

To be successful in the restaurant business, individuals need basic accounting knowledge, the ability to interact well with people, an understanding of marketing, a passion for customer service, and some culinary knowledge. Cooking or a basic working knowledge of the kitchen, service skills, accounting, and marketing can be learned through books and school. Passion for the restaurant business, enjoying human interaction, and fostering a constant desire to learn can not be bought at the local bookstore or learned in class. These traits are innate in a successful restaurant owner.

Being able to prepare great meals at home or inheriting a million dollars does not mean an individual will be able to operate a successful restaurant. Operating a commercial kitchen that serves 300 dinners nightly from a 40-item menu is much different than holding a dinner party for ten close friends.

Why People Go into Business

People venture into owning a business for many reasons: Some prefer to be their own boss; for others, running and operating a business might fulfill a lifelong dream; some people become entrepreneurs following a job loss; others may inherit the business; some may have a talent in specific areas and seize an opportunity to capitalize on that talent. Whatever the reason for opening a business, it is critical to educate yourself about every aspect of the business.

Understanding the Hospitality Industry

The unique hospitality industry requires that those who enter it as a career be passionate about serving others. The restaurant business is a major part of that industry. As you enter into this hectic, crazy, and often stressful but fun world, you must keep everything in perspective. Customers can be demanding and even rude, but it is important to remember that when they lash out, it is not a personal attack. To be successful, restaurant operators can not take these episodes personally. Some customers react in a volatile manner when their expectations are not met. Or, the customer may be working through a recent personal tragedy. Whatever the reason, the restaurant operator's job is to serve them in the best way possible and try to make their visit a pleasurable experience.

Over the past 30 years, chain restaurants have evolved into major players in the restaurant business. They have been able to do this for several reasons. They:

- deliver consistency in product and service standards;
- recruit top-notch people;
- train and develop people through written programs;
- introduce standardized systems to control costs; and
- keep up with trends and the marketplace.

Some individuals contend that these companies were cash rich and were able to grow through that money. However, that is not necessarily the case. Most chains started as single units and struggled in their infancy. Their growth periods started slowly and at times the owners had to overcome the same barriers as the single unit operations of today.

There is a tremendous amount to be learned from the chains. The systems that work for them can work in single unit operations. Inventory control, budgeting, developing people, standard operating procedures, and delivering great customer service work not only for restaurants with 100 plus units but for every restaurant.

Types of Restaurants

There are many types of restaurants and food service establishments. They range from corner delis to full-service operations and from quick serve casual to formal dining. Each type of restaurant has developed over time to fill a specific niche and to cater to a specific target market.

Quick Serve (Fast Food)—These restaurants are designed to serve a basic meal quickly and affordably. Menus are usually limited and kitchens are designed to produce high volume in short periods of time. The customer expects quick service, low price, and consistency. Some of the more well-known quick serve restaurants are McDonald's, Burger King, Kentucky Fried Chicken, Pizza Hut, and similar chains.

Family Restaurants—Family restaurants are just as the name implies—kid friendly, low cost, and very casual. One of the popular family restaurants would be Denny's.

Buffet—These restaurants have the ability to serve many people and offer many types of cuisine at the same time. They are usually low cost and affordable to families on a tight budget. Golden Corral would be an example of a buffet restaurant.

Casual Dining—Casual dining restaurants are full-service restaurants where consumers can dress comfortably, bring the kids, have table service, and not break the bank. The menus are usually simple and include basic fare such as burgers, sandwiches, pasta dishes, and chicken. The level of expectation and the price points are higher than quick serve establishments. Some of the most popular of the casual dining segment are TGI Fridays, Applebee's, Ruby Tuesday, and Olive Garden.

Fine Dining—Fine dining restaurants are more upscale, where the expectation of food quality and presentation, service, ambience, and the overall experience are first class. There are different levels within this segment. These levels range from establishments with table linens, attentive service, and first quality food to restaurants with captains, waiters, a sommelier, and all of the details in china and glassware. All these amenities are reflected in the check average. These restaurants are usually independently owned and not chain operated even though some owners will have multiple locations. Some examples in this area would be restaurants owned by Charlie Trotter, Thomas Keller, or Bradley Ogden.

Within each type of restaurant are several ranges. Other food service industries include cafeteria-style restaurants (institutional food service that includes hospitals and schools) and contract feeding (sport or entertainment venues). A leader in this field would be Aramark. The opportunities are numerous and diverse.

Why Restaurants Fail

Restaurants fail for many reasons, including undercapitalization, new and financially stronger competition, a lack of understanding about the marketplace and failure to change with the times, or failure to control costs. Failures are due to:

1. Lack of planning,
2. Loss of focus on the customer and the customer's needs or failure to react in a timely fashion to those needs, or
3. Losing focus on the cost of doing business.

The above reasons account for nearly all restaurant failures. Following are common reasons business owners give to explain their restaurant's failure. They can all be traced back to one of the three reasons above:

Undercapitalized—Reason #1: Lack of planning: undercapitalization is the number one reason restaurants fail and the main reason banks hesitate to lend money to aspiring restaurateurs. Chapter 5 of this book discusses the importance of financial planning and developing an operating budget and opening expenses.

Poor Location—Reason #1: Lack of planning: A well-planned restaurant with high quality food and service and a clean and relaxing atmosphere can still fail solely because of its location. Location does not simply mean the geographic location, but includes other factors such as being on the right side of the highway or street, ease of access, and visibility. Chapter 3 will discuss site selection in detail.

Low Sales—Reasons #1 and #2: Lack of planning and Loss of focus on the customer and the customer's needs or failure to react in a timely fashion to those needs: when sales are not high enough to pay the bills, it is no surprise that a restaurant will have a difficult time. If the restaurant is new and sales do not reach the required level, poor planning is probably the culprit. However, if sales meet the required level for a time but then slip below a minimum, acceptable level, the reason may be the loss of focus on the consumer and the market.

Costs out of Control—Reason #3: Losing focus on the cost of doing business: to be successful, a business must recognize two sides of the equation: producing sales and controlling costs. In the restaurant business, several cost areas must be managed to produce bottom line profit. Some of these areas include food and beverage; labor cost and associated payroll; and occupancy costs encompassing rent or mortgage, utilities, repairs and maintenance; and insurance. Chapter 8 covers all associated cost areas and ways to control these costs

Heavy Competition—Reason #2: Loss of focus on the customer and the customer's needs or failure to react in a timely fashion to those needs: if a restaurant blames its failure on a new restaurant, the underlying reason is easily traced to reason #2. A restaurant owner must first understand his or her clientele and the clientele's needs and then deliver on those needs. If the loyal customer base is easily eroded when a new restaurant enters the market, the owner must introspectively find out what is not being done in the restaurant to keep the customer.

The largest contributor to failing in the restaurant business is lack of planning, as this book will illustrate. The difference between failed restaurants and successful restaurants is that successful restaurants:

■ plan their course of action;

■ understand their market;

■ change with the needs of the market without disrupting core structure and standards;

■ develop a budget and fiscal discipline; and

■ pay close attention to details.

Just when an owner believes he or she has figured out the formula for success, the marketplace or the consumer's needs change. Restaurant owners must stay on top of the trends and keep their fingers on the pulse of consumer tastes.

Menu Design and Engineering

After reviewing this chapter, you will:

- Understand the importance of developing, designing, and "engineering" a menu;
- Be able to design a menu that will impact sales and profitability;

The menu can not simply be a haphazard listing of the food the kitchen produces. The menu is the restaurant's most powerful internal marketing tool. This chapter discusses the menu's importance and how a properly designed menu drives sales volume and profits.

Understanding the Importance of a Menu

The menu in a restaurant is the most critical link in tying together the restaurant **concept**—its overall identity and purpose. It is more than an item-by-item listing of the offerings. It steers all other aspects of the business and, in conjunction with the concept, determines the direction a restaurant will take. It is not a mere by-product of the kitchen design or of the kitchen equipment that has been purchased, but rather the guideline for kitchen design and equipment purchasing decisions. The menu also drives sales volume and profit margins.

The prospective restaurant owner who purchases or leases property, then buys equipment, then designs the kitchen and dining room, and finally designs and develops the menu, has taken steps in the wrong order.

The first step is to develop a concept and simultaneously a menu to complement the concept. A person venturing into the restaurant business should already have some sense of the concept and menu even if the menu is not fully developed, recipes are not finalized, and food descriptions are not written. The menu is not independent of the concept.

The next step is to determine what equipment is required to produce the menu efficiently and in a timely manner. When the equipment requirements have been identified, the owner must design and lay out the equipment. Improper design can adversely affect labor costs, customer satisfaction, and employee morale.

The Menu as a Marketing Tool

The menu is a powerful marketing tool that influences how restaurant guests will make purchasing decisions.

Menu marketing involves understanding the customer; grabbing the customer's attention; directing or influencing purchase decisions; and delivering expectations and using feedback to improve product, sales, **profit contribution,** and customer satisfaction.

It is imperative for any food service operator to understand that profit contribution is more important than food cost. Profit contribution is the actual profit in dollar terms that each item contributes to the gross profit of the business and is used to pay for fixed costs of the business. The higher the profit contribution of each item the more net profit that should be realized by the business. Food cost is an important management tool to be used to track and analyze the business operation but is expressed in percentages, which does not contribute profit in dollar terms.

Merely typing a list of items the restaurant offers does not accomplish any of these important tasks.

The **target market,** simply stated, is the type of customer the restaurant is attempting to reach and entice to frequent the establishment. Writing a menu requires understanding the customer's wants, needs, and expectations. A customer will judge a restaurant on several critical areas: food quality and presentation, service, ambience, cleanliness, and value. The menu informs customers of the choices available to them.

If the menu contains items targeted customers expect, it has passed only the first test. The menu must then grab customers' attention. If customers struggle to find the right item to order, they might not have the enjoyable dining experience that was expected. The proper placement of items on a menu can influence customers' purchasing decisions. This is known as **menu engineering.** The goal of menu engineering is not to force the customer to purchase an unwanted item, but rather to place certain items in high visibility locations. This approach accomplishes two major objectives: it influences a purchase that results in a pleasurable dining experience, and it provides a high profit contribution for the owner. This is a winning situation for both the business and the customer.

A menu is not and can not be stagnant. **Customer feedback** is vital to keep the menu fresh. Feedback from customers helps to improve product quality, which in turn increases sales and produces higher profits.

Price/Value Perception

Price/value perception means consumers believe they are receiving value for the price they are paying, whether the customers are eating in a fast food restaurant or dining in the finest restaurant in the area. The upscale dinner house must provide more than a quality steak or fresh seafood to meet the perceived value from the customer's standpoint. The decor, ambience, and service standards must all contribute to the customer's perception of the dining experience.

Menu Pricing Strategies

Properly pricing a menu will influence the way customers perceive a restaurant and the value it offers. Restaurants use several pricing methods. The method chosen depends on the restaurant concept and on marketplace expectations. Many operators settle into a comfort zone and use the same pricing strategy for all circumstances, such as setting a **food cost objective** of 32 percent. However, this is not always the most appropriate pricing strategy. Several factors influence the pricing structure:

1. Concept,
2. Target market,
3. Labor intensity of producing the product,
4. Volatility of raw cost,
5. Competition.

Concept

The **concept** a restaurant adopts directly influences the menu price points. An upscale steakhouse that advertises that it uses only prime beef, visits the piers daily to hand-select seafood, and offers attentive, professionally trained wait staff, will probably charge more for a filet mignon than would a casual dining, family-oriented restaurant.

Target Market

A target market is "a specific group of people, grouped together by age, income, gender, geographic location or any other defining manner in which an individual or group of individuals make purchasing decisions." A restaurant must decide the primary and secondary markets it will target. This will be discussed in detail in Chapter 4. However, it is important to understand the basic concept of a target market to properly determine pricing strategy.

Labor Intensity

A menu item that takes time and culinary talent to produce demands a higher price than something that is simple and quickly prepared. The associated preparation of a menu item may be restricted by the concept and target market. If a chef spends two hours a day producing a "featured" menu item in a casual dining restaurant and charges the same price as a more upscale restaurant, that menu item may not sell. Conversely, a low priced premade or prepackaged product in an upscale restaurant would diminish the dining experience.

Volatility of Cost

The **volatility of cost** is another factor, since some raw products may fluctuate daily. If the menu price is fixed, consider the cost volatility before setting the menu price. One restaurant set the price for baby back ribs at $15. The restaurant's cost was $72 per 22-pound case. Within three months, however, the restaurant's cost skyrocketed to $105 per case. Despite the 46 percent cost increase, management did not increase the menu price and make up profits for fear that an increase would negatively affect the number of ribs sold.

Competition

If a restaurant charges $5.95 for a hamburger, and a competing restaurant down the street sells the same hamburger for $4.95, the restaurant charging the higher price is likely to sell fewer burgers.

Each strategy has positive and negative aspects associated with it. A combination of these methods may be more appropriate to meet the influencing factors discussed previously. We will present only three of these pricing methods for the following reasons:

- These are the most widely used.
- Many of the other methods can be confusing and require production cost analysis. (Such analysis needs to be understood but is time-consuming—it is better utilized as a troubleshooting tool.)
- By utilizing these methods in conjunction with building a budget, an owner can determine if enough revenue will be generated to cover all costs and produce a profit.

Mark Up Pricing

Mark up pricing is probably the most widely used pricing method. This method involves dividing raw food cost by the desired food cost objective. However, restaurants should not try to achieve the same cost percentage on each item or category. The overall food cost, which is a function of individual item cost and sales mix, is the goal. Let's review the following example:

If the restaurant's goal is to have an overall food cost of 32 percent, the equation would be as follows:

Southwestern Chicken Entrée:

Menu Price = Raw food cost / Desired food cost percentage
= $3.25 / 32 percent
= $10.15

This method:

■ Takes into account only food costs and disregards other factors such as labor or any other fixed costs; and

■ may unfairly price certain menu items, making them hard to move and giving the customer the wrong value perception.

Base Price Method

The **base price method** allows the restaurant to assign a desired sale price to menu items. This price is usually competition- or market-based. If the going price for a menu item is $12, the owner has three options:

■ Lower the price in an attempt to gain market share.

■ Price the item in line with the competition and then set out to make the product better.

■ Price the item higher, making a statement to the marketplace—"Our product is better and we are marketing to the discriminating diner."

Once the price is assigned, the owner then has to back into the cost objective. If the objective for food cost is 32 percent and the menu item is $12, the chef has to figure out how to produce this product at the cost of $3.84.

Competition Pricing

In today's competitive world, a restaurant owner must constantly take the pulse of the marketplace and understand its needs in order to stay competitive.

The basic strategy of **competition pricing** is simply to compete with the other restaurants in the marketplace. The competition pricing method assumes that everything is equal between two restaurants, including overhead, raw food cost, labor, concept, and target market. If Restaurant A's occupancy costs and labor costs are higher than its competitor Restaurant B, and Restaurant A prices its menu under or at the same level of Restaurant B, its volume must be exponentially greater to produce the same profit. It is essential to be aware of the competitor's price points and refer to its pricing when analyzing and reviewing the present menu.

Another strategy used in some circumstances that is worth mention here is the prime cost method. Prime cost combines the food cost with the labor cost. This method should be understood for two main reasons:

1. Food companies develop products to save operators time. The cost of a premade product might be slightly higher than preparing the product in house, but restaurants realize a savings in the labor cost to produce that product. This can also be helpful in tight labor markets.

2. When setting menu prices or conducting menu reviews, labor intensity in both preparation and execution needs to be considered.

Figure 1–1, Menu Pricing Methods, is a chart of several menu items extracted from an actual menu being reviewed for an update.

Column A is the menu item.

Column B is the raw food cost according to the recipe.

Column C is the existing menu price.

Column D is the profit contribution of the item.

Column E is the food cost percentage.

Column F is the desired food cost percentage.

Columns G and H are the prices the restaurant would charge by using one of the pricing methods previously discussed.

Column I is the base cost or the dollar amount that can be spent to produce the menu item according to Column C, the existing menu price multiplied by the desired food cost percentage in Column F.

By setting up this chart with all of the menu items, the owner or manager can:

■ set a fair and competitive price;

■ know the profit contribution, which will help in engineering the menu; and

■ set a theoretical food cost for the restaurant to help manage the business.

This chart is a valuable tool to use in reviewing and analyzing the menu's effectiveness.

Menu Engineering and Design Strategies

Because customers use menus to make purchasing decisions, the menu design must take several factors into account:

■ the physical size of the menu as well as the number of panels of the cover or binder

■ the number of menu items

A	B	C	D	E	F	G	H	I
		Existing					METHOD OF PRICING	
	Raw Food	Menu	Profit	Actual Cost	Desired	Mark Up	Average	Base Mthd
Menu Item	Cost	Price	Contribution	Percent	Cost %		Competition	Cost
Appetizers								
Shrimp	$ 1.60	$ 5.95	$ 4.35	26.89%	30.00%	$ 5.33	8.95	$ 1.79
Mushrooms	$ 1.35	$ 6.95	$ 5.60	19.42%	28.00%	$ 4.82	7.95	$ 1.95
Mozzarella Sticks	$ 1.60	$ 6.95	$ 5.35	23.02%	28.00%	$ 5.71		$ 1.95
Nachos	$ 0.68	$ 6.95	$ 6.27	9.78%	30.00%	$ 2.27		$ 2.09
Chix tender	$ 0.96	$ 6.95	$ 5.99	13.81%	30.00%	$ 3.20		$ 2.09
Chimichanga	$ 1.02	$ 6.95	$ 5.93	14.68%	28.00%	$ 3.64		$ 1.95
Calamari	$ -	$ 6.95	$ 6.95	0.00%	32.00%	$ -		$ 2.22
Salads								
Caesar	$ -	$ -	$ -	0.00%	28.00%	$ -	$ 8.50	$ -
Chef	$ -	$ -	$ -	0.00%	30.00%	$ -	$ 8.50	$ -
HS Salad	$ -	$ -	$ -	0.00%		$ -	$ -	$ -
Sandwiches								
Bacon burger	$ 1.64	$ 6.95	$ 5.31	23.60%	30.00%	$ 5.47	$ 6.50	$ 2.09
Chicken salad	$ 2.77	$ 7.50	$ 4.73	36.93%	32.00%	$ 8.66	$ 7.95	$ 2.40
Entrees								
Southwestern chicken	$ 4.16	$ 14.00	$ 9.84	29.71%	28.00%	$ 14.86	$ 13.00	$ 3.92
Steak teriyaki	$ 5.25	$ 15.00	$ 9.75	35.00%	38.00%	$ 13.82	$ 16.00	$ 5.70
Baby back ribs	$ 4.08	$ 19.00	$ 14.95	21.47%	35.00%	$ 11.66	$ 18.00	$ 6.65
Scallops	$ 3.35	$ 14.00	$ 10.68	23.93%	28.00%	$ 11.96	$ 15.00	$ 3.92
Prime rib 12 ounce	$ 8.17	$ 12.95	$ 4.78	63.09%	35.00%	$ 23.34	$ 14.00	$ 4.53
TOTAL	$ -	$ -	$ -	0%	0%	$ -	$ -	$ -

FIGURE 1–1 Menu Pricing Methods.

- the color and type of the paper
- the script and size of the font
- the descriptions and language
- truth in menu
- number and type of categories
- how customers typically scan a menu

The more upscale a restaurant, the more a customer expects an expensive-looking menu. Family style restaurants might use pictures in their menus, but they are not normally found in fine dining establishments. Theme restaurants such as sports bars might use custom-designed menus that are unique to their concept. A restaurant that is designed to be child-friendly might use a menu designed with popular cartoon characters and games to keep the children busy.

Size of the Menu

A menu should be small enough that a customer can set it down on the table. If the restaurant has compact, intimate tables, a menu with legal-size paper would inconvenience customers searching for a place to set the menu down. If the number of items on the menu exceed what can be written on an 8.5-by-11 sheet, consider either creating a three-panel menu or decreasing the number of menu items.

Number of Menu Items

The number of items on the menu impacts:

1. the perceived variety from the customer viewpoint; and
2. the kitchen's ability to execute the menu.

Customers expect a certain amount of variety depending on the restaurant's concept. A diner-style restaurant would offer a wide variety of menu items covering three meal periods. On the other end of the spectrum, an upscale steak house would limit its menu to items such as steak, seafood, chicken, and other meats such as pork or lamb.

A menu with a wide variety of items must be matched with a kitchen that is designed and staffed to execute the menu in a timely manner and to deliver on the quality expected.

Menu Color and Paper

Restaurant owners must consider the color of the menu and the type of menu paper to use. Everything that communicates the restaurant's concept must flow in one neat package. The darker the paper, the more difficult it will be to read the menu, especially at night when restaurant lighting might be dim. In an upscale restaurant, selecting cheap, see-through paper would diminish the dining experience.

Script and Font

The menu should be easy to read. If customers have a hard time reading the print, whether it is because of the size of the font or the type of the script, they will order the first item that appeals to them. Font size should take into consideration the restaurant's lighting level and the target market age group. Consider the following:

Cajun Chicken Wrap - 10 point font

Cajun Chicken Wrap - 12 point font

Cajun Chicken Wrap - 14 point font

The size of the print makes a clear difference in the ease with which the customer can read the menu.

Some restaurant owners want fancy script on their menus. Observe the following font styles:

Cajun Chicken Wrap

Cajun Chicken Wrap

Cajun Chicken Wrap

Cajun Chicken Wrap

The following are examples of a menu written with different font sizes.

All sandwiches are served with Fries or Potato Chips and a deli pickle.

Roast Beef—Tender roast beef cooked to perfection, served on your choice of bread with horseradish mayonnaise, lettuce, tomato and red onion...............$6.95

Grilled Chicken Caesar Salad—An entrée size portion of our Caesar salad with grilled chicken, parmesan cheese, croutons and red onion...................$7.95

Chicken Salad Wrap—Our own freshly made chicken salad, with apples and celery wrapped up tightly with lettuce and tomato...................................$6.95

Cajun Chicken Wrap—Grilled chicken breast coated with Cajun spice, sliced thinly and wrapped up with lettuce, tomato and red onion with honey mustard dressing...........$6.95

The same menu with a different size font:

All sandwiches are served with Fries or Potato Chips and a deli pickle.

Roast Beef—Tender roast beef cooked to perfection, served on your choice of bread with horseradish mayonnaise, lettuce, tomato and onion...................$6.95

Grilled Chicken Caesar Salad—An entrée size portion of our Caesar salad with grilled chicken, parmesan cheese, croutons and red onion........................$7.95

Chicken Salad Wrap—Our own freshly made chicken salad, with apples and celery wrapped up tightly with lettuce and tomato...$6.95

Cajun Chicken Wrap–Grilled chicken breast coated with Cajun spice, sliced thinly and wrapped up with lettuce, tomato and red onion with honey mustard dressing...........$6.95

The font size difference in this example is only two points, but there is a tremendous difference to the customer. If customers have to struggle to read the menu, they will not be happy and their experience will not be a good one.

Consider the style of the font you are using. Script or fancy writing might look nice, but could be difficult to read. Do not confuse or frustrate the customers.

Descriptions and Language

Food item descriptions should convince the customer to make a purchasing decision by painting a picture in the customer's mind, ideally to such a degree that the customer can almost taste the food. If a customer has a hard time choosing between several dishes, it may be because the descriptions all paint vivid pictures (as in a well-written menu) or because all of the descriptions are uninspiring (as in a poorly written menu). Consider the following menu:

Calamari—Deep-fried calamari served over marinara sauce

Shrimp Cocktail—Six extra-large shrimp served with cocktail sauce

Crab Cakes—Maryland lump crab, pan-seared and accompanied with a red pepper coulis

In the above sampling of items, the description simply explains the items and adds nothing to excite or stimulate the customer. Now read the following sample of the same menu items:

Calamari—Rings of fresh, tender calamari coated with seasoned flour and deep-fried to a golden brown. Tossed with red pepper rings, scallions, and parmesan cheese and served over our homemade red sauce.

Shrimp Cocktail—Six extra-large Gulf shrimp, cooked to perfection. Served chilled with cocktail sauce and fresh lemon wedges.

Crab Cakes—Maryland lump crab mixed with a blend of special spices, coated with Japanese bread crumbs and perfectly pan-seared. Accompanied with a Cajun remoulade sauce.

From which menu would the customer more likely make a purchasing decision? A mouth-watering description will assist in making the sale. The following terms are examples of how descriptions can be made more appealing:

Home made	Infused	Home-style
Fresh	Tantalizing	Perfectly Seasoned
Secret Recipe	Juicy	Slow Roasted
Scrumptious	Award Winning	Grilled to Perfection

Tender	Locally Grown	Corn Fed
Signature	Golden Brow	Classic
Succulent	Loaded	Sautéed
Baked	Broiled	

Truth in Menu

Truth in menu means being honest in the menu description. An item should not read "locally grown" if the produce is being shipped in from out of the area. More importantly, many people are allergic to certain foods. If a menu item claims to use Maryland lump crab, then that is what should be used. If surimi (imitation crabmeat made from whitefish) is used instead, the menu should state that.

Categories

The customer's decision to purchase a specific item depends heavily on the menu design and item placement. People want variety, but *too much* variety can make the menu cumbersome.

Categorizing a menu gives the perception that a wide variety of choices are available. Categories such as Appetizers, Chicken, Pasta, Beef, House Specialties, and Dinner Combinations accomplish several objectives:

- Categories give the guest the perception that there is more variety.
- People will make quicker decisions, as they might move directly to the category that stands out and interests them.
- The customer's attention can be drawn to the more profitable menu items.

Scanning a Menu

Studies show that the majority of people look at a menu in a definitive and noticeable pattern. Often, as soon as a customer spots something of interest, he or she orders it before even reading over the entire menu. Refer to Figures 1–2 and 1–3,[1] which illustrate the high-impact areas of a multipage menu. Position 1 is where the customer's eyes go first, then the eyes drift to position 2, and so on. The pattern is basically the same regardless of what type of menu design is used. Scanning patterns are illustrated for both bi-fold and tri-fold menus. The main menu items, appetizers, and entrees should be visible upon opening the menu—not hidden on a back page. Figure 1–4 illustrates the high-impact areas of a single-page menu.

The menu items that receive the high visibility locations on the menu should be items with high profit contribution. Some of these dishes might be **signature items.** Signature items are dishes for which the restaurant is known and items

FIGURE 1–2

Menu Item Positioning, Two-Page Menu. © Bill Main and Associates.

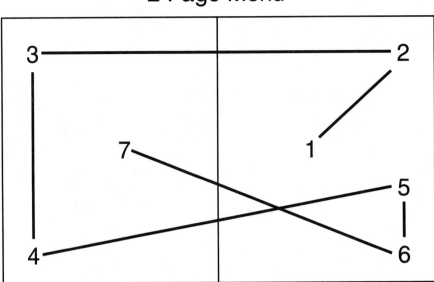

2 Page Menu

FIGURE 1–3

Menu Item Positioning, Three-Page Menu. © Bill Main and Associates.

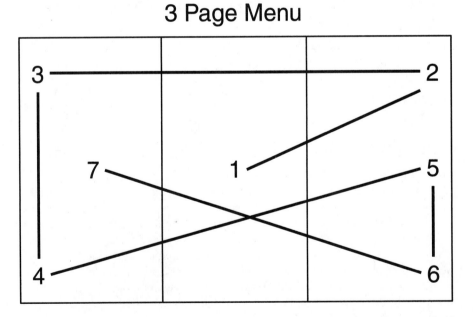

3 Page Menu

that bring customers back to the restaurant. Signature items should have a high gross profit contribution because restaurant owners should be able to charge a premium for them. By properly placing menu items, a restaurant owner can realize an increase in gross profit.

FIGURE 1–4

Menu Page Positioning.
© Bill Main and
Associates.

Appetizers

Seafood Chowder - This Award winning, creamy, seafood chowder is made in the traditional New England Style with chunks of potatoes
Cup......$2.50   Bowl.......$3.00

French Onion Soup - Traditional Onion Soup with a hint of Sherry. Served with French bread and covered with a trio of cheese - melted Swiss and Provolone Cheese and topped with parmesan cheese............................$3.50

Calamari - Fresh rings of tender calamari, lightly deep-fried and tossed with scallions, and cherry pepper rings. Topped with a hint of balsamic vinegar and parmesan cheese and served over our home-made red sauce...$6.95

Nachos - A pile of freshly cooked corn tortilla chips, topped with melted cheddar cheese, shredded lettuce, diced tomatoes, black olives, scallions and hot peppers. Served with sour cream and salsa on the side...................................$6.95

Ultimate Nachos - Our Nachos with fajita spiced chicken...........................$7.95

Peel & Eat Shrimp - A full pound of shrimp, served chilled with lemon and cocktail sauce with just a slight kick from the horseradish..........................

Wings - Large wings tossed in Buffalo sauce, served with celery, carrots and home-made blue cheese dressing. Buffalo wings are served mild, medium, hot, or *Scorching*.
Small (12).......$5.45   Large (20)..........$8.95
Extra sauces are available on the side.

Chicken Tenders - Crispy, juicy strips of chicken, deep fried to a golden brown and served with a basket of fries and a side of BBQ sauce or honey mustard. Enjoy them Buffalo style.................................$6.95

Chicken Quesadilla - Back by popular demand and a little pressure from Erin, chicken cooked with fajita seasoning and baked in the oven. Served with diced tomatoes, scallion, diced red onion and sour cream and salsa..............................$6.75

Spud Bites - Fresh Potatoes cut into bite-size pieces, deep fried and topped with melted cheddar and monterey jack cheese, bacon, scallions, and sour cream........$6.95

Maryland Crab Cakes - Our special blend of Maryland Lump crab and seasonings. Pan seared and served with a side of Cajun Remoulade...........................$8.50

Pub Ribs - *(A meal in itself)* A smaller portion of our juicy ribs, brushed with our own BBQ sauce, and served with French Fries...$8.50

Barbecue Sauce is available to take home!

High

Low

High

ICONS Icons are a great way to bring attention to signature dishes, heart healthy dishes, or new items. An icon can be any symbol that quickly identifies an item and makes it stand out from the rest of the list.

■ Vegetarian Wrap—A mixture of fresh grilled vegetables tossed with balsamic vinaigrette and served in a garlic wrap...............................$7.95

BRANDING Branding refers to building a name so that it is clearly identified in the marketplace. Many restaurants have been successful at branding and have been able to capitalize on their brand's widespread name recognition. T.G.I. Friday's Inc. has extended beyond restaurant operations to retailing both its food and bar products. The brand identity they have developed as T.G.I. Friday's has become very commonly known and the letters TGIF are automatically identified with the restaurant. Outback Steakhouse, Applebee's, and Red Lobster are other common restaurant names. They receive immediate recognition because they have developed strength in their brand. Having a strong brand provides future avenues of growth for the company, such as T.G.I. Friday's expansion into the retail market.

Developing a brand takes time and it must be part of an overall plan. The restaurant's name by itself does not brand the restaurant. The name, combined with the package and an overall plan, can develop a brand over time.

CO-BRANDING T.G.I. Friday's again is a leader in this type of marketing effort. In 2003, in the midst of the low-carbohydrate Atkins diet craze, T.G.I. Friday's partnered with Atkins Nutritionals to offer low-carbohydrate menu items.

BOXING The **boxing** concept focuses on an item or menu category, such as signature dishes, to make the category stand out. As a result, customers' eyes will be more easily drawn to that item or category. However, boxing should not be overused. Too many boxes will have a negative impact, as nothing will stand out or appear special. A profusion of boxes can easily cause confusion rather than create excitement and increasing sales.

Shading adds additional flair to the boxing concept. Look what happens to the following menu category in three examples:

SALAD BAR
Enjoy our fresh 18-item salad bar with dinner bread
and soup of the day
$8.95

or

SALAD BAR
Enjoy our fresh 18-item salad bar with dinner bread
and soup of the day
$8.95

---

or

SALAD BAR
Enjoy our fresh 18-item salad bar with dinner bread
and soup of the day
$8.95

Types of Menus

A restaurant might use several menus in addition to the main menu. Various types of menus make sense to use in specific situations and concepts:

Different Menus for Lunch and Dinner

Menus designed to offer different items or different-sized portions at various meal periods can increase revenues and maximize profits. People are more accepting of higher-priced items at dinner and are therefore willing to spend more than what they are willing to spend for lunch. Different menus are also often used at restaurants that have some downtime during the afternoon, or at restaurants that drive the majority of their sales and profits at dinner.

Having separate menus raises logistical issues, such as time needed for kitchen line changeover, and the possibility that customers returning to the restaurant for dinner will want to order items that are available only on the lunch menu.

Specials or Features Menu

A menu designed to describe the features for lunch or dinner can be printed and added to the regular menu or presented as an additional, stand-alone menu. Either way, it is important to give the specials menu the same care and attention as the everyday menu. It is also important when running specials and featured items to make sure they are indeed special. If the same special is run night after night, the specials menu will lose its effect. The customer might even perceive the specials menu as a way for the restaurant to get rid of old or non-selling items. So, make the specials menu special, or do not run such a menu. If the concept is very casual and one of the keys to success is relaxation, a specials page might be handwritten. If so, make sure the handwriting is readable and that all the words are spelled correctly. If there is any doubt that the staff will verify spelling and write legibly, type the specials menu instead of handwriting it.

When changing the specials menu, be sure to change all of the menus. If a customer receives yesterday's specials menu and decides on an item from that menu, the individual may get upset to learn that it is not available. There are several ways to ensure that your menus are properly rotated:

- Know how many menus are in the house. Collect all of the menus and count them. If the number does not match, find the other menus.
- Use a different color paper each day so that a quick glance will indicate that the wrong menu is being distributed.
- The host should open menus at the table, so if the wrong menu is being handed out it is immediately noticed and pulled away.

Opening the menu at a table also serves other purposes. If the menu is dirty or has crumbs on it, the host will notice. It also provides an opportunity for the host to interact with the customers instead of simply dropping the menus on the table and heading back to the front door.

Hosts should always carry one or two extra menus, so that they will not have to run back to the host stand if a menu can not be given out because of a problem.

Special Drink Menu

A menu describing special drinks of the house can include martinis, frozen daiquiris, or special house drinks. Special drink menus generate interest through pictures and clever names.

Late Night Menu

An easy-to-execute selection of several items is a great way to generate sales. It might not make sense to keep the entire kitchen open and serve a full menu late at night, but a smaller menu can drive bar sales, since people will enjoy eating at a bar more than they would drinking in a restaurant.

Early Bird Menu

Used in the right way, an early bird menu can generate sales during a slow or even dead period such as 4 P.M. to 6 P.M. or 3 P.M. to 5 P.M. These menus should contain a few selections that give a sampling of the regular menu at a discounted price, including dessert. It can help boost sales during down times.

Pub Menu

A menu offered at the bar only, this menu can also be used as the late night menu. A pub menu with a few appetizers could help boost sales at the bar. It might also be a way to reduce table turn times if customers enjoy an appetizer at the bar instead of at their table.

Prix Fixe Menu

A prix fixe (pronounced pree-fiks) menu offers customers several entrée selections, sides, and dessert all at a fixed price.

Wine Menus

Pricing wines can be tricky. Properly pricing a glass, bottle, or carafe of wine can entice the customer to purchase the wine. However, the same wine list if improperly priced will keep incremental sales low and wine inventory intact, and could detract from the restaurant's value perception.

Restaurateurs need to understand that wine pricing differs from food pricing. One difference is the perceived value of the purchase. Customers who know the retail price of a wine may question the considerable markup of the same wine offered at their favorite restaurant. While customers may also know the going price for filet mignon, they are willing to pay the menu price because they understand that it takes several people time to prepare the filet and the sides that accompany it. The customer may judge a bottle of wine differently because it is merely brought to the table, opened, and poured. Labor cost is minimal and the customer may not tolerate an excessive markup.

Restaurateurs also must consider their restaurant concept when developing a wine menu. Pricing wines at two or three times the average entrée price diminishes the value of the overall dining experience. In finer dining establishments that are known for wine and attract a wine-savvy clientele, this may not apply. However, most restaurant owners write their wine menus for mainstream consumers. For instance, if a couple orders an appetizer to share for $7, two entrees totaling $29, one dessert and two cups of coffee worth $11, and a glass of wine each totaling $13.50, their bill is $60.50. If they ordered the same food items with a bottle of wine, that bill could easily go up to $75. Once the tax is added (8 percent, for example) and gratuity (17 percent) the difference in the bills is $18.13 ($75.62 vs. $93.75). This is a noticeable difference to many people and, depending on the concept, the value perception might be lost. For the restaurateur, there are several positives to selling a bottle of wine at dinner and it is important that the "value added" is obvious to the guests. The positives include:

- The labor expense of serving wine is a fraction of the labor expense of producing dinners.
- The bottle of wine can add tremendous value to the dining experience.
- Gross profit contribution is improved through proper sales and marketing of wine.

Restaurant operators must understand that wine, unlike food, requires no preparation and is less perishable than raw food product. To offer wine, restaurants need only have a secured, temperature-controlled storage area and a staff training program. Conversely, the kitchen's physical plant requirements and operational expenses are much greater. Therefore, pricing wine to get the same or nearly the same margin as the restaurant gets from food should be given much thought.

Wine professionals' opinions vary regarding the way a wine menu should be written and priced. Some think that the wine menu should offer descriptions, while others believe descriptions take up too much room and are unnecessary. Some restaurants list wines from the lowest priced to the highest priced. Others list by variety.

The first step in developing a wine menu is determining what the food menu will support. If the average entrée price is $15, then having wines on the list for $50 or more would conflict with the menu and the concept. An Italian restaurant is more likely to sell wines than a Mexican restaurant. How many wines a restaurant offers by the glass, bottle, or carafe must also be considered. If the list is extensive enough to categorize by grape, such as cabernet sauvignon, merlot, pinot noir, sauvignon blanc, or pinot grigio, the menu should read that way. It should sort the wines by listing them from the lightest to the more full-bodied and robust wines. In states where the law allows, many wine purveyors will assist in writing a wine menu to promote the sale of their own wines. Many of them will even pay to print the wine menu.

Restaurateurs should be careful never to carry too many wines by the glass if the wines will not be consumed while they are still fresh.

Wine pricing has many variations. Options include doubling the price and adding a dollar; multiplying by 1.5 and adding $7; charging according to budgeted cost of goods; and adding a fixed cost to all wines, which lowers the price of high-end wines and increases the price of less expensive wines. In this scenario, the higher-cost wines will offer great perceived value.

Pricing wines is therefore a personal choice that involves the menu, the concept, and the clientele. An upscale steak house is expected to carry a better wine list with more selections and higher-cost wines than is a casual dining restaurant. A wine bar with food specifically prepared to be paired with wine will have a better selection and higher price points than most other restaurant concepts.

Taking all of these pricing strategies into account, let's review several ways to increase wine sales:

■ Increase bottle value. Tremendous values are available for all styles of wine. Search for wines that fit the restaurant concept and look for cost that will allow proper pricing. Instead of strictly seeking a 33 percent cost of goods sold (COGS), consider wines with a 40 to 42 percent cost that might warrant a slightly higher price. If a customer orders two glasses of wine at $6.75 each, that customer might find higher value in buying the bottle for $23. With the sale of the bottle, the customer and the restaurant both win. The guest has an enhanced dining experience and the gross profit goes from $8.75 to $12.

■ Increase glass selection. More wine selections may entice customers to order two glasses of different wines. They might prefer a glass of pinot noir with their appetizers but have cabernet sauvignon with dinner. Again, both the customer and the restaurant win, with the restaurant realizing higher profits and the guest enjoying an enhanced dining experience.

■ Offer flights of wine. An increased glass selection will allow the restaurant to offer flights of wine. A flight is a sampling of three or four wines, poured at three or four ounces instead of six or seven ounces. Flights give the customer the flexibility to have different wines with different courses. Or, a small group may want to sample a number of wines.

■ Offer half bottles of wine. Half bottles are a great way to increase wine sales. A table that finds a full bottle to be too much has the option of ordering a half bottle.

■ Offer carafes. While serving wine in carafes may seem to be outdated, that is not necessarily the case. A carafe is not limited to the old mason wine style. New, more interesting and elegant carafe styles are available. To increase carafe sales, the house selection must be a good value, good tasting, and even a recognizable wine. Restaurants should spare themselves embarrassment by not serving boxed or cheap wine.

■ Use point of sale materials. Depending on the concept, use table tents, additional menus, or menu inserts to promote wine sales. Somewhere on the wine list, such as under the glass selection, print *"If each guest may have more than one glass of wine, may we suggest a bottle or carafe of wine."*

■ Highlight a "wine of the month." Featuring wines for a short period of time is a great way to boost sales, add variety, and test wines for customer feedback and future wine menus. Also, many wine purveyors are more than willing to provide a knowledgeable staff member on certain nights to train the staff and to introduce their wines, offer samples to guests, and add more fun to the dining experience.

■ Train your staff. Staff members can not sell products with which they are uncomfortable or unfamiliar, or if they do not feel qualified. The staff must be motivated to sell wine. Train, train, and train the staff. When they think they have mastered the art, train some more.

Dessert Menus

Separate dessert menus that are smaller than the main menu and easy to read are a great way to increase dessert sales. They are also an effective vehicle for increasing awareness of additional avenues for sales such as port wine, after dinner liqueurs, and coffee drinks. Dessert or after dinner selections menus should be easy to read with mouthwatering descriptions. The pricing structure for a dessert menu depends on the concept. Some restaurants lower the price of the desserts, recognizing that the sale is an add-on or incremental sale. A dessert menu with low- to mid-range price points adds great value to the dining experience.

Dessert menus should carry a variety of choices such as chocolate, seasonal fruit cobbler or pie, ice cream, and crème brulée. Other dessert offerings depend on concept and the ability to produce the dessert.

Some restaurants forgo dessert sales in hopes of turning the table for a new customer. Others even have separate rooms where dessert is served. Unless the restaurant has the welcome problem of always being on a two-hour wait, the sale of the dessert, after dinner drink, and coffee enhances the dining experience and increases the gross profit from each guest.

Using a dessert tray to show the desserts is another popular method of selling desserts and can be very effective if done properly. The desserts must be fresh and appealing to the eye. If they have been sitting on the tray for some time and appear old, the method can lose its appeal and limit sales.

If a restaurant wants the server to make the dessert sale, taking the dessert menu or dessert tray to the table should be done automatically. When the server asks, "Would you like to see our dessert menu?" the customer may say "no" without considering the option of a dessert or after dinner drink.

Mistakes in Menu Design

Incomplete Menus

Menus that are incomplete or not 100 percent updated annoy guests. If a menu item is changed, make sure all of the menus are changed. If daily specials are inserted, make sure every menu has an insert.

Extra Plate Charge

Some restaurants impose an extra plate charge and justify it by telling customers that each plate is served with a full portion of side dishes. However, not everyone can eat full, dinner-sized portions. If customers want to split an entrée, they will probably be very satisfied to also split side dishes. Charging $2 for a plate because two people want to share may decrease the perceived value of the dining experience.

Misspelled Words

Use spell check and have someone other than the person who wrote the menu proofread the menu.

Improper Description with Omitted Ingredients

Some people have potentially severe allergies to certain products. In many cases, customers simply do not like certain ingredients. Failure to list the exact description can cause major problems and even lawsuits.

Smaller Portions

Not everyone wants a dinner-sized portion, especially at lunch. Larger portions bring higher prices. At lunch, a lower price point is expected and so is a smaller portion.

■ CHAPTER REVIEW

The restaurant menu is one of the most critical components in developing a successful business. It helps customers shape their perceptions of the establishment, communicates the concept, and markets the products. Menu development is also one of the first steps that must be completed in developing a restaurant. It shapes everything else that follows and ties the restaurant together.

■ KEY TERMS

base price method	menu engineering
boxing	price/value perception
branding	profit contribution
competition pricing	signature items
concept	target market
customer feedback	truth in menu
food cost objective	volatility of cost
mark up pricing	

■ REVIEW QUESTIONS

1. What is a target market?
2. What is meant by price/value perception?
3. List the five factors influencing menu pricing structure.
4. List the three pricing methods presented in this chapter and give a brief explanation of each.

Note

1. Bill Main, Menu Magic

CHAPTER 2

Marketing: Research Analysis and Building a Customer Base

After reviewing this chapter, you will:

■ Be able to define marketing;

■ Understand how to conduct basic marketing research to determine local demographics;

■ Have the knowledge to develop an effective marketing plan;

■ Understand the relationship of advertising to marketing; and

■ Learn some low-cost and effective marketing tools.

Success in business is derived from customers who are willing to pay for a product or service while keeping costs down to produce a profit. In the restaurant business, the key to success is retaining a regular customer base that frequents the restaurant while attracting new customers.

As you read the text, consider the following questions:

What is the definition of marketing?
What is the purpose of marketing?
What does a marketing plan involve?

Review these questions at the end of the chapter and compare the change in understanding of marketing's role in the restaurant business.

This chapter discusses step-by-step defining the target market (customer), researching and understanding that market, building a plan to attract and keep customers, and keeping the restaurant new, fresh, and exciting.

This chapter conveys a basic understanding of the accepted teachings of marketing and highlights the imperative role of marketing in a restaurant's success. Some

restaurants have not only survived but thrived without the owners understanding the importance of studying the market. Such restaurants are the rare exception rather than the rule. The chances of survival without effective marketing are slim. In today's world, it is highly unlikely that a restaurant can survive without owners having an understanding of marketing and its impact on success.

The Role of Marketing

Some assert that marketing is simply developing attention-getting advertising and then properly placing those ads in the media. That is a gross oversimplification. Marketing involves much more than advertising.

Marketing can be simply defined as *"constantly focusing on the customer and making business decisions based on the changing needs and desires of the customer."*

This definition provides a customer-centered vision and approach to marketing the restaurant so it will evolve and grow. The marketing plan takes all aspects of the operation into account, because all aspects will—in one way or another—affect the business and the marketing of the business.

Creating an effective marketing plan requires that the restaurant operator know customers and potential customers. It is imperative for the restaurateur to research customer preferences and desires.

Marketing research has two basic purposes:

1. To develop an understanding of the target market (potential customer) and the market segments. (A **market segment** is a smaller, more specific group within a specific target market.)

2. To formulate a plan to attract the target market to the restaurant and then meet or exceed customer expectations so the customer returns to make future purchases.

Successfully marketing any business requires that the operation be flexible enough to adapt to ever-changing customer tastes and desires. A customer may initially be attracted to a restaurant, but the customer's preferences may change over time, even if the restaurant consistently delivers an outstanding experience.

Consider the restaurant in the context of a successful theater performance. A great Broadway show will stay open for years if it brings in new actors and makes subtle changes to update the script or the staging over time. The show and the people need to be fresh and crisp during each performance, just as they were on the day the show opened. The enthusiasm that subtle changes bring to the stage attracts return audiences to the show year after year. The restaurant business is similar. Customers want every experience to be exciting and fresh. If, over time, the experience becomes stagnant, the customer may seek a new restaurant. The public has a number of dining choices and that number is constantly growing. Customers' desires and needs change, especially when they involve dining out. Today's hot menu item is tomorrow's run-of-the-mill item.

A customer's **frequency of visits** (how often a customer visits the restaurant in a given time frame, e.g., four times per month) is a vital part of any restaurant marketing plan. Frequency of visits signals consistency in maintaining the established customer base. The more frequently a regular customer visits, the less the restaurant needs to focus attention and resources on driving new trial—getting people in the marketplace to try the restaurant. Some effort must *always* be given to driving in new customers, but even more valuable are regular customers whose **word-of-mouth advertising** can be the best form of marketing a restaurant can get.

Here's a common misconception: *There is loyalty among restaurant customers.* In fact, restaurant customers can be very fickle. While customers may be loyal for a time, such perceived loyalty can be quickly lost, despite the time and effort invested in cultivating it. Customer loyalty can be lost for several reasons:

- The customer may have one bad experience with the food or service.
- A more conveniently located restaurant may open.
- The menu may become stagnant.
- There might be high turnover among the staff, creating an unsettling atmosphere. Customers are not attracted to a chaotic and ever-changing environment.

As these examples illustrate, staying in touch with customers' desires and ever-changing tastes is imperative. Every customer is important to a successful business. An excellent way to conduct marketing research is to ask the customers already in the restaurant about their desires. But do not rely solely on present customers who obviously like the restaurant. It is also important to be familiar with potential customers' preferences to attract them to the restaurant.

Figure 2–1 illustrates that success requires an ability to keep present customers while attracting new customers. Keeping the new customer is directly dependent on management's ability to execute and deliver a pleasant dining experience. Customers' expectations are developed either through advertisements or through what they have heard about the restaurant through word-of-mouth advertising. It is similar to having a great desire to see a particular movie because of the ad-generated hype surrounding the movie or because of the actors in the movie. The hype creates excitement. Viewers go to the movie with great anticipation but may leave the movie feeling disappointed if it did not meet their expectations.

Partial failure may be blamed upon:

- retaining present customers but failing to attract new customers, or
- attracting new customers but failing to retain them.

Both of these scenarios are dangerous, but failing to attract new customers is the beginning of the end. As present customers leave or perceived loyalty is lost, no new customers fill the void.

The second reason for partial failure is an inability to retain regular customers. This situation is easier to correct, as the problem is most likely with the internal operation or the expectations being set. Something is leaving the

FIGURE 2–1

Marketing Effectiveness Grid. Copyright © 1997 by Alexander Hiam, www.insightformarketing.com

High	***Partial Failure*** New customers replace lost customers	***Success*** Sales and profits grow at the maximum possible rate due to satisfied customers and the ability to attract new customers	
CUSTOMER ATTRACTION	***Total Failure*** Sales Fall as customers leave	***Partial Failure*** Sales slow or fall due to lack of new customers	
Low			
	Low	**CUSTOMER RETENTION**	**High**

Real World Scenario

A chef once told a story that directly relates to perceived loyalty. This chef worked in a popular upscale restaurant. The owners believed they had achieved success because their reservation book for the upcoming weekend was completely filled early in the week. They stopped advertising for the most part, did not network through charities or business organizations, and just sat back and enjoyed their version of success. They continued to work very hard within their four walls. They had a large base of loyal customers. But over time that customer base began to erode because of people moving and other factors. The owners had no idea how to attract new customers. To stop the erosion of their present customers, they listened to those customers' needs and changed their menu to satisfy the present customer base. They catered to their every need.

At the same time, the marketplace in the area had changed. More office space was opening and squeezing out some local residents. Nearby property values dropped. Lunch business was thriving, but the real money was in the dinner business. The owners remained an upscale restaurant but their market continued to erode. The business ended up closing and was sold to another locally owned, more casual-themed restaurant. The new restaurant was able to meet the needs of the changing market and became very successful.

The moral of the story is: Stay in touch with the entire marketplace and adapt to the needs of that market.

customer feeling dissatisfied with the experience. The best way to find out how the restaurant is being perceived is to ask the customer. Owners and managers cannot hide in an office and simultaneously build their clientele. Building relationships with customers is a vital part of the success equation. If marketing efforts are increasing dining counts, the objective must be to deliver a memorable dining experience and get those new customers to return.

Success is achieved when the ability to keep present customers aligns with the ability to attract new customers and keep them coming back. Maintaining this momentum and carrying it into the future are not simple tasks. They require defining the market, researching the market, reaching the market, and executing within the restaurant, all to gain advantage over the competition. Stay in touch with the customers and continually meet their needs while finding new customers and driving trial to the restaurant.

Target Market

The target market must be well defined. This market is the guide to developing products and services. A simple definition of **target market** is "a specific group of people with similar purchasing patterns."

The target market may be:

1. 30-year-olds and older,
2. people with higher-than-normal disposable income,
3. people living within a three-mile range of a geographic location, or
4. people that dine out two to three times per week.

Within the target market are market segments. A market segment is a subgroup in the target market that may have even more specific wants and needs. **Market segmentation** is grouping customers with similar likes and dislikes to determine how and where the group would shop, the type of car group members would drive, and what type of restaurant they would frequent. Identifying market segments requires restaurant operators to look through the eyes of the customer. What does the customer see? How does the customer feel? What does the customer expect? How does each staff member respond to the customer? A whole list of questions arise when the restaurant operator has this understanding of marketing. The questions will help to develop an effective marketing plan for the business and mold the business to fit the needs of the target market. The target market or market segment will not mold itself to the business.

The first step in developing a customer base is to define the market segment to be reached. All marketing efforts must be geared to the members that comprise that market, or the target market. The following example is condensed from an actual marketing plan.

A target market for a brew pub is 30 to 55 years of age with a higher-than-average disposable income. A brew pub, by nature, attracts a predominately male audience by offering handcrafted beers and a complementary menu listing items such as steak, ribs, and spicy foods. But, for obvious reasons, the brew pub cannot alienate the female segment of the 30 to 55 age group. A marketing segmentation of this group focuses efforts on attracting the female sector of this market. This marketing focus may involve a selection of wines by the glass, specialized drinks such as cosmopolitans, and lighter fare on the menu.

Always take into consideration what is known as the *veto vote*. The veto vote occurs when a group of individuals get together and decide where to dine. Five people choose a particular restaurant but one individual cannot find anything appealing on that restaurant's menu, so the group goes to another restaurant. In this case, the majority of the target group was satisfied, but there was no consideration for a smaller, particular segment of the target group. Appealing to the smaller segment can be done without committing the common marketing error of being all things to all people.

If a restaurant opens with a very similar concept to what is already available nearby, or does not fit into the marketplace, success may be difficult to achieve. To get a consumer to try a new restaurant and return to it, the new restaurant must be better than the competition in some manner that touches the consumer and his or her desire to make a purchase. Whether the offer is in value perception, service, convenience, atmosphere, or menu, offering something new, different, and fresh is a must.

How does a restaurant accomplish this? It must first understand that people like to be in comfort zones. The television show *Cheers* opened with a song that said, "You want to go where everybody knows your name." When the host staff, servers, bartenders, and managers know a customer, the customer's comfort level increases. Why would customers change restaurants if they are treated well and known by name? Everyone enjoys their comfort zones, whether they are in places of business, at work, or in friendships. The owner of a new restaurant must ask, "Why will people in the marketplace want to frequent this establishment instead of staying with a known entity?" The answer will lead to step one, attracting the customer, which leads to step two, delivering on expectations, and finally to step three, keeping customers coming back.

Market Research

Conducting **market research** is essential to any marketing plan. Restaurants need specific information to prepare an effective marketing plan that will contribute to sound, educated decision making. This information will directly affect the site selection process, as will be discussed in the next chapter, and will affect other business decisions, including concept direction, menu decisions, and pricing structure. Locating a restaurant in a marketplace that will support its particular type of business is critical to success. But how does a small independent operator conduct cost-effective market research? There are several options. First define the needed information:

■ Age group of the target market,

■ Lifestyle of the target market,

■ Income level of the target market,

■ The number of people in the target market living in the projected area,

■ Traffic patterns at the site,

■ Economic growth plans of the immediate area and the surrounding region,

■ Competition (both direct and indirect; the dining dollar is limited, so even indirect competition will affect revenues),

■ Crime rate of the area.

Several Web sites provide access to valuable demographic information. States also compile useful information, such as traffic-count data that is often updated approximately every two to three years. A state's department of transportation often has this information online. Refer to Figure 2–2 for an example of a traffic volume report for sections of roads in New York's Albany County.

Concept Development

Market research will reveal the type of restaurant concept a geographical area or marketplace will support. Once the marketplace and the needs of the consumers within it are understood, a concept can be developed to fill a need or niche in that market. Even a great concept in the wrong market is likely to be destined for failure.

Theme

Developing a successful restaurant requires the creation of a theme. A concept cannot be a halfhearted compilation of loose odds and ends with the hope of ending up with a product the market will clearly recognize. To tie the entire package together, the owner must methodically develop a concept to create a restaurant that is clearly identifiable in the marketplace. The concept does not stop with identifying the cuisine to be offered or the decor to be chosen for the building. It includes even the smallest detail. The concept must be reflected in every aspect of the restaurant. While the food is a key component and the name is the identifying brand, everything from the initial business and marketing plan to the design, the decor, the color schemes inside and outside the building, the

Touring Route	Section Length	Start Description	End Description	Count Year	Count AADT
		NEW YORK STATE DEPARTMENT OF TRANSPORTATION			
		2002 Traffic Volume Report for ALBANY COUNTY			
157	1.21	RT 157A S JCT	CR 256	00	485
157	3.60	CR 256	CR 311	00	814
157	0.89	CR 311	RT 85 JCT END RT 157	01	1615
157A	3.74	RT 157	ROUTE 910J JCT RIGHT	00	1052
157A	2.14	ROUTE 910J JCT RIGHT	RT 157 END RT 157A	02	1127
158	1.83	RT 146 OSBORNE CORNER	RT 20 SHARPS CORNER	01	3868
158	1.35	RT 20 SHARPS CORNER	SCHENECTADY CO LN	01	4295
335	0.46	RT 910A JCT	RT 32 DELMAR BYPASS	02	7471
335	1.31	RT 32 DELMAR BYPASS	RT 443 ELSMERE END RT 335	02	8139
377	0.24	RT 9 ACCESS ROADS SB	LAWN AVE	02	10894
377	0.16	LAWN AVE	ALBANY N CITY LN	01	8320
377	0.52	VILLAGE OF MENANDS SOUTH BOU	WARDS LANE	01	8320
377	0.84	WARDS LANE	RT 378 JCT END RT 377	01	7805
378	0.93	RT 9 JCT	RT 377 JCT VILLAGE OF MENAND	02	14544
378	1.01	RT 377 JCT VILLAGE MENAND	RT 32 UNDER	01	14704
378	0.59	RT 32 UNDER	ACC RT 7871	01	16097
378	0.34	ACC RT 7871	RENNSELAER CO LN	02	28923
396	2.33	CR 301	CR 53 S BETHLEHEM	01	2146
396	2.11	CR 53 S BETHLEHEM	RT 9W BECKERS CORNER	01	2218
396	2.14	RT 9W BECKERS CORNER	RT 144 END RT 396	01	2289
397	3.09	RT 146 ALTAMONT	RT 20 JCT DUNNSVLE END RT 39	02	2052
443	3.37	SCHOHARIE CO LINE	RT 156 BERNE	01	976
443	3.45	RT 156 BERNE	RT 910J BERNE	02	1976
443	3.57	RT 910J BERNE	START 85 OLAP	02	1736
443	2.02	START 85 OLAP	END 85 OLAP	02	4266
443	1.93	END 85 OLAP	CR 301	02	2239
443	3.85	CR 301	CR 308	01	4621
443	2.35	CR 308	VAN DYKE RD	01	4912
443	0.40	VAN DYKE RD	ELM & CHERRY ST DELMAR	00	7922
443	1.10	ELM & CHERRY ST DELMAR	RT 140 DELMAR	01	8251
443	0.67	RT 140 DELMAR	RT 335 ELSMERE	01	13796
443	1.33	RT 335 ELSMERE	ALBANY S CITY LN	02	17430
443	0.80	CITY OF ALBANY	START RT 9W OLAP	02	17430
443	0.07	START RT 9W OLAP	WHITEHALL RD	01	10344
443	1.28	WHITEHALL RD	RT 20 JCT END RT 443 END RT	00	9650
470	1.30	RT 9R JCT COHOES CITY LINE	COLUMBIA ST JCT	01	10754
470	0.43	COLUMBIA ST JCT	REMSEN ST	01	5916
470	0.23	REMSEN ST	RT 787 JCT	01	6126
470	0.80	RT 787 JCT	RENSSELAER CO LINE	98	13137
787	0.40	RTE 7871 JCT ACCESS RT 7	RTE 7WB JCT	96	35749
787	0.36	RTE 7WB JCT	ACCESS TO TIBBETS ST	01	33397
787	0.09	ACCESS TO TIBBETS ST	COHOES CITY LINE TOWN OF COL	01	28878
787	0.66	TOWN OF COLONIE COHOES CITY	ACCESS TO DYKE AVE	01	28878
787	0.52	ACCESS TO DYKE AVE	ACCESS TO BRIDGE AVE	00	26032
787	0.41	ACCESS TO BRIDGE AVE	RT 470 ONTARIO STREET	01	20834
787	0.12	RT 470 ONTARIO STREET	RT 32 JCT END 787	00	19668
7871	0.32	RT 871 INTER 23	ACC RTS 9W & 912S	96	18150
7871	0.62	ACC RTS 9W & 912S	ACC RT 32	02	44585
7871	1.03	ACC RT 32	ACC ROUTES 9 & 20	98	41486

FIGURE 2–2

Traffic Count Information, Courtesy of the New York State Department of Transportation.

price points, the background music, the standards of service, the uniforms, the vision, and the goals for the restaurant are all part of a common thread.

The whole restaurant package will determine how the paying public perceives it. The package includes the facility, food and beverage, service standards, atmosphere, and ambience.

A restaurant cannot cater to everybody in the marketplace and it should not try to do so. The menu, business plan, and marketing plan will define:

■ The specific target market,

■ The segments of that market, and

■ The plan to attract that segment of the public.

It is important to fill seats in a restaurant, but not at the expense of losing the *core* clientele.

It is critical to understand what the target market wants in a dining experience. In general, people do not go to a restaurant and critique every aspect of the facility. But when something is not right with the food, beverage, service, or value, the customer senses it. People want to leave the restaurant feeling good about their dining experience and often expect to be in a better frame of mind than when they entered. Certainly, no one goes to an establishment that will add to the stress they may already feel.

As previously noted, today's consumers have a wide variety of dining choices, from fast food for those who demand "satisfy me now," to fine dining for those who want to be king—or queen—for the night. Customers connect certain expectations to each level in this barrage of choices. At the fast food drive-in, customers may expect only a tasty morsel to satisfy their immediate hunger. But expectations at a fine dining establishment change dramatically. Customer expectations are driven by the concept.

Remember: Consumers can spend their money at a wide variety of eateries. Whatever the concept or market, without a positive and memorable impression, eventually the business will suffer. Build the business one customer at a time.

Developing a concept is not to be done hurriedly. It takes time, imagination, and an understanding of the industry and the market. This planning during the creativity phase is a critical factor to success.

People want restaurants that cater to them. Their conscious state of mind can clearly taste, smell, and see good food. Quality food appeals to several senses.

A glass of wine or an ice cold beer is also a tangible item. But intangibles such as ambience, caring, and passionate service must also be present.

It is important to choose a concept that is not too similar to other restaurants already in the market. If the concept is a stripped-down version of another, established restaurant in the same market, the chances for survival are diminished. It is not impossible to succeed, but giving the consumer too many of the same choices will most likely decrease the share of the business dollar available and make it difficult to survive.

Conversely, proven concepts outside of what is available in the proposed market can be viable concepts. Trends such as brew pubs, martini bars, and wine bars have dominated the marketplace at different times. New, aspiring owners seeking to be part of such trends would have been wise to learn from the proven, successful establishments already in existence. They would have been wise to also examine failed operations, which can also provide a bounty of valuable information. After all, owners of failed businesses had already made the mistakes and endured the trials and tribulations with which the new owners were about to be confronted. Often, the difference between the successful operation and the failed operation is that savvy operators made adjustments in stride and kept their finger on the pulse of the customer and the market, while the operators who were slow to learn or too stubborn to adapt to the marketplace closed.

Confusing the public about the concept is a critical marketing error. During concept development, it is critical to pay close attention to details. It is also essential to identify proven concepts similar to the new design. Questions to ask include:

■ What makes this concept so popular?
■ Why does this concept continue to thrive and attract new customers?

The concept developer must also examine everything making the concept work, including menu, food quality, price points, quality of people, service standards, location and ease of access to the location, decor, ambience, and cleanliness. Restaurateurs who poorly imitate successful concepts fail miserably. New operations sometimes try to duplicate part of an existing concept and haphazardly piecemeal together the balance, resulting in an ill-conceived overall package that. The customer can become confused about the concept and what it is trying to convey to the market. A concept must be all-inclusive, right to the smallest detail.

A well-planned concept is easy to identify. A popular restaurant concept clearly ties everything together into a seamless package.

Child-oriented restaurants are designed to take the pressure away from parents by entertaining the children. Chuck E. Cheese's restaurants are a prime example of this type of restaurant. Family style and casual dining restaurants' price points allow young parents on a tight budget to take their children out to an affordable restaurant. These restaurants are child-friendly and instill a family-friendly attitude in management and staff as part of the restaurant's culture. Coloring books and even a toy box may be available for children. Birthday clubs may be a part of the marketing plan to build loyalty. These restaurants build business by allowing people to relax and have some fun. They incorporate fun, friendliness, affordable price points, and consistency in their food into their package. Part of the marketing goal of this type of restaurant is to build frequency of visits.

A restaurant with higher price points that is considered in the upper end of the casual dining market may view its concept differently. The more customers pay for a product or service, the higher their expectations. The staff's knowledge of food and spirits, or lack thereof, will be more evident to the customer. Staff training will be more intense and taken much more seriously. This type of restaurant may consider itself to also be child-friendly, where children are welcome, but the pricing structure may be more than parents want to spend on children. Adults may prefer a place like this when dining with spouse or friends. The staff needs to cater somewhat to children so as not to give the parents the idea that the children are neglected. These concepts may aim for a frequency of visits of one every couple of weeks.

The more upscale a restaurant is and the higher its price points, the greater will be customers' expectations. In many markets, the more upscale a restaurant is, the fewer its frequency of visits will be. A very upscale restaurant may be known as a *special occasion restaurant*, where frequency may be once or twice yearly and only for occasions such as birthdays, anniversaries, or holidays. This sector of the business is more specialized and the customer base is usually not as large as it is in the casual dining market.

Some restaurants prefer not to have children as patrons, not because of a dislike for children, but rather to cater to a specific clientele. At times the parents find it difficult to control their children in a restaurant setting or prefer to take a break from their children by leaving them with a baby-sitter while they enjoy a fine dining meal. If the restaurant check average is $75, the person paying the bill will not likely want to tolerate a child crying or screaming during the meal.

Do not try to be everything to everybody!

It is usually detrimental for restaurateurs to attempt to attract customers any means possible. In such cases, decisions are usually knee-jerk reactions to a slow sales period. Sometimes the marketing tactics employed in attempting to drive customer counts cause the restaurant to veer off in a new direction that ultimately alienates core clientele.

Marketing Plan

A marketing plan should be written in conjunction with the business plan. A business plan sets a direction for the restaurant before beginning work on the actual development; provides a reality check on the feasibility of the undertaking; sets budgets; and determines capital needed and attracts investors. An effective

Real World Scenario

An independently owned restaurant opens in a small suburban area and flourishes for many years. Soon, chain restaurants start to open within a five-mile radius. During the first couple of months of the chain invasion, the restaurant sees sales drop. The restaurant owner begins to panic and is desperate to put people back in the seats. Grasping at straws, he signs up for any and all coupon programs available, without analyzing the effect the discounts will have on his gross profit. Over the next several months, the chains' honeymoon period ends and the public that frequented the independently owned restaurant gradually returns to the establishment. But now the customers have a coupon in hand. The deals are two-for-one, $10 off, and several others. Gross profits begin to drop. In response, the owners raise menu prices. Customers without a coupon or discount card find that the perceived value disappears. The original, loyal customers then seek a new restaurant because the restaurant they once loved has priced its menu above the market perception of value. Within three years, coupon sales account for 30 percent of gross sales. When a restaurant's gross profit drops below an acceptable level and the owners believe they have done what was necessary to drive top-end sales, the only option left is to cut costs. Lowering quality standards and purchasing inferior products may reduce costs but also further alienate the customer base. Recovery from this vicious cycle is extremely difficult.

marketing plan includes all information pertinent to locating, attracting, and retaining customers. The information contained in a marketing plan includes:

- target market and market segments
- geographic market area
- building design
- signage
- decor and atmosphere
- name selection and logo
- menu
- quality standards
- staffing and training
- customer sensitivity
- price/value perception
- sanitation and cleanliness standards
- feedback loop for product and service improvement
- strategic business units (SBUs) within the organization and within the restaurant, which may include breakfast, lunch, dinner, catering, delivery, and retail
- competitors and their strengths and weaknesses
- barriers to market entry
- promotion and advertising

Real World Scenario

A small chain restaurant opens at an approximate weekly volume of $80,000. Within six months, the restaurant has managed itself down to a "comfortable" sales volume of $32,000 per week.[1] Because the restaurant's managers earn bonus pay based on sales volume, they create ways to attract more customers, with the blessing of their small chain, which has given them independence to create a "local feel."

The unit managers believe that bodies in the seats mean sales. They bring in entertainment, offer coupons, and buy a large-screen television for sporting events with hopes of improving their bar business. The managers are so intent on increasing sales volume that they never uncover the root problem. They did not need to encourage more people to come through the door by artificial means. They simply needed to focus on their original plan and deliver great service and a great product. Once they learned this hard lesson, the managers focused on their primary customers and saw the restaurant's sales volume nearly double within two years.

Geographic Market Area

It is important to define the **geographic market area**. Start with a map of the restaurant's prospective location. Draw circles one, three, five, and ten miles from the site. The circles illustrate where the potential geographical target market is located and help to focus efforts within that range. Depending on the restaurant concept, the majority of clientele will be drawn from one of these defined areas. The information derived may answer some questions about the type of customer different concepts would attract. For example:

- one-mile range: take-out lunch business with no parking
- three-mile range: casual dining
- five-mile range: themed or more unique restaurant, or casual dining with other, outside attractions such as theaters or shopping
- ten-mile range: destination only and/or upscale restaurant

The ranges of distance do not rule out customers from outside this area, but for the time being, the simple rules above will help to focus marketing efforts. Customers do not travel far from home because of the plethora of dining choices available to them nearby their homes.

Building Design

The building design, along with exterior fixtures such as signs, props, and awnings, can form images in customers' minds as to what they can expect when they enter the restaurant. For example:

- A modern building with large plate glass windows and a dark wood interior might give the impression of upscale dining.

- A brick building with bright awnings and fluorescent signs in the window may signal a casual and relaxing atmosphere.
- An old house could convey a homey, down-to-earth feeling.

Signage

The sign is the restaurant's identification card. It will appear in advertisements and on business cards and will be visible to passersby. If the restaurant concept is easy-going, casual dining but the sign gives the appearance of an upscale establishment, the restaurant could lose customers even before having the chance to serve them.

Decor and Atmosphere

Restaurant decor should support the overall concept and not be a haphazard collection of props, as the decor helps set the tone for the atmosphere. The decor includes lighting fixtures, paint color, props (things displayed on shelves or hung on the walls, such as pictures, prints, and mirrors), flooring, tables and chairs, unique and rare items, or a distinctive story about the concept or the building. If the restaurant concept is geared toward family and fun, but decorated in a stuffy manner, the decor is self-defeating. It is not unusual to find restaurant operators buying props at flea markets, garage sales, or antique markets at a fraction of the cost if they were bought new.

Name Selection and Logo

The restaurant name and any subtitle it may use give people an immediate impression as to the type of restaurant it is. A name must be memorable and should be easy to pronounce.

Additional subscripts restaurants attach to their names, such as "Bar & Grill," "Steak & Seafood," or "Italian Restaurant" offer potential customers certain expectations. Name selection is an important part of marketing the restaurant. Try the following exercise when selecting the name:

- Choose several different names and subscripts.
- Place the names in different formats on mock up menus.
- Assemble several roundtable discussions using this format as part of your research. Do not defend your position against individuals' opinions.

Hopefully, this exercise will prove to be effective and offer some comfort with the name selection.

A logo is the restaurant's identifying mark that the public will recognize. Corporate America offers thousands of logo examples. Sometimes a logo without words is all that is needed to convey a message. In the restaurant industry, McDonald's has developed its brand and logo—the golden arches—to be automatically identifiable worldwide. Many restaurant companies do not develop a logo per se, but rather use the restaurant name as an identifier, such as Outback Steakhouse.

In addition to the logo itself, many restaurants add subheadings or mottos that immediately inform the public as to what the concept is. For example, Outback Steakhouse uses the tag line "no rules, just right" to state that customers will not experience a robotic approach to the dining experience. The staff, besides being very carefully chosen and trained, will not recite a prepared greeting, but will greet you with good manners and individual personality. The customer will be right and will enjoy the experience.

Applebee's' message is "Eatin' Good in the Neighborhood," changed from the former tag line "Neighborhood Bar & Grill." The objective is to keep the "neighborhood" associated with their name.

Menu

Menu design, menu items, and price points must also complement the restaurant concept and the target market. The menu direction may change from the initial plan to the roll out of the concept.

Quality Standards

The marketing plan must specify the restaurant's standards for food quality and consistency, beverage operations, cleanliness, and service. Clearly stating the standards in the document provides management with a written document to reference.

Investing time and money in promoting a business is wasteful if the business is unable to deliver and execute the product and services to the satisfaction of the customer. The restaurant business involves selling both a product and a service. Both must have a certain minimum quality standard. The quality and the consistency of the product is the most noticeable of the two.

Quality standards are not and should never be negotiable. The restaurant owner must set the level on these standards and never lower it. Customers will notice immediately if the standards and consistency begin to slip. The chef and manager must insist upon higher than passable quality. If either ever questions the quality and freshness of a product, there really is no debate—it should not be served. Customers sense when an organization's goals are out of alignment with its delivery. If customers sense that such a state has become the standard operating procedure, the customer base will eventually erode.

Staffing and Training

Staffing the restaurant and training the staff might seem to be outside of the realm of marketing, but that is not the case. The staff and how that staff is trained have an impact on the customer. Customer contact is a very important part of marketing. It details the product and service delivery to the customer. The marketing plan leaves no room for management or employee interpretation. Once

Real World Scenario

A brew pub planned to open in a redeveloping downtown market. The brew pub originally planned a menu of "pub fare" that included fast, plentiful, moderately priced food. Traditional bar foods such as Buffalo wings and nachos were to complement burgers, sandwiches, and salads. The menu was right for the number of office workers in the market during the day. However, the dinner-time customer base was comprised of young, affluent, and educated people, primarily as a result of the colleges and universities in the area.

The business plan took into account two theaters that were within walking distance of the brew pub and a major upscale hotel within five minutes and in close proximity to downtown.

Delays occurred in the loan procurement and set construction back by two years. In those two years, many changes occurred and several other establishments either opened or expanded their market share. A major chain also developed plans for a bar/nightclub/amusement facility less than a three-minute walk from the planned brew pub site.

The new developments created some conflict when the marketing plan was ready to be written. If the marketing plan followed the direction of the business plan, the brew pub would be in direct competition with other well-established facilities or operations that had very deep pockets to fend off competition. The different venues would compete for the same dollar. The brew pub owner considered several factors in evaluating his direction, including the decor and building location, the fact that a brew pub could take some liberties with the menu because a brew pub is not confined to a particular style of menu offerings, and that choices for casual dining with a slightly more upscale feel were minimal.

The historic building in which the brew pub was housed was designed to separate the pub area from the main dining room. The dining side decor was dark wood, with comfortable booths and a large fireplace at one end.

The owner had designed two distinct areas of the restaurant and hired a local, up-and-coming, high-profile chef to prepare menu items such as filet mignon, seafood, and unique pasta and chicken dishes for the dining area (the pub menu would feature lighter fare). Even the sandwiches were to be fresh, delicious, and presented with a certain flair.

The restaurant did not target the young college crowd because most such customers were more interested in late night venues, and they also did not have the spending power of the brew pub's target market. That target market included young, affluent people in the 30- to 35-year-old age group. The menu changes broadened the target market group to 30 to 55 and branded the brew pub as more than just a bar. Business people, theater-goers, and even young couples with families felt comfortable in the facility.

The business opened successfully. The owner, while rigid in his standards and vision, was flexible with the menu to ensure that his business carved a niche in the market and became profitable.

management develops or accepts the plan, managers also accept responsibility for its content and must be held accountable to uphold the agreed-upon standards.

The uniform the staff wears projects the restaurant image, reflects its standards, and *must* fit the theme. While many states have laws defining who is responsible for paying for uniforms, a good rule of thumb is that if the uniform or part of the uniform bearing a company logo is required, the company is required to provide the required part. In the case of uniform items such as shirts, employees may purchase additional shirts. Restaurant owners should verify local regulations with their state labor department.

The uniform is not just comprised of the shirt or skirt, pants, apron, shoes, and belt. It also includes the standards of how staff members are expected to carry themselves and the jewelry that staff members are permitted to wear on the job, especially earrings, facial rings, bracelets, and other items.

Customer Sensitivity

Customer sensitivity—the attitudes managers and employees present to the customer—is a major factor in the customers' perception of the restaurant. Consumers can spend their money in any number of restaurants. The customers in a restaurant are there because they have made a conscious decision to spend their hard-earned money in that establishment. Part of being successful in the hospitality industry is ensuring that the customer feels relaxed in the restaurant. Customers' lives are stressful enough. They come to a restaurant to alleviate some of that stress. If the restaurant adds to the customer's stress level, that customer will not dine there often, if ever again.

The restaurant owner, management, and staff must have a passionate, sincere concern for guests' total dining experiences. Customers should never feel as if they are a bother to the staff. If a customer feels this way, even if the feeling is misinterpreted, that customer will not return. Each and every customer is important to a successful business and the base of customers grows every time a positive dining experience is delivered.

Price/Value Perception

Price/value perception must be aligned with the restaurant concept. Consumers will pay for a product or service according to what they decide is a value for the product and service they receive. Failure to meet their expectations will result in lost customers.

Sanitation and Cleanliness Standards

Sanitation is a top priority in the restaurant business that cannot ever be taken lightly. Improper sanitation standards can be disastrous for business. Marketing, by definition, means that the customer is the focal point of everything you do. The restaurant must have a detailed plan to provide a clean and sanitary environment and safe, fresh food. It takes only one incident of food-borne illness to severely hurt the business and possibly force it to close.

Feedback Loop for Product and Service Improvement

A **feedback loop** is an important part of the marketing equation that is often overlooked. Restaurants strive to be attractive to their particular target market. The constant feedback received allows management to fine-tune the products and services to better serve the market and market segments. The more management stays in touch with the market, the greater the advantage a restaurant has over its competition. There must be a feedback loop that encourages this flow of information.

The feedback loop begins when a restaurant owner, staff member, or manager receives feedback from a customer, collects the feedback, and uses it for future planning. If it is difficult for a customer to communicate this information, the restaurant will never receive it or benefit from it. Staff must understand the importance of feedback. If an owner or manager defends the restaurant's position without giving the feedback proper attention and careful consideration, the staff will stop asking for feedback.

Research is actually conducted every time an owner, manager, or employee solicits input or feedback on their product or service. The various options for transmitting the feedback include:

- verbal solicitation
- comment cards
- telephone number of owner
- e-mail address
- mystery shoppers
- round tables and focus groups

VERBAL SOLICITATION Whenever an employee or manager asks a customer about the quality of the food, service, or overall dining experience, they are conducting market research. This can be a key research tool and it is not confined to within the four walls of the restaurant. Anytime a staff member talks to a restaurant patron, that staff member is gathering marketing research information.

The staff member, whether inside or outside of the restaurant, must listen without prejudice or position to the customer, with a sincere concern for the guest's experience. It is important to note that perception is reality. If a negative situation is defended or excuses are offered, customers may not provide this critical feedback in the future because they will not feel as if they can be open and honest. In the case of a negative experience, the restaurant must have a policy in place that allows employees to do whatever they deem necessary to get that customer to return to the restaurant. This not only confirms that the customer's business is valued, but it also gives an employee who is empowered to make things right a certain amount of pride in the business. If the experience was positive, that feedback should be gratefully accepted and passed on. Any feedback received must be communicated on the feedback loop.

COMMENT CARDS Comment cards are a great way to solicit immediate, real-time, anonymous feedback about a guest's experience. However, restaurants should never rely upon written comments at the expense of the personal touch. Nothing takes the place of talking with customers while they are in the restaurant.

Comment cards allow customers to comment on several aspects of the restaurant and dining experience. Information can be solicited not just on the food or service, but also on the quality and variety of menu offerings, the atmosphere, cleanliness, how guests were welcomed at the door, and so forth. These inquiries are not part of the general experience. When a dining room manager is working the floor, his or her concern is for the guests' immediate dining experience. A manager does not ask, "Is the restroom clean enough for you?"

Properly structured comment cards should not be too cumbersome for the customer to complete. A card that takes less than one minute to complete is best (see Figure 2–3). Customers also do not want to be asked to fill out a comment card every time they visit the restaurant.

Following trends is an important part of the feedback you receive. The information collected on comment cards can be altered as the need for information changes. For instance, if you are preparing to update the menu, comment cards may skip over service issues to focus on what the customers want on the menu. The questions must be short and to the point so as not to take up too much of the customers' time.

We are always striving to improve our resturant. We would appreciate if you can take a moment to complete this survey.					
1=POOR 3=AVERAGE 5=OUTSTANDING					
	1	2	3	4	5
Food Quality					
Food Presentation					
Greet at the Door					
Attitude of Server					
Knowledge of Server					
Service					
Menu Variety					
Value					
Cleanliness of Facility					
Noise Level					
Overall Experience					

Additional Comments: _____

_____

_____

If you would like to be contacted by management or would like to receive information on the restaurant please fill out the following:
Name:
Address:
E-mail:

FIGURE 2–3

Comment Card

Comment cards are also good for compiling a database of names and addresses to announce special events or employee or management promotions, promote special dinners, mail catering information, and offer gift certificates.

If a comment card is returned and is generally negative in tone, it should not be simply logged as a complaint. Face two facts:

1. Someone had a bad experience in the restaurant and no one caught it while the customer was there. In this case there was inadequate face-to-face contact while the customer was in the building. This is a critical service problem, as several people had to have contact with the customer he or she was in the restaurant, including the host, the server, possibly a bus person, and a manager. The comment card, as part of the feedback loop, indicates that something went wrong. The first step is to identify what the problem was and why the problem happened. Did the staff show any real concern for the customer? Did the staff ask the right questions? Are the staff and management trained properly to read body language and recognize problems?

2. The customer took the time to fill out the card so they are owed some response. Making direct, face-to-face contact with the customer is difficult for some people. By nature, people do not want to hear negative comments. In the hospitality industry, face-to-face contact is a must. If feedback is negative in tone, staff should not take it personally.

In response to negative comments management and staff must do the following:

- Stay calm.
- Listen completely to what the guest has to say.
- Apologize and be sincere.
- Do what it takes to get the customer back.
- Use the information to correct the situation.

TELEPHONE NUMBER OF OWNER Because the owner or general manager cannot be in the restaurant 24 hours a day, seven days a week, a telephone number for the owner should be readily available to the customer. This number should be on a table tent, menu, or the receipt. It allows a customer to make a direct call and lodge either a complaint or compliment. The fact is that some people by nature, under any circumstance, will not complain while in the restaurant. Unfortunately, these people are the easiest to lose because the owner may not know there is a problem.

If a customer calls the restaurant to lodge a complaint about a bad experience, the customer should not be placed on hold while the owner or manager is located. A short, user-friendly form for taking information about the experience should be available to anyone who answers the telephone. This information should be given to the manager or owner, who should make a personal telephone call to the customer.

E-MAIL ADDRESS Technology has enhanced the ability to communicate. While not everyone has an e-mail address, it makes it quite simple for those that do have e-mail to offer feedback on their experiences.

MYSTERY SHOPPERS Mystery shoppers, or secret shoppers, are effective when used in the proper way. Most "shops" are done for management to receive a snapshot view of how the restaurant is executing service and quality and being perceived by the public. Many owners use a shopper to provide feedback when the owner is not in the building. Some owners use shoppers to capture or prevent theft. All of these methods provide very useful information to an owner. However, shoppers can be more effective than just a snapshot of one single dining experience.

Professional shoppers can be used to gauge the overall customer dining experience. However, some shoppers—usually friends and family—might give glowing feedback instead of being honest. Such flattery does not help the business. Professional shoppers are knowledgeable in the restaurant business and can report point-by-point service standards that include the time of a greeting by a server or bartender, the time from order placement to receiving a drink or appetizer, the time between courses, whether hot food is actually being served hot, if cold food is being served cold, and so forth. As helpful as secret shoppers are, this checklist system does not tell the whole story.

Effective mystery shoppers will provide feedback on their experiences. The owner should ask questions like: "Was some emotion charged up?" "What was the overall experience?" This information is useful to give the owner insight into what the guest feels. If the entrée is taking a little more time than you would like but the guest is enjoying him- or herself, maybe the time constraint on entrée service is too tight. Again, the standard should not be changed from one experience. You should look for trends and follow up with other research.

Mystery shopping should be done randomly at both lunch and dinner, slow times and busy times. The shop should include a phone call to the restaurant before or after the visit, which helps the owner improve training standards for all employees charged with answering the telephone.

Real World Scenario

A restaurant received a mystery shop report that was done via telephone call. The shopper had called to inquire about the restaurant and none of the questions were answered properly. Through further research, the owner discovered that the dishwasher, while cleaning the dining room in the morning, answered the telephone and attempted to answer questions. He was trying to be helpful as part of the team, but he had no answers to common questions and did not realize that what he was doing could have been damaging to the restaurant.

Round Tables and Focus Groups A **round table** or **focus group** is a small group of people (usually 10 to 12 suffice) brought together to provide feedback on a particular subject or subjects. Focus groups, when done correctly, can be very effective in gathering information, especially when changing a menu, upgrading decor or physical structure, or changing or adding locations. These groups are most effective when facilitated by a professional who has market research experience. The input from the group could be misleading if the wrong questions are asked. The meeting must also have specific goals. For instance, a menu focus group should be asked the following questions:

- How often do you dine out?
- What other restaurants do you frequent?
- What is it that attracts you to these restaurants?
- What specific items do you order when dining out?
- What is most important to you in a restaurant?
- What level of service do you get from this restaurant?
- What items would you like to see on the menu?
- Do you feel you receive value for the price points of the menu?

Developing specific questions along with soliciting general input helps to gain an understanding for what customers or potential customers may want. The participants in a focus group should not be limited to regular customers, because such a focus group would narrow the feedback. Instead invite:

- frequent customers,
- customers from different meal periods,
- infrequent customers, and
- people that have never dined in the restaurant.

Strategic Business Units

Strategic business units (SBUs) are the revenue generating components of a business, which, in the case of the restaurant industry, may be comprised of any of the following:

- Lunch,
- Dinner,
- Catering,
- Takeout, and
- Retail.

Each SBU has an individual plan to drive sales. Lunch will be marketed differently than will dinner. The price points and the check average may vary. Lunch is expected to be served faster due to time constraints. Dinner is slower paced because most people do not want to rush. Lunch is also easier to drive frequency, as your customer may be more apt to eat the same dish more than once a week. The marketing plan must address each SBU separately.

Specific marketing ideas and suggestions for each area will be discussed shortly, in the Promotion and Advertising section of this chapter.

Competition and Its Strengths and Weaknesses

No marketing plan is complete without identifying the competition. After all, competing restaurants are trying to win the same dining dollar. A business must develop an advantage over the competition to expand market share. Management must be aware of what the competition is doing to attract customers, along with competitors' strengths and weaknesses.

Barriers to Market Entry

At times, barriers restrict entry into a given market. Information about such barriers is vital to selecting a viable site for the restaurant. Barriers can include zoning laws, environmental issues, labor market problems, and high costs inherent to an area or region. Research is crucial to uncovering any potential problems before making a major investment.

Promotion and Advertising

Advertising is how most people would define marketing. But, as the previous pages have shown, advertising is only one function of the marketing process. Yet advertising is what reaches most customers and gets them to first dine at a restaurant. The purpose of any advertising campaign is threefold: to attract attention, stir an emotion, and drive trial.

Effective advertising can be difficult, frustrating, and expensive to take from concept to reality. There are many forms of advertising and every salesperson of each type of media will claim that their method is more effective and will reach the most consumers. In turn, every radio station will brag about how it reaches more consumers than the next radio station. Sales representatives will pull out graphs and charts to prove their point, as will salespeople for coupon books, magazines, weekly publications, and yellow pages. If each medium was used and an ad placed in each, the cost will drown the business. Set an advertising budget and spend accordingly.

Restaurant owners spend thousands of dollars annually to attract new customers. Yet once those customers enter the restaurant, many owners and managers fail to deliver the dining experience to meet customers' expectations. It is a waste to spend so much money to get customers without having a plan of action to satisfy the customers and earn the right to serve them again. That is

Real World Scenario

A major restaurant opens on a busy, undivided, two-lane highway in a large city. The restaurant owner has four other very successful restaurants in the same city. However, this particular restaurant failed because of its location. The problem was that there were trees in front of the restaurant blocking the view of the parking lot, because the restaurant sat back about 50 yards from the road. Cars coming out of downtown and traveling at 45 miles per hour would not see the restaurant until they were passing it. So, they just turned around, right? Wrong! As cars stopped at the traffic light 100 yards ahead, there was a strip mall entrance anchored by one of the most successful restaurants in the city. In addition, three other restaurants were within walking distance of the parking lot. Even if drivers wanted to turn around and go back, there were other issues such as a small parking lot with limited spaces and no traffic light to re-enter the highway in either direction.

If diners traveled toward the downtown area, they had access to the strip mall restaurants first and still had the parking problems at the other restaurant. The food quality, service, and decor always received top scores in research. The location was just too frustrating for patrons to get in and get out.

why a proper training program is imperative and should be detailed in the marketing plan.

The purpose of advertising is to communicate available goods and services to the marketplace. There are many forms of advertising. Personal advertising is a business owner having the opportunity to engage others in a one-on-one conversation, including:

- speaking to guests already in the establishment;
- hosting chamber of commerce meetings, mixers, and events;
- making food runs to local businesses;
- sponsoring a special night for a local business or apartment/condominium complex; or
- sponsoring and attending charity events and fund raisers.

Impersonal forms of advertising include newspaper, radio, and television ads.

Personal Advertising

GUESTS IN THE RESTAURANT Speaking to guests already in the establishment is a powerful marketing tool commonly referred to as table visits. Just because a customer has decided to try the restaurant does not mean that he or she will frequent the restaurant in the future. Most customers appreciate that someone other than a server or bartender is watching out for their satisfaction. The restaurant increases the chances of gaining regular customers by showing sincere concern during a customer's initial dining experience and making a major investment in the personal form of advertising. The satisfied or delighted customer becomes the most economical form of advertising: a word-of-mouth advertisement. Friends, relatives, and business associates are more likely to respond to a personal recommendation to try a restaurant than they are from reading an advertisement.

So, by merely "closing the deal" on the customer already in the restaurant, potential future customers will hear about the restaurant and the out-of-pocket expense was $0. In fact, money was made. Doing this with each and every customer will yield tremendous results.

Each member of the restaurant team must learn customers' names and learn as much about the customers as possible. When patrons are known by name they:

■ are more likely to frequent an establishment;

■ are more likely to talk positively about the establishment;

■ are more forgiving when a mistake is made; and

■ will communicate the positives and negatives directly.

A manager can't be an ostrich and bury his or her head in the ground if something goes wrong. Many restaurateurs will find that some of their best customers are ones that did not have a great first experience, but, because the problem was handled beyond any expectation they might have had, became long-term customers. Face problems head on.

As long as there are customers in a restaurant, there is only one place for an owner or manager to be: *on the floor talking to them.*

CHAMBER OF COMMERCE The local chamber of commerce has one goal: to promote business in the community. Members of the chamber usually patronize fellow members' businesses. Many chambers hold mixers, social events intended for members to network and for the host business to show itself to the public. Contacts and referrals obtained by attending chamber functions are examples of good, low-cost advertising.

FOOD RUNS A food run is an example of low-cost, personal, direct advertising. Food runs can be used to drive lunch or dinner sales, but are probably more effective at lunch. A restaurant needs simply to locate a business in its immediate area that has 10 to 15 employees. The restaurant contacts the business to verify how many people work in the office. When the office asks why, the restaurant explains that it would like to send the office lunch on a day that is convenient for the office. On the day agreed upon, the restaurant packages samples of salads, sandwiches, beverages, and desserts, along with some menus and possibly even a card for each office employee for a complimentary appetizer. The recipient office will be startled, to say the least. Many of its workers will now visit the restaurant for lunch or dinner just to say thank you. That gives the restaurant an opportunity to earn the workers as regular guests.

Real World Scenario

A restaurant that had been open for about one year was struggling to attract a good portion of its market. The restaurant was at the bottom of a hill and on the opposite side of the road from the main flow of traffic. Cars coming off the exit of a major highway were past the restaurant before realizing it was there. Within a one-mile stretch were some of the most popular national restaurant chains. Right in the middle of these chains was an apartment complex with more than 1,000 apartments. The restaurant's objective was to get those apartment complex residents to travel toward it. Wednesday night was designated as "apartment complex residents'" night. Residents received discounts on drinks and appetizers in the lounge and a 15 percent discount in the dining room. In return, the restaurant was allowed free advertising in the complex's monthly newsletter. The restaurant catered a residents' mixer held quarterly in the complex clubhouse and also sent the office staff lunch as a thank you. Within three weeks, it was bringing 20 to 30 people into the lounge and about 15 people for dinner every Wednesday. For most, it was their first exposure to the restaurant, and the majority would return often. Restaurant management made the group feel at home. The arrangement became a great success for the restaurant.

SPECIAL NIGHTS A special night means simply designating one night of the week for a particular group. If a restaurant has a major business nearby that employs a large number of people or a major apartment or condominium complex it is trying to reach, this form of advertising is inexpensive and very effective.

TAKE-HOME MENUS Printed menus that customers can take home with them promote business. Whether customers take the menu to keep at home or at work, they will look at the menu at some point and probably show it to another person.

CHARITY EVENTS AND FUND RAISERS Charity events and other types of fund raisers are good for two reasons: restaurants get a good corporate image by giving something back to the community, and residents see that the restaurant is active and involved in the community. People remember such activities. It is impossible to donate to or attend every charitable function. But restaurant owners should choose several charities that they would like to help and find out how to get involved. Donating gift certificates can help promote business. If two people spend $50 at the restaurant, a $25 gift certificate would bring in $25 in sales. The actual cost of the donation is about $10, but $25 is tax deductible. The restaurant benefits by:

- getting its name in front of the public eye;
- getting a tax benefit that is higher than the actual cost of the donation; and
- possibly giving a customer a first exposure to the restaurant.

Impersonal Advertising

The various forms of impersonal advertising can be costly and the return on investment is difficult to measure compared to personal forms of advertising. Unfortunately, impersonal advertising is necessary, at least in the beginning. The restaurant's name must be in the public eye consistently. Consumers have short memories because companies bombard them daily.

NEWSPAPER This type of impersonal advertising is probably more likely to be within the financial reach of most restaurants compared to other forms of impersonal advertising. It is less expensive and more user-friendly than other forms of media. Newspaper ads must be properly designed to attract attention and to get the consumer to read the ad. The ad cannot merely represent facts, but must trigger some emotion in the person. Location of the ad, the size of the ad, and days the ad run are also important to having an impact. On any given day in any given market, newspapers are full of advertisements. Even consumers who are looking for a particular ad might have some difficulty locating it. Timing of advertising is also important. Advertising a restaurant on Monday is often a waste of money because most people dine out on Thursday, Friday, and Saturday.

RADIO AND TELEVISION Both of these forms of marketing speak directly to the consumer. The downside of both radio and television advertising is that they are costly and need to be repeated often to have an impact. Most consumers do not respond to an advertisement right away. Normally, they must hear or see the ad several times before making a purchasing decision.

Other Forms of Marketing

SPECIAL OCCASION TRIAL During the course of a year, people make plans to dine at restaurants for special occasions. These special occasions include but are definitely not limited to birthdays, anniversaries, Mother's Day, Father's Day, Valentine's Day, and New Year's Eve. While some members of a group may have dined at your establishment, a few in each party probably have not. Properly planning for these days or doing something special is a great way to make a positive impression on potential new customers.

CATERING AND BANQUETS If a restaurant caters any type of banquet, the occasion is advertising for the business. More so than special occasion trials, many people attending a banquet probably have not been to the restaurant. Each and every person at such a party is a potential customer. At the banquet, the restaurant staff will receive many small requests. It is important to try to accommodate any need to ensure that attendees have a positive impression of the facility and want to dine at the restaurant.

COMPLIMENTARY DESSERT, APPETIZERS, AND DRINKS Complimentary dessert, appetizers, and drinks are a great way to say thank you to customers. Too often, restaurants use complimentary items only for customers that have had problems. What about the regular customers who enjoy their visits? Times when complimentary items are effective are:

■ when you meet a new customer that tells you everything is wonderful—buy them dessert to really drive it home;

■ when someone has a special day such as a promotion, birthday, or anniversary;

■ when you just want to thank a regular customer; or

■ when a problem occurs, in which case do not try to get away cheap—do what needs to be done to fix the problem.

FREQUENT DINER PROGRAMS Frequent diner programs are a way to reward guests that are already spending money in your restaurant. Such programs are better and more advantageous than coupon programs. Coupon programs discount the product and service up front, and the consumer eventually believes that the discounted coupon price is the real price. A frequency card program may be conducted in several ways. Some of the more modern point of sale systems can track the cards and frequency of visits. Frequency cards can be redeemed as buy six get the seventh free, or buy ten get one free, and so forth.

BUSINESS CARD IN A BOWL Collecting business cards in a bowl near the front door is a great way to promote business and to build a database of names, addresses, e-mails, and telephone numbers. Simply offer a $25 gift certificate to be given to a customer drawn weekly from the business cards in the bowl. The restaurant will collect hundreds of cards in a short time.

VISITORS BUREAU Local convention and visitors bureaus are a great source of information. They can provide information on conventions in town and hotel occupancy rates, and they can guide visitors toward a restaurant. Convention coordinators look for flyers, menus, or one-time special offers to stuff into "goodie bags" that are distributed to convention goers.

THEATERS When people go to a theater to see a play or a movie, many will make a night of it. There are several ways to capture this audience:

■ Some movie theaters allow restaurants to buy movie tickets at a discounted price as long as the discount is passed on to the customer. Selling the tickets in the restaurant provides an excellent opportunity to draw people in for dinner before the movie. To kick off this program, offer a free dessert with a movie stub for about one month until customers know the theater tickets are available. The program can also generate early and late evening business.

■ A prix fixe menu can generate sales and turn tables. Theatergoers can be in the restaurant, have dinner, and be on the way to the theater before the regular dinner business gets started. It is a great way to boost sales.

■ Advertise in theater playbills and in monthly or quarterly newsletters to theater supporters.

RADIO STATIONS Contrary to popular belief, many radio personalities are not millionaires simply from being frequently on-air. Take the time to bring them some samples of the menu and a few gift certificates for the restaurant. They will remember this and may mention the restaurant on their show.

TV STATION COOKING SHOWS The Food Network has a done a tremendous favor for restaurants and chefs. Virtually every local television station does some type of in-house cooking demonstration. Contact local stations to see if you can be in the lineup to demonstrate a dish on-air.

PRESS RELEASES Press releases are a form of no-cost advertising. Before opening, a restaurant should write a press release with the details of the opening and mail it to every local media outlet within ten miles. Some will pick it up and some will not. Mail it a second time to those that did not run it the first time. Keep doing so until they respond.

CONCIERGE DINNERS If there are hotels in a restaurant's marketing area, restaurant management should become familiar with the hotel general mangers and staff. If the hotel has a concierge who is charged with taking care of guests' requests, the restaurant should have a concierge dinner to familiarize the individual with the menu and atmosphere. The better the concierge knows the restaurant and the staff, the more likely that person will feel comfortable recommending the restaurant.

FOOD REVIEWS Be prepared for food reviews. A good or decent food review can and probably will boost restaurant business. A poor review can have a negative impact. The entire restaurant staff should be trained to treat each customer as a food reviewer because, in actuality, they are.

POST-OPENING MARKET RESEARCH Most large restaurant chains have sizeable marketing budgets and can afford to conduct organized, focused, and ongoing marketing research to give them the edge on their competition. The purpose of ongoing market research is to gauge the pulse of the marketplace, but small business owners would find conducting such market research cost-prohibitive and very time-consuming. However, without regard to cost, restaurant operators must recognize the need and the importance of this research. The consumer needs to know what a restaurant can do for them. The difficult part for restaurant owners is that most consumers' wants and needs are constantly evolving and changing. However, by being in tune with consumers, the savvy operator will recognize opportunity in changing consumer wants and needs.

Market research is conducted:

■ to give a business a competitive advantage by better understanding the needs of the marketplace; and

■ to cater to those needs before the competition understands or is aware of them.

Without this advantage, a competitor will attract the consumer first and gain market edge.

■ CHAPTER REVIEW

Marketing makes the customer the focal point of every aspect of a restaurant's business. Concept development, site selection, menu offerings, and uniform standards are all influenced by market research and analysis. Formal market research includes traffic counts, market segmentation, and lifestyle clustering, but firsthand knowledge of an area and conducting research locally are also important to the market research process. Again, consider the questions at the beginning of the chapter.

■ KEY TERMS

customer sensitivity	market segment
feedback loop	market segmentation
focus group	round table
frequency of visits	strategic business units
geographic market area	target market
market research	word-of-mouth advertising

■ REVIEW QUESTIONS

1. What are the two purposes of market research?
2. What is meant by frequency of visits?
3. How does market segmentation differ from target market?
4. Explain a strategic business unit?
5. List some of the forms of impersonal advertising.

Site Selection

After reviewing this chapter, you will:

- Know how to locate, select, and evaluate a site for a restaurant concept;
- Learn how to select a general location and then refine the search to an exact location; and
- Learn that each concept carries unique characteristics and demographics for a specific location.

This chapter will review the critical, grueling, and frustrating task of locating and evaluating a site. Many opinions formed are subjective and are based on personal observations. The right location for one type of restaurant might be completely wrong for another type. The factors involved in making this determination are many and the methods presented are intended to assist in understanding the selection process.

Gathering Information

Selecting a site for a restaurant will have a direct impact on the level of success the restaurant will reach, and, at a minimum, dictate the business volume. A restaurant can be well planned and successful in one location but, even if developed with the same care and upholding the same standards, can fail or struggle if it is built in the wrong location. The **demographics** (which define the targeted age group and offer specific information about the group), market segmentation, traffic patterns, and firsthand knowledge of the site and the surrounding area are all parts of the site selection equation.

The first step in site selection is to research any zoning laws that might prevent a restaurant from being built or opened in a particular location. **Zoning laws** are local regulations that designate certain tracts of land for specific uses, such as residential, commercial, light industrial, retail, or restaurant. Going through the process of determining the viability of a site only to find out that it is restricted in its use is very aggravating. Zoning laws may also dictate parking requirements, access from adjoining roadways, building setbacks from the road or nearby houses, and even sizes of signs.

There are several schools of thought in determining which data or systems should be used during the site selection process.

The conventional approach until recently was mainly hands-on: research town plans at the city hall and physically go to the location to count cars, interview residents, observe local businesses, and so forth. Other, more modern methods include conducting studies relating to demographics, lifestyle classifications, market segmentation, and clustering. Such studies can be complicated, time-consuming, and sometimes expensive. This chapter presents the strengths and weaknesses of the various factors that should be considered and why they should be considered. For best results, the site selection process should combine both new technology and census data along with the old time-proven method of personal observation.

When researching a site, many prospective restaurant owners want to determine how far people will travel to dine at a particular restaurant. They want to know if the restaurant will appeal only to people living in an immediate neighborhood, or if customers will travel ten miles to dine there. Prospective owners should use the 80/20 rule, which asserts that 80 percent of customers will come from within a certain radius of the restaurant. The following is a guideline:

> One to two miles—lunch business or neighborhood restaurant
>
> Three to five miles—casual dining or specialty restaurant
>
> Ten miles—destination or more upscale restaurant

Most restaurants' customers fall within the three-to-five-mile range, but this is only a guideline and not a steadfast rule.

Some of the data needed to conduct a study are:

- The number of people living or working inside the target market;
- The disposable income of this group;
- Dining patterns for this group.

Often, prospective restaurant owners don't have the expertise to conduct site selection research. If a particular site is recognized as a great location, the odds are that others also see the same opportunity, and a restaurant owner could face competition from other operators who have greater access to capital or have the ability to assume more risk. Still, it is important to have a basic understanding of how to conduct research.

To assist in the process, use the form in Figure 3–1 to get an overall score of the viability of a restaurant in a given market. The scoring on this form is subjective and the person using it must be somewhat familiar with the site, the surrounding area, and certain trends. A line-by-line description shows how to score each line on the form. Each item receives a score from 1 to 10, with 10 being the best.

Location		

The scoring of this sheet is to give you a starting point for site selection.
Scoring is on a 1 to 10 basis. 1- Poor   10- Best

Demographic		Notes
Household Income		
Availability of Target Market		
Geographic Location	**Score**	
Future Area Growth Plans		
History of the Area		
Auto or Foot Traffic		
Other Business		
Restaurant Market Saturation		
Crime Trends		
Convenience of Location		
Sub Total	0	
Building and Land		
Past Problems of the Buiding/Land		
Driving Visibilty		
Parking		
Ease of Access		
Lighting in Parking Lot		
	0	
	0	
Sub Total	0	
TOTAL	0	
Average	0.00	
Weighted Average	0.00	
Seasonal Business		
Hotels		
Office Buildings		
Past Success as a restaurant		
Mass Transit		

FIGURE 3–1

Site Selection Scoring Table.

In determining the quality of a site, needed information includes:

■ Demographic data, including household income and availability of target market;

■ Geographic location data including future growth plan for the area the history of the location automobile and foot traffic near the location other businesses that would draw traffic into an area (e.g., a strip mall or shopping center) restaurant market saturation and direct restaurant competition crime trends and convenience of location;

■ Building and land issue information, including past problems of the building/land driving visibility parking ease of access and lighting in the parking lot;

■ Additional site selection data, including seasonal factors, hotels in the area, office buildings in the area past success trends, and mass transit.

Demographic Data

Demographic data on age, income levels, drive times to work, and other data can be downloaded from the United States Census Bureau at http://factfinder.census.gov (see Figure 3-2). This data is not included in the overall score but is used for reference only.

HOUSEHOLD INCOME The household income is important to understand because it directly relates to how often a household may frequent a restaurant and what type of restaurant they would frequent. For example, seniors living on a fixed income may be more likely to frequent a buffet type of restaurant.

AVAILABILITY OF TARGET MARKET The availability of the target market as defined in the marketing plan is also important so the operator can understand the number of people that live and/or work in the vicinity. This again will directly impact the potential traffic flow through the business. This can be graded as a letter (A=Excellent, B=Very Good, C=Fair) or by whatever other scale the scorer wishes to use.

Geographic Location Data

The factors included in this section, as well as the Building and Land section, are scored on the 1 to 10 scale as previously explained.

FUTURE GROWTH PLAN FOR THE AREA There are several sources of information for future growth plans, including local chambers of commerce, city halls, and organizations involved with business improvement districts, planning, zoning, and city development.

HISTORY OF THE LOCATION If an area has struggled economically and has had problems recovering, it could be difficult to attract customers.

AUTOMOBILE OR FOOT TRAFFIC Automobile traffic at the site location provides basic information about potential customers. If the site is near a main thoroughfare or leads into one, the traffic on that thoroughfare must also be considered. Again, this traffic pattern can be a strong positive or negative influence depending on the specifics relating to time of day and congestion.

Sometimes foot traffic is more critical than auto traffic. For instance, in a downtown area with offices, foot traffic at lunchtime will drive more business

Subject	Number	Percent
EMPLOYMENT STATUS		
Population 16 years and over	25,359	100.0
In labor force	18,529	73.1
Civilian labor force	18,477	72.9
Employed	17,891	70.6
Unemployed	586	2.3
Percent of civilian labor force	3.2	(X)
Armed Forces	52	0.2
Not in labor force	6,830	26.9
Females 16 years and over	12,958	100.0
In labor force	8,522	65.8
Civilian labor force	8,514	65.7
Employed	8,258	63.7
Own children under 6 years	2,640	100.0
All parents in family in labor force	1,554	58.9
COMMUTING TO WORK		
Workers 16 years and over	17,611	100.0
Car, truck, or van -- drove alone	15,303	85.9
Car, truck, or van -- carpooled	1,225	7.0
Public transportation (including taxicab)	137	0.8
Walked	115	0.7
Other means	100	0.6
Worked at home	731	4.2
Mean travel time to work (in minutes)	23.7	(X)
Employed civilian population 16 years and over	17,891	100.0
OCCUPATION		
Management, professional, and related occupations	10,126	56.6
Service occupations	1,388	7.8
Sales and office occupations	4,491	25.1
Farming, fishing, and forestry occupations	0.0	0.0
Construction, extraction, and maintenance occupations	743	4.2
Production, transportation, and material moving occupations	1,143	6.4
INDUSTRY		
Agriculture, forestry, fishing, and hunting, and mining	7	0.0
Construction	770	4.3
Manufacturing	1,604	9.0
Wholesale trade	494	2.8
Retail trade	1,860	10.4
Transportation and warehousing, and utilities	661	3.7
Information	578	3.2
Finance, insurance, real estate, and rental and leasing	1,731	9.7
Professional, scientific, management, administrative, and waste management services	2,504	14.0
Educational, health and social sciences	4,297	24.0

FIGURE 3–2

US Census Bureau Demographic Data.

than will automobiles, since people in cars may have difficulty parking. If the restaurant is located in a mall, foot traffic in the mall is more critical than how much auto traffic is on a nearby highway.

OTHER BUSINESSES If other businesses are close to the site, the consumer has more reason to be in the vicinity of the restaurant. Research any business associations in the neighborhood. These associations, if they exist, may have valuable insights into local business trends. If an association does not exist, talk to local business owners about area trends.

RESTAURANT MARKET SATURATION Several restaurants grouped in one area usually is a positive signal for business, as consumers have more options in the area. In addition, if one restaurant is extremely busy, the others have an opportunity to serve the overflow of customers, which can be a boon for the dining market in that area.

However, the dining dollar is limited. If the market becomes oversaturated, fighting for a portion of the dining dollar can be difficult. Restaurant **market saturation** takes into account all restaurants in the area. Be more aware of direct competition, which is a similar concept. If an owner is opening a steak house when there are already four established steak houses in the area, the direct competition would be a deciding factor in the site selection. This direct competition could negatively impact the market saturation score.

CRIME TRENDS Crime near your restaurant is one of the quickest ways to lose business. People need to feel safe when going out to eat.

CONVENIENCE OF LOCATION How easy is it for someone to drive to the restaurant? If the restaurant is difficult to access, it may be difficult to draw enough customers.

BUILDING AND PROPERTY ISSUE INFORMATION: PAST PROBLEMS OF THE BUILDING/LAND The condition of the building, including any problems with plumbing, sewage, the roof, or asbestos, and the land could make the property expensive to prepare for use.

DRIVING VISIBILITY When customers are driving toward the restaurant, it should be visible from the road.

PARKING Parking can be a factor in whether people will travel to the restaurant. If parking is difficult at certain times of the day, it might cause a loss of business. If parking is abundant, traffic can flow toward a restaurant solely for that reason.

EASE OF ACCESS INTO AND OUT OF THE PARKING LOT A restaurant may have more than enough parking, but if parking is cut up or access is difficult, the benefit will be diminished. If a customer is driving down a busy road and has to cross oncoming traffic and there is no turning lane in the middle of the road, the customer may get frustrated and just decide it is too much trouble entering the parking lot.

LIGHTING AND SECURITY OF PARKING LOT A parking lot is a positive factor for a restaurant, but it must be secure and well lit.

Additional Site Selection Information

The following information is for reference purposes only. These are not scored but the information is important to properly evaluate a sight.

SEASONAL FACTORS If the business is seasonal, like many found in vacation spots, can it generate enough volume to pay an owner through the off-season?

HOTELS Major hotels that attract business people and tourists or cater to large banquets or conventions can be a positive influence on business.

OFFICE BUILDINGS IN THE AREA Office buildings can drive business, though more so for lunch than for dinner. They can also be a strong negative influence on business if the area is too heavily dependent on daytime offices to drive business.

PAST SUCCESS TRENDS AS A RESTAURANT If a restaurant has existed in this location before, it is critical to know how successful it was. If a restaurant existed but failed, more research should be conducted to understand why. If more than one restaurant existed and each one failed, this is a definite red flag. The reason might relate to poor operators, but several failed operations might point to another factor. The scoring explained above may uncover the reasons for failure.

MASS TRANSIT Availability of mass transit nearby can be positive or negative. In a city location that depends on the labor force coming from outside the immediate area, mass transit is vital to attracting the workforce needed. A negative factor can be a bus stop on the same grounds as a restaurant. If the bus line is extremely busy and people are always milling about, the congestion may dissuade customers from entering the parking lot.

Scoring

In determining the viability of a site, assign a letter code from A through D. An A site is a prime location with high visibility, heavy automobile and/or foot traffic, ease of access to parking, and other businesses. Potential owners may also want to add a suffix of + or – to the letter, such as an A+ location. This is prime real estate that may not last long on the market. An A location, under normal circumstances, will carry with it a relatively high price tag or lease payment. The owner of a D location is usually happy to have someone in the spot.

Real World Scenario

A site available in a nearby city was once the location of a long-standing, very successful restaurant. The owner of that restaurant found other interests while giant chain restaurants moved into the surrounding area. The building was demolished and the land was put up for sale or lease. The price tag on the land was too high even for the most established and diverse restaurant chain. Even though it was an A+ location, the purchase price was beyond reach even for very high-volume operations.

The second number is known as the *weighted average*. The weighting is based on the geographic location carrying 80 percent of the overall score and the building and land carrying 20 percent of the overall score. The weighted score simply gives a different perspective and can signify a great general geographic area with the wrong specific location or building. If there is a large disparity in these scores, the search for a more suitable location should continue.

Scoring is as follows:

9.0–10.0: A+ location

8.5–9.0: A location

7.5–8.0: B location

7.0–7.5: C location

Below 7.0 is a D location and should be avoided.

Let's look at how the scoring works in the following three cases.

THE WINE STATION This is a wine bar with a lighter, tapas-style menu (small plates) and a demographic of 30-year-olds and older. It is heavily marketed toward professional men and women and does not allow children. The concept includes an open kitchen, wood-fired pizzas, panini sandwiches, fresh salads, a raw bar, and homemade desserts. A lounge area features a center fireplace that burns on four sides. Two dining rooms, one over the other, seat about 60 people each. The facility also has a stone patio area that is tree-lined and can seat about 30 people.

In Figure 3–3, the score for The Wine Station is 7.63, with a weighted average of 7.52. This signifies a B geographic location and a B for the specific site. But what is the site worth? There is no formula to answer this question. The worth depends on what the return on investment (ROI) is for that site. If an A+ location drives occupancy costs to the point where **breakeven**—the point at which cost and income are equal—becomes unreachable, it is not a good site, regardless of the site's score. A B location with good lease terms will suffice. On the other hand, if the concept is dependent on high volume and needs an A site to drive the necessary sales, the A site and its associated expense may be necessary.

THE SPORT CLUB This is a sports bar/restaurant with 50 televisions and a separate dining room. It has a pub fare menu with a few dinner entrees, such as New York strip and shrimp scampi. The owner has a reputation for top quality food

Location		

The scoring of this sheet is to give you a starting point for site selection.
Scoring is on a 1 to 10 basis. 1- Poor   10- Best

Demographic		Notes
Household Income	$ 68,999	
Availability of Target Market	Very Good	Occupations, employment and disposable income
		very positive for this concept
Geographic Location	**Score**	
Future Area Growth Plans	7	Area has grown extensively over the past 10 years
History of the Area	8	Very busy area for bsuiness and retail
Auto or Foot Traffic	8	Over 30,000 cars daily within 50 yards
Other Business	8.5	Offices, retail including mall, restaurants, hotels
Restaurant Market Saturation	5	Very saturated to the point chains have stopped
Crime Trends	8	Very few problems
Convenience of Location	7.5	High traffic, easy entrance, very busy at certain times
Sub Total	52	
Building and Land		
Past Problems of the Buiding/Land	8	No known problems
Driving Visibilty	8	Great from road, main road a little tough
Parking	7.5	Over 100 spots
Ease of Access	8	Middle turn lane
Lighting in Parking Lot	8	Brand New
	0	
	0	
Sub Total	39.5	
TOTAL	91.5	
Average	7.63	
Weighted Average	7.52	
Seasonal Business	N/A	
Hotels	8	
Office Buildings	7	
Past Success as a Restaurant	N/A	
Mass Transit	7	

FIGURE 3–3

Wine Station Site Score.

and for operating clean, professionally run restaurants. The target market is 21 years and older. Children are welcome and there is a children's menu.

In Figure 3-4, The Sports Club receives an average score of 7.5 and a weighted average of 7.24, a B geographically and a C for the building. This is a good score for the concept.

PRIME STEAK HOUSE This is a steak and seafood restaurant with an average dinner check of $25, not including drinks or wine. The target market is 30

Location		

The scoring of this sheet is to give you a starting point for site selection.
Scoring is on a 1 to 10 basis. 1- Poor   10- Best

Demographic		Notes
Household Income		
Availability of Target Market		
Geographic Location	**Score**	
Future Area Growth Plans	6	Talks but no action to date
History of the Area	8	Very busy area
Auto or Foot Traffic	8	Auto traffic is over 20,000 cars per day
Other Business	6.5	Many very small operations
Restaurant Market Saturation	7	Quite a few, small, niche oriented
Crime Trends	7	Some problems, late night bar area
Convenience of Location	6.5	Tough from certain parts of the city
Sub Total	49	
Building and Land		
Past Problems of the Buiding/Land	8	None that is known, part of Historic Society
Driving Visibilty	8	Quite visible
Parking	9	One of the few in this area with off street parking
Ease of Access	8	Turn Lane
Lighting in Parking Lot	8	Kept up to date
Sub Total	41	
TOTAL	90	
Average	7.50	
Weighted Average	7.24	
Seasonal Business	N/A	
Hotels	3	None in immediate vicinity
Office Buildings	5	Not within 1 mile
Past Success as a Restaurant	8	Has been established over 30 years
Mass Transit	5	Nearby

FIGURE 3–4

Sports Club Site Score.

years old and older with above-average disposable income. Children are allowed, but there is no children's menu. The facility has parking for about 40 cars. The neighborhood is marginal and has been in economic stagnation for about ten years.

In Figure 3-5, Prime Steak House has an average score of 6.25, with a weighted average of 5.82, which is a very poor score for this type of restaurant.

Scoring is on a 1 to 10 basis. 1- Poor   10- Best

Demographic	Score	Notes
Household Income		
Availability of Target Market		
Geographic Location	**Score**	
Future Area Growth Plans	5	No growth in ten years and none planned
History of the Area	5	Stagnation at best
Auto or Foot Traffic	7	Auto traffic quite heavy
Other Business	5	Some have closed, none have opened
Restaurant Market Saturation	6	For the area a few
Crime Trends	5	Several problems including drugs
Convenience of Location	5	Across a bridge and at the end of a highway
Sub Total	38	
Building and Land		
Past Problems of the Buiding/Land	8	Popular for many years
Driving Visibilty	8	Right on the main drag
Parking	6	Some but not adequate
Ease of Access	8	easy to gain entrance
Lighting in Parking Lot	7	Kept up
Sub Total	37	
TOTAL	75	
Average	6.25	
Weighted Average	5.82	
Seasonal Business	N/A	
Hotels	3	None
Office Buildings	3	None
Past Success as a restaurant	6	Up to 2 years previous very good
Mass Transit	4	Bus stop on corner near parking lot

FIGURE 3–5

Prime Steak Site Score.

Beyond Price

Sometimes larger companies have other motivations for a particular site. New York City's Times Square is a perfect example. Hundreds of thousands of people are exposed to the businesses there every week. Along with that exposure comes a heavy price tag. Most companies cannot afford the rent, even some that lease locations there. But larger companies might lease space for the name exposure alone and accept the loss or the breakeven it might bring.

Some chains also lease space in malls where they know they will lose money. However, they often encounter mall owners who own more than one mall. They lease their prime spots in other malls to restaurants that are willing to pick up a D location to help mall owners fill vacant space in lighter traffic areas.

Once a location has been researched, the prospective owner must then determine how the cost of the lease compares with the traffic the location will bring.

Sample Site Selection Problems

PROBLEM ONE Even the largest restaurant companies choose a site they believe has great potential, but the proprietor never fully understands the implications of locating at a particular site. For instance, one of the largest restaurant companies in the country leased a spot in the affluent Buckhead area of Atlanta, Georgia, based on several factors:

1. the future growth potential of the area, which was seen as promising (and which eventually proved to be correct);
2. the traffic volume from early morning to late night, seven days a week; and
3. the success of three other units of the same concept in the city, along with the concept's growing popularity.

Some important issues, however, were overlooked.

1. Crime trends in the area. This particular area was growing and growth brought with it increased crime. The site was on the edge of Buckhead closer to the midtown area. People who wanted to avoid any possibility of crime stayed more in central Buckhead.
2. Failure to research the history of the land for problems such as sewage, dumping, or any other cause that may require a costly fix. At the rear of the parking lot was a 20-foot support wall that dropped down to a small river. The wall was in complete disrepair. The needed repairs were very expensive and the owner had to close 20 percent of the parking lot for more than two weeks.
3. A bus station was built directly in front of the building one year after the restaurant opened. The bus stop had been planned for more than three years. People were at the bus stop at all hours, which was discomforting to some customers.
4. The road on which the restaurant was located was two lanes in each direction and the speed limit was 40 miles per hour. Unless patrons knew specifically where to turn, they would drive past the restaurant before seeing it. Customers driving from downtown had to make a left turn into the lot without a turning lane, making access very difficult.

PROBLEM TWO A brew pub that was having success after success in several markets opened a unit in a very affluent area. The restaurant had top-notch food, quality beer, excellent service standards, and a unique concept. There was more than enough of the targeted demographic with plenty of disposable income. The only major flaw in this site selection was that the people in the area did not understand brew pubs, regardless of the quality of the food. They thought of a brew pub as a bar rather than as a restaurant. The restaurant struggled to attract customers. If the same restaurant had opened with the same menu but called itself a wine bar, a martini bar, or even just a restaurant, it would have attracted customers much more easily.

THE BOTTOM LINE Finding the right location for a specific concept must be done methodically. Not all concepts fit all locations. Some restaurants that fail do so not because of poor quality food, poor service, or an unconcerned attitude, but simply because the restaurant was built in the wrong location. When researching a location, it is imperative to solicit input from as many people as possible. Prospective owners should distribute the site selection form and ask a variety of people for their opinions and then compile the information to use as a starting point.

The second step is to get firsthand information by visiting a site at different times and monitoring traffic patterns. It is also a good idea to go into nearby restaurants and count customers at meal periods.

Buying versus Leasing

The decision to buy a building or property instead of leasing it depends on several factors. Some people consider buying an investment in the real estate business, while others view leasing as a waste of money paid in rent with nothing to show for the expense at the end of the lease term. Often the building or even the land are not for sale, but are available only for lease.

When deciding whether to purchase, an owner must consider his or her financial position along with long-term goals and area trends. If this is a first-time venture, leasing, in most cases, ties up less capital. Also, prospective owners should consider the following:

1. If the business does not succeed, it will be easier for an owner or real estate company to re-lease the property than to sell it. The real estate company or building owner assumes that burden and is probably better suited to deal in real estate.
2. Critical working capital might get tied up in closing costs, legal fees, and the down payment for the purchase.
3. Leasing allows a new restaurant owner to concentrate on the restaurant business rather than the real estate business.

There are also some disadvantages to leasing the property instead of buying the real estate:

1. A restaurant owner has no equity position in a leased property. However, if the real estate is purchased, there will be some amount of equity, depending on the size of the down payment and length of time of ownership.

2. If the lease option is a **triple-net lease**, which is a lease that requires the lessee to pay rent, property tax, and all repairs, the lessee is paying to improve someone else's property.

If an experienced owner has *a proven track record* in business and the restaurant concept is also proven, purchasing the land and constructing a building may be the better option. The restaurant goals and the owner's financial position will determine how to proceed. This decision should always involve the business owner's accountant.

Many chain operations lease property because the belief is that their business focus should be on restaurants and not on real estate. They do not like to tie up capital in property, but would rather invest in equipment, expand to additional locations, or maintain cash reserves. To make the right determination, a restaurant owner should:

1. write down the business goals for the next five years;

2. on two spreadsheets, compare purchase vs. lease costs and project business goals for five years into the future; and

3. consider tax liability and present and future financial positions with legal and accounting professionals.

There are several opportunities for a restaurant owner to enjoy the best of both worlds by protecting cash assets and eventually owning the property:

■ The owner may lease a property with a three-year base term instead of the typical five years. The profitability of the business will be apparent within the three-year period. If the business does not succeed, the lessee is responsible only for the balance of the three-year term instead of a five-year term.

■ The proprietor can have two term options on the lease agreement: a first option for five years and a second option for seven years. Such an agreement still offers the normal 15 years for a lease, but offers protection on the front end of the contract.

■ A restaurant operator may opt to build in an option to purchase the property or, at a minimum, retain a **right of first refusal** if another potential buyer makes an offer. The right of first refusal requires the building owner to offer the property to the lessee before placing it on the open market for sale. The sale price should be agreed upon before the lease agreement is signed.

Approaching the lease in this manner allows restaurant owners to concentrate on operating their establishments while possibly having property ownership if and when the restaurant achieves success. The proprietor also has protection if the business is not as successful as planned. (No one ever wants to consider failure, but it is important to consider all options.)

Evaluating an Existing Restaurant Operation

Information and Data Collection

In making any decision, the data collected are *extremely important* in supporting the choice. There are several good sources of information about real estate:

1. City or town hall: prospective owners should look up all records for transfer of this property as far back as is noted.
2. The restaurant owner should talk with immediate neighbors about the parcel or building.
3. Owners should review past tax records.
4. Restaurant operators should talk with vendors and trades people that may do business with the present owners or who have worked on the building.
5. Real estate agents are a good source of information.
6. Owners should also consult friends and acquaintances that might know something about the property.

The purpose of such research is to verify whether the property is in good condition. Excessive bills for repair work can signal chronic problems. If the property has been sold numerous times, that may be a red flag. If a restaurant existed at the site, it is important to find out how busy and how successful it was. *If several restaurants failed at the site, it is imperative to find out why.*

Even with a lease, a restaurant owner should hire a building inspector to thoroughly inspect the building and use all the information to piece together a history of the building.

Empty Shell

If the building is an empty shell with only exterior walls and perhaps power, the cost of building out the space could be high. Equipment, contractors (electricians, carpenters, sheet metal workers, plumbers, etc.), licenses, and architects can be quite costly. Building a restaurant from the ground up will be discussed in depth in Chapter 7.

Purchasing an Existing Operation

A **turnkey** operation is one that is purchased with the intent of operating in a very similar fashion to the existing operation, thus the name *turnkey*: just put the key in the door and the business is open.

In this scenario, the new owner is, in part, paying for the hard work of the previous owner and the clientele that owner built. The new owner's hope is that the clientele will be as loyal to the new owner as they were to the previous owner. The previous owner can provide valuable experience and knowledge about the marketplace and the people in it, having made the mistakes and learning what works and what does not work. The former owner can also be helpful during transition.

Purchasing a turnkey operation can be tricky, though, because many operators will sell when every aspect of the restaurant is in need of an overhaul and the establishment is worn down.

If the building and equipment have been well maintained, however, purchasing an existing operation is probably the *most economical* way to get into the restaurant business, whether or not the concept is being changed. Many owners, when putting their businesses up for sale, are willing to hold a good portion of the asking price in a loan note to them. They do this because they understand how difficult it is to get approval for bank financing. It also makes the business more attractive to a buyer, and decreases the buyer's tax liability. The more of a loan note a previous owner is willing to hold, the more confident that person is in the continued success of the business.

There are several ways to place a value on an existing business. Many brokers use the rule of thumb of two times the net profit of the business, plus the owner's salary and discretionary cash, such as depreciation and interest expenses. The bottom line in setting a sale price is simply what a buyer is willing to pay for the business. The buyer is making an investment and business decision, not buying a job.

The way to set the multiple is to start at two times and then adjust it according to the conditions set forth below. In the case of a restaurant that is very popular with great cash flow and new equipment, the present owner will probably have enough confidence in the business's continued growth to hold a note, the multiple of which will probably be close to twice the net profit. Another common way to value a business is to calculate 20 to 30 percent of the gross sales. Both methods rely upon the same factors:

1. the condition of the equipment, furniture, and fixtures;
2. the condition of the building;
3. the lease terms being offered;
4. the sales trends over the past three years;
5. the reputation of the business; and
6. any new competition that might be opening in the area that may erode the sales line.

Financial information provided by the seller is important. This includes not merely the tax returns but also invoices, bills, loans, and payroll. All these will help the buyer reconstruct actual performance.

The purchase price must be factored into the expected return on investment. A prospective owner must compile a budget to start this process. An accountant is vital in making this decision. A new restaurant operator must not give up security to purchase a job for him- or herself. The business purchaser should make an investment that will add economic value to the present situation.

THE CONDITION OF THE EQUIPMENT, FURNITURE, AND FIXTURES Restaurant equipment is expensive. It also loses most of its value the very first time it is used. If any equipment needs replacement within three years, specifically kitchen or point of sale (POS) equipment, that cost should be subtracted from the total asking price. **Point of sale equipment** is used where servers and bartenders enter food and beverage orders for the bar or kitchen. (POS equipment plays a much larger role and will be discussed in detail in Chapter 5.) Also, the buyer should look at the cost of repair bills for other equipment, including refrigeration units, heating ventilation and air conditioning (HVAC), grills and ovens, and so forth. If the repair bills are high, chances are good that some of the equipment will soon have to be replaced. The buyer should be careful not to get hooked into paying for the previous owner's neglect.

CONDITION OF THE BUILDING Repairs to the building are also expensive. If the lessee is responsible for repairs, it is important to have the building thoroughly checked. Roof leaks because of roof-mounted equipment are common. The roof should be carefully checked out, especially while it is raining or, in the north, during a winter thaw. The condition of ceiling tiles can be a telltale sign of problems.

Compliance with the federal Americans with Disabilities Act (ADA) may also require building updates. Such costs may include (but of course are not limited to) bathroom overhauls, new doorways, ramps, and possibly even an elevator. A prospective owner should contact a building inspector to get a written statement as to what, if any, such improvements would be necessary. Even if the inspector requires no updates to comply with ADA code, the prospective owner should *have the inspector put that in writing*.

LEASE TERMS BEING OFFERED Terms of the lease are vital. The lease should detail cost, length of the lease, and responsibility for repairs. If the rent is raised, which is likely, the value of the business goes down. For instance, if the landlord raises the rent by $500 per month, the business's net income automatically decreases by $6,000 over the course of one year. Therefore, the value of the business decreases by $6,000.

SALES TRENDS OVER THE PAST THREE YEARS If the sales trend has been *positive* for the past three years, the business will demand a *higher* price. If the sales trend has been *negative*, the cost will *decrease*. For example, if the restaurant's sales trend has been down 5 percent each year for the past two years, a potential buyer could assume that sales will be down a minimum of 5 percent in the upcoming year.

NEW COMPETITION THAT MAY ERODE THE SALES LINE If new competition is moving into the area, a prospective buyer should determine the impact the competition will have on the sales line. It is possible the present owner is getting out of the business before the competition moves into the area.

■ CHAPTER REVIEW

Selecting a site is a grueling task that must be conducted with the utmost care and attention to every detail. Researching any site or location takes time and patience. Employing a scoring system allows a prospective buyer to methodically analyze all the pertinent data available on a site. The buyer should consider not only the site itself, but all of the associated costs that site entails. An A location will carry an A price tag. The restaurant concept must support such a site selection. It is possible that an A, B, or C site might satisfy the concept and anticipated volume.

■ KEY TERMS

breakeven	right of first refusal
demographics	triple-net lease
market saturation	turnkey
point of sale equipment	zoning laws

■ REVIEW QUESTIONS

1. Explain a zoning law.

2. What is a triple-net lease?

3. List five of the factors that should be considered when evaluating a site.

CHAPTER 4

Business Plan

After reviewing this chapter, you will:

- Understand the importance of a business plan;
- Be able to assemble the data necessary to write a business plan;
- Be able to write a business plan that will attract investors and set standards for the restaurant; and
- Understand the various legal entities of business.

Any businessperson, regardless of the industry, must understand the importance of a business plan. A business plan is the guiding light and road map for any business, no matter its size, number of employees, or revenue generated. This chapter introduces valuable information that will lay the foundation for formulating and building a well-organized and thorough plan.

Following the steps involved in writing the plan will enable business owners to methodically add the building blocks to guide them in building a successful restaurant.

It is important to develop the discipline to conduct market research to understand the market, develop a concept and menu, bring together the key players, and develop financial data. The business plan encompasses all of this knowledge and includes it in one document. It serves as a road map, giving management a starting point, a destination, and a clear path to success. The business plan also provides the knowledge to properly evaluate and analyze the potential and viability of any business. This road map does not show the detours that might occur on the way to the destination, but it does keep management focused.

Purpose of a Business Plan

A business plan is the road map to success for any business, whether the business is a small food service operation, a computer software company, or a

Real World Scenario

Scenario 1—A casual dining restaurant opens without a plan. The two partners in the business have opposing views of the type of menu that will best serve the needs of the market. One partner wants a more upscale menu with slightly higher price points than most of the restaurants in the market. Although there is a small market for both an upscale menu and the price points, the other partner contends that this market does not have sufficient base to drive the necessary traffic counts that would produce the dollar sales volume necessary for a thriving business. The restaurant opens with the higher price point menu and the restaurant does attract a small market. However, the traffic counts are not enough. The partners change the menu eventually to better serve the needs of the market. After a month with the new menu, they realize a slight uptick in traffic counts but still not an increase sufficient to meet their costs. The partners hire weekend musical entertainment, which upsets some of the regular customers. Concept changes take place every month or so until the business closes within a year of opening.

Scenario 2—A restaurant opens on a golf course in the Northeast with a clear business plan and focus on the market. The plan includes local market research, financials including a budget with projected sales and costs, cost control systems, the menu and price points, and the necessary members of the management team as well as operational standards for the staff. The menu was fine-tuned over the first four or five weeks, staying within the guidelines of the original plan and focusing on the target market. At the end of the first year the owner reviewed the results and compared the results to the initial plan. The owner made adjustments for the following year and planned to increase sales by 10 percent and profits by an additional 20 percent.

In the second year the owner saw an increase of almost 18 percent in sales and more than 30 percent increase to the bottom line. A sales increase of at least 10 percent was achieved for the first five years in business.

multinational conglomerate such as Darden restaurants. Whether a business has yearly revenues of a billion dollars or merely $1 million in sales, whether it has two employees or two thousand employees, without a business plan, a business will drift with the tide and necessary operational adjustments will only be made as time or energy level of the owner permits. However, a sudden increase in sales or a flood of new customers does not happen with luck. A business plan is devised to give management and investors a deep understanding of how a business will develop from a simple idea through the long process of the research and planning stages to a thriving, successful entity. It forces the businessperson (author of the plan) to do deep soul searching and consider a wide range of factors.

The business plan is not to merely present dreams, although certain parts of the business plan allow the entrepreneurial spirit, dreams, visions, and enthusiasm of an individual to be shared with others. However, the majority of a business plan is only concerned with hard facts and educated assumptions. It allows owners, managers, and investors to make informed, educated decisions on the future prospects of a business.

A business plan will:

1. force management to set long-range goals;

2. develop short-term goals and recognize important milestones in support of the overall long-range goals;

3. allow one to compare pre-opening expectations to post-opening reality such as budgeted sales and expenses to actual revenue and costs; and

4. make informed decisions about the future of the business and keep management from making knee-jerk operational decisions that can be more damaging than helpful to business.

Audience

A business plan is written for two major reasons:

1. develop conceptual and operational standards for management; and

2. attract investors.

Because there are two audiences, an owner could take the long route and develop two separate plans: One for investors and one as a guiding doctrine of operations to be used by the restaurant managers. Each plan would vary slightly because the management team is more interested in the vision of the owner and the standards they as managers will be responsible for enforcing rather than the owner's financial position. The financial strength of a company may be a weighted factor in a manager's decision to work for that company, but it is not necessary for them to know personal financial matters or the financial position of investors. Investors, on the other hand, want to know the plans for generating revenue, controlling the cost, their anticipated **return on investment** (ROI), the owner's experience in running such an operation, and how much of a vested interest the owner will have in the business. But having two plans can be confusing and a waste of time. Simply adding addendums that detail the financial data that banks or investors require is a more straightforward way to develop the plan. It also gives more detailed information to investors on the plans to operate the business, which may be a deciding factor in their decision to invest.

Contents of a Business Plan

Because it is written for two reasons—to guide the management and attract investors—a business plan, contains pertinent information for both groups:

1. Investors want sound investments and a reasonable ROI. Their decision will be based on the information about the project as well as the financial data of the plan. The investor looks for:

- management's experience and knowledge about the business;
- market research, analysis, and planning;
- financial information concerning the necessary funds to get the business started; and
- pro forma data that defines expectations for some time into the future (normally five years).

2. Managers will look to the plan as their guide for restaurant operations. The business plan will be their point of reference for making decisions on the business including but not limited to:

- concept development;
- marketing;
- capital investment;
- menu;
- pricing;
- staffing; and
- operational standards.

The following parts make up the business plan:

I. EXECUTIVE SUMMARY

II. INDUSTRY

III. VISION AND OBJECTIVES

IV. BUSINESS DESCRIPTION

V. MANAGEMENT AND OWNERSHIP

VI. MARKET RESEARCH AND ANALYSIS

VII. MARKETING PLAN

VIII. DESIGN

IX. OPERATIONAL PLANS

X. BUDGETS AND FINANCIAL PLANS

XI. RISK

Exhibits

Break-even analysis of the business. This concept will be further discussed in Chapter 5, Finance and Accounting.

Financial data of the previous business if one existed including three to five years of tax returns, personal data, **balance sheets**, income statements, and invoices from previous purveyors. This information allows the owners to draw conclusions about the operation possibly not disclosed by the previous owners.

Personal financial data of owners—This data shows the commitment level of the owners and their financial stability.

Usage of funds and investment—How the investment money and loan proceeds will be spent.

Offering of stock or ownership—What the owners are offering for consideration of investing in this project.

The Business Plan

The contents of a standard business plan follow. Text set in italic provides excerpts from a sample business plan.

I. Executive Summary

The executive summary is a brief overview of what the rest of the business plan contains. The point is to give the reader an understanding of the plan. It is also a starting point for the owner, which will be referred from here on as the "author," to share his or her enthusiasm and passion for the plan. If the author can not convey his or her enthusiasm, odds are the reader will not become enthusiastic about it.

This business plan will describe what will be known as the Heartland Grill. The Heartland Grill will be a mainstream, casual dining restaurant based on high quality, simple food that can be identified by the general population of Americans in various regions of the country: BBQ ribs and steaks from the Midwest; chowder and seafood from New England; jambalaya and gumbo from New Orleans; Southwestern cuisine to spice things up; chicken pot pie, apple cobbler, and pecan pie from the South; and traditional dishes such as hamburgers, salads, and sandwiches.

This business plan will review in detail the site, the market and segments of the market, the decor, the menu, opening and operational budgets, and the background of the management.

II. Industry

When writing about opening a new restaurant, the strength of the restaurant industry in the proposed market is a critical factor to demonstrate how viable the marketplace is presently and the potential future success of the business. The ability to convey a strong marketplace for both the industry and the restaurant concept can also be a deciding factor among investors and management. Investors do not want to invest in a tight market where choices are abundant, customers are few, and survival depends on the size of the bank accounts of the owners or investors. Also, attracting quality managers may be difficult if there is not a strong argument for the viability of the industry as a whole and more specifically the specific restaurant.

The restaurant industry as a whole continues to grow. According to the 2002 Restaurant Industry Operations Report produced by the National Restaurant Association and Deloitte & Touche, the restaurant industry produces approximately $146.7 billion in sales and employed 11.6 million people and will grow at approximately 2 percent per year for the foreseeable future. The restaurant industry in the specific region has been in a boom for the past several years, mostly fueled by chain restaurants. However, several locally owned operations have opened and appear to be successful. These locally owned restaurants are casual dining concepts and have opened in the downtown market, which is a different market from the locations where the chains opened next to each other.

Over the past several years, throughout the country, casual dining concepts have survived, and in many cases even flourished while fine dining and more upscale dinner houses have suffered. Many long-time upscale dinner houses have even closed their doors due to the recent economic downturn. Casual dining can be defined as a restaurant in which the average person can afford to frequent two to three times per week. These visits would include both the lunch and dinner periods as well as socializing at the bar. This casual dining theme must be reflected in the menu, the price points of the menu, the service standards, and the decor and atmosphere. The Heartland Grill is designed to meet the needs of the "casual dining consumer" on all fronts.

The downtown market has been in a redevelopment stage for several years and this growth continues to attract more visitors to such places as the Princetown Theater, the County Arena, and the Capitol Reparatory Theater. (The Princetown Theater and Capitol Reparatory Theater are within walking distance of the facility.) The redevelopment of the downtown market is not complete and much of it is happening in and around the immediate area of the restaurant site, including office buildings; the Governors Hotel, which is the site of the restaurant; and new court buildings. Our research tells us that there are plans to develop condominiums within walking distance. This is part of the city's overall redevelopment plan.

Most of the restaurants and pubs that have opened in the downtown area direct their marketing efforts toward the college-age crowd that is in a different demographic than what the Heartland Grill will set out to attract. The college-age group does not have disposable income to dine out often. According to Deloitte & Touche, the demographic that dines out most often with the disposable income is 35 to 55 year olds. This is the demographic the Heartland Grill will target.

III. Vision and Objectives

Painting a picture for the audience is a great way to get readers caught up in the excitement, passion, and vision the author has for the project. Again, touching the emotion, on which some people will base decisions, is key. In this part of the plan the author can put forth the vision and state clear objectives that can easily be understood by the audience.

The vision is to open by late summer of 2005 and to open with an operations manual in place that includes job descriptions, position training programs, inventory control programs, and human resource programs.

Having these programs in place ensures a quality operation and allows us to concentrate on the customer and deliver a great dining experience each and every visit. Management is determined to create a dining experience that will generate positive "word of mouth" advertising from each and every guest served.

The downtown market is desperately lacking banquet facilities and meeting space. The hotel has a banquet facility and a meeting space that can hold 65 people and 60 people respectively. These two rooms are next to each other and separated by a moveable wall that allows the room to be opened for a larger banquet. Two other meeting rooms that can hold 25 people each. These rooms will be aggressively marketed by both the hotel and the Heartland Grill.

IV. Business Description

A detailed description of the business allows the reader to paint a very clear picture of the vision. This section of the plan is where detail is added so the reader can picture the restaurant. This part of the plan includes the proposed menu, price points, decor, target market, and any information that will help the reader more clearly understand the entire business.

If this business is being purchased, describe the business as it exists today and its positive and negative points, including an explanation of trends and the reason for the sale.

The Heartland Grill will be located in a 4,400 square foot space adjoining the hotel through a large foyer. The banquet and meeting rooms as well as the restrooms will be located in the foyer area. The restaurant has a separate entrance to the public and this entrance is located on the corner of the building, which makes it visible to automobile and foot traffic, and a large parking area across the street.

The kitchen design must be able to handle two separate business units: a 130-seat dining area, 25-seat bar, and the previously mentioned banquet facility. This design will enable the banquet area of the kitchen to operate independently of the dining facility. Refer to Figure 4–1.

V. Management and Ownership

The management of the business is probably the most critical piece of information for an investor. This is true in large companies or small local businesses. Stock prices on the New York Stock Exchange rise and fall depending on the hiring, firing. or retirement of senior company officials. If the owner and management have proven, positive track records in the business, investors feel more comfortable with their investment. Although having any business experience is a positive, having experience in the restaurant business could be a deciding factor. The plan should contain detailed background of the owners and any managers that are presently on board with the owners.

Provide detailed job descriptions and responsibilities, including reporting structure, in this part of the plan. This management hierarchy will remove any ambiguity of responsibility and gives the investors as well as future managers and chefs an idea of exactly what is expected of them.

Ownership will be set up in a corporation and the exact type of corporation has yet to be determined. This will be done through legal and CPA counsel. Investment will be described in the Budget and Financial section of this plan.

Management of the restaurant will be by David Williams. David will have direct control over day-to-day operations and all operational decisions affecting the business. David's

FIGURE 4–1

Line Drawing—Heartland Grill.

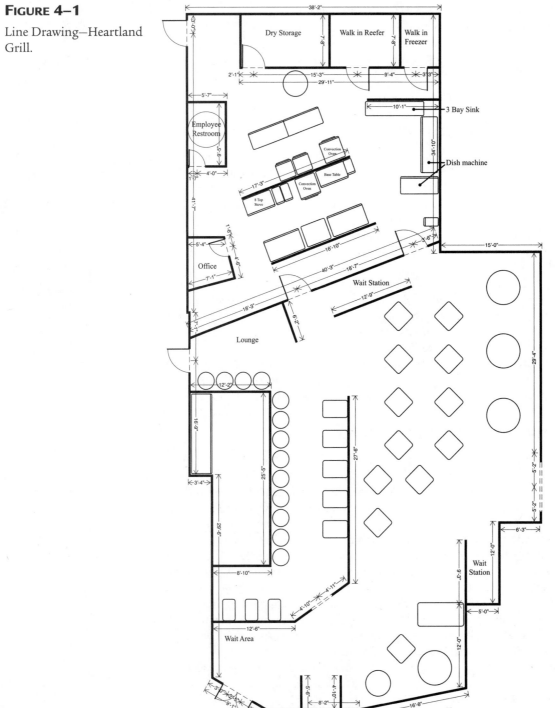

background is extensive with more than 20 years' experience in the restaurant business including:

- *vice president for a small chain of 40 restaurants;*
- *writer of several published articles on the restaurant business; and*
- *present owner of a very successful restaurant.*

Key positions will be filled once financing is in place. These key positions include:

1. *executive chef (presently filled—see attached resume);*
2. *sous chef;*
3. *front of the house manager; and*
4. *bar manager.*

David is capable of personally performing each of these key positions, which is critical in the future if one of these positions ever remains open for a period of time.

Note: This leaves several positions unfilled, specifically any front of the house or dining room managers, if any will be hired, and a sous chef if volume warrants. Even if the job has not been filled, place a job description here so the investors see that the author knows exactly the type of person being sought.

Job descriptions for all positions are included in the appendix of this book. They are not duplicated here.

VI. Market Research and Analysis

As discussed in Chapter 2, Marketing: Research Analysis and Building a Customer Base, no business should be opened without first doing some degree of market research. The restaurant can have the best product and service in the world but if the product or service does not have people willing to pay for it, the business will not survive. A summary of the marketing plan should be written in this section:

SITE SELECTION This part of the plan describes both the exact address as well as conveys why this location fits in with the target market. Banks are very familiar with the cities or towns where they operate. It is their business to know where the development is and what the plans are for the town. They also know the decision makers in the city or town.

The site of the Governor's Hotel is a perfect location for the Heartland Grill. It is located on the corner of Sheridan and Cardinal streets. It is in the heart of the capitol redevelopment and close to I-887 and has parking for over 200 cars. The hotel has 165 rooms, which will offer a captured audience. Several major roadways access the downtown market. The major route, I-887 has an off-ramp and on-ramp one block from the hotel. The other major routes I-89 and I-90 enter into I-887 within one mile of the restaurant. Additional arterial routes also enter the downtown market within 2 miles of the restaurant. This makes access to and from the downtown area very easy. I-887 has over 87,000 cars traveling daily according to the New York State Department of Transportation.

Other restaurants in the area that are direct competition for the dining dollar to the Heartland Grill (i.e., Michaels, Prime Steak and Seafood, Giovanis; McGovern's, New York Brewery and Restaurant, State Café, Orleans) even if their menu or theme is different. The Heartland Grill, from the outset, will have to differentiate itself from these other restaurants in several areas: menu, quality food, quality attentive service, value and atmosphere, and the ability to handle small office parties and banquets. The operations manual will define all of these differences.

The menu that is provided has been proven in the content, quality, value, and public appeal. Much of the menu has been tested at the Rivers Edge Golf Club in Atalon, which David now operates and has for the past five years. It can be argued that the golf club has a captured audience for the menu. However, this is a public course and due to extremely harsh weather conditions last spring, the golf course was off of previous year sales by 20 percent while its restaurant sales were up approximately 15 percent through the first 3 months of the year. This is due to the high percentage of local, non-golfer clientele that have discovered the restaurant over the last four years. Marketing toward local clientele was part of the initial business plan and we have achieved that goal.

We will have the same goal for the Heartland Grill. We will set out to market our restaurant to:

1. *people that live or work in the area;*
2. *people that visit one of the downtown entertainment venues;*
3. *the meeting and banquet facilities of the hotel;*
4. *the hotel guest; and*
5. *people that have, as of yet, not discovered what the downtown market has to offer.*

State, county, and city office buildings surround the site. These buildings will lend to a high potential of lunch and after-work business. It also offers people a place close to their office to escape for a small meeting. The proximity to entertainment venues gives the restaurant potential for dinner customers. Parking, which is a rare commodity in this market, is also available to people dining in the restaurant.

COMPETITION *As previously noted there are several restaurants in the area. These restaurants range from fast food or takeout restaurants, cafes, casual dining, and two upscale dinner houses. The fast food and cafes are not recognized as direct competition to our establishment and the upscale dinner houses are more expensive but will attract some of our older demographic. Our concentration for this plan was on the casual dining segment.*

VII. Marketing Plan

The full marketing plan is a separate document, but a summary of the plan needs to be written in the business plan. The business plan will hold steady over time with some adjustments. The marketing plan is a living document that will change with market conditions and needs of the consumer and the business.

Restaurant	Concept	Distance from Restaurant	Strengths	Weaknesses
Michaels	Steak & Seafood Upscale	1/2 mile	Established for over 80 years High Profile Chef	Parking is minimal Seating is packed tightly Owner sometimes loses focus
Prime Steak & Seafood	Steak & Seafood Extremely upscale for marketplace	2 blocks	Very established operator with 4 other operations Parking directly behind the building	Extremely pricy for the market High break even due to square footage of restaurant
Giovanis	Italian Casual Dining	1 mile	Long established Value Valet parking	Food is at times mediocre Neighborhood is neglected
McGoverns	Casual dining Irish pub	1 block	Visibility	High priced Markets to college crowd
NY Brewery and Restaurant	Brew pub and Restaurant	2 blocks	Parking in front Visibility to Highway Large very uniqe atmosphere	Owner loses focus High turnover in the kitchen
State CafŹ	Casual dining/pub	1/2 block	Expanded dining room Good pub fare Patio	Owner is not from a food background Depends on foot traffic
Orleans	Cajun/creole	2 blocks	Unique menu High traffic area Recently expanded	Several bad food reviews Market to college age

FIGURE 4–2

Chart of Restaurant Competition.

VIII. Design

The design of the restaurant includes:

1. drawings (architectural if available, but if hand drawn, use mechanical tools from office supply;
2. stores and draw to scale) of both the interior and exterior of the restaurant;
3. pictures of the building if the facility was used as a restaurant previously;
4. color schemes and props that will be used for the decor;
5. floor plans of the dining room, kitchen, and storage facilities; and equipment position.

This is the where the plan starts to come to life. The audience can see the layout of the restaurant and the picture previously painted begins to take a more defined shape. The more detailed the plans, the easier it is for the audience to understand the plan and share the vision.

IX. Operational Plans

The operational plans include:

1. detailed standards of execution such as delivery time of the appetizers and entrees;

2. an addendum including employee manual, job descriptions, training programs, daily accounting procedures, and manager shift responsibilities.

All forms and checklists are included in the appendix. They are not duplicated here.

The quality and time standards for the restaurant will be taught to the staff and enforced by management. The time standards for delivery of food will be:

■ *server to the table—within 1 minute of being seated;*

■ *drink time to the table—3 to 5 minutes;*

■ *appetizers—8 to 10 minutes;*

■ *lunch—12 to 15 minutes;*

■ *dinner entrees—15 to 20 minutes; and*

■ *dessert—5 minutes*

All staff members will receive a detailed training program for their position as well as a service class so they understand the importance of taking care of each and every customer.

X. Budgets and Financial Plans

Investors as well as managers want to see the projected financial data. This financial data supports assumptions made in previous parts of the plan. This data includes:

1. projected month-by-month sales and expenses for five years (pro forma);

2. operational expenses breakdown of contracted maintenance and services, including trash removal, cleaning services, knife sharpening, carpet cleaning, pest control, and so on.

3. any data that will support the entries on the main budget such as:

    a. *customer count projection for each strategic business unit (SBU) including lunch; dinner; bar, and so on-traffic flow will include number of customers and the per person average sales;*

    b. sample labor schedule with associated costs;

    c. advertising costs extracted from the marketing plan;

    d. insurance quotes; and

    e. INSERT BUDGET, PRO FORMA AND ASSOCIATED COSTS

Per person average sales, sample labor schedule and costs, and budgeting information mentioned above is discussed further in the Chapter 5, Finance and Accounting.

XI. Risk

In any new venture there are roadblocks and some degree of risk. For management to avoid addressing these risks and their ramifications is a fatal flaw in the planning process. Of course, the ideal situation is to never have these problems surface. However, the author of the plan gains tremendous credibility from the audience when the roadblocks and risks are foreseen, their ramifications are understood, and a plan is developed to deal with these issues should they arise.

Several roadblocks may prevent the restaurant from reaching its goal and there are some risks associated with a restaurant, some inherent to the industry and some specific to this restaurant. The following details these possible roadblocks and risks and the plans that management has developed to reduce or eliminate these risks and roadblocks:

1. *Liquor license approval—The liquor license paperwork has not been completed as of this plan writing. However, David has been through this process and we do not foresee any problems for approval.*

   ACTION: We have hired an attorney versed in the liquor laws of the state and he has personally handled over 40 licenses.

2. *Staffing due to labor shortages—Although the entire restaurant and hospitality industry has been affected, this area has struggled due to the tremendous growth of the industry here.*

   ACTION: The general manager and the chef have successfully operated in this area for several years and have a very good reputation among restaurant employees. Several of these restaurant employees have made verbal commitments to the owners.

3. *Possible move for an 1,800 person office building—There is an office building 1.5 miles from the restaurant that employs over 1,800 state employees. There has been talk about moving part or all of the staff to different offices.*

   ACTION: After talking to several people employed in that building, the move has been a discussion for three years but nothing solid has been established. Their understanding is that if it does occur it would be a shifting of personnel and their offices will be filled within a couple of months.

4. *Increased competition—There is only one other site available for a restaurant in the immediate vicinity. The owner of the land is looking for a premium price at 150 percent more than the going rate. This makes any project on this site cost prohibitive.*

5. *Sales not meeting budgeted level—Projected sales are the owner's best educated guess computed by figuring average lunch check, average dinner check, multiplied by the number of customers and added to the projected daily bar sales. These estimates have been based on customer counts and trends in other restaurants in the area.*

   ACTION: If the projected sales levels are not keeping pace with the budget, we will monitor customer satisfaction, review the menu for profit contribution, analyze where our sales are lacking, and in keeping with our business plan develop a marketing campaign to bolster sales.

Exhibits

BREAKEVEN ANALYSIS The breakeven point and its importance are detailed in the Chapter 5.

PERSONAL FINANCIAL DATA Personal financial worth is important to banks as a safety net for their loan.

SOURCE OF FUNDS AND USAGE The **use of funds and investment** describes to the bank or investors how money will be raised and exactly how the money will be used. There are pre-opening expenses and cash reserves for operation and cost overruns during the construction phase. Investors, and more importantly banks, want to make sure the business is sufficiently capitalized so management is not returning for cash 30 days into the project.

OFFERING OF STOCK This is known as a prospectus. If offering an investor an opportunity to purchase stock in the company, the investor will want to see exactly what is being proposed, how and when their investment will be paid back, and their projected return on investment.

Business Structure

Choosing a business structure such as a corporation, partnership, or proprietorship is a critical decision for starting a new business. The decision will affect business from its conception and well into the future. The owner, an accountant, and an attorney should determine the business structure, as it will have several influencing factors such as tax, liability, controlling votes, and transferability issues. Whatever the structure, there needs to be clearly defined roles for everyone, including any silent partners, who usually are not that silent.

Possible business structure include:

1. sole proprietorship;
2. partnership;
3. limited liability company;
4. subchapter S corporation; and
5. subchapter C corporation.

Sole Proprietorship

Sole proprietorship is the simplest from of a business operation. Simply stated, when an individual operates a business for the purpose of producing a profit, a sole proprietorship exists. This form of business entity taxes the business for income tax purposes at the individual rate for any profit produced.

If the business produces a profit of $50,000, the owner claims that profit as his or her income. Liability is assumed by the individual and any suits brought against the company also brings suit against the owner and any assets of the owner.

Partnership

A **partnership** is formed when two people engage in a business for the purpose of producing a profit. A partnership does not have to be a written, formal agreement between two people, even though many times these agreements do exist. These agreements will normally define the roles of each partner with respect to the business. Each partner assumes equal risk and liability for the actions of the other. Liability and tax implications are equal for each person.

If a couple enters into business and only one is actively involved in the business but the other does any work such as payroll, both are equally liable for any suits brought against the partnership.

Corporation

A corporation is a legal entity similar to a person, which has its own Federal Employer Identification Number (EIN) just as a person is assigned a social security number. The form is Federal form SS-4 and is available from the Social Security Administration (1-800-829-3676 or www.irs.ustreas.gov). A corporate entity can enter into contracts, assume debt, pay taxes, and be liable in a lawsuit. A corporation is formed by filing the appropriate papers with the secretary of state in the state in which the restaurant will conduct business, and pay the associated fee.

Stockholders who purchase shares of stock in the company own the corporation. The level of management and control in the corporation will depend on the type of corporation selected, which will be discussed in the Chapter 5. The stockholder, as an owner of the corporation does not stake any claim to the assets of the business and in most cases[1] is not personally liable for the debt or possible suits of the corporation. Stockholders' liability is limited to their investment in the shares of stock they own.

There are several choices of corporations. The choice made depends on several factors mainly income tax, qualification restrictions, and benefits, which should always be discussed with professionals such as attorneys and accountants.

Subchapter C Corporation

A **C[2] corporation** is the most common form of corporation. This type of corporation is unlimited in the number of stockholders it can have. "C" corporations will normally pay an income tax on the profit then distribute the profit in the form of dividends to shareholders who in turn pay income taxes on their dividends. This is known as double taxation[3] because both the corporation and the stockholders are paying tax on the same profit.

To reduce profit at the corporate level, stockholders may lease assets to the corporation, which are deductible expenses to the corporation. This can result in a short-term loss for the stockholder but a long-term capital gain. For instance, George wants to start a restaurant in a building he presently owns. Not being a restaurateur, George brings in a well-respected chef and several investors. Because George already owns the building and does not want to share the ownership of the building he sets up a realty trust that leases the building to the newly formed business. The lease expense is deductible to the restaurant and claimed as income to George's realty trust. However, over time George can claim depreciation, taxes, interest, and expenses on the building against the income from the rent. Although this may give George a short-term loss, he would more than likely face a capital gains tax if and when he sells the building.

Stockholders might also choose to loan money to the corporation in lieu of stock ownership. The stockholder in this case becomes a creditor to the corporation. The interest on the loan is deductible to the corporation and claimed as income to the individual.

Subchapter S Corporation

The **S corporation** offers the same limited liability for its stockholders as a C corporation but the profit is taxed at the individual level. This profit is taxed even if it is not distributed, where in a C corporation only the dividends, the actual amount received by the stockholder, is taxable. Most small companies do not concern themselves with this issue since the stockholders are normally employees or the operators of the company and most if not all of the profit would be distributed in the form of compensation. (There should be some reserve for capital expenditures as will be discussed in subsequent chapters.)

The S corporation does have a few limitations that restrict qualification for filing this type of entity:

1. it must have less than 35 stockholders, which might limit the ability to raise capital;
2. there must be only one class of stock;
3. the stockholder must be a person, so a corporation, most trusts, or a venture capital company would not qualify; and
4. no resident aliens may hold stock in such a company.

These are usually not issues for a small business.

Limited Liability Company

A **limited liability company** (LLC) is a relatively new business structure that is now recognized in all 50 states. An LLC is not a corporation because there is no issuing of stock but it does offer the limited liability protection of a corporation along with the "pass-through" taxation characteristics of a sole-proprietorship or partnership.

An LLC has some other advantages over the corporate structures available:

- LLCs offer greater flexibility in management and business organization;
- LLCs do not have ownership restrictions of S corporations making it ideal for foreign investors; and
- LLCs accomplish this without IRS restrictions of S corporations.

An LLC, like any other form of organization, also has some pitfalls. Transferability of ownership is usually restricted in the agreement made between the members of the LLC.

A restaurant business by its nature—the selling of alcoholic beverages and the high traffic flow of people in the building and cars in the parking lot—will increase exposure to liability. Because people want to limit their personal exposure to liability, a corporation would be the only way to enter into business. The type of corporate structure depends on the previous descriptions of these structures and consultation with legal and accounting professionals.

The decision-making process depends on the structure chosen. This process should be detailed in the corporate documents known as the articles of incorporation or the LLC agreement. Clearly defining roles of stockholders, corporate officers, and the board of directors prevents ambiguity among managers and micro-managing by individuals outside the day-to-day operations. One of the quickest way to failure is to have too many bosses making decisions as they see fit. Disparate views from the owners sends confusing messages to management and staff, who will be confused as to whom is running the business and to whom they must answer.

A general manager or some designated individual needs to have complete control over the operation. This individual might be one of the corporate officers or members of the LLC, which would normally be the case in a small operation. Either way, the staff and management team must recognize this individual as their leader. The involvement by the rest of the investors needs to be clearly documented so as to prevent potential problems.

■ CHAPTER REVIEW

A business plan plays a dual role in the formation and operation of a business. It is the operational guide for the business and management. It details the operation, management roles, standards, expectations, and execution methods to bring the plan to fruition. It also contains pertinent information for investors. It details financial data, marketing research, and how the business will achieve its goals.

■ KEY TERMS

balance sheets

breakeven analysis

C corporation

financial data

limited liability company

partnership

return on investment

S corporation

sole proprietorship

use of funds and investment

■ REVIEW QUESTIONS

1. Who are the two major audiences for a business plan?

2. List some of the differences between sole proprietorship, partnership, LLC, C corporation, and S corporation.

Notes

1. There are some circumstances where as a stockholder who is also an officer of the corporation might be personally liable for their actions if he or she uses the corporation as a shield in such a way that can be deemed harmful through negligence on his or her part.

2. A C or S designation is from the IRS code that governs corporate bodies.

3. At the time of this writing, there was a bill in front of Congress to abolish the "double taxation" of dividends at the stockholder level.

CHAPTER 5

Finance and Accounting

After reviewing this chapter, you will:

- Understand accounting terms impacting the restaurant business;
- Complete an annual budget;
- Develop, analyze, and interpret profit and loss statements;
- Understand the balance sheet;
- Project monthly and weekly sales and costs;
- Understand ratios and breakeven point;
- Use data to make informed decisions;
- Comprehend financing a restaurant including the small business administration (SBA); and
- Know all the state and federal agencies governing the business.

Understanding the language of business is an important part of operating a successful restaurant. From initial financing to budget development to analyzing the operation, this chapter offers basic knowledge and in-depth understanding of this language of business.

Accounting Principles

Accounting is the language of business. It is an accepted set of practices to account for the revenue a business generates, the expenses incurred in generating the revenue, and reporting and interpreting the data. The accounting process develops information that a business owner can use to analyze the profitability and direction of the business and use to make informed business decisions. Today, business owners have help in the accounting process from computers and software programs such as Quick Books or Peachtree accounting.[1] The programs set up the accounting process and the owner simply makes entries. However, the basic accounting principles are important to understand, because restaurant owners need to analyze the reports and make decisions. Every business owner should have an accountant review the business's reports for general record keeping accuracy, depreciation expenses, and tax planning.[2]

As in any business, a restaurant owner must possess a basic understanding of accounting principles. A restaurant operator must understand how revenue is generated; how costs are incurred; the tax implications involved in generating a profit; how to interpret ratios such as check average, seat turnover, and quick ratio; the break-even sales point; developing and analyzing the profit and loss (P&L) statement and understanding the balance sheet. The owner of a cash business must also be disciplined with the cash that flows through the business, because cash in the register does not equate to available discretionary cash to spend.

Accounting in the restaurant business is not accomplished simply by adding the daily receipts and paying the invoices incurred during the course of the day. There are other considerations and liabilities incurred, including sales taxes collected on behalf of the state, payroll and payroll related taxes, workers' compensation, unemployment insurance, and disability insurance costs (in states where applicable). Other liabilities also accrue daily and funds must be readily available to cover those liabilities. At the first of each month, the rent or mortgage is due unless the building is owned outright. The business has to pay utilities such as gas and electric bills every month. It is also a good idea to have some reserve cash for capital improvements or slow business periods. A successful business striving to survive long into the future will not achieve success by operating out of its cash drawer in the hopes that a busy week will generate enough cash to pay the rent or meet payroll obligations.

Accrual Method of Accounting

There are two accepted methods of accounting: accrual and cash basis. The accounting method a restaurant implements is known as the **accrual method of accounting**. The accrual method accounts for sales and expenses as they are incurred, and not when the cash changes hands for the sale or purchase. For example, during the course of a week a restaurant receives two truck deliveries from its main food supplier, along with beer, wine, and liquor deliveries. Even though a supplier may offer terms of 14 days to pay an invoice, the invoice needs to be accounted for when the deliveries enter the building. By using this method, at the end of the week, there are real-time data to analyze the operation by comparing current week sales to invoices accrued that generated that sales level.

Accounting Period

The yearly **accounting period** for most restaurants is the calendar year and starts on January 1 and ends on December 31 of the same year. Each calendar month within the year comprises an accounting period, because many fixed costs such as rent and utilities are billed monthly. Each month is broken down into weekly periods, which allow operations to be analyzed in real-time without having to wait until the end of the month to identify possible problems.

Reports

Record Keeping

Keeping track of sales and all costs is the dreaded "management" of the business. These data produce the report card indicating how well each person in the restaurant is doing their job.

Daily record keeping allows an owner to compare actual sales and incurred costs against projected sales and costs. If the accounting process is not set up properly, managing the business will become difficult and frustrating, as there will not be hard, real-time data to analyze and to support decisions. Record keeping is easier in today's business world due to computerized point of sale (POS) systems, back office systems, and accounting software programs.

Computer Systems and Programs

Modern POS systems allow managers to extract just about any information they could want, including hourly sales, menu mix, hourly labor costs and guest check monitoring all in real time. Some POS systems also include programs that handle employee scheduling and inventory.

Scheduling programs allow managers to plan their labor costs and adjustment to staffing levels accordingly during the course of the day.

Keeping inventory is a must to have accurate information in determining cost of goods sold (COGS). The COGS is the cost of products purchased for resale either in their raw form or in a recipe.

Profit and Loss Statement

The most commonly used financial statement a restaurant owner is concerned with is known as the **profit and loss statement (P&L)** or income statement, shown in Figure 5–1. The first part of the P&L shows the sales categories where revenue is generated, such as by sales of food, beer, wine, liquor, soft beverages, catering, retail sales, and any other forms of income that the owner would want to isolate for analysis. The second part of the P&L shows the expenses associated with generating the revenue, including inventories, rent, utilities, payroll, and other variable and fixed costs associated with operating the business. The difference between revenue and expenses produces either a pre-tax profit or a loss for the business.

The sale of food and beverages and possibly other items such as retail products generates revenue. The breakdown of these sales categories of the

FIGURE 5–1

Profit and Loss
Statement.

		TOTAL	
SALES	$	1,430,500	
Food	$	929,825	65.00%
Wine	$	135,898	9.50%
Liquor	$	114,440	8.00%
Beer	$	243,185	17.00%
Soft Beverage	$	7,153	0.50%
Catering	$	-	0.00%
TOTAL	$	1,430,500	100.00%
COGS			
Food	$	302,193	32.50%
Wine	$	48,923	36.00%
Liquor	$	29,754	26.00%
Beer	$	68,092	28.00%
Beverage	$	1,073	15.00%
Catering	$	-	32.00%
Other	$	-	0.00%
COGS	$	450,035	31.46%
			200.00%
Gross Profit	$	980,465	68.54%
Labor	$	282,000	18.80%
Operating Expenses	$	64,500	4.51%
Operating Profit	$	633,965	44.32%
Occupancy			
Rent	$	74,340	5.20%
Property Taxes	$	13,250	0.93%
Trash Removal	$	5,200	0.36%
Water and Sewer	$	27,500	1.92%
Insurance	$	11,500	0.80%
Utilities	$	38,500	2.69%
Equipment repairs	$	1,500	0.10%
Building repairs	$	4,500	0.31%
Total Occupancy	$	176,290	12.32%
Indirect Expense			
FICA, Payroll Burden	$	51,332	18.00%
Workers Comp	$	9,971	0.70%
Disability Insurance	$	2,500	0.17%
Advertising	$	7,800	0.55%
Credit Card	$	16,093	1.13%
Telephone	$	4,200	0.29%
TOTAL INDIRECT	$	91,896	6.42%
Manager labor	$	190,000	13.28%
Bonus	$	12,500	0.87%
Profit / Loss	$	163,279	11.41%
Loan Payment*	$	37,200	0.00%
Equipment Lease	$	-	0.00%
Net Profit/Loss	$	126,079	8.81%

operation's P&L is determined by how much information an owner wants or
needs for analysis. Soft beverage sales are often lumped into food sales by assigning soft beverage as a subcategory of food and then analyzing it as a part of food
cost.

Cost of Sales or Cost of Goods Sold (COGS)

The **cost of goods sold** (COGS) is the restaurant's cost for the food and beverage inventories purchased to generate the sales. It is important to calculate the percentage of COGS as well as the dollars spent because it gives the owner or manager data to properly analyze these costs and locate potential problems or areas of opportunity to improve. The percentage of the COGS is calculated by dividing the cost by the sales generated in a specific category such as food, wine or beer. In the following example food cost is being calculated.

$$\{(\text{Beginning inventory (\$Value)} + \text{Purchases}) - \text{Ending inventory (\$ Value)}\}/\text{Sales} = \% \text{ of cost}$$
$$\{(\$5,000 + \$3,000) - \$4,000\}/\$11,500 = 34.78\%$$
$$\text{Food cost is } 34.78\%.$$

Gross Profit

The **gross profit** is calculated by subtracting the COGS from the revenue.

Expenses

Expenses associated with operating a restaurant are many. The P&L breaks these expenses into categories for easy analysis:

1. **Labor**

Labor includes direct management and hourly payroll expenses, but does not include associated costs such as benefits, FICA (otherwise known as social security, and instituted by the Federal Insurance Contribution Act), workers' compensation, unemployment insurance, and other insurances where applicable by law. These expenses will be entered as separate line items.

2. **Operational Expenses**

Operational expenses are the daily expenses incurred in operating a restaurant. They include items such as linen, paper products, china, silverware, glassware, and office and computer supplies.

3. **Occupancy**

Occupancy includes rent or mortgage, property taxes, water and sewer taxes, insurance, utilities, and repairs. These items are all included in occupancy costs, because in analyzing the viability of a site, an owner must consider all associated costs with that site. Although the rent might be reasonable, the combined expenses might put the site out of financial reach. Other expenses that might have to be calculated here are percentage rent and common area maintenance (very common in mall or strip mall settings).

4. **Indirect Expenses**

These expenses are usually associated with other expenses that have been incurred. These expenses include associated payroll expenses, employee benefits and **credit card discount rates.**[3]

5. **Management Labor and Bonus**

Management is normally paid by salary and adjusting the schedule to save labor costs on the bottom line. Control of this cost is determined annually, so it is separated from hourly labor. Some operations pay a bonus based on performance of the restaurant and possibly goals set by management.

6. **Loan and Lease Payments**

Loan and lease payments are made to banks or leasing companies. By understanding the P&L and balance sheets, an owner can make an informed decision about the amount of debt the restaurant can assume. Only the interest on the loans is tax deductible.

Depreciation

Depreciation is a noncash, tax-deductible expense that allows for the decrease in usefulness of equipment and plant assets. Therefore, it is not accounted for on an operational P&L. An accountant should be consulted to properly account for this expense.

The Balance Sheet

ASSETS AND LIABILITIES All pieces of property a business owns are considered assets. These assets can be in the form of equipment, land, buildings, inventories, cash, and so on.

Liabilities are all debts owed to creditors such as banks and suppliers. Owner's equity is what remains once all liabilities are paid from the assets of the business, as shown in the following equation. Liabilities, because creditors have "preferred" rights to assets, are placed before owner's equity.

$$\text{Assets} - \text{Liabilities} = \text{Capital or owner's equity}$$

CURRENT ASSETS Current assets are those **assets** that can reasonably be realized as cash by the business within a year or less. In the restaurant business, these assets include food and beverage inventories, accounts receivable if accounts are carried, and possibly retail items the restaurant may offer. Fixed assets are those assets that would be used to generate revenues such as the building, equipment, or land that would house those assets.

CURRENT LIABILITIES Current liabilities are those **liabilities** due within a year such as invoices from purveyors and loan payments that are due within a 1-year period.

The difference between current assets and current liabilities is known as **working capital**. Working capital is the cash the business will have to meet its current debt load. The current ratio is used to determine the solvency of a business. The ratio is computed by dividing the current assets by the current liabilities.

	2005	2004
Current Assets	$50,000	$35,000
Current Liabilities	$20,000	$24,000
Working Capital	$30,000	$11,000
Current Ratio	2.5:1	1.46:1

$$\text{Current ratio} = \frac{\text{Current assets}}{\text{Current liabilities}}$$

If the current assets exceed current liabilities, the ratio greater than 1:1 and the business is believed to be solvent. The **quick ratio** is more readily acceptable for restaurants. It removes some of the assets from the equation, including inventory, and deals strictly with the cash, marketable securities, and accounts receivable.

$$\text{Quick ratio} = \frac{\text{Cash, marketable securities, accounts receivable}}{\text{Current liabilities}}$$

A restaurant will always carry an inventory. If the quick ratio is less than 1, it could indicate solvency issues and that sales are only generating enough capital to buy more inventory, and not enough to cover fixed costs, other debt, or liabilities.

Bank Accounts

Restaurant owners are famous for being poor accountants. Every restaurant must follow these steps to get better control of finances. First, the owner should buy an accounting program such as Quick Books. Quick Books is an easy to use, comprehensive accounting software program.

Secondly, the establishment should open three separate bank accounts. Although charges will be incurred with each account, having three accounts serves two purposes:

1. it disciplines the restaurant to use specific funds for specific expenses, and

2. it will show the restaurant operator at a quick glance whether the establishment has positive cash flow, and the operator can make this determination without going through other paperwork.

The three accounts are:

1. operations,

2. escrow, and

3. payroll.

Operations Account

The operations account is for actual operational expenses, such as product purchases and operational supplies. Operational supplies are those that are consumable commodities needed to sell product and keep the restaurant clean. All of these product purchase and operational supply bills should be paid on time when they come due. If the money is not in the bank, the restaurant has a cash flow problem.

Escrow Bank Account

The escrow bank account is for fixed costs such as rent, insurance, utilities, and accrued monies such as state sales tax and quarterly payroll expenses. The owner should know what monthly bills are coming due. This information may come from the budget or past bills and includes such bills as rent, taxes, insurance, utilities, and any other fixed costs. At the end of each week, a corresponding portion of this expense should be placed in the escrow account. Then, when the bill comes due, the money is in the account to pay for it. Also, the manager or owner should deposit each day's sales tax collections into this account.

Escrow Tracking Worksheet

This worksheet (refer to Figure 5–2) informs managers of the total amount that should be available in the escrow account. This worksheet, when used properly, dictates how much cash should be in the escrow bank account. By following this discipline, bills can be paid when they come due without an owner relying on a busy weekend to meet the expense. If there is not enough cash to fund this account, management can immediately recognize a cash flow problem and take corrective action. To use this form:

August A	B MONTHLY BILL AMOUNT	C PREVIOUS BALANCE	D Week 1	E Week 2	F Week 3	G Week 4	H Week 5	I Week 6
Insurance	$500		$ 125	$ 125	$ 125	$ 125		
Workers Comp	$40		10	10	10	10		
Sales Tax		$11,234	1495.00	1148.00	1149.00	1313.00		
Payroll Taxes		$350	180	195	185	180		
Utilities	$3,000		$ 750	$ 750	$ 750	$ 750		
Rent	$6,500		$ 1,625	$ 1,625	$ 1,625	$ 1,625		
Unemployment Tax Accrual		$1,969	$ 328	$ 318	$ 330	$ 325		
Property Tax	$200		$ 50	$ 50	$ 50	$ 50		
Water and Sewer	$150		$ 38	$ 38	$ 38	$ 38		
Loans	$650		$ 163	$ 163	$ 163	$ 163		
Leases	$900		$ 225	$ 225	$ 225	$ 225		
Contract Obligations	$800		$ 200	$ 200	$ 200	$ 200		
TOTAL ESCROW			5188	4846	4849	5003	0	0

FIGURE 5–2

Escrow Tracking Worksheet.

1. Column A lists the different cost areas.

2. Column B is a recurring amount that is either extracted from the budget or based upon trends over the previous few months. The monthly amount can be entered and then divided over the number of weeks in that particular accounting period. In this example there is a 4-week accounting period.

3. Column C is for any line items that have previous balances and not paid in the previous month but due quarterly.

4. Columns D through H represents the weeks within the present accounting period

5. Several entries are made weekly when the dollar amount is known. These entries include:

    a. sales tax is generated weekly and extracted from the sales report;

    b. employer payroll contributions; and

    c. unemployment taxes.

At the end of each week, the total escrow amount should be in the bank ready to pay these bills. If this amount is not in the account or was used for operational purposes, there is a cash flow problem.

Payroll Account

The payroll account is exactly as the name implies: to meet payroll obligations to staff and any associated payroll expenses. If the pay period ends on Sunday and payroll is distributed on the following Friday, the restaurant owner should not need the coming week's receipts to meet the accrued payroll obligation. The payroll account should be funded by the end of the incurred pay period, which in this example is Sunday.

Funding each of these accounts can be accomplished is several ways. The payroll account should be funded according to the amount of dollars spent on each day's labor. The amount deposited should also account for employer portion of social security, federal unemployment insurance, and state unemployment insurance. The amount for each state will vary. For instance, if management payroll is $7,000 weekly, and hourly labor costs, which will vary by the day in accordance with volume, are:

	HOURLY	MANAGEMENT	DAILY DEPOSIT
Monday	$300	$1,000	$ 1,300
Tuesday	$400	$1,000	$ 1,400
Wednesday	$500	$1,000	$ 1,500
Thursday	$600	$1,000	$ 1,600
Friday	$800	$1,000	$ 1,800
Saturday	$800	$1,000	$ 1,800
Sunday	$400	$1,000	$ 1,400
		TOTAL	$10,800

Budgeting

To properly analyze a profit and loss (P&L) statement, there must be a base of information to compare. This information is compiled by developing a budget. A budget is a planning tool that, unfortunately, is not always given the attention it needs. Projecting sales, anticipating costs, setting standards of acceptable cost margins, and documenting this process is known as budgeting. The budget, as used in a restaurant, is to plan for the future of the operation.

Many people use budgets at home to keep spending within their income means and plan for the future. It includes savings and investment plans, retirement accounts, planning for major purchases such as a car or new house, and future tuition expenses. Why is it that most restaurant owners do not build budgets for their businesses? Although developing a budget can be time consuming, it is a critical step in operating a restaurant successfully and planning properly.

A budget forces management to plan periodically and work toward preset goals, giving an owner or manager information to make informed decisions for the long-term business success. By understanding how to develop and implement a budget and how to analyze a P&L statement, management prevents itself from making knee-jerk decisions and is able to plan for future growth.

Because the P&L statement is the report that will be used to analyze operations, the budget should follow the same format using the same line items in the same order. A budget is shown in Figure 5–3.[4]

Components of a Budget

The first step in the budgeting process is to determine projected sales. This determination needs to be made in a logical progression and not simply by making up a number. If the check average for lunch is anticipated to be $9 per person, management must make an educated guess as to how many people per day the restaurant will serve at lunch. If the estimate is 40 on Monday, 60 on Tuesday, 80 on Wednesday, 120 on Thursday and 150 on Friday, with only 60 on Saturday and 20 on Sunday, the total is 530 customers for lunch. At a check average of $9 per plate, the total lunch sales would be $4,770. This calculation needs to be done for dinner sales, bar sales, off-peak hours, such as 2 P.M. to 5 P.M., and late night. If there is a separate room for small parties or banquets, sales for that part of the business also need to be projected.

Once sales have been projected, the percentage cost of each sales category must be calculated. This number can not be randomly generated. Menu prices, along with the cost calculation sheets that were presented during the menu development process, should be used to generate these cost percentages.

This section discusses how cost areas are defined and calculated for budgeting. Costs are either fixed, variable, or a combination of the two. These costs are defined as follows:

		JANUARY	FEBRUARY	MARCH	APRIL	MAY	JUNE	JULY	AUGUST	SEPTEMBER	OCTOBER	NOVEMBER	DECEMBER	TOTAL
SALES		$ 100,000	$ 100,000	$ 105,000	$ 110,000	$ 120,000	$ 125,000	$ 120,000	$ 120,000	$ 95,000	$ 95,000	$ 100,000	$ 110,000	$ 1,300,000
Food	E	$ 60,000	$ 60,000	$ 63,000	$ 66,000	$ 72,000	$ 75,000	$ 72,000	$ 72,000	$ 57,000	$ 57,000	$ 60,000	$ 66,000	$ 780,000
Wine	E	$ 9,000	$ 9,000	$ 9,450	$ 9,900	$ 10,800	$ 11,250	$ 10,800	$ 10,800	$ 8,550	$ 8,550	$ 9,000	$ 9,900	$ 117,000
Liquor	E	$ 10,000	$ 10,000	$ 10,500	$ 11,000	$ 12,000	$ 12,500	$ 12,000	$ 12,000	$ 9,500	$ 9,500	$ 10,000	$ 11,000	$ 130,000
Beer	E	$ 20,000	$ 20,000	$ 21,000	$ 22,000	$ 24,000	$ 25,000	$ 24,000	$ 24,000	$ 19,000	$ 19,000	$ 20,000	$ 22,000	$ 260,000
Soft Beverage	E	$ 1,000	$ 1,000	$ 1,050	$ 1,100	$ 1,200	$ 1,250	$ 1,200	$ 1,200	$ 950	$ 950	$ 1,000	$ 1,100	$ 13,000
TOTAL SALES		$ 100,000	$ 100,000	$ 105,000	$ 110,000	$ 120,000	$ 125,000	$ 120,000	$ 120,000	$ 95,000	$ 95,000	$ 100,000	$ 110,000	$ 1,300,000
COGS														
Food	P	$ 20,400	$ 20,400	$ 21,420	$ 22,440	$ 24,480	$ 25,500	$ 24,480	$ 24,480	$ 19,380	$ 19,380	$ 20,400	$ 22,440	$ 265,200
Wine	P	$ 3,150	$ 3,150	$ 3,308	$ 3,465	$ 3,780	$ 3,938	$ 3,780	$ 3,780	$ 2,993	$ 2,993	$ 3,150	$ 3,465	$ 40,950
Liquor	P	$ 2,600	$ 2,600	$ 2,730	$ 2,860	$ 3,120	$ 3,250	$ 3,120	$ 3,120	$ 2,470	$ 2,470	$ 2,600	$ 2,860	$ 33,800
Beer	P	$ 5,800	$ 5,800	$ 6,090	$ 6,380	$ 6,960	$ 7,250	$ 6,960	$ 6,960	$ 5,510	$ 5,510	$ 5,800	$ 6,380	$ 75,400
Beverage	P	$ 150	$ 150	$ 158	$ 165	$ 180	$ 188	$ 180	$ 180	$ 143	$ 143	$ 150	$ 165	$ 1,950
COGS		$ 32,100	$ 32,100	$ 33,705	$ 35,310	$ 38,520	$ 40,125	$ 38,520	$ 38,520	$ 30,495	$ 30,495	$ 32,100	$ 35,310	$ 417,300
Gross Profit		$ 67,900	$ 67,900	$ 71,295	$ 74,690	$ 81,480	$ 84,875	$ 81,480	$ 81,480	$ 64,505	$ 64,505	$ 67,900	$ 74,690	$ 882,700
Labor	P	$ 18,000	$ 18,000	$ 18,900	$ 19,800	$ 16,800	$ 17,188	$ 16,500	$ 16,800	$ 12,825	$ 12,825	$ 15,000	$ 19,800	$ 202,438
Operating Expenses	IS	$ 3,000	$ 3,000	$ 3,117	$ 3,235	$ 3,469	$ 3,586	$ 3,469	$ 4,669	$ 4,083	$ 4,083	$ 4,200	$ 4,435	$ 44,345
Operating Profit		$ 46,900	$ 46,900	$ 49,278	$ 51,656	$ 61,211	$ 64,101	$ 61,511	$ 60,011	$ 47,597	$ 47,597	$ 48,700	$ 50,456	$ 635,918
Occupancy														
Rent	F	$ 6,195	$ 6,195	$ 6,195	$ 6,195	$ 6,195	$ 6,195	$ 6,195	$ 6,195	$ 6,195	$ 6,195	$ 6,195	$ 6,195	$ 74,340
Property Taxes	F	$ 1,000	$ 1,000	$ 1,000	$ 1,000	$ 1,000	$ 1,000	$ 1,000	$ 1,000	$ 1,000	$ 1,000	$ 1,000	$ 1,000	$ 12,000
Trash Removal	F	$ 450	$ 450	$ 450	$ 450	$ 450	$ 450	$ 450	$ 450	$ 450	$ 450	$ 450	$ 450	$ 5,400
Water and Sewer	F	$ 1,950	$ 1,950	$ 1,950	$ 1,950	$ 1,950	$ 1,950	$ 1,950	$ 1,950	$ 1,950	$ 1,950	$ 1,950	$ 1,950	$ 23,400
Insurance	F	$ 694	$ 694	$ 694	$ 694	$ 694	$ 694	$ 694	$ 694	$ 694	$ 694	$ 694	$ 694	$ 8,333
Utilities	F	$ 3,500	$ 3,500	$ 3,500	$ 3,500	$ 3,500	$ 3,500	$ 3,500	$ 3,500	$ 3,500	$ 3,500	$ 3,500	$ 3,500	$ 42,000
Equipment repairs	V	$ 50	$ 50	$ 53	$ 550	$ 600	$ 63	$ 60	$ 60	$ 48	$ 48	$ 50	$ 55	$ 1,685
Building Upgrades	V	$ 500	$ 500	$ 525	$ 550	$ 120	$ 625	$ 600	$ 600	$ 475	$ 475	$ 500	$ 550	$ 6,020
Total Occupancy		$ 14,339	$ 14,339	$ 14,367	$ 14,889	$ 14,509	$ 14,477	$ 14,449	$ 14,449	$ 14,312	$ 14,312	$ 14,339	$ 14,394	$ 173,178
Indirect Expense														
FICA and Payroll Expenses	VE	$ 6,120	$ 6,120	$ 6,282	$ 6,444	$ 5,904	$ 5,974	$ 5,850	$ 5,904	$ 5,189	$ 5,189	$ 5,580	$ 6,444	$ 70,999
Workers Comp	VE	$ 690	$ 690	$ 713	$ 735	$ 660	$ 670	$ 653	$ 660	$ 561	$ 561	$ 615	$ 735	$ 7,941
Disability Insurance	VE	$ 100	$ 100	$ 100	$ 100	$ 100	$ 100	$ 100	$ 100	$ 100	$ 100	$ 100	$ 100	$ 1,200
Advertising	V	$ 1,500	$ 1,500	$ 1,575	$ 1,650	$ 1,800	$ 1,875	$ 1,800	$ 1,800	$ 1,425	$ 1,425	$ 1,500	$ 1,650	$ 19,500
Credit Card	V	$ 540	$ 540	$ 567	$ 594	$ 648	$ 675	$ 648	$ 648	$ 513	$ 513	$ 540	$ 594	$ 7,020
Telephone	F	$ 350	$ 350	$ 350	$ 350	$ 350	$ 350	$ 350	$ 350	$ 350	$ 350	$ 350	$ 350	$ 4,200
Employee benefits		$ 800	$ 800	$ 800	$ 800	$ 800	$ 800	$ 800	$ 800	$ 800	$ 800	$ 800	$ 800	$ 9,600
TOTAL INDIRECT		$ 10,100	$ 10,100	$ 10,387	$ 10,673	$ 10,262	$ 10,443	$ 10,201	$ 10,262	$ 8,937	$ 8,937	$ 9,485	$ 10,673	$ 120,460
Manager labor	F	$ 16,000	$ 16,000	$ 16,000	$ 16,000	$ 16,000	$ 16,000	$ 16,000	$ 16,000	$ 16,000	$ 16,000	$ 16,000	$ 16,000	$ 192,000
Bonus	V	$ -	$ -	$ -	$ -	$ -	$ -	$ -	$ -	$ -	$ -	$ -	$ -	$ -
Profit / Loss		$ 6,461	$ 6,461	$ 8,524	$ 10,093	$ 20,440	$ 23,181	$ 20,881	$ 19,300	$ 8,348	$ 8,348	$ 8,876	$ 9,388	$ 150,280
Loan Payment*	F	$ 3,087	$ 3,087	$ 3,087	$ 3,087	$ 3,087	$ 3,087	$ 3,087	$ 3,087	$ 3,087	$ 3,087	$ 3,087	$ 3,087	$ 37,044
Interest Expense	F	$ -	$ -	$ -	$ -	$ -	$ -	$ -	$ -	$ -	$ -	$ -	$ -	$ -
Provision for taxes														
Net Profit/Loss		3,374	3,374	5,437	7,006	17,353	20,094	17,774	16,160	5,208	5,208	5,736	6,248	$ 113,236

FIGURE 5–3

Budget Spreadsheet.

- **fixed costs** are recurring costs that do not fluctuate with volume;
- **variable costs** are defined by a percentage of sales and the associated dollar cost is directly impacted by sales volume;
- combination costs are calculated as a fixed dollar cost in addition to a percentage of sales (e.g., rent might be paid as a fixed dollar amount plus a percentage of the gross sales).

Fixed costs include:

- rent or mortgage payment—negotiated and contracted;
- property taxes—may change from year to year, but the assessed value as determined by the town or city tax department will not fluctuate within the year;
- insurance costs—determined at the beginning of the year;
- management payroll exclusive of bonus;
- contracted maintenance;
- utilities;
- loan payments—not based on sales volume; and
- equipment lease payments—contracted and not subject to volume influence.

Notes: Another term that might more universally fit management payroll cost categories is "manageable or controllable" fixed costs. Utility costs will fluctuate slightly and can be managed by understanding how gas and electric costs are charged and how the impact of cleaning and maintaining equipment can reduce costs. However, a certain, fixed amount is associated with continually operating refrigeration, gas appliances, and lights. Therefore, to more accurately represent these costs and calculate a more precise budget, all of the above will be represented as fixed costs and, later in the book, ways to manage and reduce these costs will be discussed.

RENT OR MORTGAGE PAYMENTS In determining the viability of the business, it is important to know what this payment is and to plan for any future increases in this payment, and to know the methods used to determine such increases. The entry in this budget example is for a straight-dollar rent. If the lease calls for additional rent based on a percentage of sales to be added to the base rent, the calculation on the spreadsheet should be changed to reflect this. Percentage rents are mostly used in mall or strip mall rentals where there are several occupants in a building or complex. Common area maintenance fees for security, trash removal, and other services may also be charged.

PROPERTY TAX The town or municipality where the property is located levies property tax. The property tax can be passed to the lessee of the property if the lease was written to reflect this. Property tax can change from year to year, but will normally remain steady once it is set for the year you are budgeting, so it is entered as a fixed cost.

INSURANCE COSTS Insurance to cover liability and the property will normally stay constant throughout the year. When applying for insurance, the length of time an operator has been in business (experience factor) is considered, along with the number of claims previously made against the business. Adjustments are made yearly.

MANAGEMENT PAYROLL In most situations managers are salaried employees. This amount is a fixed cost, as it will be constant throughout the year. If a pay raise is anticipated during the year, it should be entered in the month the pay raise is expected.

CONTRACTED MAINTENANCE To operate a restaurant properly and safely, certain regular maintenance is required. Maintenance contracts would include such line items as extermination, landscaping, hood cleaning, carpet cleaning, knife sharpening, fire suppression system (ansul) inspection, and any other contracts to keep the building and equipment operating properly and safely. Due to the potentially high number of possible contracts, this category is listed on the "operational expense" worksheet and entered as a combined line item on the budget under operating expenses. This worksheet will be discussed later in this chapter.

WATER AND SEWAGE If the lessee is responsible for the water and sewage charges, this expense must be entered and accounted for. This number might fluctuate with an increase in business, but for the most part will remain relatively steady.

UTILITIES Besides heat and air conditioning, the walk-in coolers and freezers require quite a bit of energy, as do stoves, ovens, fryers, bar refrigeration, and other equipment. Although this cost can fluctuate slightly and can be managed to some degree through understanding utility charges, it is entered as a fixed cost because it will remain relatively steady and is not entirely a function of sales volume.

LOAN PAYMENTS This entry is the total payment of principal and interest. The budget is not concerned with just the interest, which can be charged off against taxes. The budget includes the entire payment because it reduces available cash flow for business operations.

LEASE PAYMENTS If the restaurant leases any equipment, the lease payment should be entered here. Many restaurants lease kitchen equipment, refrigeration, and possibly other furniture to free up capital.

Variable costs need to be entered after the fixed costs are filled in. It must be noted that some costs can be considered fixed or variable depending on how a restaurant operator chooses to budget. For instance, advertising can be budgeted as a fixed dollar amount to be spent monthly. If this is the case, then the cost is fixed. However, if the amount spent on advertising is a percentage of sales volume, then the cost is variable and the dollar amount fluctuates depending on sales. Variable costs include:

■ hourly labor and associated costs including payroll taxes,

■ operational expenses,

■ equipment repairs,

■ building repairs,

■ advertising,

■ credit card expenses, and

■ projected management bonus earnings.

LABOR The cost of labor, along with food costs, are the two major expenses in restaurant operations. Labor has associated costs that are sometimes overlooked, including FICA contributions, workers' compensation, disability insurance, and state and federal unemployment taxes.

OPERATIONAL EXPENSES Operational expenses are those expenses constantly incurred in business operations, such as linens, paper supplies, dishwasher chemicals, and plate and glassware replacement. These expenses as stand-alone items do not account for large chunks of the budget, but combined can add up to 6 percent to 8 percent of total sales.

The next step is to budget operational expenses (refer to Figure 5–4). This worksheet is designed to help managers understand and account for operational expenses, which can easily get out of control. Because each of these cost areas might be insignificant on its own, managers tend to neglect these cost areas. In column B, the percentage of sales budgeted by management should be entered. If the entry is a fixed dollar cost, the dollar amount instead of the percentage is entered as such. The total dollar amount of operational expenses is entered as one line item on the main budget for each month.

EQUIPMENT REPAIRS Unfortunately, equipment breaks and needs to be repaired from time to time. By planning for breakdowns, there is no need to scramble to make the bill payments. If the restaurant projects a certain percentage of sales to be set aside for breakdowns, calling a repair company to do the repair will not ruin the restaurant operator's day. If the restaurant consistently spends more than is projected, management may need to evaluate the situation to determine whether purchasing or leasing new equipment is in order.

BUILDING REPAIRS Depending on the lease terms, the lessee might be responsible for building repairs. Budgeting for this expense, just as equipment repairs, will take the bite out of these inevitable problems occurring.

A	B	JAN	FEB	MAR	APR	MAY	JUN	JUL	AUG	SEP	OCT	NOV	DEC	TOTAL
OPERATING EXPENSE :		$ 100,000	$ 100,000	$ 105,000	$ 110,000	$ 120,000	$ 125,000	$ 120,000	$ 120,000	$ 95,000	$ 95,000	$ 100,000	$ 110,000	$ 1,300,000
Percentage of Sales Expenses	Budgeted % of Sales													
LINEN	0.80%	800	800	840	880	960	1,000	960	960	760	760	800	880	10,400
KITCHEN SMALLWARES/SUPPLIES	0.15%	150	150	158	165	180	188	180	180	143	143	150	165	1,950
F.O.H. SMALLWARES/SUPPLIES	0.15%	150	150	158	165	180	188	180	180	143	143	150	165	1,950
DISHWASHER SUPPLIES	0.20%	200	200	210	220	240	250	240	240	190	190	200	220	2,600
BATHROOM SUPPLIES	0.10%	100	100	105	110	120	125	120	120	95	95	100	110	1,300
TELEPHONE CALLS	0.20%	200	200	210	220	240	250	240	240	190	190	200	220	2,600
MISCELLANEOUS	0.10%	100	100	105	110	120	125	120	120	95	95	100	110	1,300
POSTAGE EXPENSE	0.02%	15	15	16	17	18	19	18	18	14	14	15	17	195
PAPER SUPPLIES	0.15%	150	150	158	165	180	188	180	180	143	143	150	165	1,950
GENERAL & OFFICE SUPPLIES	0.02%	15	15	16	17	18	19	18	18	14	14	15	17	195
COMPUTER SUPPLIES	0.02%	15	15	16	17	18	19	18	18	14	14	15	17	195
CHINA	0.15%	150	150	158	165	180	188	180	180	143	143	150	165	1,950
SILVERWARE	0.15%	150	150	158	165	180	188	180	180	143	143	150	165	1,950
GLASSWARE	0.15%	150	150	158	165	180	188	180	180	143	143	150	165	1,950
MENUS/PRINTING	0.00%	-	-	-	-	-	-	-	-	-	-	-	-	-
UNIFORMS	0.00%	-	-	-	-	-	-	-	-	-	-	-	-	-
Fixed Dollar Contracts - Monthly	**Enter Monthly Charge**													
LANDSCAPING	$ -	-	-	-	-	-	-	-	-	-	-	-	-	-
CARPET CLEANING	$ 250	250	250	250	250	250	250	250	250	250	250	250	250	3,000
KNIFE SHARPENING	$ 30	30	30	30	30	30	30	30	30	30	30	30	30	360
BEER CLEANING	$ 50	50	50	50	50	50	50	50	50	50	50	50	50	600
CLEANING COMPANY				-	-	-	-	-	1,200	1,200	1,200	1,200	1,200	
MUSIC/CABLE	$ 75	75	75	75	75	75	75	75	75	75	75	75	75	900
FRY OIL REMOVAL														
PROFESSIONAL FEES	$ 250	250	250	250	250	250	250	250	250	250	250	250	250	3,000
EQUIPMENT RENTAL														-
SECURITY	$ -	-	-	-	-	-	-	-	-	-	-	-	-	-
EXTERMINATION	$ -	-	-	-	-	-	-	-	-	-	-	-	-	-
Fixed Dollar Contracts - Quarterly	**Enter Quarterly Charge**													
HOOD CLEANING														
GREASE TRAP														
Yearly Charges	**Enter Yearly Charge**													
LICENSE AND PERMITS														
	$ -												-	-
	$ -													-
DIRECT OPERATING EXPENSES		$ 3,000	$ 3,000	$ 3,117	$ 3,235	$ 3,469	$ 3,586	$ 3,469	$ 4,669	$ 4,083	$ 4,083	$ 4,200	$ 4,435	$ 38,345

FIGURE 5–4

Operational Budget Analysis.

ADVERTISING Advertising the business, to some degree, is necessary. A designating percentage of sales or straight dollar amount for this purpose should be part of the budget.

CREDIT CARD EXPENSES An often overlooked expense is the fee companies charge to process credit card sales. The processing companies are not necessarily the banks issuing credit to consumers. The processing company might be an independent business that charges the restaurant that accepts credit cards. This expense is also known as the **discount rate** and can be up to 2.5 percent of sales on Visa, Master-Card, and Discover cards and 3.5 percent of sales for American Express. If a customer spends $100, the restaurant would actually receive just $96.50 to $98.50, depending on the credit card the customer used and the associated discount rate.

Over the course of a year a restaurant projects that credit cards will be used 50 percent of the time for purchases and projects an average discount rate of 2 percent. If that restaurant's total sales are $1 million and credit cards are used to pay $500,000 (50 percent of $1 million), it will cost the restaurant $10,000 paid in the discount rate.

MANAGEMENT BONUS Some owners pay managers a performance bonus. These bonus payments may be based on sales, cost controls, or other specific goals the owner would like to meet, such as low employee turnover. Bonus payments are made to improve performance of the management team.

Training Expense In recent years, many restaurateurs have included staff and management training and development as a fixed cost of doing business. Managers can continue to develop their skills in a wide variety of areas by attending seminars, lectures, and workshops. Owners now recognize this as a benefit to their teams and seek out such seminars. Whether for hiring and training new staff or continuing staff education, training and development is a recurring cost that should be accounted for in the budget.

Breakeven Sales Point

A business's breakeven sales point is an important concept and number to understand. The **breakeven point** (BEP) is the sales volume the restaurant needs to generate to reach a point where neither a profit nor a loss is realized. This number is merely the business's survival point where bills can be paid but no profit is generated. If sales fall below this number, the restaurant will need a cash injection just to pay the bills and keep afloat. Knowing the breakeven point will assist a business owner in making investment and marketing decisions and will assist in the site selection process discussed earlier. The breakeven point is not the only consideration in any decision, but is a valuable tool that assists an owner in making clear decisions for the future.

To calculate the breakeven point, the business's fixed and variable costs need to be determined. There are several ways to calculate the breakeven sales point. The formula that will be used for this calculation is:

$$S = \text{Fixed costs (in dollars)} + \text{Variable expenses}$$
$$\text{(as a percentage of net sales)}$$

where S is the breakeven sales volume.

For example, if total fixed costs are $158,768 per year, that number is inserted into the formula.

$$S = \$158,768 + \text{Variable expenses (as a percentage of net sales)}$$

Each variable expense is calculated as a percentage of total net sales and not as a percentage of a specific category. For instance, if food sales generate 80 percent of total revenue and total revenues are estimated at $1,000,000, food sales will be $800,000. If the food cost objective is 30 percent, food will cost $240,000. As a percentage of overall sales, food will cost 24 percent ($240,000 of $1,000,000), not 30 percent.

$$\frac{240,000}{1,000,000} = 24\%$$

All other costs (expressed as a percentage of total sales) are added to the food cost total of 24 percent.

If the total variable costs are estimated to be 63.28 percent of sales, the equation becomes:

$$S = \$158{,}768 + 63.28\%$$
or
$$36.72\% = \$158{,}768$$

This means that $158,768 is 36.72percent of the breakeven point. But we need to see what 100 percent of the breakeven point is. To get that answer, $158,768 is simply divided by 36.72 percent to calculate a breakeven point of $432,374. This means that the restaurant must generate $432,374 in sales and keep costs at projected levels before it starts generating a profit.

The breakeven point will fluctuate if any of the cost areas are not managed to meet the budgeted cost objective. If the food cost is projected at 30 percent of food sales but the cost area is not managed and actual food cost is 33 percent, the overage will negatively impact the breakeven point. Cost areas must therefore be managed to ensure the breakeven point is real.

Example: If food cost in the previous example climbs to 33 percent of the $800,000 in food sales, the cost in dollars climbs to $264,000 or 26.4 percent of overall sales. The variable total is now 42.28 percent plus 26.4 percent or 68.68 percent. Plug this number into the equation for breakeven.

$$S = \$158{,}768 + 68.68\%$$
$$31.32\% = \$158{,}768$$
$$BEP = \$506{,}922$$

The original breakeven point was $432,374.

$$\$506{,}922 - \$432{,}374 = \$74{,}548$$

The difference of $74,548 is due to the inability to control food cost. The breakeven point increases dramatically and directly affects bottom line profit.

Another advantage of understanding the breakeven point and how to calculate it is that a restaurant owner can calculate the specific operating income required to generate a given profit. To modify the formula for this calculation, the operator must simply add the desired operating income to the end of the equation:

$$S = \text{Fixed costs} + \text{Variable costs} + \text{Operating income}$$
$$S = \$158{,}768 + 63.28\% + \$80{,}000$$
$$36.72\%S = \$238{,}768$$
$$\text{Sales} = \$650{,}239$$

Analyzing the Financial Reports

The restaurant owner now has the necessary information available to properly analyze the establishment's financial statements and make informed, intelligent decisions affecting the business. The financial reports will be analyzed in two ways. First is the execution and operational analysis of the restaurant. This analysis is concerned with day-to-day sales operations and the ability to control costs. The second analysis is concept analysis, which is primarily covers the restaurant's overall performance and its market position. This analysis examines ratios, the restaurant's ability to attract and keep customers, how the restaurant controls fixed costs (including facility and occupancy costs), and the facility's capital expenses.

Execution and Operational Analysis

Because the business would be unwise to wait until the end of the year or even the end of the month to determine operational problems or areas of opportunity, the operational analysis should be reviewed weekly. The first step in analyzing any data is to ensure that all data are current. The data would include:

1. sales information,
2. copies of all invoices and other expenses,
3. physical inventory of all food, beverage and supplies on hand,
4. payroll data, and
5. budget.

Analyzing the P&L to the Budget

By analyzing the budget (Figure 5–3) and the P&L statement (Figure 5–1), management can make better decisions on sales, costs, future investments, pay raises, and the direction of training issues. The analysis should include the following steps.

1. Management compares the top line, sales, and the bottom line, pre-tax profit. In the example, the actual top line sales exceeded budgeted sales by $130,500. However, net pre-tax profit was only $12,843 more than the original projection.

2. The restaurant operator then examines the COGS and the corresponding percentages. In this case, the actual COGS was 31.46 percent and the budgeted COGS was 32.1 percent. This tells management that costs, at the inventory levels, costs are being tightly controlled.

3. The manager then examines the operating profit line, which demonstrates that, even with better-than-projected sales and tight control on COGS, there is still less of an operating profit than was projected in both dollars and percentage. The budgeted operating profit was $635,918 or 48.61 percent, but the actual P&L was $633,965 or 44.32 percent.

4. The next step is for management to investigate the difference between the budgeted operating profit and the actual operating profit by reviewing labor and operating expenses, where it is apparent that both categories exceeded the budget. The manager should flag these areas and return to them after the entire analysis is complete.

5. In looking at occupancy costs, management sees that the performance was close to budget in dollars and percentage.

6. Finally, the operator observes that the management labor line is slightly higher than budgeted and that a non-budgeted management bonus was paid.

Review Flagged Areas

LABOR In the example, hourly labor expenses were higher than budgeted. Although the overage might appear to correspond to an increase in expected sales, it should be noted that the actual percentage was also higher. As the dollar sales increase, the percentage should decrease to some degree. (*This is referred to as* **economies of scale**. *There will always be a base cost to properly operate the restaurant. If the base cost is $5,000 a week to cover the expected volume and an increase in business warrants additional staff, the restaurant only has to schedule enough extra staff to handle the additional business. The $5,000 a week base cost is adequate for $30,000 in weekly revenue, and that cost percentage is 16.66 percent. If an additional $500 in labor is necessary to handle $35,000 in revenue the percentage of labor is only 15.7 percent.*) Management discovered several problems with labor. Management realized it were not keeping control on weekly schedules nor controlling costs during the shifts. Turnover was high and the constant training placed a burden on labor cost. Management had made a business decision in the beginning of the year to use some payroll expense to develop the staff. Therefore, some of the cost was viewed as an investment and not a pure cost and management was willing to absorb that additional cost.

OPERATING EXPENSES Because the operational expense category has many components, each line item must be analyzed. In analyzing the operational budget, management recognized several issues:

- several contracts were not accounted for in the initial budget, which cost management the bulk of overspending,
- linen costs were higher than budgeted,
- dish chemical usage was extremely high,
- silverware replacement costs were slightly more than budgeted, and
- telephone expense was high.

The following were found to be the problems and management was able to develop a plan to reduce future cost:

- contracts for maintenance were reviewed and negotiated for the following the year;
- the linen overage was found to be mostly a training issue—employees were improperly handling dinner napkins and the kitchen staff was overusing kitchen towels;

■ dish chemical usage was also a training issue—dishwasher employees were running the dish machine with only two or three items in it, improperly pre-cleaning items, and were also running items through several times and changing the chemicals before the containers were empty;

■ there were two silverware issues—management underestimated the initial amount of silverware needed for the opening and the silverware was being thrown in the trash when plates were cleared; and

■ staff members were using the telephones to make personal calls, accounting for the telephone being over budget.

Occupancy Water charges—Water use was over budget because of an increase in volume and because the dishwasher employees were running the machine more often than needed.

Indirect Expenses FICA and payroll expenses—The original calculations for these items were wrong. Management adjusted the lines for future budgets.

Workers' compensation—Employer workers' compensation contributions were directly impacted by the increase in labor expense.

Advertising—Due to higher than expected sales, the advertising budget was curtailed.

Credit card—Credit cards were used less than expected, so the discount rate was less than budgeted.

Through this process, it is obvious that management can pinpoint exact problems and take steps to correct them. Although this specific analysis is based on a yearly P&L, it can and should be done at least biweekly. Such a review helps to manage costs in real time, to catch problems early, and to make adjustments.

Concept Analysis

Concept analysis is directly concerned with decisions made concerning the business's long-term success. This analysis includes:

1. check average and its impact on profitability,
2. ratios in determining:
   a. sales per seat,
   b. sales per square foot,
   c. seat turnover,
   d. inventory turnover, and
   e. solvency.

Check Average The **check average** is the average amount each customer spends. By nature, the lunch check average is different than the dinner check average, and the bar generates yet another check average. The check average for each profit center should be kept separately to help make more informed decisions. Check average is determined by dividing the revenue by the number of customers:

$$\text{Check average} = \frac{\text{Revenue}}{\text{Number of customers}}$$

If the check average is lower than desired or has fallen, the appropriate action is not simply to raise menu prices. An increase in prices, no matter how slight, could have an adverse affect on your goal of increasing sales by having a negative impact on customer counts. This information must be used as part of the decision-making process. But it is important to remember that no part of the equation stands alone.

SALES PER SQUARE FOOT Sales per square foot will assist in making decisions about utilizing space, design of the facility, and expansion.

$$\text{Sales per square foot} = \frac{\text{Sales}}{\text{Square feet}}$$

The higher the sales per square foot, the better the space is being utilized. It may also indicate the future need for expansion.

SEAT TURNOVER **Seat turnover** tells how often a customer fills a seat during a particular shift. The lunch period has a shorter span than the dinner period. The calculation for this is:

$$\text{Seat turnover} = \frac{\text{Number of customers}}{\text{Number of seats}}$$

If, during the lunch period, 100 customers are served and there are 150 seats, the seat turnover is 0.66 times. Obviously, there is a problem in generating lunch sales. If 150 customers are being served, the seat turnover is 1, again showing room for improvement. The higher the seat turnover, the better the utilization of the seating capacity. To increase seat turnover, several actions may be taken, but execution of the operation is the most critical.

INVENTORY TURNOVER **Inventory turnover** is the cost of the inventory divided by the value of the inventory.

$$\text{Turnover} = \frac{\text{Cost of inventory}}{\text{Value of inventory}}$$

Inventory turnover varies depending on the type of restaurant under consideration. A quick service restaurant may turn its inventory two to three times a week, whereas a full-service restaurant may turn its inventory three to five times per month. The value to an owner in understanding this ratio is that, if too much inventory is on hand, then capital is being tied up in inventory instead of being used to pay bills. By calculating this ratio weekly, along with tracking inventory levels, restaurants will be able to set a dollar value on the inventory levels they should keep on hand. This will discipline management to spend available cash more wisely.

Planning and Control

Monthly and weekly planning and reporting include several tools to assist managers in running the business better and more profitably. These tools include:

- weekly sales and labor projections,
- scheduling programs,
- declining budgets,
- weekly food cost control forms,
- monthly sales reports,
- profit & loss statements, and
- escrow tracking forms.

These forms are easy to use and take little time to complete. The forms and reports are meant to help manage the business, not to overwhelm management, waste time, or cause confusion.

Blank forms, with the exception of the scheduling program, in spreadsheet format can be found on the online student companion to this book.

Weekly Sales and Labor Projections

Once a yearly budget has been developed, projected monthly and weekly sales and budgeted expenses can be extracted from it. Adjustments can be made to sales during the year based on actual trends. Directly controlling labor cost is critical and this worksheet will assist in accomplishing that goal. Many modern day POS systems have software that can write schedules and give management a daily cost figure.

If the POS system does not offer this function, the calculation still needs to be done.

Refer to Figure 5-5. This chart illustrates a simple program that can be used by management to adjust labor cost. Under each day, fill out the projected daily sales. Column B is a percentage of sales for the corresponding category. The daily sales for each category are then calculated for each day. Management can then calculate daily labor cost for each position and enter that total on the chart. The weekly cost is then calculated and will give an indication of whether the schedules were written within the budget guidelines. If the cost percentage is higher

Restaurant Name

WEEKLY SALES AND LABOR FORECAST
August Week 1
2005

WEEKLY SALES PROJECTION		1-Aug	2-Aug	3-Aug	4-Aug	5-Aug	6-Aug	7-Aug	8-Aug
		MONDAY	TUESDAY	WED	THUR	FRIDAY	SAT	SUNDAY	TOTAL
Projected Sales		$2,000	$2,500	$3,000	$3,500	$4,000	$4,000	$5,000	$24,000
Catering									
SALES:		Projected	Projected	Projected	Projected	Projected	Projected	Projected	Projected
FOOD SALES	60.00%	1200	1500	1800	2100	2400	2400	3000	14400
BEER SALES	31.00%	620	775	930	1085	1240	1240	1550	7440
BEVERAGE SALES	1.00%	20	25	30	35	40	40	50	240
WINE SALES	2.50%	50	63	75	88	100	100	125	600
LIQUOR SALES	5.50%	110	138	165	193	220	220	275	1320
CATERING		0	0	0	0	0	0	0	0
OTHER	0.00%	0							
TOTAL SALES	100.00%	2000	2500	3000	3500	4000	4000	5000	24000
LABOR:									
KITCHEN									
COOKS		130	160	200	220	160	240	140	1250
DISHWASHERS		65	73	65	88	88	88	56	523
									0
TOTAL KITCHEN		195	233	265	308	248	328	196	1773
% KITCHEN LABOR		16.25%	15.53%	14.72%	14.67%	10.33%	13.67%	6.53%	12.31%
FRONT OF HOUSE									
SERVER		90	90	120	120	120	145	155	840
BARTENDER		85	85	100	100	110	120	85	685
HOST					60	70	80		210
RUNNER					20	30	35		85
BUSSER						30	0		30
OTHER									0
OVERTIME									0
TOTAL FOH		175	175	220	300	360	380	240	1850
% FOH LABOR		8.75%	7.00%	7.33%	8.57%	9.00%	9.50%	4.80%	7.71%
TOTAL LABOR COST		$ 370	$ 408	$ 485	$ 608	$ 608	$ 708	$ 436	$ 3,623
TOTAL LABOR %		18.50%	16.32%	16.17%	17.37%	15.20%	17.70%	8.72%	15.10%

FIGURE 5–5

Labor and Sales Projections.

than the budget, management can rewrite the schedule and trim labor hours. (Specific recommendations to trim labor cost and the rest of this chart will be discussed in Chapter 5!!!).

During the shift, adjustments can be made in accordance with the sales volume. If sales are meeting projections, then keeping staff is the right decision. If sales are falling short of projected sales, then staffing cuts can be managed through the shift scheduling.

Scheduling

By scheduling staff for specific "clock-in and clock-out" times and having the proper number of staff scheduled, management accomplishes two goals:

■ customer needs are satisfied by ensuring staffing levels meet the needs of the projected customer count, and

■ labor costs are controlled.

Declining Budget

A **declining budget** is used to track operational expenses as explained previously. As a review, operational expenses are expenses incurred daily in the normal business operations, covering basically consumable restaurant commodities such as linen, paper goods, office supplies, and contracted maintenance (landscaping and cleaning contracts).

The declining budget worksheet is shown in Figure 5-6.

To effectively use this worksheet, managers should take the following steps:

■ Operational items to be expensed should be entered in column A.

■ Column B is the percentage of total sales permitted for the category or, in some cases, such as maintenance contracts and license fees, or other fixed dollar amounts.

■ The monthly projected sales is taken from the yearly budget or from recent trends and entered in box "1."

■ The percentage in column B is multiplied by projected sales to calculate the total monthly dollar allowance for that expense category.

■ At the end of week 1, management enters the actual expense for each category under week 1, column C. This cost information should be found on the P&L statement, which should be printed weekly (weekly P&L information is only accurate if all invoices accrued during the week have been entered into the book keeping program). Columns D through G are for the balance of the weeks in the month.

■ Column H shows the running total that has been spent up to that period of the month.

■ Column I displays how much money is left in the month to cover each expense.

Box 1

PROJECTED MONTHLY SALES	$93,000								
A		**B**	**C**	**D**	**E**	**F**	**G**	**H**	**I**
	Column2 Budget		WEEK 1	WEEK 2	WEEK 3	WEEK 4	WEEK 5	TOTAL SPENT	REMAINING
OPERATING EXPENSE :	%	$	ACTUAL	ACTUAL	ACTUAL	ACTUAL	ACTUAL	MO. TO DATE	BUDGET
LINEN	0.80%	$744						-	744.00
KITCHEN SMALLWARES/SUPPLIES	0.15%	$140						-	139.50
F.O.H. SMALLWARES/SUPPLIES	0.15%	$140						-	139.50
DISHWASHER SUPPLIES	0.20%	$186						-	186.00
BATHROOM SUPPLIES	0.10%	$93						-	93.00
TELEPHONE CALLS	0.20%	$186						-	186.00
MISCELLANEOUS	0.10%	$93						-	93.00
POSTAGE EXPENSE	0.02%	$14						-	13.95
PAPER SUPPLIES	0.15%	$140						-	139.50
GENERAL & OFFICE SUPPLIES	0.10%	$93						-	93.00
COMPUTER SUPPLIES	0.02%	$14						-	13.95
CHINA	0.15%	$140						-	139.50
SILVERWARE	0.15%	$140						-	139.50
GLASSWARE	0.15%	$140						-	139.50
MENUS/PRINTING	0.00%	$0						-	-
UNIFORMS	0.00%	$0						-	-
Fixed Dollar Contracts		Enter Monthly Charge							
LANDSCAPING	$	-						-	-
CARPET CLEANING	$	250						-	250.00
KNIFE SHARPENING	$	30						-	30.00
HOOD CLEANING	$	-						-	-
BEER CLEANING	$	50						-	50.00
CLEANING COMPANY	$	600						-	600.00
MUSIC/CABLE	$	75						-	75.00
PROFESSIONAL FEES	$	250						-	250.00
EQUIPMENT RENTAL	$	-						-	-
SECURITY	$	-						-	-
EXTERMINATION	$	30						-	30.00
Yearly Charges		Enter Yearly Charge							
LICENSE AND PERMITS	$	2,400.00							
			-		-	-	-	-	$ 3,545

FIGURE 5–6

Declining Budget.

By using this form, management can make adjustments in real time and plan spending. The form can also show problems in control or even in the budget. If linen is budgeted at 0.8 percent of sales but is consistently running at 1 percent, management can focus on reducing linen usage. If, after focusing and setting controls, the percentage does not drop to the original budgeted amount, the budget itself may need revision. This review can be done with each line item.

Weekly Food Cost Planning

The purpose of the weekly food cost planning worksheet, Figure 5–7, is to assist in planning and controlling food cost. By following the instructions and making the entries, the weekly food cost planning form can reveal a food cost problem without taking a full inventory. For example, if the food cost objective is 30 percent and projected sales are $10,000, the chef has $3,000 to spend on food purchases. If sales projections are in line with actual sales and the chef consistently spends

WEEK 1 Purveyor	2-Aug Monday	3-Aug Tuesday	4-Aug Wednesday	5-Aug Thursday	6-Aug Friday	7-Aug Saturday	8-Aug Sunday	TOTAL
								0
Sysco								0
								0
Produce								0
								0
Seafood								0
								0
Dairy								0
								0
								0
								0
								0
TOTAL	$ -	$ -	$ -	$ -	$ -	$ -	$ -	0
Food Cost Objective	36.00%							
Projected Food Sales	$ 1,200	$ 1,500	$ 1,800	$ 2,100	$ 2,400	$ 2,400	$ 3,000	$ 14,400
Actual Food Sales	1500	1200	0	0	$ -	$ -	0	$ 2,700
Difference	$ 300	$ (300)	$ -	$ -	$ -	$ -	$ -	$ -
Actual $ Spent	0							
Running Food Cost	0.00%							
Additional Sales to hit budget	$ (2,700)							

B — Food Cost Objective
A — Projected Food Sales
D — Actual Food Sales

Weekly Allowance beginning of Week	$ 5,184
Left to Spend ○	$ 5,184

E   C

F

FIGURE 5–7

Weekly Food Cost Projection.

more than $3,000, there is a cost problem that must be addressed. Such a trend can become evident over a period of only 3 weeks.

The weekly food cost planning worksheet will assist management in allocating the weekly amount that can be spent on food purchases. This worksheet is included on the online student companion to this book. To use it:

■ Enter the projected food sales for each day in the "projected food sales" row (row A).

■ In the food cost objective (box B), enter the food cost objective percentage.

■ In box C, the weekly allowance in dollars is calculated by multiplying the projected food sales by the food cost objective percentage. This is the initial dollar amount that is allowed to be spent. This amount will change depending on actual, daily food sales.

■ Each day an entry is made in the corresponding box for invoices that are received from various purveyors.

■ Enter actual daily food sales in row D. By completing information daily, management generates two different numbers to guide decisions:

1. box E informs the manager how much money is left to spend before going over budget; and

2. box F indicates the additional sales needed to hit the food cost budget.

Capital Expense Budgeting

Although restaurant owners must concentrate on running their businesses in the present and focus on day-to-day challenges, they must also look to the future.

Capital budgeting covers future business planning to meet long-range goals. The capital budget includes future investment in equipment, land, and building expansion.

Equipment wears out or becomes outdated and facilities age or their size becomes inadequate, potentially prohibiting growth. To ensure long-term success, these factors must be considered and plans should be made to address them. Along with recognizing the need to update facilities or equipment, owners must also consider how to raise capital. There are several options:

1. retained earnings from the business (net income retained in the business and not distributed to owners or stockholders),

2. traditional loan sources (banks, credit companies),

4. leasing equipment to be paid with future revenue (kitchen equipment, telephone system),

5. investment from personal accounts,

6. the sale of stock, and

7. taking on a partner by offering an equity position.

Capital decisions must be based on long-range goals. Expansion to add another unit might require an investor, which will decrease the owner's liability and risk. If the owner only needs to replace worn or outdated equipment, the capital decision might be to lease the equipment so future revenues pay for the upgrade and cash on hand remains in the bank as a cushion or as operating revenue.

In most cases, raising capital through offering an equity position to an individual or group will be more expensive than traditional borrowing. Although a bank may seek 7 percent to 10 percent interest for the life of the loan, the investor will want a premium because of the considered high risk of restaurant investment. That could mean a 15 percent to 18 percent return on investment. Also, a bank will not have a stake in the financial profit of the business once the loan has been retired. However, an investor will have a claim on profits for the life of the business or at least until the end of an agreement.

One way to plan for capital improvements is to design the budget in such a way that a percentage of sales is set aside for future investment. Such decisions should be made after seeking advice from a professional, such as an accountant, as several factors (including tax implications) are involved in capital decisions.

Pro Forma Statements

A **pro forma** statement makes predictions about the future of the business. The predictions are based on management's best estimates of future operations. Typically, projecting 5 years into the future allows an owner and investors to predict future earnings potential. See Figure 5–8.

	Year 1		Year 2		Year 3		Year 4		Year 5	
SALES	Dollars	Percent	Dollars	Percent	Dollars	Percent	Dollars	Percent	Dollars	Percent
Food	$ 780,000	60.00%	$ 801,840	60.00%	$ 865,987	60.00%	$ 917,946	60.00%	$ 963,844	60.23%
Wine	$ 117,000	9.00%	$ 120,276	9.00%	$ 129,898	9.00%	$ 137,692	9.00%	$ 143,200	8.95%
Liquor	$ 130,000	10.00%	$ 133,640	10.00%	$ 144,331	10.00%	$ 152,991	10.00%	$ 159,111	9.94%
Beer	$ 260,000	20.00%	$ 267,280	20.00%	$ 288,662	20.00%	$ 305,982	20.00%	$ 318,221	19.89%
Soft Beverage	$ 13,000	1.00%	$ 13,300	1.00%	$ 14,364	1.00%	$ 15,226	1.00%	$ 15,835	0.99%
Catering	$ -	0.00%	$ -	0.00%	$ -	0.00%	$ -	0.00%	$ -	0.00%
Other										
TOTAL SALES	$ 1,300,000		$ 1,336,336		$ 1,443,243		$ 1,529,837		$ 1,600,210	
COGS										
Food	$ 265,200	34%	$ 272,626	34%	$ 294,436	34%	$ 312,102	34%	$ 327,707	34%
Wine	$ 40,950	35%	$ 42,097	35%	$ 45,464	35%	$ 48,192	35%	$ 50,120	35%
Liquor	$ 33,800	26%	$ 34,746	26%	$ 37,526	26%	$ 39,778	26%	$ 41,369	26%
Beer	$ 75,400	29%	$ 77,511	29%	$ 83,712	29%	$ 88,735	29%	$ 92,284	29%
Beverage	$ 1,950	15%	$ 1,995	15%	$ 2,155	15%	$ 2,284	15%	$ 2,375	15%
Catering	$ -	0%	$ -	0%	$ -	0%	$ -	0%	$ -	0%
Other										
COGS	$ 417,300		$ 428,975		$ 463,293		$ 491,090		$ 513,855	
Gross Profit	$ 882,700		$ 907,361		$ 979,950		$ 1,038,747		$ 1,086,355	
Labor	$ 202,438	15.57%	$ 227,177	17.00%	$ 238,135	16.50%	$ 244,774	16%	$ 272,036	17%
Operating Expenses	$ 44,345		$ 69,489	5.20%	$ 75,049	5.20%	$ 79,552	5.20%	$ 88,012	6%
Operating Profit	$ 635,918		$ 610,695		$ 666,766		$ 714,422		$ 726,308	
Occupancy										
Rent	$ 74,340		$ 74,341		$ 78,714		$ 78,714		$ 83,087	
Property Taxes	$ 12,000		$ -		$ -		$ -		$ -	
Trash Removal	$ 5,400		$ 2,800		$ 3,000		$ 3,200		$ 3,500	
Water and Sewer	$ 23,400		$ 3,800		$ 4,000		$ 4,200		$ 4,300	
Insurance	$ 8,333		$ 12,000		$ 12,500		$ 12,000		$ 12,500	
Utilities	$ 42,000		$ 15,500		$ 16,500		$ 17,000		$ 17,500	
Equipment repairs	$ 1,685		$ 1,000		$ 1,500		$ 2,000		$ 2,500	
Building Upgrades	$ 6,020		$ 1,500		$ 1,200		$ 1,500		$ 3,500	
Total Occupancy	$ 173,178		$ 110,941		$ 117,414		$ 118,614		$ 126,887	
Indirect Expense										
FICA and Payroll Expenses	$ 70,999	18.00%	$ 65,577	15.00%	$ 67,220	15.00%	$ 69,716	15%	$ 80,326	16%
Workers Comp	$ 7,941		$ 4,800		$ 4,800		$ 5,000		$ 5,500	
Disability Insurance	$ 1,200		$ 1,200		$ 1,200		$ 1,400		$ 1,500	
Advertising	$ 19,500		$ 8,000		$ 6,500		$ 6,000		$ 7,000	
Credit Card	$ 7,020		$ 9,500		$ 10,000		$ 10,300		$ 10,800	
Telephone	$ 4,200		$ 4,000		$ 4,000		$ 4,000		$ 4,000	
Employee Benefits	$ 9,600		$ 4,800		$ 5,500		$ 6,500		$ 7,500	
TOTAL INDIRECT	$ 120,460		$ 97,877		$ 99,220		$ 102,916		$ 116,626	
Manager labor	$ 192,000		$ 210,000		$ 210,000		$ 220,000		$ 230,000	
Bonus					$ 10,000		$ 15,000		$ 25,000	
Profit / Loss	$ 150,280		$ 191,877		$ 240,132		$ 272,891		$ 252,795	
Loan Payment*	$ 37,044		$ 37,044		$ 37,044		$ 37,044		$ 37,044	
Interest Expense										
Net Profit/Loss	$ 113,236	8.71%	$ 154,833	11.59%	$ 203,088	14.07%	$ 235,847	15.42%	$ 215,751	13.48%

FIGURE 5–8

Pro Forma Statement.

IRS and Other Federal and State Agencies

Several agencies at the state and federal level are charged with collecting the different taxes associated with operating a business. These taxes include:

- income tax on profit,
- unemployment insurance for both the state and federal government,
- sales tax, and
- payroll taxes.

Income tax is paid to the Internal Revenue Service (IRS) on company profits. Income tax rates change from time to time and depend on the type of entity established. A limited liability corporation (LLC) or S corporation pays tax at the individual rate because profit is income an individual owner or ownership group. In a subchapter S corporation, income tax is paid whether or not profit is actually distributed to stockholders. If an S corporation retains profits and reinvests in the business, stockholders are still liable for their share of taxes. A C corporation pays tax on profits at the corporate taxable level, and each of the shareholders pay tax on any distribution of profits they receive according to their stock ownership and the amount the corporation decides to distribute.

A corporation is required to file quarterly reports with the IRS and make estimated tax payments. This is done through tax form 1040-ES.

Unemployment insurance is paid to both the state and federal governments. The state rate varies from state to state, but the federal rate is constant. Fluctuating state rates depend largely on the type of business being operated, the length of time in business, and past claims against a company. The rates are normally only charged up to a limit of gross income. Prospective restaurant owners should check with the controlling state agency to determine what their rates will be.

Federal unemployment rates are constant and usually limited at less than the state level. For example, in 2003, the unemployment insurance rate the federal government charged was 0.8 percent of gross income limited to $7,000 of gross pay per individual.

Payroll taxes are additional costs business owners assume. These additional costs are owner contribution to FICA (social security) and owner contribution to Medicare. For example, in 2003, business owners were responsible for matching employee contributions to social security, which were 6.2 percent of gross wages up to $84,000. In addition to the FICA contribution, the federal government requires employers to contribute 1.45 percent of gross wages to Medicare. The Medicare contribution has no gross wage limit and is charged to all wages an individual earns.

Restaurant owners, when writing a payroll budget, should be careful not to overlook tips employees earn. Tips are subject to tax, including FICA tax. This FICA tax is also subject to employer contribution. Tips that employees receive are subject to income tax, including any cash tips received directly from customers or charge tips from the restaurant paid through credit cards. Employers must report this tip income on Form 4070. The report is due on the 10th day of the month after the tips are received.

TIP MYTHS

Myth 1—Only 12 percent of sales have to be claimed for tax purposes
Myth 2—Only tips from credit cards need to be claimed on taxes

---

Both myths are wrong. All tips must be claimed and taxes must be paid on those amounts. The employer must ensure that the total tip income reported is 8 percent of the total receipts for that period. The IRS Publication 531 provides this "tip allocation" method. Restaurant operators may use one of several methods to calculate this allocated amount. Complete information is available on the IRS website <www.irs.gov/business>.

Tax Fraud in the Restaurant Industry

The IRS investigates tax fraud. In a report dated January 2003, the IRS lists the following as violations most frequently committed:

■ deliberately underreporting or omitting income,

■ overstating the amount of deductions,

■ keeping two sets of books,

■ making false entries in books and records,

■ claiming personal expenses as business expenses,

■ claiming false deductions,

■ failing to pay employment taxes to the IRS, and

■ hiding or transferring assets or income.

Financing a Business

A restaurant owner has several options for financing a business:

1. personal savings,

2. conventional bank loans,

3. loans from friends and family,

4. investors,

5. partners,

6. Small Business Administration (SBA), and

7. a combination of two or more of the above.

When the time comes to get the business started, a restaurant owner must consider how he or she will finance the establishment. The financing consideration is after a concept has been developed, the business plan has been written, market research has been conducted, a menu has been designed, and several sites have been selected. How to finance the business involves several considerations and should warrant as much, if not more, careful thought than every other aspect of the process. Keep several points in mind while seeking the financing to open a restaurant.

■ It is not prudent to put an entire life savings at risk.

■ The restaurant business is a business. Prospective owners should not buy a restaurant simply to "buy" a job.

■ The restaurant needs some financial cushion to rely on if the business struggles.

■ It is a bad idea to fully mortgage a house to finance the operation.

■ Prospective owners should keep their retirement accounts intact, rather than cashing them in to open a restaurant.

■ If a restaurant operator is involving family members, the family members should be made aware of their investment risk and that they are liable for their investment with no personal guarantees for performance.

■ Partners should consider how well they know each other, what their job responsibilities and areas of accountability are, and the implications of becoming partners with a family member (this can carry its own set of problems).

Investing in a restaurant should be a combination of some of the above. The first step is to determine how much capital is needed, including:

■ opening expenses: costs of training, advertising, keeping a reserve for additional supplies, higher than normal labor, food and beverage costs during the opening period, and costs associated with a grand opening or a friends and family dinner,

■ operating capital for at least 6 months,

■ personal reserves for 12 months of living expenses, and

■ an additional 30 percent of the estimated building costs.

Construction costs very rarely stay within their budgeted allotment. Many contractors bid low and make up their margins on change orders during the building process.

Opening expenses are not built into the yearly budget. Opening expenses are separate and have their own budget. When a restaurant first opens, it needs more staff to be scheduled because on opening day, the staff is not yet a cohesive team. It takes time to develop the team, and, because the staff is not yet a cohesive team, there will be more food and beverage ordering and preparation mistakes. A grand opening or a "friends and family" dinner should be built into the opening budget if such an event is planned.

Operating capital in reserve allows the business to operate and make adjustments without panicking and without making possibly devastating knee-jerk decisions.

Personal reserves should be set aside and not touched for any reason other than personal expenses. That way, the business owner does not have to make any immediate withdrawals from the business to meet personal obligations. Making decisions when personal finances suffer is stressful and difficult.

Once the amount of needed capital has been determined, the next step is to decide how much personal money can be safely invested. The balance will have to be raised through other means. *The **cost of capital** and level of assumed risk must be considered.*

When financing a business:

- short-term assets should be financed with short-term loans;
- long-term assets should be financed with long-term loans;
- loans from friends and family can end in personal conflicts that will last forever if the business does not work; and
- bank loans may offer an advantage.

Banks *need* to make loans because loans are a major source of their income. A bank's major concern is whether the loan will be repaid. If the bank is concerned about the loan repayment, it might ask for collateral. The advantages a bank may hold over offering equity positions to investors are:

1. a lower interest rate, as investors may demand a premium equal to the risk,
2. once the loan is paid off, the bank is no longer a "partner" and future payments do not need to be made, and
3. the business develops a "track record" with the bank.

A combination of these could be the answer. Let's review some options:

Total Capital needed	$1,000,000
Personal cash	–$200,000
Equity positions	–$100,000
Capital needed	$700,000

Small Business Administration

If conventional financing does not work, consider the Small Business Administration (SBA) for a guaranty. The most popular program is the 7(a) Loan Guaranty Program. Through the program, private-sector lenders grant loans and the SBA guarantees that to 85 percent of the principal will be repaid. Approximately 5,000 U.S. lenders grant SBA loans.

DOCUMENTATION   As discussed in previous chapters, documentation is important. Investors, bankers, and the SBA want to know how you will pay them back. The business plan details all of this information. However, one other important area a local banker will consider: the site selection. Bankers know their area and the neighborhoods in their community. It is not unusual for a banker to go to a site and watch traffic patterns, count cars, and determine accessibility in and out of the parking lot. The site selection analysis completed before the financing phase will make a strong argument for the loan.

Small Business Administration Loans

This information is derived directly from the SBA:

GENERAL DESCRIPTION   The 7(a) Loan Guaranty Program is one of SBA's primary lending programs. It provides loans to small businesses that are unable to secure financing on reasonable terms through normal lending channels. The program operates through private-sector lenders that provide loans, which are, in turn, guaranteed by the SBA—the agency has no funds for direct lending or grants.

Most lenders are familiar with SBA loan programs, so interested applicants should contact their local lender for further information and assistance in the SBA loan application process. Information on SBA loan programs, as well as the management counseling and training services offered by the agency, is also available from the local SBA office.

LOAN AMOUNTS AVAILABLE UNDER SBA LOAN PROGRAMS   Effective December 22, 2000, a maximum loan amount of $2 million has been established for 7(a) loans. However, the maximum dollar amount the SBA can guaranty is generally $1 million. Small loans carry a maximum guaranty of 85 percent. Loans are considered small if the gross loan amount is $150,000 or less. For loans greater than $150,000, the maximum guaranty is 75 percent.

WHAT SBA SEEKS IN A LOAN APPLICATION   Repayment ability from the cash flow of the business is a primary consideration in the SBA loan decision process, but good character, management capability, collateral, and owner's equity contribution are also important considerations. All owners of 20 percent or more are required to personally guarantee SBA loans.

WHO IS ELIGIBLE FOR AN SBA LOAN   Although most small businesses are eligible for SBA loans, some types of businesses are ineligible and a case-by-case determination must be made by the agency. Eligibility is generally determined by four factors:

1.   Type of businesses eligible:

The vast majority of businesses are eligible for financial assistance from the SBA. However, applicant businesses must operate for profit; be engaged in, or propose to do business in, the United States or its possessions; have reasonable owner equity to invest; and, use alternative financial resources first, including personal assets. It should be noted that some businesses are *ineligible* for financial assistance.

2. Size of eligible businesses:

The Small Business Act defines an eligible small business as one that is independently owned and operated and not dominant in its field of operation. The act also states that, in determining what is a small business, the definition shall vary from industry to industry to adequately reflect industry differences. The SBA has therefore developed *size standards* that define the maximum size of an eligible small business.

If a potential borrower is close to these standards, size eligibility should be discussed with the local SBA office. Also note that the standards for a particular business may change from time to time and some exceptions do apply.

When affiliations exist with other companies (for example, through common ownership, directorships, or by contractual arrangements), the primary business activity must be determined both for the applicant business as well as for the entire affiliated group. In order to be eligible for financial consideration, the applicant must meet the size standard for its primary business activity and the affiliated group must meet the standard for its primary business activity.

3. Use of proceeds:

The proceeds of SBA loans can be used for most business purposes. These may include the purchase of real estate to house the business operations; construction, renovation or leasehold improvements; acquisition of furniture, fixtures, machinery, and equipment; purchase of inventory; and working capital.

4. Proceeds of an SBA loan cannot be used:

- to finance floor plan needs;
- to purchase real estate where the participant has issued a forward commitment to the builder or developer, or where the real estate will be held primarily for investment purposes;
- to make payments to owners or pay delinquent withholding taxes; or
- to pay existing debt, unless it can be shown that the refinancing will benefit the small business and that the need to refinance is not indicative of imprudent management. (Proceeds can never be used to reduce the exposure of the participant in the loans being refinanced.)

Special Circumstances

Certain other considerations apply to the types of businesses and applicants eligible for SBA loan programs.

SBALowDoc

- further streamlines the making of small business loans;
- The maximum loan is $150,000;
- calls for a response from the SBA within 36 hours of receiving a complete application; and
- guaranty percent follows 7(a) policy

HOW IT WORKS Once a small business borrower meets the lender's requirements for credit, the lender may request a guaranty from the SBA through SBALowDoc procedures. It's a quick, two-step process:

- the borrower completes the front of the SBA's one-page application, and the lender completes the back; and
- the lender submits a complete application to the SBA and receives an answer within 36 hours.

INTEREST RATES Interest rates can be negotiated between the borrower and lender, may be fixed or variable, are tied to the prime rate (as published in the *Wall Street Journal*), and may not exceed the following SBA maximums:

Follows 7(a) Interest Rate structure

COLLATERAL

- To secure the loan, the borrower must pledge available business and personally owned assets. Loans are not declined when inadequate collateral is the only unfavorable factor.
- Personal guaranties of the principals are required.

MATURITY Length of time for repayment depends on:

- ability to repay, and
- the use of the loan proceeds.

Maturity is usually 5 to 10 years. For fixed-asset loans it can be up to 25 years.

ELIGIBILITY A business is usually eligible for the SBALowDoc if:

- the purpose of the loan is to start or grow a business;
- the existing business employs no more than 100 people, has average annual sales for the preceding three years not exceeding $5 million, and the business including affiliates;
- the business and its owners have good credit;
- and the business owners are of good character.

Issue	SBALowDoc
Loan limit:	$150,000
Maximum SBA Guaranty percent:	85%
Guaranty fee:	1% on guaranteed portion
Eligibility Decision:	Relies heavily on lender checklist but SBA still reviews
Revolving lines of credit:	Not permitted
Turnaround time:	100% within 36 hours
Forms:	Revised one-page application form that requires more data, but same for *all* SBALowDoc loans regardless of amount
Collateral:	Follows 7(a) policy—lack of available collateral will not be the sole basis for decline of any loan
Credit decision:	By SBA with credit scoring
Reconsideration:	Permitted in field offices under SBALowDoc or regular 7(a) policies and procedures.
Secondary market:	Can be sold
Lender oversight:	Field offices responsible for lender review as coordinated with OFA and OFO in HQ
Liquidation:	Lender liquidates non-realty *before* buyback

Smaller Business Loans

The Newly Enhanced SBAExpress:

■ Makes it faster and easier for lenders to provide SBA guaranteed small business loans of $250,000 or less.

■ Allows most lenders to use SBA's more efficient and streamlined loan review processes.

■ Includes fewer SBA forms and procedures.

■ Offers special lender incentives to provide very small SBA loans, especially revolving lines of credit.

■ Loans processed centrally with usually instantaneous SBA response.

How It Works Lenders participating in the New SBAExpress:

■ use mostly their own forms and procedures for loans up to $250,000,

■ use a newly streamlined process to request a 50 percent agency guaranty,

■ take most servicing actions without prior SBA approval, and

■ may request expedited SBA purchase on small loans or in situations where liquidation may be delayed.

LENDER PARTICIPATION You may be eligible to become an SBAExpress lender if you:

- currently participate with SBA and meet certain portfolio standards-now there are no minimum SBA loan volume requirements to begin making SBA Express loans,
- are a non-SBA lender that currently makes a reasonable number commercial loans of $50,000 or less, and
- meet certain other participation requirements.

   Contact your SBA district office for more information.

COLLATERAL The SBA's general collateral policy requires guaranteed loans to be fully secured; with SBAExpress, lenders are not required to take collateral for loans up to $25,000 and may use their existing collateral policy for loans over $25,000 up to $150,000.

MATURITY Loan maturity generally depends on the borrower's ability to repay and the use of the loan proceeds. But note the new SBAExpress allows revolving loans up to 7 years with maturity extensions permitted at the outset.

INTEREST RATES Lenders and borrowers can negotiate the interest rate. Rates are tied to the prime rate (as published in the *Wall Street Journal*) and may be fixed or variable, but they may not exceed SBA maximums. Lenders may charge up to 6.5 percent over prime rate for loans of $50,000 or less, and up to 4.5 percent over the prime rate for loans over $50,000.

MAXIMUM LOAN AMOUNT The maximum loan amount for SBAExpress is $250,000.

SMALL BUSINESS ELIGIBILITY SBA *Express* loans help small businesses start, build, or grow. To qualify for the program, a business must meet the SBA's industry size standards. These standards are based on the average number of employees over the preceding 12 months or the average sales over the previous 3 years.

FOR MORE INFORMATION The SBA has offices located throughout the United States. For the one nearest you, look under "U.S. government" in your telephone directory, or call the SBA Answer Desk at 1-800-U-ASK-SBA. To send a fax to the SBA, dial 202-205-7064. For the hearing impaired, the TDD number is 704-344-6640. For information on your rights to regulatory fairness, the telephone number is 1-800-REG-FAIR.

   SBA Home Page: <www.sba.gov>
   U.S. Business Advisor: <www.business.gov>

Information Technology

Point of Sale System (POS)

Point of sale (POS) equipment is the technology that delivers the financial data discussed in this chapter.

A POS system is a computer-based order-entry system that:

1. allows front of the house staff to easily enter food and beverage orders;
2. keeps track of food and beverage orders for each table or guest;
3. acts as an accounting tool to track sales, cash due, and method of payment; and
4. gives management various reports including:
   - hourly sales,
   - menu items sold, and
   - payroll information when the system is used for employees to clock in and out.

The computer system accepts the orders through POS terminals, which are set at various locations throughout the restaurant. Each terminal has various "screens" for the server to enter the order. The order is entered and the computer prints out a "chit" to the kitchen or bar in a readable, easy-to-understand format. Each time the server or bartender wants to access the system they must first log in using a pre-assigned number or by their name. Once entered into the system, that individual is able to select a particular check or table number to either start a new check or add orders to previously opened checks.

When the chit arrives in the kitchen or at the bar, it has more information on it than simply the food or beverage item. This information is for tracking purposes and includes such information as:

- time the order was placed to help the kitchen control the time the order will be ready for the guest,
- table number,
- number of guests at the table to be matched with the number of entrees ordered, and
- server name and number.

POS systems can also offer management tools such as schedules, inventory, gift card sales, and credit card processing. These tools are sometimes acquired at an additional cost.

There are many makes and models of POS systems. The selection should be considered thoroughly to ensure that it meets the needs of the restaurant, as it will be part of the restaurant for some time. POS systems can be costly and can range from a few thousand dollars to $20,000 or more. The system needs to fit the concept, the volume, and the information needed to manage the business. A POS should be easy to use for operators.

Some of the information you should consider when purchasing a POS system is:

1. how user friendly it is (for the server/bartender/manager),

2. how quickly it gives the kitchen or bar the information needed and whether that information in a readable format,

3. whether it allows for changes to the screens (menu items, specials, pricing, etc.),

4. whether it can quickly produce manager reports including sales, open checks, open tables, and employees on the clock,

5. whether it produces necessary back office reports,

6. Whether it can write schedules,

7. whether it allows employees to clock in/out,

8. whether it has available and knowledgeable technical support,

9. whether it allows for upgrades,

10. whether it is cost effective, and

11. the number of years the product has been on the market.

USER FRIENDLY A POS system is designed to assist in managing a business, just like a written system. If a POS system is difficult to learn or time consuming to use, the staff will become frustrated, which will defeat the purpose of the POS, which is supposed to make work easier and more efficient. This is also true on the office side. Updating daily specials, changing prices, changing the menu, and adding new employee information should all be relatively simple to do.

INFORMATION IS EASY TO READ From the kitchen and bartender standpoint, the chits that come through the respective printers needs to be understandable in a quick glance. Time spent reading and interpreting the chit will frustrate the employee and the wrong item may be prepared. Chits are sometimes limited to the number of characters that can be displayed. Use readable and understandable abbreviations in programming the computer system.

ALLOWS FOR CHANGES Changes to prices or menus, particularly daily features, should be easy.

QUICK REPORTS AT THE TERMINAL The dining room manager needs quick access to certain information that will help manage the restaurant. Some of those reports include sales clock in and clock out status of employees, open tables, or open checks.

PRODUCES NECESSARY BACK OFFICE REPORTS Some older models might produce reports directly at the POS system in the dining room and not use a back office setup. These reports are usually not as detailed as the reports printed from a more modern POS system. The cost of the system and the amount of data needed will factor into what and how much information needed. Some typical reports for analysis would be:

- daily sales report with income type breakdown;
- menu item sales with sales category and item percentage;
- labor for the day with employee breakdown;
- sales per server;
- checks that are comped *(the restaurant buys the dinner or drinks for a regular customer or due to a bad dining experience)*—comped checks are still subject to sales tax; and
- checks that are voided (this is usually done when a check or part of a check should not be in the system, which can be due to several factors such as items placed on a wrong check.

SCHEDULES Some systems allow schedules to be written at the back office terminal and labor cost calculated and updated to the terminal, allowing employees to clock in only when scheduled.

EMPLOYEE CLOCK IN AND CLOCK OUT Most modern systems allow employees to clock in and clock out right at the POS terminal. This allows for the manager to track labor cost more accurately. It also allows managers to monitor employees clocking in late or those forgetting to clock out. If an employee is scheduled to clock in at 10:30 A.M., the system will set a "window of opportunity" where the employee must clock in within 5 minutes of that time. If the employee is more than five minutes late, they would have to get the manager to sign them in. This helps monitor tardiness.

TECHNICAL SUPPORT AVAILABLE Easy access to competent technical assistance is critical to the decision in purchasing a POS system. If the support team is located too far from the restaurant, system down time will cause too much undue pressure on the staff and management and the guest experience will suffer. The technical support must be competent and knowledgeable in both the system and restaurant operations.

ALLOWS FOR UPGRADES Upgrades are added to systems on a continual basis. If there is a need for the system to grow with the business, purchase a relatively new system. The older the system, the less likely upgrades will be available for it and even less likely into the future.

COST EFFECTIVE The volume of business expected and the need for information will determine the amount spent on a system. A small, independent restaurant with less than $1 million in sales, may find a low-cost, suitable POS system, even a used, refurbished system that may not offer all of the features.

NUMBER OF YEARS SYSTEM HAS BEEN ON THE MARKET There are several well-established POS systems with representatives and technical support nationally. There are also systems that have been around a relatively short period of time. Longevity is an important factor. The last thing an owner needs is a POS system that was produced by a defunct company.

Depending on the size of the operation, features and modules can be added or subtracted. If it is not needed, don't buy it. Some of these additional modules might include inventory, gift card tracking, multi-unit interface, and scheduling.

Back Office Systems

In today's world it is almost expected that a restaurant owner and manager have some amount of computer knowledge. But surprisingly many operators have not come into the computer age. Back office systems allow for better management of the restaurant through programs such as accounting, labor schedulers, sales reports, menu item sales analysis, and a host of other programs available on the market.

As competition heats up for restaurant business, POS manufacturers produce units that have comprehensive back office units that interface with the terminals in the front of the house. Older units have limited or sometimes no computer interface with the back office.

The software available to restaurants to assist in managing the business is abundant. Ordering on-line from suppliers, recipe costing, banking on-line, and catering are some of the examples of software packages.

■ CHAPTER REVIEW

A restaurant owner must possess a basic understanding of finance and accounting. Planning the future course of the business can only be accomplished by having the ability to analyze the present performance of the operation. Understanding the basic principles of accounting, equations essential to the restaurant industry, and how to apply this knowledge is crucial in analyzing the operation. The systems an operator uses to help manage the business must be easy to use and not make the operator a slave to these systems.

■ KEY TERMS

accounting period	breakeven point
accrual method of accounting	check average
assets	cost of capital
balance sheet	cost of goods sold

credit card discount rate

declining budget

discount rate

economies of scale

fixed cost

gross profit

inventory turnover

liabilities

point of sale

pro forma

profit and loss statement (P&L)

quick ratio

seat turnover

variable cost

workers' compensation

working capital

■ REVIEW QUESTIONS

1. What is the formula for calculating food cost?

2. Define the following:

    a. current assets
    b. current liabilities
    c. working capital

3. Are the following fixed or variable costs?

    a. insurance
    b. hourly payroll
    c. loan payments
    d. rent
    e. equipment repairs
    f. advertising

4. Explain a declining budget.

5. What are the three most committed violations in reporting to the IRS?

Notes

1. Quick Books© and Peachtree© are registered trademarks. They are examples of easy-to-use software accounting programs designed to make the accounting process easy for the end user.

2. As in any industry, there are accepted accounting practices for the restaurant industry. Some of these accounting practices are in place to analyze data throughout the industry. The information contained in this section is used by the author in real life situations to assist restaurants in understanding their business and directly correlates the budget to the P&L report. Although it complies with generally accepted accounting practices it may differ slightly in the format.

3. Credit card companies make a portion of their income by the merchant paying a "user" fee for accepting a particular card. The fee paid by the merchant is known as the discount rate. It is a variable expense dependent on the types of cards used and the amount of sales that are paid by credit card.

4. To assist in developing a budget, please refer to the web page listed with this book.

CHAPTER 6

Building the Restaurant

After reviewing this chapter, you will:

- Design a functional restaurant including kitchen, dining room, storage facility, restrooms, and exterior;

- Obtain the permits and licenses needed to start construction;

- Research all applicable local and state ordinances and codes including electrical, plumbing, fire, health, and the federal Americans with Disability Act (ADA); and

- Work with architects, general contractors, and inspectors to ensure a timely and cost-effective opening.

OVERVIEW

Thus far, this book has laid the groundwork for arriving at the point where it is time to build the physical plant. This is when the dream, the vision, investment, and learning process come to fruition. In a $1 million project, a 1 percent mistake in planning can mean a $10,000 drain on the bank account. Therefore, doing the research and homework and navigating methodically through the maze is critical.

Planning, Design, and Construction

Several phases comprise the planning, design, and construction process with each phase dependent on the others. The first phase is to gather as much information as possible on the building approval process. Prospective restaurant owners must contact the local building and planning boards to learn about local codes and regulations and the project approval process. Many of the codes and regulations were established to shield owners from construction companies using subpar building materials, to meet municipal zoning laws, and to protect employees and the public, as in the case of fire codes. Not following the codes can have serious repercussions. In February 2003, 21 people died in a Chicago nightclub fire that the Chicago fire inspector had ordered closed. The owners had not closed the business and were charged in the 21 deaths. The following week, 98 people perished in Rhode Island in a fire started by pyrotechnics and subpar ceiling material.

Many of these laws not only affect new construction, but apply to existing structures if business or property ownership changes hands. Zoning laws are enforced when there is a change of real property. However, **grandfather clauses** are sometimes allowed, which enable structures to continue to operate in their current business form without updates to current laws, which may also include ADA modifications. Grandfather clauses are allowed for several reasons. One of these reasons might be that the upgrades to the building in order to bring it within current code compliance may be cost prohibitive. To find out more information about local code and zoning ordinances, contact the building inspector in the jurisdiction. Do not assume that not asking about codes will mean that any violations will be ignored. In addition, inspectors may require any unapproved work to be demolished and any new work be approved before construction.

Licenses and Permits

In opening a new business or taking over an existing business, restaurant owners must obtain various licenses and permits to cover local, state, or federal regulations. Contact local agencies for any specific requirements. The following is a list of typical licenses and permits:

1. **Building permit/local permit**—A building or local permit is normally needed for any new construction. A permit is also needed if a certain percentage of an existing building is to be modified. A construction permit might require approval by the town planning or zoning commission. Buildings with historical significance and those registered as historic buildings may be very limited as to what modifications can be made. Permits cover construction and additions, plumbing, electrical, and structural changes. Any local, reputable builder should be familiar with local codes and the requirements of the building.

2. **Other building permits**—Depending on the location of the building, a restaurant may need other permits to get started. New operators should always check with the local building code enforcement before starting any work. Below is a sample listing of other permits that may be needed:

   a. demolition,

   b. dumpster,

   c. erection of temporary or long-term scaffolding,

   d. elevator and dumbwaiter,

   e. change of use/tenant,

   f. sprinkler,

   g. temporary walls or partitions,

   h. awnings,

     i.   signs, or

     j.   patios/platforms.

3. **Certificate of Occupancy (CO)**—The building inspector issues this certificate, which allows for public assembly in a building. This certificate is issued after all inspections have been completed by the overseeing agency. These inspection agencies can include electrical, plumbing, structural, fire, and health. In small communities, one person may inspect all of the building work.

4. **Health permit**—A health permit is issued by the overseeing health department, which might be at the local, county, or state level. This permit is usually issued after a thorough inspection of the facility. A follow-up, working visit might also be done at some point after opening.

5. **Liquor license**—Laws and procedures for obtaining a liquor license vary from state to state. In some states, restaurant operators own the licenses and they are recognized as business assets. In other states, the state issues the license and the restaurant must complete an application and send it to a state agency known as the state liquor authority, alcohol license control board, or a similarly named agency. Requirements to obtain these licenses vary and are sometimes controlled by local authorities. To obtain a liquor license, the restaurant owner must contact the controlling authority in the state or county. The licensing process may take several months.

6. **Federal Employment Identification Number (FEIN)**—An FEIN is obtained from the federal Social Security administration. This number is mandatory, with few exceptions, to conduct business in the United States.

7. **Sales and use tax license**—Restaurant operators obtain the sales and use tax license from the state department of taxation. Once this number is assigned, the owner becomes an agent of the state to collect and pay the appropriate agency the sales tax on products sold.

Design

The next step in the process is designing a "to scale" **line drawing** of the structure. The expense of hiring an architect to lay out the building at this point in the process is hard to justify. This first rendition is merely a design for interior flow and must include the legal requirements set forth by the Americans with Disabilities Act (ADA). In a new building, the amount of space available for the physical structure of the property might be restricted by zoning or code requirements such as the number of parking spaces needed, landscape or "greenery" requirements, and **road set backs**. The building's exterior is the first physical impression the paying public will have of the restaurant. No matter what preformed opinions potential customers may have, whether positive or negative, the building is the first impression they will receive from the restaurant. The design of the structure, lighting, signage, and color of paint, trimwork, and awnings will comprise the vision of the restaurant the public will remember.

SPATIAL REQUIREMENTS During the design phase it is imperative to maximize the use of all space.

The space allowed for the kitchen must include room for line equipment, room to prepare product, and storage facilities including dry goods, refrigeration, paper goods, and sanitation facilities. The kitchen needs to be large enough to produce and execute the menu for the proposed number of seats. If kitchen space is too tight, it limits the number of customers the kitchen can handle.

When designing a restaurant, an operator must answer several questions while keeping in mind the most important point: all designs must revolve around the restaurant concept.

Is there a point of focus in the restaurant? Examples of restaurants with specific points of focus include a brew pub, where the brewing equipment is the focus point, or an open kitchen concept, where the food preparation and cooking areas are the focal point. An open kitchen may provide entertainment appeal to the customer, or may give the customer the feeling of "being part of the entire dining experience." Some maintain that if customers can see what is going on in the kitchen, they have a higher comfort level, because they know the kitchen is clean and that the restaurant is not afraid to let customers see "behind the scenes."

The interior design should start with the kitchen, because the kitchen design must support the menu. If the restaurant design starts in the dining room, it is possible to end up with a great looking restaurant that is impractical or nonfunctional. The square footage needed for a kitchen cannot be arbitrarily decided. If the kitchen is designed for 1,000 square feet even though the concept required 1,200 square feet, kitchen staff will become frustrated, because the kitchen will always seem busy. In addition, the inadequate kitchen workspace will impede future growth. Conversely, if the kitchen could be functional at 900 square feet but is built at 1,000 square feet, the restaurant is losing 100 square feet of dining space, which equates to a seating area for eight people. If that lost seating area is multiplied by 1.5 turns per night times seven nights a week, poor planning will have cost the restaurant 84 potential customers per week.

How much space is enough? This is one critical question that the menu will directly influence. The business plan outlined in Chapter 4 described the Heartland Grill. As a review, the business plan estimated that the first full year's food sales at $630,000, plus banquet sales of $156,000. Because the plan includes banquet sales, the kitchen must be arranged so that the restaurant and banquet prep areas can operate somewhat independently of each other, even though the small business units may share some equipment. The kitchen staff cannot sacrifice service to one group (banquets) to better serve the other (dining room).

In contemplating kitchen design, the restaurant operator should complete the "Menu Distribution Chart." This chart illustrates what line position will be responsible for preparing and plating each menu item. Refer to Figure 6–1. An

X in the corresponding box means the menu item is the primary responsibility of that position (some menu items may have two positions designated as primary if each does an equal amount of work to produce the product). An S represents a secondary position, for example, the fry station. The fry station worker adds French fries to each sandwich dish because it is less time consuming than cooking

Line Position	Grill	Middle Utility	Fry	Saute	Cold
Item					
Chowder				X	
Gumbo				X	
Calamari			X		
Lobster stuffed mushroom		X			
Spinach and artichoke dip				X	
Clams casino		X			
Wings			X		
Chicken quesdailla		X			
Crab cakes		X		X	
Grilled chicken cobb salad	X				X
Chicken pot pie				X	
Fish and chips			X		
Ribs	X		S		
BBQ combo	X		S	X	
Jambalaya				X	
Chicken salad wrap			S		X
Monterey chicken sandwich	X		S		
Heartland triple decker			S		X
Pulled BBQ pork			S	X	
Classic burger	X		S		
Bacon cheeseburger	X		S		
BBQ burger	X		S		
Roasted salmon	X				
Hawaiian tuna	X				
Crab stuffed scrod	X				
Maryland crab cakes	X			X	
Seafood medley				X	
New York strip	X				
Porterhouse steak	X				
Rib eye steak	X				
Pork tenderloin	X				
Aztec grill	X				
Plated salads					X
Desserts					X

FIGURE 6–1
Line Distribution Drawing.

a hamburger to temperature. This illustration is only an example, as positions are menu and concept dependent and will vary widely among restaurants.

The next area to consider in designing the kitchen is the amount of storage needed, including dry storage, a walk-in cooler, and freezer space. Storage must account for:

■ the amount of raw ingredients required to be on hand: refrigerated, frozen products, dry goods, and prepped products, including banquet products (prep products include any product made in-house from raw ingredients and stored for service such as soup, sauces, and dressings);

■ the frequency of food deliveries; and

■ any beverages, such as wine or beer, that may be stored in the walk-in cooler.

The final part of the equation in determining needed kitchen space is the projected sales volume.

The design must account for production efficiency. If a cook has to go to ten different areas and make eight steps to each area to gather the ingredients for a single dish, valuable time is being wasted.

To start the design process, refer to Figure 6–2. This is the line design for the Heartland Grill, which is located in a hotel and has a separate entrance.

Once the kitchen and storage areas are designed, the restaurant operators can turn their attention to designing the front of the house.

Maximizing space in a restaurant is vital to the facility's success. Wasting space can result in lost seating capacity. Sales per seat and sales per square foot are important financial tools in determining a restaurant's potential and value. For practice, a helpful exercise is to visit restaurants and try to determine the number of seats available and the percentage of time those seats are filled (according to Deloitte & Touche, the average number of turns in a casual dining restaurant is two per day).

Seats produce top line profits. Wasted space costs money.

Another consideration is whether customers will be dining in large groups or in smaller groups of two to four people. The answer to that question determines what size and shape (round, square, rectangular) tables the restaurant needs to best use the space. The restaurant operator also must consider structural issues when designing the dining room, such as stanchions, support beams, or bearing walls. A bearing wall supports the building and therefore cannot be moved without compromising the structural integrity of the building.

The dining room arrangement must also meet some important goals, including having comfortable and adequate customer seating. Customer seating is considered adequate at 13 square feet per person while 15 square feet is comfortable and 18 square feet is considered roomy. Local codes may dictate the minimum number of square feet per person. Server traffic flow (aisles with clearance for two people to pass with adequate room for service trays) and server side stations, small areas in the dining room that allow servers to better address the needs of the customer by having items nearby that the customers might request. There should be adequate room to allow two to three staff members to sim-

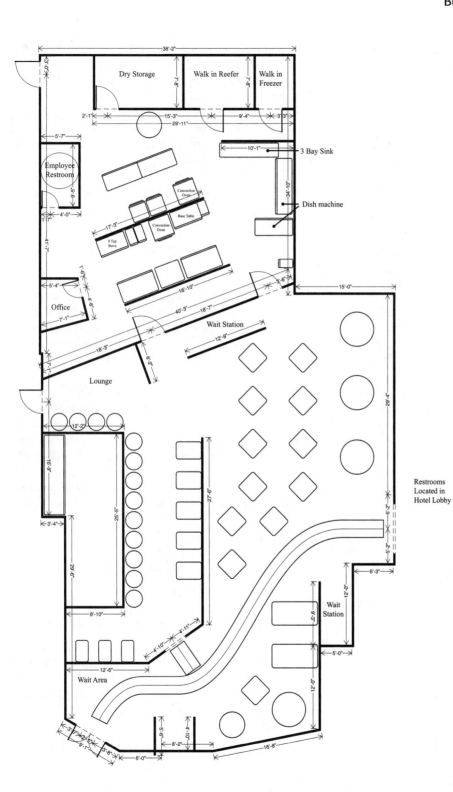

FIGURE 6–2
Construction Line
Drawing.

ultaneously work at a server station. The server station is equipped with POS machine, glassware, ice, coffee, tea and soft beverages, silverware and small plates, condiments, and menus, including dessert and wine menus. Each station should carry adequate supplies for approximately 45 minutes to 1 hour of service. Stations should not require constant restocking. Seating capacity and the maximum number of staff expected to be on the floor at any one time will dictate the number and location of side stations. All this equipment with room for two to three people to move in and out may take up 50 to 60 square feet per station.

There are places where people are not comfortable sitting and care should be taken to design the dining room with them in mind. People do not want to sit:

1. near a bathroom,
2. in the middle of the dining room if the rest of the restaurant is wide open, or
3. too close to a noisy kitchen.

Service flow has to be convenient and must allow for maximum staff productivity. The distance a staff member has to travel to get to the kitchen, the design and set up of the kitchen, and the flow of traffic within the kitchen all must be considered. The time a server or busperson spends in the kitchen because of poor design keeps them away from spending time in the most important place: with the customer.

Safety is also an issue. More slips and falls happen in the kitchen than anywhere else in the restaurant. Any injury leaves the restaurant short-staffed and can cause a financial burden if a lawsuit is filed or if the restaurant's workers' compensation insurance rates increase. If a staff member must walk any distance in the kitchen to retrieve food or to drop plates, their chances of a slip or a fall increase. It is also important that the kitchen is never crowded. The least number of people as possible should be in the kitchen at any given time. Designing for smooth traffic flow will ensure that congestion stays at a minimum.

Accessibility to the bar to pick up beverages allows a server to serve the guests more quickly. Too often, the service bar area is inconvenient or located in an area where customers congregate, making it difficult for servers to reach their drinks.

Other requirements to be considered are:

■ utility room—one or more utility spaces or rooms may be required to store electrical panels and water heaters;

■ supply storage—space for reserve plates, glassware, and silverware along with other supplies should be allotted, including any catering equipment;

■ office space—small as possible while still being functional: although offices do not produce sales, they are necessary for the owner, GM, and chef to keep organized and store a safe for cash on hand;

■ restrooms—the number of toilet stalls or urinals is not necessarily a random

number an owner selects: local codes may dictate the required number of
stalls or urinals based on maximum occupancy allowance;

- and **means of egress**—the ease with which occupants can exit the building
  in case of emergency: local fire codes will determine the number of exits a
  building must have, clearance in front of and to next to the exit, and possibly
  the exit locations. A standard rule of thumb is that a building needs one
  exit for every 75 people. The kitchen is not normally counted as an exit for
  customers.

Architect

Once the handwritten design is approved, the restaurant design should be
brought to an architect. An architect is responsible for building several sets of
plans from the line drawing. The plans serve the following purposes:

1. The first set of plans develop the line drawing into actual, scale computer-
    generated schematics that account for wall thickness, ensure adherence to
    local codes, ADA requirements, and additional space requirements for duct
    work, heating, ventilation, and air-conditioning (HVAC) systems and other
    mechanical systems.

2. The architect will also design the building's exterior, including architectural
    design, color scheme, windows, awnings, and doors. Any logos or signs that
    will be used should also be included in these plans.

3. A separate set of drawings will include structural design, and electrical and
    plumbing systems. Even though the initial drawings would allocate and
    designate space for a water heater, boiler, water softener, and electrical
    panels, the initial plan can become cluttered and confusing with all the
    information. The architect should be familiar with local codes and regula-
    tions. The architect's plans should also include the quality of building
    materials the contractors should use.

The architect's plans must be submitted to **local planning boards** for
approval. If all of the codes or local ordinances are not met, the planning board
will reject the plans and recommend that they be redrawn to meet the requirements, or ask that a **variance** be obtained. A variance is a waiver of a certain zone
or building use requirement. Variances can be political issues and can be costly.

General Contractor or Construction Manager

A **general contractor** (GC) will either subcontract some of the work to specialists
such as electricians, plumbers, and sheet metal workers, or they may have some
of these trades represented in their own company. A **construction manager**
(CM), unlike a GC, will usually oversee a project and monitor, direct, and plan
the work, which will all be performed by subcontractors (for the purpose of this

chapter, this individual or company will be referred to as the GC).

How does an operator locate and hire a GC? There are several methods:

PLACE THE JOB OUT FOR BID To do this, the operator must detail the work to be performed and whose responsibility it will be to complete each phase of the job. There is a cost associated with this bid information, as the architect will have to prepare the data. The prospective restaurant owner should research GCs to find those interested in the type of project being proposed and contact several qualified GCs to gauge their interest in doing the job. Some companies will not accept jobs below certain dollar levels. That is, if a GC normally bids out jobs at a minimum of $5 million, a $1 million dollar restaurant job may not pique that GC's interest. If the GC is willing to contract a job below the normal level, it might be an indication that the GC expects to make a higher than normal profit.

HIRE A GC Early on in the process, the restaurant operator may hire a GC who wants to assist in the design process. The restaurant owner would give the GC the basic plans and would most likely want to have some input and control over the process, including the authority to make some changes to the original architectural plans.

BECOME THE GC This is a tricky approach and can be costly. GCs earn their livelihoods from building. If building is not a restaurant owner's area of expertise, tackling the building process may be difficult. Reputable GCs leverage quality work with the promise of hiring trades people for future construction. The restaurant owner does not have this leverage and may not be able to hire local building trades people because the odds are that it is the only time the trades people would work for that individual.

Before entering into an agreement with a GC, the restaurant owner must gather the following information:

1. Has the GC built restaurants before? Restaurants present some unique building and code challenges. GCs that have built restaurants before have learned the intricacies involved, and are familiar with ansul and fire suppression systems, hoods, restaurant-specific ADA requirements, and other restaurant industry issues.

2. Is the GC bondable? Bonding companies issue bonds to ensure that the work will be completed. It is difficult for companies to be bonded if they have a shaky work history.

3. What is the GC's reputation for completing work on time and within budget?

4. Is the GC willing to accept limitations on changes without prior management approval?

One method to ensure timely, satisfactory work within budget guidelines is to offer the GC a bonus on completion of the project. A bonus incentive increases the chances of getting the restaurant open within the initial time frame and having it built properly.

WORKING WITH A GC Once the GC has been hired, actual building construction cannot start until all permits have been obtained and any variances are approved.

During the construction phase, some decisions will have to be made on the spot. Such decisions require a **change order** or field change. These changes are made to the plans on the spot to address issues that were not foreseen in the planning process and could involve items such as a plumbing route that has to be diverted because an unknown steel beam was discovered after demolition. The GC makes these decisions, usually with the owner's knowledge if it is a major change or expense. Changes may not be necessary and may serve as a vehicle for shady contractors to increase their profits. Often, a contractor is hired for a job because that contractor was the low bidder. The contractor can boost profits by adding many change orders during the building process. This practice is underhanded, but is common.

Once the building work is complete, the appropriate inspectors conduct a final inspection. Sometimes, there is a **punch list** of items to be completed before inspectors give their stamp of approval to the building. The restaurant owner must take care of the punch list items immediately and to the standard and satisfaction of the inspector. If the issues are not dealt with properly, the restaurant opening will be delayed because the inspectors do not want to waste time on repeated visits to the site to find that the work is not done to their satisfaction. Once the final inspection is complete and passed, the owner is given a Certificate of Occupancy (CO). The CO allows for public assembly to occur in the building, but it does not automatically allow a restaurant to open. The health inspection and the liquor license still must be obtained and regulations normally require that the restaurant have the CO before the other permits and licenses can be issued.

Construction

It is important that a restaurant owner have an understanding of building structures and systems. Because the structures and systems account for most of the budget, a business owner should be educated about these systems to ensure that the GC or subcontractors do not cut corners.

HVAC

Heating, ventilation, and air conditioning—an HVAC system—is designed to control temperature, humidity, purity, and distribution of conditioned air throughout a building. Heating and cooling a large structure such as a restaurant can be very expensive. Properly designing the system to accommodate the size of the room and the number of people that will occupy the room is critical to guests' comfort and the owner's expenses. Depending on the geographic location of the restaurant, electrical or gas costs to operate the HVAC system could erode a substantial amount of the business's gross income.

An HVAC system can be roof mounted or ground mounted. Roof-mounted systems can cause roof damage because of vibration.

An HVAC system works in the following manner:

1. It pulls air from the outside and mixes it with return air from inside the building.
2. The combined air is pulled through a filter to remove impurities.
3. The air is then circulated through heating coils, which activate when the room temperature falls below the temperature setting, or is circulated through cooling coils that activate when the room temperature rises above the temperature setting.

Air is then supplied to the ductwork and enters a room through diffusers that are distributed throughout the building. Diffusers have controllable slats to deflect air in several directions.

One of the purposes of an HVAC system is to make guests comfortable. Cold, drafty areas or areas where air is being forced directly at an individual can be annoying and can cause the loss of a customer. Losing a customer to discomfort is unnecessary.

The outside air pulled into the HVAC system is filtered. The filters should be changed regularly, as the dust and dirt that is pulled through them will clog the filters and force the HVAC system to work much harder. Clogged filters will increase the restaurant's electric bill and could cause a system breakdown, increasing maintenance expenses.

Roofing

Roofing can be flat or sloped. Many restaurants mount equipment on the roof, requiring a flat roof. However, modern designs allow equipment to be mounted on the building's exterior, so roof mounted equipment is not necessary. The type of roof may be influenced by the desired architectural design of the building.

Whatever the style, the roof must be designed to support its own weight, the weight of any equipment that may be mounted on it, and the weight of any rain or snow that may accumulate on it, adding significant weight. Flat roofs must be sloped slightly to allow water to run off. The recommended slope is ¼ inch per foot. Drainage must also be incorporated to allow water to run off.

A flat roof would require the following:

1. a wear course,
2. drainage layer,
3. roofing membrane,
4. thermal insulation, and
5. vapor retarder.

To prevent water from leaking into the building's interior, flashing must be installed. Flashing is comprised of thin pieces of sheet metal or other material that prevent water from penetrating a joint. Flashing is used around chimneys, where a vertically sloped roof meets a horizontal roof; around a roof drain or vent pipes; or where there is any change in the roof pattern. Drains should be located in the roof's lower points to help clear water and keep weight off of the roof. Sloped roofs allow for the use of a variety of construction materials, depending on the degree of the roof's slope. A sloped roof is more desirable when architectural design is a priority.

Exterior Walls

Exterior walls are usually load-bearing walls that support the physical structure of the building and also protect the building's interior. There are two basic types of exterior walls:

1. concrete or masonry, and
2. metal or wood stud.

Concrete masonry walls require reinforcement. They can be left exposed and can add architectural enhancement to the building. Metal and wood stud walls allow for vapor barriers and insulation to be installed in the cavities of the walls. These walls need to be finished and cannot be left exposed.

Windows

Windows affect appearance, view, lighting, and ventilation in a building. In designing a building, windows first are considered based on the building design and then selected for the desired view for the customer. The type of window selected can also affect the customer's comfort. Glass windows are insulated by using two or more sheets of glass, separated by hermetically sealed air space. Window thermal efficiency is increased by using tinted or low-emissive coating on both sides of the window. Customers do not want to sit by windows that are drafty or transferring cold air.

Lighting

Exterior lighting serves two purposes:

1. It illuminates the building so the public can see the restaurant and that it is open, and
2. It provides a safe environment.

Exterior lights should be positioned so that all areas of the building, the parking lot and immediate adjoining spaces are clearly visible.

Interior

INSULATION Insulation is designed to stop heat loss in the winter and prevent heat gain in the summer. The following chart shows recommended minimum thermal resistances of building insulation.

ZONE	CEILING OR ROOF	EXTERIOR WALL	FLOOR OR UNHEATED SPACE
Minimum recommended	19	11	11
Southern zone	26	13	11
Temperate zone	30	19	19
Northern zone	38	19	22

ELECTRICAL SERVICE AND PANELS The restaurant owner or contractor should contact the local power company early in the planning phase to ensure that the site or existing building has the capacity to handle the restaurant's required energy load. To calculate the load requirement, it is necessary to know the individual equipment requirements, which are available from the equipment suppliers. In Figure 6–3, the electrical (and gas) specifications for kitchen equipment are shown. (Prices are shown in this example to offer some cost basis.) The owner should give this information to the architect to calculate into the overall power needs.

Electric service panels should be located for easy access. All panels should be clearly marked and the electrician should review the panel with management. The electrician should review such things a shutting down three-phase switches during a power outage to protect the circuit when power is resumed.

WATER HEATERS AND BOOSTERS Hot water is necessary for cleaning and sanitizing dishes, glasses, and cooking utensils. Sometimes, a booster is needed to bring the water to the proper temperature for the dishwashing machine. The water heater must be the proper size and capacity to heat water constantly. The type of dishwashing machine used and projected volume will be used in calculating the size heater the restaurant needs.

WATER SOFTENER Water softeners are not always required, but should be used in areas with hard water to prevent lime build-up. Lime build-up in dishwashing machines can be costly. The restaurant owner should have the water tested.

GREASE TRAPS Grease traps can be located inside the building or outside of the building. The purpose of the traps is to prevent grease from entering the sewage system. Traps need to be cleaned out periodically. The size of the trap and the location of the trap depends on several factors. The restaurant owner should check with local authorities to find out if any local laws need to be addressed regarding grease traps.

Kitchen Equipment

Symbol	Item	Brand	Code	Qty	Dimensions	Electrical/Gas Requirements	Cost ($)	Total ($)
	Line Equipment							
A	Refrigerated equipment stand	TRUE	5T790	1	50.25Wx30 1/2D	120v--1/3 HP	2,359	2,359
B	Pizza Unit	TRUE	5t825	2	67"x35 1/4D	120v	2,539	5,078
C	Fryer	Frymaster	5F105	3	15 7/8Wx28 1/2D	100,000 BTU	999	2,997
D	8 top stove 24" griddle	Vulcan	5v319	2	48"Wx33D	26k btu top/35k btu oven	3,399	6,798
E	Convection oven	Vulcan	5v254	1	Single 40W x 41 1/2 D	120v	3,949	3,949
F	Broiler	Wolf	2W246	1	Will sit on Ref. A	14,500 BTU burners/8 burners	2,649	2,649
G	Work table	Eagle	9E450	2	48"	None	259	518
H	Cheesemelter	Vulcan	5v114	1	36"	30k btu gas	1,785	1,785
I	Microwave	Amana	5D163	2	21 5/8W x 11'9" D	120v 1000 watts	529	1,058
J	Hand wash sink			2	12W x 18D	None	129	258
	Major Equipment						-	-
K	Walk in refrigerator	Rapids	WIC852	1	7'10"W x 11'9" D	1 HP	2,800	2,800
L	Walk in freezer	Rapids	WIF68	1	5'10"W x 7'10" D	1 1/4 HP	2,619	2,619
M	Freezer compressor	Rapids	FR100XD	1		1 HP	2,459	2,459
N	Walk in compressor	Rapids	RH87B	1		1 HP	1,519	1,519
	Wine/beer cooler	*****		1		1 HP	5,000	5,000
	Wine/beer cooler compressor			1		1 HP	2,400	2,400
Q	Ice machine	Manitowoc	MB1300	1	1320 lb 48"W	208 or 230v	3,449	3,449
Q	Storage bin	Manitowoc		1	760 lb	None	965	965
R	3 bay sink	Eagle	7E446	1	108"W	None	600	600
S	Shelving units			6		None	300	1,800
T	Refrigerated pizza unit	Bevair	4b533	1	60"	120v	1,519	1,519
U	Dish machine	Jackson		1	Electric	208/230v (Single, 3 Phase)	7,599	7,599
U	Dish shelving units			3	Soiled/Clean	None	500	1,500
	Water heater			1		None	800	800
	Ansul system			1		220v	1,200	1,200
	Stainless for walls			12		None	200	2,400
	Prep Area							
W	Convection oven	Vulcan	5v254	1	Single 40W x 41 1/2 D	120v	3,949	3,949
Y	Jacketed kettle			1		60 amp, 3 phase	8,500	8,500
AF	Slicer	Globe		1		120v	800	800
AA	2" prep table		4p773	1		None	135	135
AB	6" work table		9e362	2		None	299	598
AD	Mixer		6p637	1	40 qt	115v 60/1 1.5 HP	5,250	5,250
AE								
	Hood			1		120v 60hz--0-20 amps	12,500	12,500
AC	Alto shaam	Alto sham		2	double stack	125v--2100 watts-60hz	8,500	17,000
	Shelves			4		None	200	800
	Miscellaneous*			1		None	5,000	5,000
						TOTAL	97,658	120,610

FIGURE 6–3

Equipment Specification.

ACOUSTICS A bustling restaurant can become very noisy and a high noise level can upset guests. The noise level can be controlled by acoustically designing the restaurant. Noise needs to be absorbed rather than reverberating back at the guests. Windows reflect noise, as do low, hard material ceilings, hard wood, and concrete floors. Window treatments, acoustic ceiling tile, and other materials can help reduce noise.

There are four considerations in selecting a ceiling:

1. decor,
2. acoustics,
3. fire rating, and
4. light-reflecting value.

The first consideration in selecting a ceiling its fit with the decor, but the other three factors must also be considered. When making the choice, the restaurant operator should ask the ceiling manufacturer about the acoustics, or noise reduction coefficient. A ceiling should absorb sound to reduce the restaurant's noise level.

The ceiling fire rating may be a standard set by either the state or the local fire marshal. This information is readily available from either the local planning board or fire inspector.

The ceiling should reflect light rather than absorb light. The more light the ceiling reflects, the less electrical power it takes to light the restaurant.

FLOORING Flooring is a major decision that must be considered carefully. The type of floor selected will have long-term cost implications and inherent advantages and disadvantages associated with it: maintenance, repair, replacement costs, and traction must all be considered in the selection process. Traction is critical because slips and falls are the most frequent injuries reported by restaurant employees.

Local health codes may require a certain kind of kitchen flooring in the kitchen because many health departments will not permit porous floors. Porous floors are difficult to clean because they absorb and trap grease and oils.

	ADVANTAGE	**DISADVANTAGE**
Asphalt Tile	Low cost Large color selection Moderate maintenance	Affected by oils Least resilient Possible cracking
Vinyl Tile	Wide color and pattern selection Resistant to oils and solvents High resiliency	Prone to scratching and scuffing
Carpeting	Sound absorbent Decorative Comfortable	High maintenance needs Moderate to high initial cost Show spills
Linoleum	Available in sheets or tiles Wide color range Low cost Good resilience	Lacks resistance to moisture
Terrazzo	Decorative Durable Low maintenance	High initial cost Unusable for areas subject to spillage
Wood	Decorative Comfortable	Unusable for areas subject to excess moisture or spillage Moderate care and maintenance
Concrete	Durable Low maintenance Low to moderate initial cost	Dusting and blooming Hard on back, knees, and feet

In choosing a floor, it is imperative that the restaurant operator considers these advantages and disadvantages. Once the floor is installed, it is important to follow the manufacturer's suggested cleaning method. Using the wrong cleaners on the floor might decrease its life span. Carpets should be professionally cleaned monthly or at least bimonthly. Carpets absorb oils and, if not cleaned, the oil will become a permanent part of the carpet.

LIGHTING   Some considerations in choosing interior lighting are:

1.   lighting the dining room so guests and employees can see,
2.   adding to the ambience and atmosphere,
3.   bringing out the colors and accenting the decor,
4.   wattage usage, and
5.   ability to dim the lights if necessary.

There are many building considerations in both starting from the ground up and in locating a restaurant in an existing building. Restaurant owners must learn as much as possible about construction, equipment, zoning laws, contracts, materials, and building systems. Thirty to 40 hours of research can save tens of thousands of dollars in the long run.

Construction Budget

Compiling a budget is extremely important. As discussed, construction costs can be staggering. Figure 6–4 is an outline for compiling a construction budget. As the job is put out to bid, the budget can be filled in, and it can be referred to when contractors present bills. This listing is for totals only to offer some idea of construction cost. Each line item will have several subitems listed. When comparing bids it is imperative to compare all aspects of the bid. These items should be listed with brand, quantity, hardware included, and whether the installation is included.

Figure 6–5 is a listing of bar equipment, front of house equipment, and furniture that also needs to be estimated into the budget.

Insurance

Insurance is a necessity in business. Insurance is contracted to cover liability, workers' compensation, and, in some states, disability. A restaurant needs to have insurance coverage for:

- building structure,
- equipment,
- injuries that occur on the property,
- sickness from inferior or contaminated product,
- liquor liability, and
- power outages that might cause product spoilage.

		Bid Amount	Change Orders	Total	Comments
1	Demolition				
2	Excavation				
3	Foundation				
4	Utilities to Building				
5	Rough Plumbing				
6	Framing				
7	Rough Electrical				
8	Sound System Wiring				
9	Roofing				
10	HVAC				
11	Masonry				
12	Windows				
13	Exterior Doors				
14	Insulation				
15	Drywall				
16	Interior Doors				
17	Restroom Build Out				
18	Flooring/Carpeting				
19	Wall Finishing				
20	Finish Electrical				
21	Finish Plumbing				
22	Light Fixtures				
23	Window Treatments				
24	Landscape				
25	Clean Up				

FIGURE 6–4
Construction Budget.

The level of insurance coverage might be dictated by the landlord or by state policy. The building owner normally requires the lessee to assign the owner as an "also insured" to cover the structure from any damage caused by the building's occupant. When shopping for insurance, a restaurant owner should check with a reputable insurance agent that has insured restaurants in the past.

If a customer makes a claim against the business, the owner should only take information, such as the person's name, address, telephone number, and complaint. The owner should apologize for any inconvenience to the individual and then contact an attorney for advice. It is important that the business owner never admit to wrongdoing or claim that the restaurant is at fault. Frivolous lawsuits are filed frequently, and scam artists hope a business owner will just offer a cash settlement to keep the business name out of papers. Sometimes the claims are idle threats, but sometimes they are very real. They should all be taken seriously.

Over the last decade, liquor liability has become a major problem for restaurants. As the legal limit for blood alcohol levels are lowered in the fight against

Symbol	Item	Brand	Code	QTY	Dimensions	Electrical Requirements	Cost $	Total $	Page
	Bar Equipment								
A	3 Bay Sink	Krowne	22-43-L	1	48" L X 18.5"D	water	539	539	64 rapids
B	Hand Wash Sink			1	12"x12"	water	160	160	
C	Ice Bins	Krowne	PT-2436	1	36" L x 24" D	drain	589	589	65 rapids
CC	Ice Bins	Krowne	22-36-DP	1	36"l x 16.5D	drain	535	535	
D	Back Bar Cooler	TRUE	TBB4G	1	90 3/8x27x37	120v	2189	2189	D
E								0	
F	Soda Gun	Supplied						0	
G	Speed Racks	Not Spec'd		2			150	300	
H	Bottle Cooler	TRUE	TD -50-18	1	50" x 26 5/8 x 33 3/8	120v	1189	1189	E
I	Under Counter Liquor Rack	Supreme	CLR -24	1	23" l x 20 1/4 D		425	425	219 nex da
J	Under counter Glass Washer	Glas Tender	3g620	1	18"wx24"dx381/2"h	208v single phase	3269	3269	66 rapids
K								0	
L								0	
M								0	
N								0	
O								0	
P								0	
Q								0	
Q								0	
R								0	
S								0	
T								0	
U								0	
U								0	
V								0	
								0	
	Small Supplies							0	
	Total							1500	
	Breakdown separate								
	FOH Furniture								
	Bar Stools			31			135	4185	
	Tables							0	
	2 tops			6			130	780	
	4 tops			12			175	2100	
	High tops			6			200	1200	
	Bar low living room style			5			150	750	
	Chairs for dining Room			60			135	8100	
									0	
						Total		9970	27810

FIGURE 6–5
Front of House Equipment.

drunk driving, lawsuits and liability are on the rise. Programs such as Bar Code, an intervention program developed by the National Restaurant Association, trains employees to recognize and handle intoxicated individuals. Liability can be reduced through training and awareness.

Business owners assume liability as soon as a customer or noncustomer sets foot on their property. Awareness of the liability helps owners focus on eliminating, or at least minimizing, problems that can cause injury and be attributed to owner negligence. Slips and falls, both in the restaurant and outside of the restaurant, are a major concern for restaurant owners. Maintaining the parking lot by filling in potholes and clearing snow and ice is a must. Slips and falls on ice will not only cause a claim against the restaurant, but it will also keep customers away because they do not want to risk slipping. Inside the restaurant, it is not only the customer that is prone to slips and falls, but also staff. More staff injuries are reported because of slipping in the kitchen than any other injury, including cuts and burns. There are several hazards in the kitchen, such water, food, and grease on the floor. These hazards, combined with a hurried staff, create the perfect conditions for someone to slip and suffer a major injury.

Following are some ways to prevent kitchen falls:

1. Install nonslip floors that are approved for restaurant use.
2. Require all staff to wear nonskid shoes.
3. Keep all floors clean and clear of debris.
4. Clean up spills immediately.

Another unfortunate occurrence in the restaurant business is a customer's becoming sick and blaming the sickness on the restaurant food. By following strict standards from receiving, preparation, storage, line preparation, and service, restaurants can minimize the possibility of food-borne illness (see sanitation section, cleanliness, and sanitation standards).

Blame for food-borne illness is often misplaced on restaurants. Such illness can be acquired from food that was eaten up to 48 hours or more before dining at the restaurant. Unfortunately, most people blame the illness on their most recent meal. The restaurant owners should take information, investigate the incident, and document the findings.

Americans with Disabilities Act

The **Americans with Disabilities Act** (ADA) prohibits discrimination on the basis of disability in employment, state and local government, public accommodations, commercial facilities, transportation, and telecommunications.

To be protected by the ADA, one must have a disability or have a relationship or association with an individual with a disability. An individual with a disability is defined by the ADA as a person who has a physical or mental impairment that substantially limits one or more major life activities, a person who has a history or record of such an impairment, or a person who is perceived by others as having such an impairment. The ADA does not specifically name all of the impairments that are covered.

The above two statements are the opening paragraphs of *A Guide to Disability Rights Laws* (see http://www.ada.gov/cguide.htm). In short, the ADA was written and is in place to protect the working rights and right to access public facilities for disabled Americans. The ADA will have an impact on the restaurant building design. Some of the major concerns when building include but are not limited to the following:

1. parking requirements,
2. ramps,
3. entranceways,
4. passageways,
5. access to dining room and bar area,
6. bathroom accessibility,

7. counters and bar height and length requirements,

8. telephone height, and

9. elevators.

It also applies to employees and the accessibility they have to workspace.

Parking

Parking requirements include the number of handicapped spaces and the size of these spaces to accommodate vans and maneuverability.

TOTAL PARKING IN LOT	REQUIRED ACCESSIBLE SPACE
1 to 25	1
26 to 50	2
51 to 75	3
76 to 100	4
101 to 150	5
151 to 200	6

One in every eight accessible spaces, but not less than one, shall be served by an accessible aisle that is at least 96 inches wide.

Ramps

Interior and exterior ramps and curb ramps must be provided. A slope of 1 foot per 10 feet or 1 foot per 12 feet is allowed for a maximum rise of 6 inches. A slope of 1:8 or 1:10 is allowed for a maximum rise of 3 inches.

Entranceways

Entranceways need to be accessible and ADA requirements include the size of doorways, the number of entranceways, and the number of emergency exits. At least 50 percent of all public entrances, those that are not loading or service entrances, must comply with this law. All doorways must have a minimum opening of 32 inches and open 90 degrees. At least one entrance must be at ground level.

Access to Dining Room and Bar Area

In new construction, all dining areas, including raised or sunken dining and out-door seating, shall be accessible. In nonelevator buildings, an accessible means to the mezzanine is not required under the following conditions: (1) the area of mezzanine seating measures no more than 33 percent of the area of total accessible seating; (2) the same services and decor are provided in an accessible space usable by the general public; and (3) the accessible areas are not restricted to use by people with disabilities. In alterations of existing buildings, access to raised or sunken dining areas or to all parts of outdoor dining is not required provided that the same services and decor are available in an accessible space usable by the general public and are not restricted to use by people with disabilities.

Passageways

Wheelchair passage width for a single wheelchair is 32 inches at a point and 36 inches continuously. Wheelchair turning space is 60 inches to make a 180-degree turn.

Bathroom Accessibility

Compliance with bathroom accessibility laws can be accomplished in several ways. New construction must comply with the latest standards. These standards include:

■ Toilet stalls—The stall shall have a minimum depth of 56 inches.

■ Grab bars—Grab bars must be mounted 18 inches to 27 inches above the finished floor. Other requirements include size, strength, and positioning.

■ Urinals—Mounted no higher than 34 inches above the finished floor. Urinals used primarily by children aged 6 through years shall be mounted no higher than 24 inches.

■ Flush controls—Flush controls must be mounted no higher than 44 inches above the finished floor.

■ Sinks—Sinks shall have a knee clearance of at least 27 inches with the counter or rim no higher than 34 inches. Maximum depth of the sink shall be no more than 6½ inches. A clear floor space of at least 30 inches by 48 inches shall be provided in front of the sink to allow forward approach. Any drain or hot water pipes must be insulated to protect against contact. Lever-operated, push-type, touch-type, or electronically controlled faucets are acceptable.

Counters and Bar Height Requirements

At any counter that is more than 34 inches high where customers can consume food or drink there must be a portion of the main counter that is at least 60 inches long provided for customers in wheelchairs. The height of this section of the counter can be from 28 to 34 inches above the finished ground floor with a minimum knee clearance of 27 inches in height, 30 inches in width, and 19 inches deep.

Telephone Height

Public telephones must be approachable and have clearance of 30 inches by 48 inches, allowing for parallel or forward approach. The height of the telephone must be 15 to 54 inches, depending on several factors, including forward or side reach and forward or parallel approach (refer to full document).

Elevators

If a structure has three or more floors and at least 500 square feet per floor, an elevator is needed, even if the floors are not accessible to guests. This requirement is to protect individuals with disabilities from not being allowed to work in such a building.

These are just highlights of how the ADA affects building plans. Business owners should review the full document.

Opening Process

Much of the groundwork and preparation for opening has been discussed in previous chapters. This section of the book details the phase that begins with the initial small wares order and includes the hiring and training phase, finally opening the doors to the public, making an impact on that public, and keeping the doors open.

This part of the process has many aspects. Opening a restaurant is fun, induces anxiety, causes sleepless nights, and generates nervous energy. New restaurant owners should know that the human body can run on adrenaline for a limited time before it begins to tire. Although sleep may be the furthest thing from the owner's mind, it is important to get enough rest during this phase. Being in a constant state of fatigue can be dangerous, not only to the individual's health, but also to the business. When people are overly tired, they become irritable and may make bad decisions. Restaurant owners should follow these recommendations through this critical phase:

1. Keep the daily routine as normal as possible. Eat three nutritious meals and take time to digest these meals.
2. Go for a walk in the afternoon to relax and re-energize.
3. Set goals and timelines for projects. Every day, build a task list from these goals and timelines to maximize productivity.
4. Delegate tasks and follow up. Delegating is not merely assigning work. Delegating requires that the manager properly communicate the task, give clear deadlines as to when milestones within the task are to be accomplished, and a detail clearly what the expected outcome is.

Soft versus Hard Opening

PRE-OPENING CELEBRATION Many restaurants use a pre-opening party to celebrate their new venture. Although this usually attracts many dignitaries, businesspeople, friends, and well-wishers, it may—depending on how it is done—have a slightly negative impact on the business. Example: a grand opening cocktail party is held on Tuesday with local dignitaries and business leaders and the press cover the party. Because of the media exposure, the public now knows the restaurant is open. By Friday, customers are waiting for a table. This is known as a **hard opening**. If the wait is legitimate and operations are smooth, all is well. The restaurant is a hit and the staff is coping with the crowd. Everyone is leaving with a positive experience. However, it is nearly impossible to have a smooth-running operation after just a few days and the odds are that people are leaving with a bad or not-so-great attitude. Restaurants and their employees need time to fine-tune the operation. This is normal, as the team will begin to meld together through working alongside each other.

New restaurants also have to determine the direction in which the public will drive the menu decisions. If, at opening, the owner believes that the filet mignon and Chilean sea bass will be the largest selling menu items, but the porterhouse and the scallops are outselling them, preparation and ordering need to be adjusted.

A **soft opening**, on the other hand, allows the team to work out problems and make adjustments. A soft opening simply means that the restaurant opens to the public with minimal advertising and lets word-of-mouth spread over the first week or so. The resulting trickle of business allows the team to meld and the menu to take on a life of its own.

Opening Operations Budget

The opening budget (Figure 6–6) is separate from the operational budget. The opening budget incorporates pre-opening expenses including:

1. license fees
2. hiring expenses
3. pre-opening labor budget
4. advertising
5. office expenses
6. menu and printing expenses
7. small wares orders (sample small wares chart is in the appendix of this book)
8. Pre-opening celebration

We now have several budgets that have been developed:

Liquor License	$	3,500
Health License	$	250
Hiring Ads	$	1,000
Opening Marketing	$	5,000
Opening Training	$	4,500
Friends and Family Night	$	3,500
Food for Prep and Training	$	2,500
Professional Fees	$	6,000
Small Wares Supplies		
China	$	7,500
Silver	$	1,500
Glass	$	1,500
Paper	$	1,000
Kitchen Supplies	$	8,500
FOH Supplies	$	4,500
Uniforms	$	2,000
Menus and Printing	$	1,500
Opening Inventory	$	27,000
TOTAL	$	81,250

FIGURE 6–6
Opening Operations
Budget.

1. Construction—Figure 6-4, which covers planning, designing, constructing, and equipping;
2. Kitchen equipment—Figure 6-3;
3. Front of the house equipment and furniture—Figure 6-5;
4. Opening operations—Figure 6-6;
5. Yearly-operations budget—Figure 5-3.

These budgets are management's best estimate of the total cost to open the restaurant.

■ CHAPTER REVIEW

Designing and building a restaurant is a large undertaking and prospective restaurant owners are normally not proficient in this skill. There many, many considerations, including local zoning laws, state and local fire codes, and hiring contractors. The process can be very draining physically, emotionally, and financially. Although the prospective owner will not have the time to become completely qualified to design and construct the building, it is imperative that the new restaurant owners learn everything possible about the process.

■ KEY TERMS

Americans with Disabilities Act	line drawing
building permit	liquor license
Certificate of Occupancy	local planning board
change order	means of egress
construction manager	punch list
Federal Employment Identification Number	road set back
general contractor	sales & use tax license
grandfather clause	server station
hard opening	soft opening
health permit	variance
heating, ventilation and air conditioning	

■ REVIEW QUESTIONS

1. List five permits that may be needed to start a building project.

2. What authority issues the following licenses?

    a. Federal Employment Identification Number (FEIN)

    b. Sales and use tax

    c. Liquor license

3. What is a variance?

4. What are the advantages of a soft opening of a restaurant versus a hard opening?

Sanitation Management

After reviewing this chapter, you will:

- Develop an in-house sanitation management program to ensure serving safe food in a clean environment;
- Teach staff how to keep the facility clean and free of bacteria;
- Monitor suppliers to ensure that they meet and follow local sanitation standards; and
- Conduct periodic inspections of the facility.

The purpose of this chapter is to create a reference guide for food service operators to teach managers and employees the basics of food service sanitation management. Sanitation management means understanding, controlling, planning, teaching, implementing, and upholding the standards and importance of food safety. All food service operators have an obligation to the public to prepare and deliver a safe food product in a clean, sanitized environment for customers' enjoyment. A restaurant will not remain in business long if the facility and the food are not considered to be safe and clean.

*This information in this chapter does not take the place of any approved, or, in some localities, required health courses from local or state health departments, such as **ServSafe®** and other certified courses. These courses, even if not required by local health departments, are highly recommended for management, kitchen staff, and key employees. Contact the health department for local requirements.*

Health Agencies and Their Roles

Operating a clean, safe, and sanitary restaurant is imperative to continued operation and long-term success. The Food and Drug Administration (FDA) and state and local health departments and inspectors are not enemies of the food business—though some food service operators may treat them as such. The goal of these groups and the individuals that work for them is to protect the public from health risks in the environment including food-borne illness. A **food-borne illness** is a sickness that humans contract through ingesting spoiled or tainted food. A food-borne illness, if traced back to a restaurant, can be costly in the form of lawsuits, loss of business, and even bankruptcy. The FDA, along with other agencies, such as the Centers for Disease Control and Prevention (CDC) and the United States Department of Agriculture (USDA), are charged with establishing and enforcing general food safety guidelines and regulations.

Many of these guidelines in a restaurant can be implemented by simply training personnel to understand the regulations and the ramifications of not following them. Other guidelines and regulations are somewhat more difficult to implement, and management may have to make an investment in resources to conform to these regulations.

Food and Drug Administration

The **Food and Drug Administration** (FDA) is the central federal agency charged with ensuring the health and safety of the public through food, drug, and cosmetic manufacturing and sales. The FDA, in addressing food and food safety, is mainly concerned with setting and enforcing standards and regulations at the source of the food including livestock, produce, seafood, and dairy, and manufacturing, packaging, and distribution. State and local health agencies are responsible for the retail trade of food, but the FDA writes the guidelines for standards. State and local agencies use the standards put forth by the FDA; some use these standards exactly as they are written and some with minor changes to them.

U.S. Department of Agriculture

The **United States Department of Agriculture** (USDA) has several responsibilities and many agencies within its office. This book is only concerned with the USDA's responsibility in the food service industry. In dealing with the nation's food supply, the USDA is responsible for the inspection and grading of meats, meat products, poultry, dairy products, eggs and egg products, and fruits and vegetables shipped across state boundaries. The USDA logo is displayed on these food items.

Centers for Disease Control and Prevention

The **Centers for Disease Control and Prevention** (CDC) investigates outbreaks of food-borne illness, studies the causes and control of disease, and publishes statistical data.

National Sanitation Foundation International

The **National Sanitation Foundation** (NSF) International sets standards for equipment manufacturers. Manufacturers can request NSF International evaluation to receive its stamp of approval, which can be used on manufacturers' equipment. Most restaurant equipment suppliers will not carry equipment and storage containers for sale unless they meet these rigid standards.

Occupational Safety and Health Administration

Occupational Safety and Health Administration (OSHA) oversees the working conditions of employees to ensure that they comply with the Occupational Safety and Health Act of 1970. The law sets standards of a hazard-free workplace and safe equipment and job procedures. OSHA requires that any hazardous chemicals used for cleaning have a material safety data sheet supplied by the manufacturer and that it is kept on file at the restaurant. Local health departments will request to see this file during an inspection.

State Health Agencies

State health agencies are responsible for developing standards and ordinances for their individual state. States use the knowledge and expertise of the FDA in creating these standards. Some states require certification by food service operators in food service sanitation. This standard is becoming more popular among state health agencies and it is probable that, in the near future, this standard will be adopted nationwide.

Local Health Agencies

The local agency is normally the agency with which the food service operator will work. The local agency can be the town, city, county, or state in which the restaurant is located. The FDA standard is to inspect all facilities every 6 months. Depending on the budget and staffing of the local inspection agency and past violations that occurred in a particular restaurant, the inspections might only take place once a year or more than twice a year.

The licenses and permit fees will be paid to the local office. The local health agencies will perform the routine inspections to ensure compliance with state and local codes, in states where required they will conduct **hazard analysis critical control point** (HACCP) inspections and offer classes to the management and staff.

Some violations are considered critical and others are minor infractions. The critical violations usually bring fines and can be cause for a hearing to temporarily suspend operation or, in extreme cases, cause for immediate shutdown of a business.

Possible shutdown is why it is so critical to understand and manage the standards within a restaurant and use the experience and knowledge of inspectors. Their job is not to close the restaurant, but to protect the public. When inspectors arrive, the restaurant operator should follow them closely to see what they do in the process of an inspection, take notes, and follow up on the issues immediately. Whenever possible, the restaurant owner should have another manager or chef follow along. The knowledge they will receive can be invaluable.

Some newspapers and local television and radio stations publish serious violations via print or the airwaves. A restaurant does not need this type of attention and media.

Each state and locality has different standards and penalties for violations. Because it would be too extensive to list all the differences from state to state, interested individuals should connect online (www.cdc.gov/other.htm) for a direct link to their state of operation.

Food-Borne Illness

Many of the factors causing food-borne illness are directly under the restaurant's sphere of influence (storage, equipment, preparation, service), some are partially within the sphere of influence (employee's hygiene, purveyors used), and other factors are completely out of the restaurant's control (farms, packing houses). An outbreak of food-borne illness is defined as two or more people developing an illness related to food that was consumed.

The CDC estimates 76 million cases of food-borne illness each year resulting in 325,000 hospitalizations and 5,000 deaths per year. Food-borne illness is also responsible for $5 to $6 million dollars in medical expenses and lost worker productivity.[1]

More than 250 food-borne illnesses have been identified. Food-borne illnesses have several sources, including:

1. bacterial,

2. viral, and

3. parasitic.

Bacteria are the foremost concern for food service operators because most cases of food-borne illnesses are bacteria-related and include Escherichia coli (E. coli), salmonellosis (salmonella), shigellosis, campylobacter, and botulism. **Bacteria** are living organisms that take nutrients through their cell walls. Each cell, in time, splits in two, and this process continues until outside sources stop the process. This bacterium will cause illness in one of two ways: as a pathogen itself, which is a disease-carrying organism, or by discharging toxins and waste that are poisonous to humans.

Several conditions promote the growth of bacteria: *f*ood, *a*cidity (pH level), *t*ime-*t*emperature, *o*xygen, and *m*oisture (FATTOM). The ideal environment for the rapid growth of bacteria is warm, moist, protein rich, and having a low or neutral acid level. High temperatures (above 140°F) normally kill bacteria but not all bacteria will be killed in this manner.

FATTOM Categories

FOOD Bacteria prefer high protein foods or those high in carbohydrates such as poultry, meats, seafood, dairy, and cooked potatoes.

ACIDITY The measurement of acids in foods is defined as the **pH level**. The lower the pH level, the higher the acidity. For instance, citrus fruits, commercial grade mayonnaise, and items with an acid additive, such as vinegar, have low pH levels, which help prevent the growth of bacteria. pH levels that promote the growth of bacteria would fall in the range of 4.6 to 7. Foods with a pH level greater than 4.6 are considered to be potentially hazardous foods.

TEMPERATURE Temperature and time are the two main enemies of food. The "temperature danger zone" in which bacteria will grow is between 41°F (5°C) and 140°F (60°C). This range dictates that refrigeration must hold all products at less than 41°F and warming units must hold all heated foods above 140°F. Freezers must maintain a temperature at or below 0°F (–17°C).

TIME Time is a major ally in promoting bacterial growth. Under proper conditions, bacteria can double every 15 to 30 minutes. Some bacteria have been found to double approximately every 10 minutes.

Some bacteria create a thick wall called a spore that protects the cell in extreme temperatures. If the conditions once again become favorable to cell growth, the bacteria will begin to reproduce.

There are several phases of bacteria growth. The first phase is known as the **lag phase**—where the bacteria become familiar with the surroundings, but do not multiply. Refrigeration, freezing, canning, and irradiation extend the lag phase of bacteria. The next phase is known as the **log phase.** At this phase bacteria growth is the most rapid. The next phase is the **stationary phase**—the number of new cells are equal to the number of cells that are dying. The **decline phase** is where the cells are killed off. However, all efforts must be made to kill all of the cells, because if they are not killed, enough cells will be left to start the process again.

OXYGEN Bacteria differ in their needs for oxygen. Some cannot exist without it (aerobic), some can not exist with it (anaerobic—found in canned goods and airtight sealed packages), some can exist either way (facultative), and some need small amounts (microaerophilic).

MOISTURE Bacteria need moisture to grow. This moisture in food is found in the water content of that food. Removing water can be accomplished in several ways. One method is to freeze the food. Frozen food products remove the availability of moisture because the freezing process changes the water from a liquid state into a frozen state. Other methods would include drying and smoking.

Bacterial Food-Borne Illness

E. COLI Escherichia coli, better known as E. coli, was first discovered in the United States in 1982. Several harmless strains of E. coli are found in the intestinal tract of warm-blooded animals. However, food-borne illness in humans is normally related to people eating food or drinking water that has been infected by cattle feces. Some of the other sources where E. coli have been found include lettuce, contaminated well water, and unpasteurized milk and apple cider.

The symptoms of E. coli begin within 2 to 5 days of consuming contaminated food or water and can last up to 8 days. The symptoms include:

- nausea,
- severe and painful abdominal cramps,
- severe and bloody diarrhea, and
- vomiting and low-grade fever, in some cases.

The CDC reports that in approximately 3 percent to 5 percent of cases, hemolytic uremic syndrome (HUS) can occur several weeks after the initial symptoms. This complication can lead to kidney failure. Children and the elderly are most prone to the complications.

Some of the preventive measures that can be taken are:

- eat only thoroughly cooked beef (internal temperature of 160°F),
- avoid unpasteurized juices, cider and milk, and
- wash fresh fruits and vegetables before eating raw or cooking.

SALMONELLA Salmonellosis (salmonella) is caused by salmonella bacteria, of which *Salmonella typhimurium* and *S. enteritidis* are the two most common strains. In 1984, a new strain of salmonella was discovered in the United States that is resistant to antibiotics used to treat other strains. The bacteria are found in the intestines of birds, reptiles, and mammals. The CDC receives reports of more than 40,000 cases per year but estimates that 1.4 million people are actually infected and approximately 1,000 deaths each year are caused by salmonella.

The major concern for the food service industry for salmonella bacteria are raw poultry, eggs, beef, and even unwashed fruit and vegetables. Some health departments have reported salmonella in raw alfalfa sprouts and scallions. The infection can occur from raw fruits and vegetables or fruit or from handling reptiles.

The symptoms of salmonella are:

- diarrhea,
- fever,
- abdominal cramps, and
- headache.

Though most cases clear up within 5 to 7 days, more severe complications from salmonella can occur, including Reiter's syndrome and typhoid fever. Reiter's syndrome can last for months and lead to arthritis. Typhoid fever is mostly found in underdeveloped countries and places where sewer systems overflow.

To prevent salmonella:

■ drink only pasteurized milk,

■ do not eat food products containing raw eggs,

■ cook eggs thoroughly,

■ cook poultry to an internal temperature of 170°F for breast meat and 180°F for thigh meat, and

■ wash hands immediately after handling raw poultry, raw eggs, reptiles, or contacting pet feces.

SHIGELLOSIS Bacillary dysentery, also known as shigellosis, is caused by shigella bacteria. The CDC estimates that more than 40,000 cases occur every year in the United States, even though only 18,000 cases are reported to the CDC. There are four main types of shigella infection: *Shigella dysenteriae, S. flexneri, S. boydii,* and *S. sonnei.*

Shigella bacteria is transmitted by:

■ eating food or drinking beverages contaminated with the bacteria from food handlers that did not wash their hands,

■ eating food contaminated by flies that were bred in infected feces,

■ drinking or swimming in contaminated water, and

■ eating vegetables grown in contaminated fields.

Only a small amount of organisms are needed to pass the disease and often can be passed by people that do not show any symptoms. The CDC recommends that any food service worker that shows symptoms should not serve food or water until laboratory tests show that infection has passed.

Symptoms of shigellosis usually begin within 2 days and will pass within 5 to 7 days. These symptoms include:

■ fever,

■ tiredness,

■ watery or bloody diarrhea,

■ nausea and vomiting, and

■ abdominal pain.

Most people that contract shigella recover completely, but one of the complications of *S. dysenteriae* type 1 produces shiga toxin and may lead to life-threatening HUS; the same infection that occurs in some cases of E. coli.

Steps to prevent shigellosis include:

■ washing hands thoroughly after using the bathroom or changing diapers and always before handling food and beverages,

- disinfecting diaper-changing areas,
- avoiding swallowing swimming pool water, and
- teaching children to wash their hands after using the bathroom.

CAMPYLOBACTERIOSIS Campylobacter bacteria causes the infectious disease known as campylobacteriosis. *C. jejuni* is the most common type of infection, but there are also types *C. fetus* and *C. coli*. *C. jejuni* is the leading cause of bacterial diarrhea and affects an estimated 2.4 million people every year. It primarily affects children under 5 years old and young adults. Few people die from the infection. The infection is transmitted from handling raw poultry, eating undercooked poultry, drinking nonchlorinated water or raw milk, or handling animal or human feces. Poultry and cattle waste are the most frequent sources, but the bacteria has been found in feces from puppies, cats, and birds.

Symptoms appear within 2 to 5 days, but some infected people show no signs of the infection. The infection can last up to 10 days, but normally passes within 2 to 5 days. The symptoms include:

- diarrhea (often bloody),
- abdominal cramping and pain,
- nausea and vomiting,
- fever, and
- tiredness.

There are several ways to prevent the spread of campylobacteriosis:

- wash hands immediately after handling raw poultry or meat or preparing any food,
- use hot water and soap to wash all food surfaces and utensils that have come into contact with raw meat or poultry,
- cook poultry products to an internal temperature of 170°F for breast meat and 180°F for thigh meat,
- drink only pasteurized milk or chlorinated or boiled water, and
- wash hands after handling pet feces or visiting zoos.

BOTULISM Botulism, although rare, is a serious illness caused by botulinum toxin, which is a poison produced by *Clostridium botulinum* bacteria. Only about 10 to 30 cases of food-borne botulism are reported each year, but can be fatal if not treated quickly and properly. The toxin affects the nerves and can cause paralysis and respiratory failure.

The toxin *C. botulinum* is anaerobic, which means it can survive with little or no oxygen and is most common in home-canned foods with low acid. These home-canned products include asparagus, green beans, beets, and corn. The bacteria can also be transmitted in sources such as tomatoes and improperly handled baked potatoes wrapped in aluminum foil.

Symptoms of food-borne botulism usually begin within 18 to 36 hours, but may not appear for 10 days or in as little as 6 hours. These symptoms include:

- double vision and drooping eyelids,
- slurred speech,
- dry mouth and difficulty swallowing, and
- weak muscles.

Food-borne botulism can be detected by the use of laboratory tests. If diagnosed early, antitoxins can be used to block the disease from becoming worse. *C. botulinum* is one of the most potent toxins in nature. Exposure to the toxin in aerosol form can be fatal. Some ways to prevent food-borne botulism include:

- refrigerate oils with garlic or herbs, and
- keep foil-wrapped baked potatoes hot until served or refrigerated.

Viral Food-Borne Illness

Viruses, unlike bacteria, do not reproduce in food, but merely use the food to transmit the virus. A **virus** is the smallest living organism known and attacks living cells, reproduces in those cells, and then explodes, releasing the virus to attack more cells. The two viruses of most concern to the food industry are hepatitis A (HAV) and norovirus.

HEPATITIS A Hepatitis A is carried only by primates. The virus, after ingestion, lives in the gastrointestinal tract, and subsequently replicates in the liver. HAV is excreted in bile and high concentrations are found in stool samples. The incubation period is approximately 28 days, with a range of symptoms occurring from 15 to 50 days.

The CDC receives about 25,000 reported cases a year, but estimates that the true average is probably around 263,000 cases per year. HAV can occur at any point in the food's life cycle. One of the main food groups infected by HAV is shellfish. The only method to prevent spreading HAV through shellfish is to cook the shellfish, which is still not guaranteed to kill the virus. The food service operator has control over the product only once it has entered the restaurant, and food handlers are the main prevention of HAV infection among coworkers or to customers. HAV can be passed 1 week before the onset of symptoms and 2 weeks after the symptoms appear. The symptoms include:

- vomiting,
- diarrhea,
- dark urine, and
- jaundice.

To prevent the spread of HAV:

■ wash hands thoroughly before touching any food items,

■ wash hands thoroughly after using the rest room,

■ reduce bare hand contact with raw or undercooked foods,

■ use food service gloves when touching any food items, and

■ encourage food service workers to remain out of work and seek medical attention when ill.

NOROVIRUS Norovirus is a member of a group of viruses known as caliciviruses, previously known as Norwalk-like viruses. The virus attacks the stomach and intestines and many times is referred to as the stomach flu. This virus is not related to influenza, which is a respiratory virus. Some of the symptoms include:

■ nausea,

■ vomiting, sometimes violently and without warning,

■ diarrhea with abdominal cramps, and

■ sometimes headaches and muscle cramps.

Symptoms usually surface within 24 to 48 hours after ingestion of the virus and usually only last a couple of days. There is no specific treatment besides drinking fluids to keep from dehydrating. The virus can be passed through:

■ eating food or drinking liquids infected with the virus,

■ touching a surface that has been infected with the virus and then touching the mouth, or

■ having direct contact with a person who is infected.

Even though the virus does not multiply outside the human body, it can make a person sick once the food or liquid has been infected. It takes only 100 particles to infect the food or beverage. This makes it very easy to become sick from the virus. The main source of norovirus is oysters that are harvested from contaminated waters, but the virus has been found in produce and frozen strawberries. Prevention measures include:

■ enforce strict, thorough hand washing standards before handling food and always after using the restroom,

■ food service workers should not work for 2 to 3 days after feeling better,

■ obtain oysters from only reputable, approved sources, and

■ wash raw vegetables.

Parasitic Food-Borne Illness

Parasites are another way that food-borne illness occurs. The parasites most common to food-borne illness are trichinellosis, toxoplasmosis, and cryptosporidiosis.

TRICHINELLOSIS Trichinellosis (trichinosis) is caused by consuming raw or undercooked meat from animals infected with the larvae of a species of worm known as trichinella. The infection is common in wild carnivorous animals but also occurs in pigs. Pork is the main concern for the food service operator.

Trichinosis occurs when meat is consumed that is infected with trichinella cysts. The acid in the stomach dissolves the hard covering of the cysts and releases the worms. The worms pass to the small intestine within 1 to 2 days and lay eggs. The eggs develop into worms and travel through the arteries to the muscles. The worms curl into balls and encyst.

Symptoms include:

■ nausea,

■ diarrhea,

■ vomiting,

■ fatigue,

■ fever, and

■ abdominal pain.

After these initial symptoms there is an onset of headaches, chills, cough, eye swelling, aching joints, itchy skin, or constipation. The symptoms can be severe and in some cases cause death. The disease is rare in the United States and only about 12 cases a year are reported to the CDC.

To prevent trichinosis:

■ cook meat to an internal temperature of 170°F,

■ freeze pork that is less than 6 inches thick for 20 days at 5°F to kill worms, and

■ clean meat grinders thoroughly after grinding meats.

TOXOPLASMOSIS Toxoplasmosis is caused by a single-celled parasite, *Toxoplasma gondii*. The CDC estimates that over 60 million people in the United States carry the disease, but the human immune system is capable of keeping the parasite from causing illness. However, pregnant women and those with weakened immune systems are at a higher risk.

The infection occurs by consuming food or water that has been contaminated with the parasite. Pork, lamb, and venison are at most risk. Cats are also carriers of the parasite and cat owners are at risk.

Most people are not aware that they have been infected but the leading symptom is a flu-like feeling with swollen lymph glands or muscle aches that may last for a month. Severe toxoplasmosis can cause damage to the brain, eyes, or other organs.

To prevent the spread of toxoplasmosis:

■ wear gloves when gardening or changing cat litter, and

■ sanitize all cutting boards and cutting utensils immediately after use.

CRYPTOSPORIDIOSIS Cryptosporidiosis is caused by a microscopic parasite known as cryptosporidium. The parasite lives in the intestine and passes through the stool. The parasite is protected by a hard shell, which allows it to survive for long periods of time outside the body. Cryptosporidium is found in soil, food, water, and surfaces that have been contaminated. The parasite is spread by:

■ consuming something that has come into contact with the feces of an infected animal or human,

■ swallowing water from recreational facilities (cryptosporidium can survive in chlorine-treated water for several days),

■ eating uncooked food such as fruits or vegetables, and

■ swallowing the parasite from surfaces that have been contaminated, such as toys.

Symptoms occur within 2 days but may take as long as 10 days to surface. The symptoms include:

■ dehydration,

■ weight loss,

■ stomach cramps or pain,

■ fever,

■ nausea, and

■ vomiting.

To prevent cryptosporidium, follow these guidelines:

■ do not swallow recreational water, and

■ wash or peel raw vegetables.

Sanitation Management

A food service operator is responsible to the public to deliver safe food and beverages. The information revealed in the previous sections combined with an understanding of the guidelines set forth by the FDA and USDA, along with all of the

offices of these groups, and the local and state health agencies, give a food service operator more than enough information to develop an internal sanitation
management program. A **sanitation management program** uses this information to implement controls and programs within the owners' sphere of influence
and shares with others (employees, delivery people) the responsibility of delivering safe food and beverages to the consuming public. The sphere of influence
within the restaurants control can be broken into two major parts:

1. receiving and storing, and
2. preparation, storage and delivery.

Receiving and Storing

The restaurant's sphere of influence in the receiving and storing phase of food
would include:

■ purveyors,
■ receiving area,
■ staff training,
■ storage guidelines, and
■ cleaning and sanitizing procedures posted for equipment and facility.

PURVEYORS Purveyors are only in a limited sphere of influence for the food service operator. Certain controls can be put in place to ensure the restaurant is
receiving quality, safe food products. The area of influence where the restaurant
has no control over would include the farms where the fruits and vegetables are
grown and the livestock are raised, the transportation used by these farmers; the
slaughter houses; the packing houses; the transportation used for delivery to the
purveyor; and the storage facility of the purveyor. Restaurants depend on the FDA
to do its job in protecting them from receiving tainted or contaminated food.

The sphere of influence the restaurant has control over is selecting the right
purveyor that enforces standards set by the FDA and USDA. As mentioned earlier in the book, it is the responsibility of the food service operator to visit the
facility of the purveyor to ensure their standards are acceptable with their facilities, equipment, and personnel. If any of these areas are not acceptable or are of
concern, the food service operator should not purchase product from this purveyor. The following example standards are the minimum for starting a quality
sanitation management program. These standards should be developed for all
purveyors:

MEAT, POULTRY, AND FISH PURVEYOR

1. purchase from approved sources with proper licenses and permits;
2. refrigeration is maintained and in proper working order;

3. request information and documentation for delivery days they receive product—the older the product is when arriving at the purveyor, the less shelf life that product will have when it arrives at the restaurant;

4. sanitation standards of :

    a. receiving area should be clean and free from dirt buildup and debris;

    b. storage areas should be proper temperature, rotation of stock should be evident—floors, walls, and shelves should be clean and sanitary;

    c. cutting area should have sinks and cutting board sanitation sinks;

    d. shipping area should be clean, free from debris, and properly cooled;

    e. delivery trucks should be sanitized daily both inside and cleaned outside (keeping the exterior of the trucks clean indicates the company is aware of the importance of cleanliness and are making the effort keep the trucks clean);

    f. employees should follow sanitation procedures and all rules for washing hands, cutting surfaces, and storage areas;

    g. employee changing area should be separate and their clothes for work should not be worn into or out of the facility; and

    h. trash area should not be close to receiving, shipping, or the cutting area.

All areas should have sanitation and cleaning procedures posted. Cleaning supplies should be properly stored and used. Check deck drains for cleanliness as build up can lead to problems such as flies and rodents.

Ensure a pest management program from a reputable company is in place both inside the facility and around the perimeter of the facility. Controlling rodents is difficult, but the company must make every effort to do so and eliminate any problems.

PRODUCE PURVEYOR

1. check all refrigeration for proper temperatures;
2. check receiving and loading dock for cleanliness and sanitation;
3. check truck to ensure they have been cleaned and maintained;
4. the facility should be clean and free of debris and boxes;
5. a pest management program should be in place;
6. check for rotation of product; and
7. employee sanitation standards are posted and practiced.

RECEIVING AREA The receiving area of the restaurant is the first physical point of control that completely falls within the restaurant's sphere of influence. Some recommendations for the receiving area would be:

1. keep trash area separate from the receiving area;
2. keep doors open only when actively unloading deliveries;

3. clean receiving areas at least once daily; and

4. have an active rodent elimination program in place.

All products that are delivered should be properly inspected. All refrigerated product needs to arrive at or below 41°F. If the temperature is higher, bacteria may have had time to start to reproduce. An infrared thermometer allows for measuring the surface temperature of food without breaking the seal. Canned goods should show no signs of damage such as dents or expansion. These cans are prime targets for the growth of botulism. If cans are found to be damaged, they should be removed from the storage area, marked "DO NOT USE," and stored away from any access. An office space is recommended. Immediately contact the proper purveyor about the product. All products should immediately be stored in its proper location.

STORAGE GUIDELINES Storing and rotating product properly is a major step in preventing food-borne illness. The **first-in, first-out** (FIFO) method should be used. This method of storage ensures the oldest product is used first. Simply rotate old product forward or to the top and the new product to the back or bottom of the storage unit. Dairy, seafood, produce, meats, and poultry have certain storage standards that will prevent cross-contamination and also extend food shelf life. All refrigeration has areas that are colder and less exposed to temperature fluctuation due to opening and closing of the refrigerator door. Some basic guidelines for storage follow:

1. *all* storage, including dry storage, freezers, and refrigeration must be a minimum of 6 inches off the ground;

2. poultry and dairy should be stored on a bottom shelf away from the door and close to the compressor because this is the coldest area of the cooler;

3. produce should be stored away from any other product;

4. in-house prepared products should be stored on separate shelves away from all raw products and should follow approved guidelines for cooling, marking, rotating, and covering (these standards will be discussed later in this chapter); and

5. shellfish tags should be kept on file for approximately 90 days. Check with the local health agency for specific information. In some states a separate license is required to offer shellfish on the menu.

CLEANING PROCEDURES There is an old term: "inspect what you expect." Detailed cleaning procedures for all equipment should be posted. If the staff knows their work will be inspected, they are more likely to follow up and complete the work to expected standards. These procedures would include facility and equipment.

The cleanliness and sanitation standards of the facility are at the heart of the restaurant's sphere of influence. The facility includes the exterior and interior of the building, which encompasses: the trash area, landscaping, exterior building walls, parking lot, entranceways, dining room, kitchen, storage areas, and bathrooms.

Germs and bacteria will breed on unsanitary equipment. If that unsanitary equipment is then used to prepare other food, the bacteria that is breeding will cross-contaminate any food that it comes into contact with the unsanitary equipment.

INSPECTIONS Local health authorities will inspect a facility at least once a year. In some areas this may be as often as twice a year and even more often for facilities not passing the standards set forth by the authority. As mentioned above, a food service operator should follow these inspectors and learn from them. Use the inspection time to learn what could be done better to ensure the safety of the food and beverage being served. The food service operators that ignore or fight the inspector are probably more likely to have problems.

PREPARATION, STORAGE, AND DELIVERY The next major step is preparation, storage, and delivery phase. During the preparation stage, food passes through several or all of these control points:

1. thawing,
2. cooking,
3. cooling,
4. storing,
5. reheat,
6. hold, and
7. service.

At each of these points bacteria can be introduced to the food and allowed to multiply.

THAWING Many people in their home will thaw meat or other products by simply pulling the product from the freezer and setting it on a counter. What people do in their own home is up to them but this is not acceptable practice in a restaurant. The reason is that the exterior of the product may thaw in a couple of hours but the interior of the product may take several hours more to thaw all the way through. The outside of the product during this phase of thawing can reach the danger levels of between 41°F to 140°F allowing bacteria to start its growth phase. Also, remember that any bacteria introduced to the product before it was frozen will again multiply if the previously frozen food is allowed to sit at room temperature. Freezing does not destroy all bacteria.

Proper thawing is accomplished by pulling the product from the freezer and allowing it to properly thaw under refrigerated conditions. However, this not always feasible, and there is another method accepted for foods that need to be completely thawed in under 2 hours: running the food under drinkable water where the water temperature is less than 70°F. Microwave defrost is also acceptable for foods that will immediately be cooked.

COOKING Requirements for the cooking phase depend on what is being cooked. Minimum standards for internal temperatures of hot foods are set as follows.[2]

PRODUCT		TEMPERATURE
Ground beef, pork veal, lamb		160°F
Ground turkey, chicken		165°F
Fresh beef, veal, lamb	Medium rare	145°F
	Medium	160°F
	Well done	170°F
Fresh pork	Medium	160°F
	Well done	170°F
Chicken and turkey, whole		180°F
Poultry breast		170°F
Leftover and casseroles		165°F

COOLING After food is cooked thoroughly it needs to be cooled down to 70°F within 2 hours and down to 41°F within 6 hours. This can be accomplished in several ways:

1. Ice bath—An ice bath is surrounding the pot the food was cooked in with ice. The ice quickly cools down the product. However, the size of the pot can negatively affect the cool-down time. If the pot is too large to properly cool the product, the product should be separated into several smaller containers and each container should be set in its own ice bath.

2. Ice sticks—Ice sticks are long, plastic tubes that NSF approved and filled with cold water and frozen. The sticks are placed into the pot to assist in cooling the product down more rapidly. The food can then be stored in a walk-in cooler to help cool the product.

3. Refrigeration—Place cooked product such as rice or vegetables in shallow pans and refrigerate immediately.

STORING Cooked food should be stored in proper, approved containers with the National Sanitation Foundation (NSF) designation. Food should be stored in refrigeration that is in proper working order and can maintain a temperature not to exceed 40°F. When opening and closing the doors of refrigeration units, the internal temperature of the unit will fluctuate but should be able to recover quickly. Storage of hot products in refrigeration, either in ice baths or with cooling sticks, should be done so the hot product is not below any other stored and cooled product. If hot product is stored below other cooled product, it could heat the cooled product to an unsafe level and also introduce moisture into the product. Approved lids are to be placed immediately on the cooked product once the product has been cooled to under or at 41°F.

Once food is covered it should be marked with the product name, date it was made, and who prepared it. Separate batches should never be mixed with each other. Reminder: Rotate food using the first-in, first-out (FIFO) method.

PROPERLY REHEATING FOOD Cooked food, such as soups and sauces that have been refrigerated and need to be reheated to serve, has to be reheated to 165°F in less than 2 hours for at least 15 seconds. Once this internal temperature is reached, it can be held at 140°F.

HOLDING TEMPERATURES Food must be held at a minimum of 140°F. Highly perishable foods should not be reheated more than once. Cream soups, gravies, and custards need to be discarded after one reheat.

SERVICE Service of the food is where more people will come into contact with the prepared food than at any other time. The cook, the expediter, the food runner, or server, and the customer will all come into contact with the food during this stage. The staff must understand the importance of properly handling and carrying of dishes during this phase. Fingers should not be on the rim of the plate, fingers should not touch any part of the silverware the customer will use, and plates should not be carried in such a manner that bottom of one plate touches the food on another plate.

Servers should wash their hands as often as possible during a shift. If they carry dirty dishes to the dish room, they should wash their hands before returning to the floor and especially before carrying any food to other customers.

Customers can also be carriers of food-borne illness and can transmit problems through several means.

1. If the customer returns food for any reason, they probably touched the plate and the silverware. If the customer are not sanitary in personal hygiene, bacteria can be transmitted to the server when the server picks up the plate.

2. If there is a salad or food bar, customers can transmit bacteria and other diseases through touching the utensils or by having the utensils touch a previously used plate. It is highly recommended that customers be encouraged to use a new plate each time they return to the salad or food bar.

3. Through the drinking glass on the table. The mouth is full of germs and can easily transmit infectious diseases by drinking from a glass and a server or bus person picking that glass up from the rim or placing their hands inside the glass.

STAFF TRAINING People are the number one line of defense for preventing food-borne illness. Educating the staff is the best way to prevent food-borne illness. Their education should include understanding the damage that can be done by not following sanitary procedures. Several points need to be taught and continually enforced to ensure a safe food handling program.

- Clean hands—Hands must be washed after smoking, eating, combing hair, handling soiled dishes in the dish room, after using the toilet, or any contact that may cause contamination. Washing one's hands is the best defense against the spread of food-borne illness.

- Combing hair and hair restraints—Hair should always be kept clean and neat. Hair should be combed in restrooms and not in food preparation areas. Hair should be kept off the shoulders of service staff. Kitchen staff with long hair should keep their hair intact under a cap or net.

- Jewelry—Jewelry collects oils from the body and will promote germs. Jewelry should be worn sparingly and extra bracelets, rings, and visible body piercing should not be allowed.

- Clothing—Uniforms should be clean at all times. Uniforms worn at work should be put on at work and removed before leaving.

- Chewing gum—Gum chewing is an unsafe act in food preparation areas. Service staff should not chew gum.

- Fingernails and nail polish—Long fingernails might be the personal touch of a staff member, but long nails are a potential health hazard in the food business. Germs and bacteria can build up under the nails and be transferred easily. Long nails can also break and end up in food, which is more than just embarrassing, it is a physical hazard. Nail polish can chip and cause the same problems as broken nails.

- Drink containers—Drink containers should not be left around a service area or in the kitchen. If a staff member drinks from a cup, that cup should be sent to the dish room. Germs gather on the rim of the glass or bottle and can easily be transferred to the hands when you bring the glass or bottle to the mouth to take a drink. After drinking, hands should be washed immediately.

- Open cuts or abrasions—Open wounds will harbor germs and bacteria. Nobody with an open cut or abrasion should ever handle food or beverages in any manner. Cuts or abrasions, no matter how small, should be covered with an approved covering. If on the arm, a long sleeve shirt should be worn over the covering. If on the hand, a plastic glove should be worn.

- Handkerchief—If someone sneezes, a handkerchief should be used and hands should be washed immediately. No one with a cold, flu, or symptoms of a cold or flu should be allowed to work.

- Rubbing eyes—The mucous membranes of the eyes can harbor germs and bacteria. Germs and bacteria can also be transferred to employees by rubbing or touching their eyes.

- Tasting food—During the course of the day, it falls into several people's job description to taste the food for quality and freshness. The way this should be done is to place the food in a bowl or plate and taste it with a spoon or fork, which should be used only once.

Employees need to be taught these standards from the very first day and these regulations should be enforced at all times. But what if something does happen and a customer blames the restaurant for an illness? First, listen to the complaint, apologize for the way they are feeling and fill out a complaint form such as the one in Figure 7–1. The complaint form helps the manager gather information on the symptoms, the exact illness, and to help trace the potential problem. Recommend the customer see a physician. Do not admit to any fault but inform the person that an investigation of the issue will be made and they will be notified. Remember that some symptoms can appear days after infection. In addition, review the steps and determine whether there was anything that might have caused this to happen. Then, review with the staff the problem and conduct a hazard analysis critical control point to determine where a problem may have been introduced, such as time or temperature problems. (Hazard analysis critical control point or HACCP will be discussed further later in the chapter.) Some localities and states require the food service establishment to contact the controlling agency about any reported problems.

According to the National Restaurant Association, the following is a list of frequently cited factors for causing food-borne illness outbreaks:

1. failure to properly cool food;
2. failure to thoroughly reheat or cook food;
3. infected employees who practice poor personal hygiene at home and the workplace;
4. foods prepared a day or more before they are served;
5. raw, contaminated ingredients incorporated into foods that receive no further cooking;
6. foods allowed to remain at bacteria-incubation temperatures;
7. failure to reheat cooked foods to temperatures that kill bacteria;
8. cross-contamination of cooked foods, or by employees who mishandle foods, or through improperly cleaned equipment.

Hazard Analysis Critical Control Point (HACCP)

This system of food inspection was first developed for NASA to ensure the astronauts were receiving safe food on their trips to space. The system follows food from the raw state to the prepared state when it is served to the customer. There are critical points during the process where the food is most susceptible to bacteria and other germs. These critical times are known as critical control points.

The FDA applies this process to the seafood industry and juice production and packaging. Several state and local health departments have adopted this

| Name: |
| Address: |
| Telephone Number: |

| Date food was ordered: | Time Consumed: |
| Number affected: | |

| Food item: |

Illness complaint:

Diarrhea _____	Vomiting _____
Nausea _____	Cramps _____
Fever _____	Other _____
Dizzy _____	

Summary:

Was a doctor contacted?   Yes   No

Names and addresses of other consumers:

Action for resolution of complaint:

Contact of health department:

Manager Signature _____   Date _____

FIGURE 7–1 Customer Complaint Form.

process and will conduct HACCP inspections on a wide range of foods in a food service establishment during the course of the year. However, it is recommended that each food service establishment adopt this approach and develop an in-house HACCP program. This program, once it is developed for in-house use, is a great training tool for employees.

Understanding the HACCP Process

To understand the HACCP process, it is necessary to have some knowledge of the potential hazards a particular food might have. It is also important to understand the consequences of that food not being handled properly through its stages of receiving at the back door to the time it is served to the customer. HACCP involves seven principles:

1. analyze hazards—potential hazards associated with food are identified;
2. identify critical control points—points in a food's production life cycle, from its raw state through processing and to serving to the consumer, at which point hazards can be controlled or eliminated;
3. establish preventive measures with critical limits for each control point;
4. establish procedures to monitor the critical control points;
5. establish corrective actions to be taken when monitoring shows a critical limit has not been met;
6. establish procedures to verify the system is working properly; and
7. establish effective record keeping to document the HACCP process.

A flow diagram can be drawn on any product and a chart set up to address each potentially hazardous point in the preparation process. At each level the description of the potential hazard along with any control measures that would ensure its safety should be documented. The flow chart, Figure 7–2, shows the cycle of a frozen turkey breast from the time it arrives to the time it is served.

In Figure 7–2, the HACCP decision tree illustrates the first step of the process. At each level there are steps that allow for hazards to be introduced to the food. For instance, the first step, which is the delivery, the following would be examples of possible points where hazards could be introduced to product:

1. Is the truck properly refrigerated?
2. Is all packaging intact with no cans dented and all seals tight with no tears?
3. Are sample temperatures taken of refrigerated products?
4. Are frozen products properly frozen and nothing has started to thaw?
5. Are products immediately and properly stored?

This process is recommended by the FDA to determine if a particular food is hazardous and needs further controls put in place.

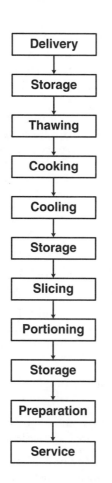

FIGURE 7–2
HACCP Decision Tree.
From the Food and Drug
Administration.

Developing a HACCP Program

One way to ensure safe handling, storage, cooking, and serving of all food items is to develop an in-house HACCP program.

To accomplish this, identify all the items on the menu and then develop a flow chart as previously discussed for each item. During the process if it is determined that a critical control point does not exist for a particular product, no further action needs to be taken.

Health Inspections

The FDA recommends health inspections twice a year. But, as discussed previously, many local health departments do not have the budgets or manpower to conduct such inspections. Once a year may suffice especially if standards are high and these standards are enforced. If an establishment has problems, particularly critical violations, the more often the inspector will be on the premises. To prevent constant inspections, having an in-house HACCP program along with an understanding of the health department regulations is key to passing these inspections.

Each state has its own standards for inspections, and restaurant managers and owners should obtain a food inspection worksheet or other information from their local health inspection agency to familiarize themselves with local standards and codes.

General Areas Covered

Receiving Area—Receiving area should be free of debris and not used as a trash storage area. Floors should be clean. Orders should be put away immediately.

Doors—Doors should be able to close tightly. Seals should be intact to prevent rodents from entering the building.

Hand Washing Sinks—Hand washing sinks should be available in food service areas and be stocked with soap and paper towels at all times. Hand washing sinks should never be blocked with dishes, pots, or any other item that can prevent access to the sink.

Sanitation Buckets—These buckets should be available in all food service areas and especially on the line.

Cutting Boards—Cutting boards can not be worn and cut into. Different colored boards can be designated for poultry, vegetables, and so on.

Bathrooms—Bathrooms must be cleaned, have soap and paper towels, and have signs posted for employees to wash hands after using the facilities.

Clothing Storage—Personal items can not be stored in food service areas.

Ice and Food Scoops—Scoops used for ice or food such as flour or sugar should be stored outside the bin so the handle does come into contact with the food.

Food Service Gloves—Most states and local health departments require approved food service gloves when handling any food. In some locations, not using these gloves is a major violation and can carry fines.

Storage and Shelves—Storage must be NSF approved and can not be rusted out with a minimum clearance of 6 inches.

Thermometers—All refrigeration must have thermometers. Some refrigeration units are equipped with thermometers that are hard-wired to external displays. Some areas still require thermometers to be placed inside the unit. Stem thermometers, also known as bi-therms, are required to test soups, sauces, and food items on the kitchen line for service. All line cooks should carry these at all times.

Food Temperatures—Food temperatures should be taken at different intervals during the course of the day. Remember the 41°F and 140°F rule. Keep foods covered when not directly accessing it.

Dish Machine Operation—Inspectors will check the operational capacity of the dish machine, as many food-borne illnesses can be eliminated through the proper operation.

Pest Management

The goal of pest management is to prevent or eliminate any problems with pests, particularly rodents, roaches, and flies. An integrated pest management program should be placed in the hands of professional pest managers. Open traps or glue strips to trap mice or rats are not acceptable and fly strips for flies are not acceptable in most areas. Chemicals and pesticides in food service areas are not allowed. Some health departments do not allow such products even on the premises. A contract with a professional pest management company is required in some areas.

Many of these pests are brought into a building from boxes or crates. Roaches can live in the corrugated cardboard and can be transferred very easily. To help prevent the transfer, cut boxes immediately and get rid of the boxes.

Small black boxes that allow rodents to enter but not exit can be placed around the exterior of the building and used in strategic places inside the building. Flies and insects can be controlled by special units placed by professional companies.

■ CHAPTER REVIEW

A sanitation management program is critical to the long-term success of any restaurant. The program must incorporate an understanding of food-borne illness and the bacterial, viral, and parasitic causes of food-borne illness. This understanding can not stop at the management level. It is the responsibility of management to educate the entire staff and to hold each member of the staff accountable for the overall success of the program. Educating the staff needs to start from the first day of employment and should continue every day.

Owners, managers, and key employees should attend and become certified through local, state, or an industry approved sanitation classes.

■ KEY TERMS

bacteria	pH level
Centers for Disease	decline phase
Control and Prevention	first-in, first-out

Food and Drug Administration

food-borne illness

hazard analysis critical control point

lag phase

log phase

National Sanitation Foundation

parasite

sanitation management program

ServSafe®

stationary phase

United States Department of
Agriculture

virus

■ REVIEW QUESTIONS

1. What is a food-borne illness?

2. Describe sanitation management.

3. What is the main concern for the USDA?

4. How many cases of food-borne illness does the CDC estimate occur each year in the United States?

5. What does FATTOM stand for?

6. What are three preventive measures for spreading salmonella?

7. Explain FIFO.

8. What is HACCP?

9. Develop a HACCP flow chart for the following:

   a. New England clam chowder

   b. Turkey—from the frozen state to serving

   c. Rice—from cooking to serving

   d. Roast beef—from receiving to cooking to serving

10. Describe some of the symptoms of hepatitis A.

Notes

1. Centers for Disease Control, "Foodborne Infections-General Information." September 3, 2003.

2. USDA national consumer education campaign 2004.

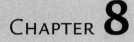

CHAPTER 8

Restaurant Management and Operations Analysis

OBJECTIVES

After reviewing this chapter, you will:

- Define the personnel needs of the restaurant;
- Develop training programs for each position of the restaurant; and
- Analyze the operation and develop plans to correct problem areas.

OVERVIEW

During the planning phase, priorities change, deadlines get pushed back, and there always seems to be more time tomorrow. Now, as the restaurant opens, the deadlines are constant and exist with every customer.

One individual cannot run a restaurant alone. Caring, passionate managers and staff must contribute to the overall success. To ensure that everyone to contributes, each individual staff member must be developed. This chapter addresses two objectives: to present training methods that will enable managers and key employees to develop the skills necessary to operate a successful restaurant, and to educate owners how to analyze their businesses and adjust to become or remain profitable.

Building the Team

Management

Every day brings new challenges and new opportunities. Decisions must be made constantly that may affect the customer, employee, or the physical plant. The restaurant must have a "go-to" person readily accessible and capable of making those decisions. This individual should be held accountable for all decisions and therefore must have the knowledge and the competence to call the shots. The designated decision maker, whether it is the general manager, assistant manager, chef, or some other individual, needs to be given the space to maneuver and to make choices. Wrong decisions should be used as a training tool to fine-tune that individual's ability to make better judgments in the future. Investors, owners, or part owners who are not directly responsible for daily operations should not make decisions that will affect customer loyalty, employee, or management morale or any other segment of the day-to-day business. If someone other than the designated decision maker takes charge, it sends a confusing message to the staff and the management team, potentially causing frustration that will become evident in staff behavior.

Attitude, passion, work ethic, and understanding the business are the elements that comprise the fuel that drives success. When an owner is setting out to build a team, it is important to start at the top. The management's knowledge and experience should be enhanced with individuals on staff that have complementary and diverse strengths.

Choosing the management team is a critical step and should be approached as follows:

1. identify key positions required;
2. detail personal strengths and weaknesses through the development of job descriptions;
3. determine the pay scale for each position; and
4. set a time line for opening the restaurant and include "start dates" for each position to assist in determining when the interview process needs to start to bring the right individuals aboard at the proper time.

The following positions and responsibilities are examples of the chain of command that might be established in a restaurant. Refer to the appendix for Areas of Accountability form and all corresponding job descriptions.

General Manager The general manager (GM) has overall operational responsibility for the restaurant. The GM must take responsibility for the day-to-day operations and is accountable to the owner, board of directors, investors, and regional director of a chain operation. Specific tasks may be delegated, but the ultimate responsibility for the entire operation lies with the GM.

A general manager needs to possess many skills as well as personality. Some of the skills a good GM has are:

■ the ability to hire, train, and develop the staff—a GM must be extremely proficient at staff development, as this skill will affect every other aspect of the business;

■ an understanding of federal, state, and local laws affecting the restaurant business;

■ a working financial knowledge of a restaurant;

■ the marketing skills to understand the needs of the target market and the ability to promote the business;

■ proficiency in conflict management;

■ an ability to set and meet budgets;

- a working knowledge of the kitchen;
- a good time manager;
- a high energy level;
- the ability to be calm under pressure;
- good decision-making skills involving the guest, investor, and employee;
- a working knowledge of computers and POS systems;
- good communication skills;
- high moral and ethical standards;
- a great eye for detail; and
- strong leadership skills.

CHEF/KITCHEN MANAGER The chef or kitchen manager is responsible to the GM for kitchen operations. These tasks can, of course, be delegated, but the final responsibility lies with the chef. Responsibilities include:

- menu development,
- recipe development,
- food cost,
- health and sanitation standards,
- hiring and training,
- ordering,
- scheduling,
- enforcement of standards, and
- kitchen equipment repair and maintenance.

All chefs are not created equal and their management skill sets vary greatly. Some chefs have experience in hotel and banquet dining, some in fine dining, and some in casual dining. The skill sets will vary greatly depending on their experience.

1. *Fine dining chefs* are creative and work alongside sous chefs and cooks. Their on-hand inventory is low and they usually order frequently from vendors. They may even personally shop for certain items. Fine dining chefs work with small groups, many of whom are dedicated to the culinary arts and are hungry for culinary knowledge. Their skills lie in creativity.

2. *Hotel or banquet chefs* have a cast of players and may delegate some responsibilities to others. The steward controls the storage areas and much of the inventory. The large number of kitchen employees may be unionized and their employment may be protected by organized labor, which limits the power of the chef. Hotel or banquet chefs may be serving several dining rooms, room service, and banquets simultaneously, putting the chef in a largely supervisory and oversight capacity.

3. *Casual dining chefs* run a kitchen with a medium-sized staff, hire, complete paperwork and training, personally interact with staff daily, and are directly responsible for inventory, cost, cleanliness, and sanitation. In this role, casual dining chefs do not to be as creative as fine dining chefs and developing menus may not be their forte. They are not required to have the solid planning skills of a hotel chef. But casual dining chefs bring a wealth of knowledge about meeting weekly budgets and producing quality food in a fast-paced environment.

ASSISTANT MANAGER An assistant manager is exactly what the name implies—the individual who assists in managing the restaurant. Under the direction and supervision of the GM, the assistant takes the GM's place when the GM is not present and helps to ensure smooth operations with or without the GM's presence. An assistant manager is normally in the learning phase of overall operations and may not be allowed to make decisions as the GM would, but rather would support the GM's values and standards.

DINING ROOM MANAGER A dining room manager has the responsibility of ensuring that floor operations run smoothly. These responsibilities may include staff hiring and training, scheduling, and guest interactions while the restaurant is open. Some restaurants do not have a staff member with the specific dining room manager title. The responsibility may fall to an "on-scene" manager, such as the GM or an assistant. If a manager is the dining room manager during a given shift, that individual should be in the dining room during the shift and not in an office.

BAR MANAGER A bar manager is responsible for hiring and training the bar staff; teaching the service staff about wine and spirits; enforcing adherence to local and state liquor laws; ordering beer, wine, spirits and supplies for the bar; controlling inventory; and ensuring that health standards are followed. The bar manager might be a bartender or an assistant manager who has the bar as a designated area of responsibility.

PURCHASING MANAGER The purchasing manager position is for larger individual or chain operations where purchases are made from a central location or individual. This person is responsible for negotiating the best deals for the restaurant and ensuring that the quoted prices are what the restaurant is charged.

Cost Controls and Systems

Any business's profits are driven by two things: sales and expenses. When people see a restaurant that is always busy, they assume that the restaurant is extremely successful. However, to achieve a profit, there must be a portion of cash from a sale left over after all of the restaurant's variable and fixed expenses are paid. The cash left is pre-tax profit, and when that amount is positive, a restaurant can be considered successful. To be successful in business, each cost or expense must be managed. The first step to control costs is to develop a budget as discussed in earlier chapters. The budget is the guideline to control costs and to drive as much profit as possible to the bottom line. If an owner invests a significant portion of time finding ways to bring customers into the restaurant and enticing them to return, it makes sense to learn how to keep as much of that income as possible.

This section will discuss the expenses and systems that can help control these expenses, including:

- food cost;
- alcoholic beverage costs;
- soft beverage costs;
- labor costs;
- operational costs; and
- occupancy costs, including rent, insurance, utilities, and building and equipment repairs.

The many cost control systems can become overwhelming and cumbersome. These controls are designed to help an owner and management operate the business more efficiently, not to enslave them to the cost control programs. If an owner or manager becomes a slave to the systems and spends too much time on them, the systems become lose value in comparison to the benefit realized.

Food and Beverage Cost Controls

In the restaurant business, controlling food and beverage costs should be a major focus for every employee. Both of these cost areas, along with labor costs, com prise the majority of a restaurant's expenses. A 1 percent cost sway in either direction will have a major impact on the bottom line profit.

Food Cost

Controlling food cost is not only the responsibility of the chef, sous chef, kitchen manager, and kitchen staff. Although the majority of food cost responsibility may fall on their shoulders, controlling food costs requires contributions from the entire team. Everyone that comes into contact with the food, from the dishwasher to the servers and bus staff to the bartenders and managers, bears some responsibility in controlling food costs. Part of the senior kitchen staff's responsibility is to teach both the kitchen and front of the house staff to understand the importance of controlling food cost and how each member of the team can have an impact on it.

The next section presents the life cycle of food and every aspect that can impact food cost, from menu development through ordering, preparation, and serving the prepared dish.

FIGURE 8–1

Life Cycle of Food.

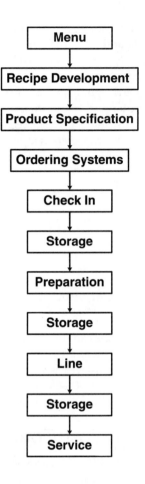

Menu Fine-Tuning and Updating

The menu should be updated at least twice a year or seasonally, adding new items and removing items that are out of season, not selling well, or not contributing the necessary gross profit. However, making final menu decisions includes several other considerations.

The first step, determining the sales/profit contribution, is depicted in Figure 8-2.

This chart was first introduced in Chapter 1 and will now be referenced to illustrate how this information is used to update and reengineer the menu.

The next chart is illustrated in Figure 8-3. This sales mix chart will be used to graph the menu items for each category. (For the purpose of this illustration only the entrees will be used.) In Figure 8-3 the columns represent the following:

■ A Menu item

■ B Number of menu items sold

■ C The menu price

ORIGINAL MENU

A	B	C	D	E	F	G	H	I	J	K	L
		Existing				METHOD OF PRICING			New		
	Raw Food	Menu	Profit	Actual Cost	Desired	Mark Up	Average	Base Mthd	Menu	Profit	Food Cost
Menu Item	Cost	Price	Contribution	Percent	Cost %		Competition	Cost	Price	Contribution	Percentage
Appetizers											
Shrimp	$ 1.60	$ 5.95	$ 4.35	26.89%	30.00%	$ 5.33	$ 8.95	$ 1.79	0	$ -	0.00%
Mushrooms	$ 1.35	$ 6.95	$ 5.60	19.42%	28.00%	$ 4.82	$ 7.95	$ 1.95	0	$ -	0.00%
Mozzarella sticks	$ 1.60	$ 6.95	$ 5.35	23.02%	28.00%	$ 5.71		$ 1.95	0	$ -	0.00%
Nachos	$ 0.68	$ 6.95	$ 6.27	9.78%	30.00%	$ 2.27		$ 2.09	0	$ -	0.00%
Chix tender	$ 0.96	$ 6.95	$ 5.99	13.81%	30.00%	$ 3.20		$ 2.09	0	$ -	0.00%
Chimichanga	$ 1.02	$ 6.95	$ 5.93	14.68%	28.00%	$ 3.64		$ 1.95	0	$ -	0.00%
Calamari	$ -	$ 6.95	$ 6.95	0.00%	32.00%	$ -		$ 2.22	0	$ -	0.00%
Salads											
Caesar	$ -	$ -	$ -	#DIV/0!	0.00%	#DIV/0!	$ -	$ -	0	$ -	0.00%
Chef	$ -	$ -	$ -	#DIV/0!	0.00%	#DIV/0!	$ -	$ -	0	$ -	0.00%
HS Salad	$ -	$ -	$ -	#DIV/0!	0.00%	#DIV/0!	$ -	$ -	0	$ -	0.00%
Sandwiches											
Bacon burger	$ 1.64	$ 6.95	$ 5.31	23.60%	30.00%	$ 5.47	$ 6.50	$ 2.09	0	$ -	0.00%
Chicken Salad	$ 2.77	$ 7.50	$ 4.73	36.93%	32.00%	$ 8.66	$ 7.95	$ 2.40	0	$ -	0.00%
Entrees											
Southwestern chicken	$ 4.16	$ 14.00	$ 9.84	29.71%	28.00%	$ 14.86	$ 13.00	$ 3.92	0	$ -	0.00%
Steak teriyaki	$ 5.25	$ 15.00	$ 9.75	35.00%	38.00%	$ 13.82	$ 16.00	$ 5.70	0	$ -	0.00%
Baby Back ribs	$ 4.08	$ 19.00	$ 14.92	21.47%	35.00%	$ 11.66	$ 18.00	$ 6.65	0	$ -	0.00%
Scallops	$ 3.35	$ 14.00	$ 10.65	23.93%	28.00%	$ 11.96	$ 15.00	$ 3.92	0	$ -	0.00%
Prime Rib 12 ounce	$ 8.17	$ 12.95	$ 4.78	63.09%	35.00%	$ 23.34	$ 14.00	$ 4.53	0	$ -	0.00%
TOTAL	$ 36.63	$ 137.05	$ 100.42	26.73%						$ -	0.00%

FIGURE 8–2

Menu Item Costing.

Enter number of menu items in this category						5				

A	B	C	D	E	F	G	H	I	J
Item	# Sold	Menu	Total	Food Cost	Food	Category	Profit Contr	Profit	Menu Mix	Cont. Mar.
		Price	Sales	Percentage	Cost $	Menu Mix %	Per Item	Contribution	Percentage	Category
Southwestern chicken	33	$ 14.00	$ 462	31.50%	$ 4.41	15.79%	$ 9.59	$ 316	15.79%	Low
Steak teriyaki	39	$ 15.00	$ 585	32.27%	$ 4.84	18.66%	$ 10.16	$ 396	18.66%	Low
Baby Back ribs	66	$ 19.00	$ 1,254	35.11%	$ 6.67	31.58%	$ 12.33	$ 814	31.58%	High
Scallops	44	$ 15.00	$ 660	23.67%	$ 3.55	21.05%	$ 11.45	$ 504	21.05%	High
Prime Rib 12 ounce	27	$ 13.00	$ 351	48.46%	$ 6.30	12.92%	$ 6.70	$ 181	12.92%	Low
CATEGORY TOTAL:	209		$ 3,312					$ 2,211		
Profit contribution per customer		$ 10.58	Equals column I divided by column B							

FIGURE 8–3

Charting Sales to Profit.

- D Total sales in dollars
- E The food cost percentage of the item
- F The food cost of the total units sold expressed in dollars
- G The percentage of the menu item sold as compared to the entire entree category
- H The profit contribution of each individual menu item sold expressed in dollars
- I The total contribution to profit from all of a specific item sold

The information derived from this chart will be used to place each menu item on the sales/profit contribution graph Figure 8-4. This graph will place each item in one of the following categories:

FIGURE 8–4

Sales to Profit Graph.

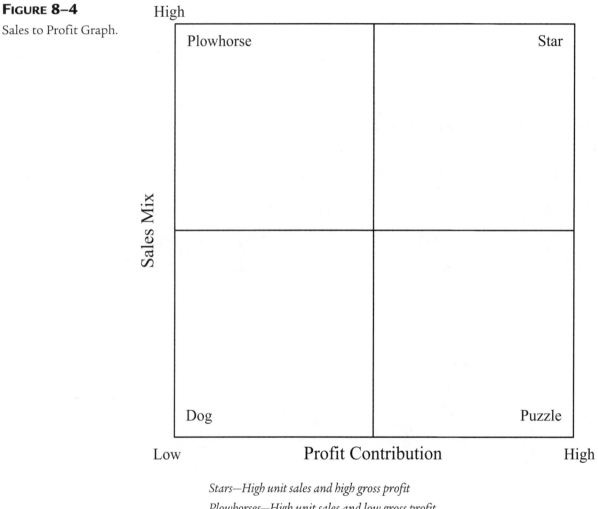

Stars—High unit sales and high gross profit

Plowhorses—High unit sales and low gross profit

Puzzles—Low unit sales but high gross profit

Dogs—Low sales and low gross profit

Stars

HIGH UNIT SALES AND HIGH GROSS PROFIT Stars are the popular menu items that people talk about, purchase on return visits, and love to order. They are also the items that contribute the most to profit.

Plowhorses

HIGH UNIT SALES WITH LOW GROSS PROFIT Plowhorses obviously have appeal and are the best candidates to turn into stars. They are items that people enjoy and frequently order, just like the items in the Star category, but the profit contribution is less. However, before an operator raises prices, consider several factors.

1. The market and customer sensitivity—The targeted market or customer might not accept a price increase on a particular item because the price increase may put it beyond the perceived value.

2. Product ingredients—Can the cost of producing the product be lowered by working out the recipe so the raw cost is less, which would increase the gross profit? For example, can the chef use margarine instead of butter or use half and half used instead of heavy cream? Any decision about ingredients should never diminish the product's quality.

3. For every problem, there should be several options for a solution, none of which can be an off-the-shelf, sure-fire answer for every situation. If the item is a "must keep" item for the concept, then the answer might be options such as the following:

    a. raise the price to an acceptable gross profit contribution level;

    b. remove the item from the menu, which will probably trigger customer complaints. Then bring the menu item back with a slight price increase. The customers might be grateful enough for the chance to purchase the item that they will forgive the price; or

    c. work on the recipe to decrease cost and increase the gross profit contribution.

Puzzles

LOW UNIT SALES AND HIGH GROSS PROFIT Puzzles are the type of menu item that deliver a high gross profit but demand is weak. Some options with such a menu item might be to:

1. position the item in a better, more visible spot on the menu;

2. rework the recipe and presentation to increase the appeal;

3. see if a slight lowering of the price would still offer an acceptable gross profit and increase unit sales;

4. reword the item name and description on the menu; or

5. combine some of the above options.

Dogs

LOW UNIT SALES AND LOW GROSS PROFIT Dogs have both low unit sales and low margin contribution. These types of items need immediate attention. Valuable space is being wasted on the menu with the Dogs.

In Figure 8–4 the four menu categories are represented with the horizontal axis representing Sales Mix and the vertical axis representing Profit Contribution.

The horizontal axis is set by dividing the number of menu items in a category into one and multiplying by 80 percent. Eighty percent is an acceptable level of sales for an item in reference to its own average unit volume.

In Figure 8-4 we position both the horizontal and vertical axes. To position the horizontal axis, take the total number of items in the category expressed as a fraction. (If there are five items in the category, then each item is one-fifth of the total) and multiply by the 80 percent acceptable level and then multiply the total by the total number of items sold.

$$(1/5 \times 80\%) \times \text{Total number of items sold}$$
$$16\% \times 209 \text{ (Number of items sold)}$$
$$33.44 \text{ (Acceptable number of sales per item)}$$

The vertical axis is set by dividing the total dollar sales by the number of customers:

$$\text{Total sales/Number of customers } \$3{,}312/70$$
$$= \$10.58 \text{ profit contribution per customer}$$

Using 33.44 units per item sold and $10.58 as the acceptable profit contribution, columns J, Contribution Margin Category, and K, Sales Item Category, are filled out as low or high. Refer to Figure 8-3 as follows:

1. Southwestern chicken sold 33 units at a contribution level of $9.59 per sale. This falls below the acceptable level for both contribution and units sold. Therefore, we would enter a low in both column J and column K.

2. Complete this step for each item and then place the position of each on the chart.

This spreadsheet is available on the online companion to the book and will calculate the menu item designation automatically.

Once this has been charted, it will illustrate in which category each item falls: Star, Plowhorse, Puzzle, or Dog.

The sales/profit contribution is only one consideration when analyzing the menu. Other considerations that help in analyzing the menu and making final decisions are:

1. repurchase intent,
2. intensity to produce, and
3. raw item usage.

Repurchase Intent

Repurchase intent refers to the probability that the customer will return to the restaurant intending to repurchase a specific item. Certain items may not have a high number of units sold, but the item is unique and builds a loyal following. That loyal following can constitute the veto vote or be responsible for bringing other customers to the restaurant.

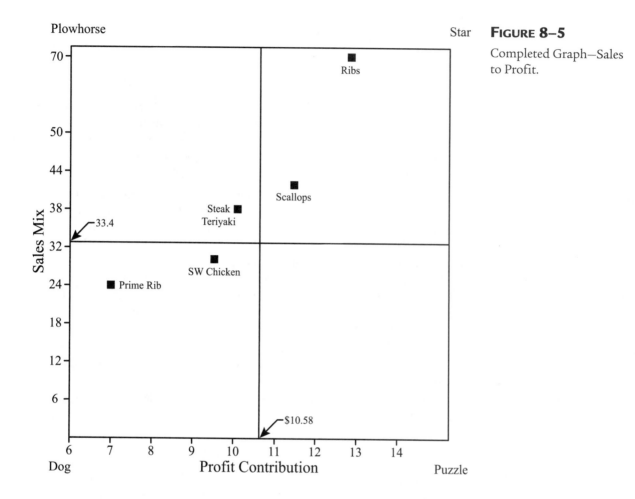

FIGURE 8–5

Completed Graph—Sales to Profit.

Intensity to Produce

It is easy to defend menu items that are popular and contribute to restaurant profit no matter how intense their production. However, an item that is time-consuming in production and either not popular or not contributing to profit may be difficult to defend. Production intensity may be the final factor in deciding whether to remove an item and replace it with something less intense and hopefully more popular with a higher profit contribution.

Raw Item Usage

Raw item usage refers to the raw items used to prepare a product. To keep freshness, raw product should be used in as many products as possible. However, if an item has a high unit sales volume, good contribution to the gross profit, and high repurchase intent, then the single use items do not present a problem.

Results and Decisions

Finally, review the results. Before doing so, recall that any tool used is merely to give management a starting point to investigate possible issues. This chart in itself cannot direct the decisions on needed changes. If sales of one item increase, the boost can skew the chart. For instance, in the sample menu analysis, baby back ribs are almost off the charts in terms of popularity and profit contribution. Because of the price of the ribs, it might make some of the other items appear to be weak in both popularity and profit. The menu analysis produced the following results:

1. Southwestern chicken was approaching both lines of falling within the acceptable level of contribution and popularity. The recipe was adjusted to add more intense Southwest flavor, the specific item was marketed for one month and it was repositioned on the menu.

2. Steak teriyaki was relatively popular but not contributing an acceptable level of profit. Management conducted a focus group, part of which was to determine if a seven ounce cut of steak could be served in place of an eight ounce cut. It was unanimous. The price remained the same, which increased the profit contribution and did not harm sales or popularity.

3. Prime rib was not popular and the cost was high. The item was dropped from the menu.

4. Ribs and scallops were contributing acceptable profit and were both popular items.

Recipes

Having written recipes that the entire kitchen staff follows accomplishes some primary objectives:

1. item cost can be projected if everyone follows the same recipe—giving management a better idea of the overall food cost; and

2. customers will receive a consistent product on each visit.

In Figure 8-6 is a recipe cost chart. This sheet should be completed for each menu item. First develop a cost for the batch and then divide by the serving size to determine the cost of the serving. In the example given, New England seafood chowder has a batch cost of $44.65. There are two serving sizes, a 7-ounce cup and a 9-ounce bowl, with costs of 0.65¢ and 0.84¢, respectively.

Systems

Several systems can be implemented to control food costs. These systems include:

1. vendors, order guides and specifications,
2. order guides,
3. accepting orders,
4. storage and organization,
5. pull thaw,
6. preparation,
7. storage and rotation,
8. line production and storage,
9. order entry,
10. service to the guest,
11. sales mix, and
12. inventory.

ITEM:

Chowder			
Serving Size	7 and 9 ounces		
Clam juice	2 cans	$	2.97
Clams	4 cans	$	25.61
Flour	3 lbs	$	0.23
70 ct potato	8 each	$	2.26
Red potato	12 each	$	0.75
Half and half	3 each	$	3.81
Onion	3 each	$	2.50
Butter	3 lbs	$	4.35
Surimi	8 ounces	$	1.10
Seasoning		$	1.00
Crackers		$	0.07

Yield in Ounces   Total 480

Per Ounce

		Cup	Bowl
$	44.65	7 ounces	9 ounces
$	0.093	$ 0.65	0.84
Menu Price		$ 2.50	$ 3.00
Cost %		$ 26.05%	27.91%
Gross Profit $		$ 1.85	$ 2.16

FIGURE 8–6

Recipe Cost Chart.

VENDORS, ORDER GUIDES, AND SPECIFICATIONS Setting standards and specifications for raw product will have a direct impact on the quality and cost of food produced and the associated menu price. If recipes call for a particular quality of raw product (specification or spec), whether that product is produce, spices, meat, seafood, or canned product, anything below that quality will undermine the desirability of the finished product. A better quality product will cost more, so that cost must be calculated into the menu price to give the expected cost percentage.

Once specifications, pack size, projected usage, and brand—if there is one—has been established, the information should be charted. Refer to Figure 8–7.

This type of chart can be used for each category. Distribute one to each potential supplier and compare the total cost. The projected usage is necessary because one supplier may low bid their price on low-usage items but not come close to meeting the quality or package price of some higher-use items.

Comparing the name brand or exact specification of a product is imperative to maintain the quality standard. Also, the person placing the order must confirm with the sales representative that the price is steady and not just a special 2-week price to get the restaurant's business.

The location of the facility can also help determine whether it is practical to use a particular supplier. If the restaurant is a far distance from the warehouse, it might be on the tail end of the delivery route. Also, if a restaurant employee has to pick up products from the supplier, the distance to the warehouse should be a factor.

ORDER GUIDES Using an order guide is the best way to ensure that enough product will be on hand. An order guide simply consists of:

FIGURE 8–7

Product Specification.

Item	Brand	Pack Size	Projected Usage	Cost per Unit

- product name,
- pack size,
- column for the *on-hands* inventory,
- par level (once it has been established), and
- quantity needed.

Figure 8–8 illustrates a produce order guide.

To properly use the order guide, the first step is to take a physical, on-hand inventory. Then order according to the **par level**. The par level is the minimum quantity of a product that should be in the restaurant. To help establish pars, these order guides should be kept and tracked over a period of time. If four cases of tomatoes are used per week the par might be five. The additional case protects the restaurant from running out of product.

When an order is placed to a warehouse, the person calling in the order merely circles the product once it is called to the person taking the order as a way to ensure the product had been ordered and also to communicate the order to the opening kitchen person.

ACCEPTING ORDERS This step in the food cost process marks the first time the food actually comes through the back door. Accepting and checking orders should be done carefully, paying attention to detail, and at the chef's or kitchen manager's pace and not the pace of the delivery person. The delivery person wants to drop the order and continue on the route. Why should the delivery truck driver care if something is missing or is not right?

Verify the following when orders come in:

1. ensure that orders match what was actually ordered and what is on the invoice;

2. be certain that the product brand or spec is what was ordered—*if the normal, specified product is out of stock, the supplier may substitute a similar product;*

3. ascertain that weight and counts are correct;

4. determine that the product is fresh and will have a normal, accepted shelf life;

5. check to see that boxes are intact and not damaged;

6. place frozen and refrigerated products in their appropriate locations (dairy, chicken, meat, and fish should be immediately refrigerated and placed in their appropriate location and rotated after the check-in is complete);

7. make sure that the person checking the order puts the order away and rotates the product immediately—don't accept "I'll get to it before I leave";

8. walk out to the delivery truck, look for problems in the sanitation of the interior and exterior of the truck—if the truck is not being kept clean, it could indicate substandard of the warehouse sanitation, bringing bugs or rodents into the restaurant.

ITEM	ORDER SIZE	PAR	Monday OH/Order	Tuesday OH/Order	Wednesday OH/Order	Thursday OH/Order	Friday OH/Order	Saturday OH/Order	Sunday OH/Order
Apples	Dozen	112 each							
Carrots	1 pound pack	3 lbs							
Celery	Buch	3 bunches							
Corn	Case	as needed							
Cucumbers	Each	6 each							
Eggs	Dozen	10 dz							
Garlic, Peeled	Gallon	.25 gal							
Ginger	Pound	3 lbs							
Lemons	200 count case	.25 case							
Lettuce Iceburg	Case	1/2 case							
Lettuce Kale	Case	1/2 case							
Limes	60 Count Case	20 each							
Milk	Gallon	Gallon							
Mushrooms, Small	5 pounds	.25 case							
Onion - Red	25 pound bag	1/4 bag							
Onion - Yellow	50 pound bag	1/4 bag							
Peppers, Green	Each	6 each							
Peppers, Red	Each	6 each							
Potato	70 count	.25 case							
Potato Red B	10 pounds	2 pounds							
Romaine - Case	Case	.5 case							
Scallion - Bunch	Bunch	2 bunches							
Salw Mix	Case	2 bags							
Spinach	Bag	1/2 bag							
Spring Mix	Case	1/2 case							
Squash	Each	as needed							
Tomato	5x6 pink	.5 case							
Tomato - Cherry	Flat	.25 flat							
Zuchinni	Each	6 each							

FIGURE 8–8

Produce Order Guide.

It is important to have some tools available when receiving orders:

1. order guides: to compare what was ordered to what is coming in;

2. stem thermometer or infrared thermometer with a laser (infrared thermometer can take a surface reading in one-half second): take sample temperatures of meat, poultry, fish, and dairy;

3. pound scale: spot weigh products such as meat, seafood, and produce;

4. box knife: cut boxes open to ensure the quality of the product;

5. day stickers and use first stickers: this will assist in proper rotation. If a product does not have an expiration date, the day stickers can be placed on the product to tell when it came in. "Use First" stickers signify which product is to be used first; and

6. marker: to mark boxes if necessary (i.e., a case of prime rib is received and it is for a banquet)—mark the box in such a way that no one will use it.

STORAGE AND ORGANIZATION Being organized prevents many stressful moments and thousands of dollars in improperly rotated product. The assertion comes to mind from the disorganized executive: "don't go near my desk I know exactly where everything is!" Unfortunately, in the restaurant business, more than one person will go into the storage area to locate a product or put products away. Most of the staff at one time or another will have to go to the storage area to search for something. If staff members cannot find what they are looking for in about 10 seconds, they will look no further. If a cook walks into the walk-in cooler, goes to where the soups are normally kept and does not see any more chowder, he or she might automatically assume that the restaurant is out of chowder. So, they "**86**" (86 in a restaurant means the restaurant is out of the item) the product and then make a new batch. The night cook might then come in and say, "I made chowder last night." The night cook looks in the walk-in cooler and says "there it is, right next to the produce." But the chowder is stored two shelves over from where it belongs. As a result:

■ time was wasted because the soup was prepared twice;

■ money was wasted because the soup won't be used within the shelf-life; or

■ the guest was upset about being told the restaurant was out of the desired item.

No one wins in this situation. *Staying properly organized saves money, time, and frustration.*

When storing produce, use a box blade to cut boxes down to the minimum possible height. Trimming the top of the box allows cold air to reach the vegetables, which keeps them fresher longer. Also, when making counts to place orders, it is easier to see the actual amount of product in the box.

PULL THAW *Pull thaw* is a phrase that describes the pulling of product from the freezer and placing it in the cooler to thaw so that it may be used at some point in the near future. Pulling frozen product from the freezer and storing it in the cooler creates health concerns as well as food cost concerns. Proper storage for thawing, especially with poultry, is outlined in local health codes and standards. These standards were reviewed in Chapter 7.

PREPARATION Preparing food properly is a concern from both the quality and the cost perspectives. If food is not prepared properly, it may have to be thrown away and the order or item may have to be started over from scratch. If this happens, the restaurant doubles its food cost. If making a product costs $20 per batch and a batch is not prepared properly, the cost becomes $40. To prevent product loss during this phase:

■ provide detailed training for the person preparing the dish so the individual knows exactly how to make it;

■ have written recipe cards detailing the exact measurements and cooking procedures;

■ have a clean, sanitized work surface; and

■ have the proper equipment and utensils available to the cook.

Cooks should always use **prep sheets**. A prep sheet accomplishes several objectives:

■ specifies what product needs to be made and in what quantity;

■ maximizes staff productivity; and

■ prioritizes the workload for the staff.

The prep sheet in Figure 8–9 contains:

■ item name;

■ par level (amount needed);

■ on-hands amount (written in the same unit of measure as the prep amount); and

■ prep amount.

STORAGE AND ROTATION As a review, food must be stored in accordance with local health guidelines, which include approved storage containers and the proper cooling of product.

Tools for proper storage:

■ containers and lids approved by the health department;

■ cooling sticks;

■ plastic spatulas;

■ product labels; and

■ markers.

Containers should be the proper size, made of approved material for food storage, and have proper lids. When transferring the product from the container in which it was made into the storage container, use a plastic spatula to get all of the prepared product so as not to wash any of it down the drain. Any product washed down the drain costs money. Example: An ounce of salad dressing costs 8¢ and a restaurant carries five dressings. If 20 ounces of dressing are wasted per week, the cost is $1.60 per week or $86.20 per year. If staff

ITEM		MONDAY	TUESDAY	WEDNESDAY	THURSDAY	FRIDAY	SATURDAY	SUNDAY
	PAR	OH/PREP	OH/PREP	OH/PREP	OH/PREP	OH/PREP	OH/PREP	OH/PREP
Apple BBQ Sauce								
Baked Beans								
Blue Cheese								
Bread for French Onion								
Chicken Salad								
Chowder								
Clean Fryer								
Clean Grill								
Cole Slaw								
Cook Pork								
Cook Turkey								
Crab Cakes								
Crème Brulee								
Early Bird dessert								
French Onion Soup								
Hot Sauce								
Marinara Sauce								
Marinate Chicken								
Quesadilla - Chicken								
Quesadilla - Vegetable								
Remoulade Sauce								
Ribs								
Russian Dressing								
Salad of the Day								
Saute Onions								
Saute Shrooms								
Saute Spinach								
Scrod juice								
Spicy BBQ Sauce								
Twice Baked Potatoes								
Veg of Day								
White Wine Marinade								
Wild Rice Pilaf								
Wing Sauce - Mild								
Wings								

FIGURE 8–9

Preparation Sheet.

do this with all other products, it is quite easy to see how the cost can add up. Attention to detail can save hundreds or even thousands of dollars in the course of a year.

The same process should be used when **marrying down** product. Marrying down refers to transferring product from a large storage container to a smaller container for more efficient use of storage space, or getting the product ready for line storage. Also, the marrying down process frees up the larger container for storage of newly made product. Once the food has been transferred from the pot, kettle, or bowl into the storage container, properly cool the product in accordance with health standards. Then, clearly mark the container. Proper marking would contain such information as:

- product name;
- date made;
- preparer's name; and
- shelf-life of the product.

Proper product rotation saves both labor and food expenses. Rotation simply requires setting up a system that ensures that the oldest product is sold first (first product in, first product out, or FIFO, in accounting terms). New product should be placed behind or under the old product. When a team employee retrieves the product, the storage will be set up so that they have to pull the old product first. The savings from the food perspective is evident. Labor savings is achieved by not having a staff member produce the product again because of improper rotation.

LINE PRODUCTION AND STORAGE Product should be brought to the kitchen line only when it will be used for the next shift. Portion control on certain items can add up to big savings. If a sandwich requires 5 ounces of turkey but a cook freely puts turkey on the sandwich when preparing it, the cook can misjudge the amount by only 1 ounce. If the restaurant prepares 200 sandwiches per week, that equals 12.5 pounds of turkey wasted every week, or 156.25 pounds wasted per year. At a cost of $2.40 per pound, the restaurant is wasting $375 per year on one single product. However, the manager needs to a balance food cost savings and labor cost.

ORDER ENTRY POS systems were reviewed in Chapter 5. If a restaurant uses a POS system, it should be used to its full potential. The POS system can easily track that sales mix information previously discussed, making a menu analysis rather easy.

SERVICE TO THE GUEST Hot food needs to be served hot and cold food needs to be served cold. Once food is prepared, it needs to be delivered to the guests' table immediately. Recooking food because it is not delivered immediately should never occur.

SALES MIX A **sales mix** is a system used to track the quantity of items sold per day. This system, if used properly, documents a history of the quantity of product on hand each day to properly serve the customer. The sales mix chart will also be referenced to establish par levels and write proper prep sheets to maximize labor productivity. See Figure 8–10.

There is one sales mix sheet for each day of the week. This sheet lists each item on the menu and should be filled out daily so information is accurate.

INVENTORY Controlling food cost without an inventory program is almost impossible. Many inventory systems are available on the market. The system implemented needs to fit the particular operation and sales volume. An inventory system gives accurate, up-to-date information on actual food cost.

Inventory should be monitored weekly until costs are under control. Then the inventory can be taken biweekly to save time. Conducting a physical inventory is a good way to follow up on rotation, storage, cleanliness, and provide training for kitchen staff about controlling costs. In smaller operations with less manpower, taking inventory only on high-cost items such as meat, fish, and chicken could be sufficient to discover any cost problems.

Some basic information is needed for an accurate inventory. See Figure 8–11.

- previous week's on-hand inventory;
- amount of New York strip steaks purchased during the week;
- last price for the steaks; and
- physical inventory count at the end of the week.

The actual number of items sold, as shown on the inventory valuation sheet, Figure 8–12 (Column H), should match the actual number of units sold on the Inventory Usage Sheet (Column F). In Figure 8–11 the inventory shows a usage of 46 New York strips. If the POS only accounts for 40 sold, six steaks are missing. Management needs to find the discrepancy and implement a plan to correct this difference. If there were two steaks improperly cooked, the chef

Item	1-Apr	8-Apr	15-Apr	22-Apr	23-Apr			
Southwestern Chicken	6	8	8	9	7			
Teriyaki Steak	8	5	6	7	7			
Scallops	12	14	15	14	14			
Ribs	18	22	21	22	24			
Prime Rib	8	7	7	8	6			

FIGURE 8–10

Sales Mix Chart.

| Inventory Usage | | | | | | Ending | Usage |
	Beginning Units	Units Purchased	Total	Ending Units	Usage	Unit Price	Value	Value
Ribs	40	80	120	30	90	$ 5.80	$ 174	$ 522
NY Strips	20	36	56	10	46	$ 7.80	$ 78	$ 359
Scallops	15	30	45	20	25	$ 2.60	$ 52	$ 65
Burgers	45	120	165	38	127	$ 1.25	$ 48	$ 159
						Total	$ 352	$ 1,105

FIGURE 8–11

Inventory Usage.

| Actual Inventory Valuation | | | | | | | | |
	Beginning	Purchases	Total	Ending	Sales	Cost	Actual Units	Missing
Ribs	$ 232.00	$ 464.00	$ 696.00	$ 174.0	$ 1,615	32.32%	85	5
NY Strips	$ 156.00	$ 280.80	$ 436.80	$ 78.0	$ 720	49.83%	40	6
Scallops	$ 39.00	$ 78.00	$ 117.00	$ 52.0	$ 330	19.70%	22	3
Burgers	$ 56.25	$ 150.00	$ 206.25	$ 47.5	$ 776	20.45%	115	12
Total	$ 483.25	$ 972.80	$ 1,456.05	$ 351.5	$ 3,441	32.10%		

FIGURE 8–12

Inventory Valuation.

should have documented that information or there may also be a theft problem that needs to be addressed.

Figure 8-13, theoretic inventory valuation, illustrates the cost of sales for each item represented. As a reminder food cost is calculated as follows:

((Beginning inventory$ + Purchases$)–Ending$)/Food sales

This theoretic valuation is based on the actual number of units sold. This cost percentage is 29.3 percent as shown in the total cost box. However, Figure 8-12 illustrates what happens to food cost when the actual usage does not equal actual number of units sold. Food cost increases from 29.3 percent to 32.1 percent, a difference of 2.8 percent. If this difference remains at this level across the menu for the entire year and food sales are $1 million, that 2.8 percent equates to $28,000 directly taken out of the bottom line.

SOME ADDITIONAL TIPS FOR FOOD COST CONTROLS

■ conduct daily inventory on major, high-cost items—compare the actual usage against the actual unit sales;

■ use a lockbox in the walk-in for high cost items such as steak;

■ enforce rotation, first-in, first-out (FIFO), and organization;

■ plan food sales for the week—don't just let things happen;

Theoretic Inventory Valuation						
	Beginning	Purchases	Total	Ending	Sales	Cost
Ribs	$ 232.00	$ 464.00	$ 696.00	$ 174	$ 1,710	30.53%
NY Strips	$ 156.00	$ 280.80	$ 436.80	$ 78	$ 828	43.33%
Scallops	$ 39.00	$ 78.00	$ 117.00	$ 52	$ 375	17.33%
Burgers	$ 56.25	$ 150.00	$ 206.25	$ 48	$ 857	18.52%
Total	$ 483.25	$ 972.80	$ 1,456.05	$ 352	$ 3,770	29.30%

FIGURE 8–13

Theoretic Inventory Valuation.

- use a waste chart to write down anything that is improperly cooked, thrown away, or overprepped;
- do not allow employees to exit the building near storage areas;
- do not allow backpacks or book bags to be kept in storage areas and do inspect these bags once in a while; and
- continually shop prices but do not be quick to jump ship to a new supplier. If the present supplier offers good service and has always been fair and honest, let the supplier know that a better pricing structure is being offered from someone else but the present relationship is valued, giving the supplier the opportunity to meet or match the price.

Controlling Beverage Costs

The bar is an area where restaurant owners become paranoid and start to worry that every employee is stealing. This is not always the case, and the way to remove the paranoia is to have systems in place to control costs. When the bar staff knows that inventories are conducted, the cash drawer will be checked periodically, mystery shoppers are part of the control system, and register tapes are reviewed nightly, they will be more likely to remain honest and play by the rules.

A bartender may buy a drink for a customer for several reasons: to show the customer appreciation for the business, to increase their tip, or to allow a friend to have a free drink. Buying a drink for a customer in appreciation of their continued support of the business is good business and a tradition that is expected by many customers (if state liquor laws allow this). However, if a bartender does it for the selfish reason to increase his or personal financial gain through a larger tip, that is stealing. Giving away free drinks is intolerable, and the bartender should be immediately invited to find employment elsewhere.

The following guidelines will help in controlling alcoholic beverage costs.

BARTENDER TRAINING Once a staff member becomes a bartender, the individual takes on a different personality. They believe that they have moved into a different class of employee. The employee's attitude changes a little, as he or she perceives having been promoted. A bartender is responsible for more than pouring drinks. Bartenders need to be very social, outgoing people. A bar customer, in most cases, enjoys some interaction and prefers that the bartender not read a newspaper at the end of the bar. The bartender should also be very involved in teaching the staff about wine, spirits, and beer.

Pour standards for each drink should be written and easily accessible on a chart for quick reference. If a martini and a Manhattan call for 2.5 ounces of liquor, then each and every drink should be made to that standard. All drinks should be standardized. Some restaurants use measured glasses or a meter pour system, which controls costs, but may give the guests the perception that they are being ripped off. The cost control choice is strictly a personal preference. Proper training and testing of a bartender's ability to pour the correct amount will accomplish the same goals.

Proper pouring of wine and draft beer is imperative. The bartender needs a working knowledge of a draft beer system: What causes the beer to come out foamy? What pressure should the CO_2 gauges be? If 2 ounces of beer are wasted for each 16 ounces poured, the waste will be 220 ounces per barrel of domestic beer (import kegs normally carry less than the American standard of 15.5 gallons per half barrel). At an average cost of a half-barrel of beer at $70, the cost for improper pouring is $15.40 per half-barrel. When that number is multiplied by the number of half-barrels purchased, it is evident that a significant amount is being poured down the drain.

With wine, it is important to have a consistent pour from one bartender to the next. A standard wine pour is 6 ounces. Each bartender should pour 6 ounces every time.

Bartenders need to be trained in the proper use of the POS as well. Usually, the bar POS is programmed somewhat differently with quick screens so that the bartender does not have to ring up a check for each drink sold.

Server Training Servers must also be trained to control beverage costs. Servers must be knowledgeable in drink recipes, types of liquor, and beer and wine selections. If a server is taking a drink order but does not understand the order, not only will the customer get frustrated, but there is a good chance the server will order the wrong drink from the bartender. Servers will also not up-sell liquor or offer wine if they are unfamiliar with them.

Inventory There needs to be an inventory system for beverages, just as there is for food. To control the theft of alcohol, a **perpetual inventory** system can be used as shown in Figure 8–14. A perpetual inventory system works as follows.

1. A par level is set for the quantity you need for quick access to back up the in-use bottles. This quantity varies depending on your sales. For instance, the bar may only need one bottle of Drambuie, but three bottles of Absolut vodka.

| Item | In Liquor Room | Deliveries | Available | Bottles Exchanged for Empties | | | | | | | Total Usage | Sales Reports Usage | Difference |
				Mon.	Tues.	Wed.	Thurs.	Fri.	Sat.	Sun.			
Seagrams 7	6												
Dewars	12												
Seagrams VO	6												
Jack Daniels	6												

FIGURE 8–14

Perpetual Inventory System.

2. Liquor, beer, and wine needed to operate the restaurant is taken from the storeroom and set at the bar.

3. When a bottle of liquor or wine is completely used, the inventory level at the bar needs to be brought up to par and the manager needs to bring the total quantity up to par.

4. The empty bottle is exchanged for a full bottle and the empty bottle is placed in the liquor store room.

5. At the end of the night, the manager logs the empty bottles on a chart that allows him or her to track how often that particular beverage is being replenished.

6. The manager can then compare the actual usage against sales reports from the POS system.

With this system, the manager does not have to wait for a weekly or biweekly inventory report to spot problems. This system also places accountability on each bartender, as the manager will know immediately if there is a problem and who worked the shift. When bartenders know this is happening consistently, they are much less likely to over pour or give away drinks.

The same system can be employed for bottled beer. All empties should be placed in the case. When the bartenders restock the beer at the end of the shift, they should break out only what is needed and the total should match with the number of empties and the sales report.

PROPER TOOLS One of the prevalent obstacles to overcome in delivering great and fast service is to properly furnish all the tools the staff needs (i.e., glassware, mixing tins, strainers, etc.). When a bartender does not have the tools to do the job, the bartender may get tense as the person knows he or she is "on stage" and wants to make the drinks as quickly as possible. When a bartender's stress level and blood pressure go up, that person is more likely to cut corners or make mistakes. It is less expensive to supply the bar with the proper tools then it is to absorb the cost of mistakes.

AWARENESS Bartenders, managers, and service staff need to be constantly aware of what they are doing. If bartenders know that management can quickly spot overpours, wrong glassware, or that a perpetual inventory system is used, they will be less likely to give drinks away. The manager must know drinks and the standards set.

Walking behind the bar and doing register spot checks a couple of times per shift gives the bartender a warning that the manager is in tune with what is going on. All drinks should be rung into the register or written on a tab.

TRACKING LOGS FOR MISPOURED DRINKS OR BROKEN BOTTLES A log to enter improperly poured drinks and broken bottles is a tool that will help keep track of the inventory. The log should include the date, the item, the amount, the reason, and the bartender. This log is useful to keep an eye on bartenders. If one bartender's name appears continuously, there may be a problem that needs to be confronted.

REGISTER CONTROLS The bar POS system is different from the server POS system in that the bartender has access to cash. This may present a whole new set of problems. There should not be many times when a bartender has to use the "NO SALE" command to open the register. Use of the key should be monitored closely. POS systems can usually provide information on how often this happens.

Pilferage: Here are some common tricks bartenders use to steal:

- charging the customer for a drink but not ringing it up and placing the money directly into the tip jar;
- giving away free drinks for bigger tips;
- working in collusion with a server where the server may charge a customer for a drink but not ring it in—this scenario is more common with cocktail servers who charge the customer directly each time the customer orders a drink;
- improperly counting tips and changing with the house drawer;
- underpouring for one guest in order to over pour for another guest, the latter being someone who is known to leave large tips; and
- overpouring or giving away drinks, then the bartender drops the bottle, claiming breakage when the bottle is about one-quarter full. This is why a separate log should be kept for tracking breakage.

UNIT COST AND INVENTORIES A tool that assists management in controlling beverage costs is knowing the unit cost of all liquor, beer, and wine. The unit cost relates to the per-ounce cost for liquor, glass wine and draft beer, and bottle cost for beer and bottles of wine. This knowledge helps the manager set the price and track abuse.

Inventories should be conducted weekly on all alcoholic beverages. Two people should conduct the inventory count. The individuals should be changed periodically to ensure that no one individual or individuals can fake the numbers. For example, if the GM is counting with a bartender for 2 weeks, the following week the GM may count with the bar manager or another bartender. Inventory counts and valuations are done the same way as discussed in the food cost control section of this chapter.

Labor Cost Awareness

UNDERSTANDING PAY RATES AND PAY RANGES A restaurant owner must be aware of current, acceptable rates for restaurant positions in the market. These positions include:

Managers	Chefs	Sous chefs
Sommeliers	Bartenders	Servers
Hosts	Food runners	Bussers
Line cooks	Prep cooks	Bookkeepers

Each of these positions carries with it a range of reasonable rates of pay. The economic climate and the cost of living in a geographic area directly affect these pay scales and the ranges of the pay scales. However, all employees need to be treated fairly and pay should equal their value to the restaurant. A grill cook in an economically sound area where competition for staff is fierce might command $15 per hour, where, in an economically depressed area, that same job might only pay $10 per hour. Pay scales can vary greatly and have a definite impact on the budget. The range of pay for each position allows a manager to hire individuals with varying degrees of experience and to set goals for the staff and attach increases to these wages when the goals are met.

The following guidelines will help control the labor budget and make appropriate adjustments:

1. through the annual budget, set a percentage of sales allowed for overall labor expense;
2. break down the annual budget into monthly budgets, which will help divide the money weekly;
3. divide the projected dollars between the departments in the restaurant such as kitchen, wait staff, bar, and so on;
4. write a schedule including clock in and clock out times for employees and multiply the cost—schedule them in 15-minute increments instead of a half hour or an hour;
5. make adjustments to the schedule to ensure compliance with the weekly budget guidelines;
6. post the schedule;
7. before and after every shift, check to see that everyone has punched in and out correctly;
8. monitor shift changes to avoid overtime—do not allow employees to cover a shift without your approval because it may result in someone less qualified

working a shift, affecting the service standards and possibly put a team member into overtime;

9. maximize staff productivity—if there is nothing to do (which does not occur often) send some of the staff home, leaving enough staff on to handle the volume;

10. have lower paid employees do mundane task work and have higher-paid employees perform tasks requiring more talent—this gives the lower-paid employee some training in new skill sets as a step to advancement;

11. stay aware of daily sales objectives and cut staff when business volume warrants;

12. reduce employee turnover—decreases labor costs because training new staff is expensive;

13. cross-train employees—if staff members can perform multiple job functions there is more flexibility to replace a qualified, competent employee who took the day off.

Operational Costs Controls

Linen Costs A restaurant uses many kinds of linens including kitchen towels, bar towels, tablecloths, napkins, walk-off mats, dishwasher shirts, and chef coats. Not all restaurants use all of the items, but using some of these items is unavoidable. Some restaurants also wash their own towels instead of using a linen company. When making the decision to use a linen company or washing towels in-house, consider several points:

1. expense of a commercial washing machine (a household washer will not be able to handle the amount of grease and oils a kitchen towel absorbs);

2. expense of the chemicals;

3. maintenance and repairs;

4. initial cost of the towels and their replacement cost; and

5. pressing the linens.

It is very rare that cleaning towels and linens in-house is more cost-effective than using a linen company. However, linen costs, like all other costs, can spiral out of control if your staff is not paying attention. Follow these guidelines to control linen costs:

1. Compare local companies that deliver for product quality and service as well as costs. Although undercutting unit cost, one company may cost more in other ways. If every fifth towel or linen napkin is unusable because of improper cleaning or because it is worn, then the cost of that linen is spread over the other four towels. If one towel costs 8¢, the useless towel increases the cost by 20 percent.

2. Good customer service on the part of the linen company is also imperative. Many linen companies' drivers put linen in the designated storage area as

a service to the restaurant. If the driver places the linens in a place where they get wet or soiled, they become unusable and the restaurant will absorb the cost.

3. Try to check the delivery while the driver is still present. Pull out some towels or linen from the packaging and count the towels. Shorting the bundle—while most likely not deliberate—could cause the restaurant to pay for a service it did not receive.

4. Store linens in a locked cabinet. If employees have free access to linens, the linens will be abused.

5. Keep a separate bag for linens that are delivered soiled or unusable from those that have burns or pressing problems. Linen companies will give credit for the unusable amount.

6. A standing order with a linen company is normal operating procedure. Monitor your actual usage and adjust as necessary. Linen companies operate very similarly to each other, but can vary to some degree. Some operational difference may include:

   a. Linen companies will charge an automatic replacement cost for each category. This is because the linen company automatically expects a restaurant to lose or destroy 2 percent of the linen delivered to it. This charge is added to the bill and is determined by the quantity of linen on the standing order. For instance, if the standing order is 100 bar mops (kitchen towels) per week, the bill will automatically be charged for 102 towels.

   b. Some companies may charge additional costs, such as environmental charges and inventory levels. An environmental charge is a charge levied to linen companies in certain states for the chemicals they use to clean the linen. Inventory levels are used for items such as chef coats. If 30 chef coats are needed per week, the linen company will put 60 coats into the inventory. They will supply 30 coats per week while the other coats are being cleaned. Some companies will charge for the inventory amount.

KITCHEN SUPPLIES Kitchen supplies are any items purchased for the kitchen to enable kitchen staff to perform their jobs properly, such as chef's knives, measuring utensils, pans, and so on. Kitchen supplies have to be replaced over time due to normal wear and tear and, unfortunately, abuse and sometimes theft. Some cost control tips:

■ hold the staff members responsible and accountable for the supplies they use; and

■ have designated storage areas for all supplies including measuring utensils, knives, pots, and pans (this designated location will also cut down labor and frustration by avoiding wasted time looking for utensils to perform the job).

Front of House Supplies Front of house supplies are those that servers or bartenders use to do their jobs. They include sugar caddies, salt and pepper shakers, fuel for table candles, coasters, and so on. Again, savings can be achieved in this category by holding employees accountable for their use of the supplies. Restaurants can save money on items like fuel cells for table top candles by only burning them when necessary. Before they leave for the night, servers should be required to check their aprons for supplies that they may have put in them during the shift. The amount of beverage napkins, guest checks, coasters, and even sugar (even though that is food cost) kept in the restaurant can save hundreds of dollars in the course of a year.

Dish Chemicals Depending on the type of dish machine in the restaurant, the price for chemicals will vary. Low temperature dish machines use more chemicals than high temperature dish machines. This is because low temperature machines rely on more chemicals and sanitizers to do the cleaning, while high temperature machines use a more concentrated detergent and rinse additive. Use the following tips to save on dish costs:

1. Train the dish staff in the proper use of the dish machine. This training should include turning the machine on; learning when to use the machine (partial loads will use the same amount of water and chemicals as full loads); learning how to clean the dish machine and all of the filters (clogged filters will cause improper cleaning and put a strain on the machine).

2. Have the machine tuned up at least twice a year. The person supplying the dish chemicals can recommend someone and may even provide this as a service. The tune-up will check for proper chemical draw, water temperature, the softness of the water, and even staff training.

3. If the water supply is hard water (heavy lime content), de-lime the machine at least every other week. Hard water clogs the jets and the dishes will not be cleaned properly. As a result, the dishwasher runs the dishes through twice, using twice as much chemical to clean the same amount of dishes.

4. Proper spraying of dishes. The dishwashers should spray away any debris on the plates before sending the dishes through the machine.

Bathroom Supplies Bathroom supplies include any chemicals used for cleaning the bathroom, along with toilet paper, paper towels, soap, and so on. Before deciding to use a particular company to supply these products, do some comparison shopping. Some companies sell paper for less than the next company, but offer less yardage on the roll. Some soap dispensers only use one type of soap, which might be self-contained soap units that are more expensive than pourable soap.

Paper supply companies supply the holders for paper towels and toilet paper. Paper towel systems that allow customers to grab too much paper, such as C-fold towels, are not recommended.

Store paper towels in a dry area that cannot inadvertently become wet.

PROFESSIONAL FEES Professional fees include accountants, attorneys, and payroll services. The cost may fluctuate a little, especially with the payroll service, because the restaurant will be billed according to the number of payroll checks printed. It is possible to save some expense by completing paperwork in-house, however, professionals doing any tax work will protect the business from mistakes being made, the penalties and interest of which can add up very quickly.

Shop around before hiring professional services agents. Attorneys should only be used to review contracts and will have a major impact early on through the purchase phase and entity establishment. After that time, attorneys should be used only when needed, as they are costly. An attorney should always review major contracts before signing.

The type of accountant needed depends on the size and volume of your business. A certified public accountant (CPA) is recommended in most cases. The accountant should be responsible for completing, or at least reviewing, any paperwork sent to state or federal agencies, such as quarterly tax returns, unless the payroll service completes them. A CPA can also do some tax planning. If the business is profitable, tax planning should be reviewed at least twice a year.

There are many payroll services. When shopping for this service, it is critical to understand exactly what services will be provided. A payroll service, besides issuing paychecks, should:

1. complete and file all state and local paperwork with the appropriate agency;
2. completely explain all associated payroll costs and inform the owner of any payments that will come due at some point in the future; and
3. complete and mail all W-2 forms to employees.

SECURITY Restaurants use several security measures, including hidden video cameras, an office safe, and an armored car service. There needs to be a return on investment (ROI) for any services provided. It is important to be careful about long-term contracts.

CHINA China has to be replaced constantly, due to breakage, carelessly throwing of china in the trash, and simply wearing out. The cost can add up quickly, because one dinner plate can cost between $10 to $15 in a casual dining restaurant and even more in a fine dining establishment. Servers, cooks, and dishwashers handling plates need to be aware of the cost and the precautions that should be taken to prevent excessive breakage. Stacking dishes too high for storage or carrying is dangerous. Setting the plates down with too much force is another common reason for breakage.

SILVERWARE The biggest of silverware loss is servers and dishwashers inadvertently throwing silverware in the trash as they clear plates. A catch-all with magnets is the easiest way to cut silverware waste. Another way to prevent this from happening is to conduct trash audits. A trash audit requires rummaging through the trash with a large stick, looking particularly in folded napkins or deli paper for accidentally discarded silverware. Some silverware will walk out the door in servers' uniforms or will be stolen by customers.

GLASSWARE Glassware, just like plate ware, will break or become scratched and unusable over time. Dropped glasses, overstacking, and not paying attention will cause most problems.

MENU/PRINTING The cost of printing or making copies including menus, business cards, and letterhead can add up over time. Depending on the number of copies you make, it might be worth investing in or leasing a copier.

SERVICE CONTRACTS Restaurant owners must enter into many contracts properly and safely to operate their businesses. These contracts may include hood cleaning, knife sharpening, carpet cleaning, and landscaping. The companies performing these services are not looking for small dollar or short-term contracts, because those might not be worth their time. Therefore, they try to sell additional services that may not be needed. When looking for service companies to perform these services, consider competitors and see which companies they are using. Get references from at least five other sources. The information needed is price, quality of work, responsiveness, honesty, and professionalism. Never enter into a long-term contract. Some companies will ask for 5-year contracts and write the contracts in such a way that they are difficult to break. *Do not sign any contract for that length of time!* The reason the companies want 5 years is that they have to supply equipment and usually use the contracts as proof of business to a bank or a leasing company for access to capital or lines of credit. These companies should be responsible for bankrolling their own businesses and not putting that burden on the restaurateur.

A company with a long-term contract lacks the motivation to do the job correctly because the restaurant is committed to them. In the contract, the restaurant needs to include a clause allowing cancellation of the contract if the work is not performed satisfactorily. Reputable companies do not dispute such provisions. These companies know they will perform the necessary service professionally, quickly, and at a fair price.

CABLE/SATELLITE/MUSIC Using either cable or satellite will improve reception and offer a wider variety of choices for news, sports, and other entertainment. If the business is such that it will attract people on the basis of what is on television, such as a sports bar, then such an investment may be required.

Restaurants must be very careful when dealing with music companies. There are several such companies in existence, and they usually ask for long-term contracts to provide the equipment. Two agencies—BMI and ASCAP—monitor music being played in public. This monitoring ensures that music publishers receive their royalties. In some areas, these companies are very aggressive and will enter businesses at very odd hours, and may sometimes even demand the equipment or payment. They must leave the premises when asked, as they have no authority to take anything. Restaurant owners should check with other restaurants in the marketplace to find out what they do. Sometimes a small, yearly fee will license the establishment to play music from personal equipment.

Facility Cost Control

Operating a facility is expensive. There is no way around it, but controlling the costs of operating a facility usually does not get much attention or focus. Facility costs include any expense related to the operation and preservation of a facility.

RENT Rent is negotiated between a landlord and restaurant owner before the owner can even begin work on the building. There are different types of rent, and each type affects occupancy expenses differently. This has been discussed in depth in Chapter 4.

COMMON AREA MAINTENANCE FEES Malls, strip malls, or small shopping centers normally charge common area maintenance fees to offset the costs of maintaining the property, such as lighting, security, trash removal, parking lot cleanliness, and landscaping. All tenants share the costs, although stand-alone buildings, unless on a mall pad-site, are not usually charged this fee.

UTILITIES Utility costs in a restaurant are expensive. Besides refrigeration that runs 24 hours a day, the cost of equipment that is powered up daily, such as stoves, grills, and fryers all add up quickly. Here are some tips on how to save on utility costs:

1. Do not power up at one time—Powering up all gas and electrical equipment simultaneously is not only unnecessary, but also can cost more throughout the day by having a *surge*, or *demand,* multiple added to the utility bill. The additional charge is incurred because of the large demand placed on the utility company at once. The surge is a computation the electric company uses to multiply the actual kilowatt and fuel usage. The more immediate the demand, the higher the multiple is, resulting in a higher bill during the course of the entire day.

2. Know the warm-up time for each piece of equipment and *power up* the equipment when needed. If all gas equipment is turned on at one time:

    a. a demand surge affects the bill for the rest of the day; and

    b. air conditioning kicks in to fight the heat, as the make-up air needs to be put into the restaurant.

3. When equipment is not needed, turn it off. At the end of lunch, if there will be some downtime, any equipment that is not needed at that point, such as one side of the grill or an extra fryer, should be turned off. Management should know the warm-up time for each piece of equipment to have it ready for the next shift.

4. Use plastic drapes on the front of walk-in coolers and freezers to keep the cold air in.

5. Set thermostats to operate air conditioning and heat. Never turn the systems all the way off. If the air conditioning unit is turned off at night, two things might happen: it will take more power (and cost more money) to get the building cool the next day than what was saved by turning it off; and turning the unit off might freeze up the coils from the humidity;

6. Use lockboxes on thermostats so employees or customers cannot operate them. Servers and bartenders will complain about being hot and want the air conditioning turned up. These employees forget that the comfort level is for the guests. The servers and bartender will feel warm because they are running around.

7. Have a cleaning and maintenance program in place for all electrical and gas-operated equipment. These cleaning procedures should be listed by the manufacturer in the documentation received with the units. Clogged filters and dirty grills and fryers take more energy to operate properly.

Conducting energy audits will assist in identifying problem areas. An energy audit should be conducted at least once a year. From this audit a plan can be developed to reduce waste. An energy audit in a restaurant should include:

1. locating drafts,
2. checking insulation in walls,
3. checking glass for proper glazing,
4. locating cracks in walls or ceilings,
5. doors that do not close properly, and
6. maintenance systems in place to keep equipment clean.

Water A restaurant uses water for cooking, cleaning, serving customers, and restroom facilities. Focusing on this area is everyone's responsibility.

1. Defrosting frozen food by running water, while accepted by most health departments, wastes a tremendous amount of water.
2. Have automatic shut off valves on bathroom sinks.
3. Properly maintain the dish machine.
4. Offer water to customers instead of automatically bringing water to a table (if the concept would warrant such a move).
5. Fix faulty plumbing immediately.

Furniture, Fixtures, and Equipment Replacement costs for furniture and equipment can be staggering. As mentioned previously, maintenance programs for refrigeration and ventilation should be set up early on in the building project. Furniture, such as chairs and barstools, should be checked periodically for any parts that have become loose. Carpet cleaning is normally the responsibility of the lessee, but remember who pays for carpet replacement due to wear and tear.

BUILDING REPAIRS AND MAINTENANCE Building and equipment repairs can be costly, but knowledge is power. Restaurant owners and managers must be familiar with the operation of all equipment and the common problems that are inherent to the equipment. Having a maintenance program that includes all equipment can save hundreds and even thousands of dollars in utility costs, equipment downtime, repairs, or even replacement. Follow these steps to building an effective maintenance program.

1. Collect all the manuals for all equipment. If any manuals are missing, contact the distributor or the manufacturer.

2. Build a maintenance program in accordance with the manufacturer's specification and time lines.

3. Decide what maintenance can be performed in house and what needs to be contracted by outside companies.

4. When hiring outside companies, do some homework and ask the following questions:

   a. Please provide references for other restaurants that your company handles.

   b. Does your company offer 24-hour service?

   c. How long has the company been in business?

   d. Does the company stock most of the major components of the equipment they are repairing?

   e. Does the company have qualified, competent, and courteous staff?

   f. Is the company authorized by the manufacturer as a warranty repair house?

   g. Is the company licensed and insured?

5. When repair companies do come in, spend time with them as they do the repair work. Learn as much as possible about the equipment.

6. Have the repair company save any of the old parts that they are replacing.

Safety and Security

All restaurant owners are responsible for providing a safe and secure workplace. This includes minimizing unsafe conditions through training and awareness and supplying equipment and supplies that help prevent unsafe conditions. Such supplies include items like mats to prevent slipping and cutting gloves to help prevent knife cuts. The most common accidents that cause lost work time and insurance claims are slips and falls, burns, and cuts. In addition to worker's compensation claims, lost labor hours in a tight labor market can add stress and unnecessary overtime expense.

Theft and robbery are two major security issues that must be addressed. Loss prevention standards must be in place and enforced at all times. The safety of the staff and customers is critically important to a high morale among staff and a safe feeling for customers. An unsafe environment can lower morale and affect sales if employees and customers do not feel safe.

Proper lighting of the exterior building and parking lot, unobstructed entrances, secured back doors, and patrolling of a parking lot will ensure that customers and employees feel safe.

Safety

A restaurant presents many safety challenges. Wet floors, grease, knives, hot pots and pans, steam, and open flames all present challenges to operating a safe restaurant environment. However, these are part of the business. Injuries can be prevented through the proper training and by focusing on these very real issues. Although many aspects of the restaurant environment pose threats, the biggest threat to a safe environment is not having a safety program in place and not training the staff about how to avoid the dangers. Although dangers exist, human error or indifference open the door for injury.

Human error can be eliminated or at least minimized through proper training and awareness.

Cuts Cuts can happen by using improper knife techniques, moving mechanical slicing or food equipment without regard to safety, because of broken glass or dishes, and even due to poorly designed equipment.

1. Knife techniques

   Anybody that uses a knife needs to be trained in the proper technique. Cooks are not the only staff members that use knives. Bartenders use them to cut fruit for the bar, and servers may use a knife to cut fruit or bread. Usually a chef or kitchen manager knows the proper techniques of using a knife and should be enlisted to train each member of the staff.

2. Slicers and other food preparation equipment

   Much of this equipment is very dangerous and should only be allowed for use by trained personnel. When anyone uses this equipment, they must focus on the slicer, regardless of how long they have been using the equipment. More important, when cleaning and sanitizing this equipment, extreme care should be taken. More injuries occur when cleaning the slicer than when actually using it. State laws dictate the required age of an employee who is permitted to use certain pieces of equipment. Contact the state labor department for specific guidelines.

3. Broken glasses and dishes

   Broken glass can cause damaging cuts. Dishwashers and bartenders are most prone to being cut by broken glass or dishes. When placing glasses in a rack or removing them, care should be taken to handle glasses properly. *Do not* overstack glasses, as they can break when separating them. Never place a glass in a dish sink. Other, heavier equipment placed on top can cause breakage. If someone reaches into the sink, they can severely hurt their hands. Bartenders need to pay attention when washing glasses, especially if electric glass washers are being used.

BURNS Hot grease, pots, pans, drinks, plates, and steam can all cause burns. All employees are at risk of burns, not just kitchen employees. Even though the kitchen staff is more susceptible to burns because of the nature of their jobs, service staff is also threatened by burns from hot plates and hot beverages. To help prevent burns, training is key and the following steps should be taken:

1. kitchen staff should wear long-sleeved chef coats;

2. all pans and pots—and especially their handles—should be considered hot at all times and handled with dry towels or gloves;

3. equipment should be turned on to proper temperature;

4. equipment should be maintained at optimum operating efficiency in accordance with manufacturer specifications;

5. communicating with appropriate staff that something is hot is imperative (i.e., if a cook puts a hot pan into the sink, the dishwasher needs to be told the pan is hot and the dishwasher should respond that they heard the cook); and

6. be cautious of steam—it is very dangerous and can easily cause burns.

SLIPS AND FALLS Slips and falls are very common and probably the most costly of all restaurant injuries. Slips and falls can case sprains, broken bones, or other more severe injuries. In addition to lost time, the cost for medical bills or lawsuits can be devastating.

The most common causes of slips and falls are wet or greasy floors, unacceptable floor material, and improper shoes. To help prevent slips and falls:

1. spills should be cleaned up immediately and the area should be wiped dry;

2. wet floor signs should be available and used whenever something is spilled;

3. mats should be used where appropriate to insulate the staff from the floor, especially on the kitchen lines and behind the bar; and

4. all staff should wear nonslip shoes. Specially made shoes for the food industry are available.

SWINGING DOORS Doors that swing in service areas can be dangerous and cause injury. Any door that is accessible to people entering or exiting the same space should be clearly marked and have a window so activity on the other side can be seen.

CHAMPAGNE CORKS Corks are under pressure and can be very dangerous. These corks sometimes need no prodding to pop. Once the wire safety is removed, a champagne cork can pop at any time. Proper training, including holding the champagne bottle pointed away from any person or item that may cause the cork to ricochet, holding a towel over the cork, and properly opening the champagne bottle are all part of the training program.

CIGARETTES AND FIRE Burning cigarettes are a hazard when emptied into a trash container. Cigarettes can smolder for some time and ignite any flammable material.

FIRE TRAINING All staff members should be trained on where the fire extinguishers are, how to use them, and how to fight specific fires. They should also know which fires they should not attempt to fight, and should instead exit the building and call the fire department.

CHOKING Choking is a hazard in a restaurant and staff should be trained on proper techniques of the **Heimlich** maneuver. Posters should be posted in designated areas.

FIRST AID KIT A fully stocked and accessible first aid kit should be available.

Theft and Robbery

Theft and robbery are two very real issues facing restaurants and restaurant employees. The people that commit these crimes know that there is cash in a restaurant and that many of the employees are carrying cash at the end of a shift.

Theft is often an internal issue and may not always involve cash. Food, supplies, and alcohol can all be targets of theft. Personal property of staff is also at risk if there is a thief in the building. Staff should be very careful where they put personal items and should not leave cash or valuable items in the open.

Many times, robberies that occur in a restaurant are committed by former employees or friends of former employees that know the building and the routine. The following steps can assist in implementing security:

1. Have a system of accounting for all cash in the restaurant. Do not count large sums openly. Store the money where there is access to a busy area. Even though no one wants people to be staring at them while they count, the closer to activity, the harder it will be for a thief to steal the money and get away with it. There needs to be activity outside the office.

2. Have panic buttons in the freezer, the walk-in, the office, and at the bar. These should be for manager use and knowledge only (bartenders need to be aware of the one at the bar).

3. Do a complete walk-through while people are still in the building. Corners, access through ceilings tiles, unlocked doors, and even bathroom stalls can provide hiding places for thieves.

4. Do not establish a routine pattern—vary it occasionally.

5. Many robberies occur during a trash run, right through the back door. Set a time where nothing will be taken from the building after a certain time; 10 or 10:30 P.M. is good. And always do trash runs with two to three people and instruct them to close the door behind them. The trash haul should take place when there are still employees and guests in the building. The more people that are around, the tougher it will be for someone to commit a crime.

6. Do not allow staff to walk alone to their cars at night. Make sure they walk in groups of two or three.

7. Make bank deposits during daylight hours. Try to avoid using night deposit boxes.

8. Never leave anyone in the building alone. At the end of the evening, the manager, the bartender, the dishwasher, and anyone else in the building should all leave at the same time.

■ CHAPTER REVIEW

Controlling costs is part of the successful business equation. Even if the business generates a great deal of revenue, controlling each and every cost area is what determines if the business is profitable. However, controlling costs at the expense of the customer, will never produce long-term, positive results. Serving a subpar product to protect the cost will eventually have a negative impact on the sales. Costs are controlled by setting standards and implementing systems.

Safety and security were also discussed in this chapter. These are two key issues in the restaurant business. Cash businesses are vulnerable to robbery. Be aware of this and take preventative measures to ensure the safety of the staff and the customers.

There are many ways people can be injured in a restaurant. Slips and falls, burns, and cuts are just a few. Pay close attention to detail. Teach proper knife techniques and ensure the staff knows the importance of these techniques. Clean spills immediately.

Take nothing for granted with the safety and security of everyone.

■ KEY TERMS

86	Heimlich
dogs	marrying down

par level

perpetual inventory

plowhorses

prep sheets

puzzles

raw item usage

repurchase intent

sales mix

stars

◼ REVIEW QUESTIONS

1. List some of the skills necessary for a restaurant general manager.
2. Define the following terms as used when analyzing a menu:
   a. Stars
   b. Plowhorse
   c. Puzzles
   d. Dogs
3. Why is it important to inspect a delivery truck?
4. What is meant by the term repurchase intent?
5. Explain a personal inventory system.

CHAPTER 9

Customer Service

After reviewing this chapter, you will:

- Understand how to develop a standard of delivering excellent customer service;
- Teach the standards to the staff;
- Recognize service problems and be able to correct them;
- Instill the knowledge in the staff to recognize and correct customer problems; and
- Understand how to develop positive customer service stories in your restaurant.

An owner may invest millions of dollars in opening a restaurant, the location can be perfect, and a notable chef can develop a mouthwatering menu. However, unless the entire staff, from the owner to the cleaning person, understands how to execute and deliver a great experience, everything else is meaningless.

The energy level and attitude of a restaurant starts at the top and filters through everyone in the building. If the manager has a low energy level or a poor attitude, it will show in the rest of the team. The customers will sense it. However, if the manager is positive, upbeat, energetic, and passionate and shows a sincere concern for the needs of the guest, the attitude will have almost magical powers.

It's All About the Customer

There is no doubt that being in the restaurant business or any hospitality-based business can, at times, be frustrating. However, it is important to always remember in the restaurant business that THE CUSTOMER IS KING. Everyone, including the leadership and the staff, has one goal—*please the customer and ensure that the restaurant will be their dining choice in the future.*

At any given time, each restaurant guest is the most important person in the world. Treat each guest as if he or she is the most important person in the world and the business will flourish. Say hello, get to know customers as people and not simply as customers, and learn to say thank you.

A restaurant owner must have many attributes and skills to be successful. Above all, the owner must have *passion* for the business and a *deep, sincere concern for the guest*. Without these two attributes, the business is doomed to failure, because everything else flows from these attributes. Everyone that works in the restaurant business must be passionate about food and beverage quality, service, atmosphere, cleanliness, and—most of all—a passion to deliver an outstanding dining experience to each and every guest each and every time the guest decides to spend his or her hard-earned money in your restaurant.

Webster's dictionary defines **passion** is defined as an "intense, overwhelming feeling or conviction—strong liking or desire for or devotion to some activity, object or concept."

If a restaurant owner or manager possesses this passion, he or she must instill it in the other members of the team: the management, the service staff, bartenders, host staff, bus people, chefs, cooks, and dishwashers.

An article written in *USA Today*[1] illustrates the powerful impact that anyone who cares about delivering outstanding service can have. It emphasizes the point of expectations for restaurant industry customers. Unfortunately, not everyone *gets it*. The article listed the top 10 problems restaurant customers encountered regularly. Although the data may be somewhat outdated and the numbers may have changed, the points are still valid and probably have not changed dramatically. Customers complained about these issues:

1. slow service—82.5%
2. inattentive waiters—68.5%
3. forgetful waiters—56%
4. waiters who don't know the product—55.5%
5. unclean plates—40.5%
6. rushed waiters—38.5%
7. intrusive waiters—32%
8. rude waiters—30.5%
9. unwillingness to meet special needs—20%
10. incorrect billing—13.5%

Eight out of 10 were directly attributed to service and held the top five spots.

If a restaurant's staff training program is based on passion and concern for the guest, instead of scoring a 90 on the food test, the staff will develop a deep understanding of the restaurant's vision, goals, and standards. With this passion, when a team member does not deliver, it will weigh on his or her conscience. Passionate, caring people are harder to find than people that can score a 90 on a written food test.

This chapter discusses how to develop passionate, caring people, shares some outstanding customer service stories, and identifies ways any staff can inspire their own *outstanding stories* and discover the benefits of adopting the attitude of "It is my pleasure!"

Remember that good customer service must be managed and bad customer service happens all by itself!

The Art of Customer Service

The hospitality industry is about people. Period! People are responsible for delivering an outstanding dining experience to guests who opt to spend money at your restaurant—purveyors and salespeople, insurance agents, state and local authorities, and landlords.

The term **internal customer** has been around for some time and offers a unique way of viewing employees or team members. If a manager truly desires to deliver excellent customer service, he or she must start with the internal customers. If management views employees as customers that need attention, then management acts differently toward employees. Sincere concern for the employees' well-being is rewarded by having a staff that shows and delivers that same level of service and concern to the restaurant guests.

But the internal customer involves not only the management-to-employee relationship, but also the employee-to-employee relationship. Team members must treat each other as though part of their job description is to take care of each other. First, this camaraderie makes for a comfortable work environment. Second, it encourages a higher level of customer service. Karl Albrecht, author of *Service America!: Doing Business in the New Economy* (1985) wrote,

"If you're not serving the customer, you'd better be serving someone that is."

So, if one server is taking care of a customer and another server has no immediate customer, then the server without customers should help the server with customers.

The days of "Do what I tell you because I'm the boss" are long gone. Just as customers have increasing options for dining elsewhere, employees also have increasing employment options. According to Deloitte & Touche, the National Restaurant Association's 2002 annual report indicated that locating and hiring quality employees will remain the number one obstacle for the restaurant business for the foreseeable future. This trend does not mean that employees should be allowed to do as they please. But it means standards of excellence must be in place that are taught and instilled in the staff. Employees are not allowed to treat customers poorly, and owners and managers cannot treat employees poorly.

Management must find ways to satisfy all individuals, including the employees, who are now considered "internal" customers. Owners and managers must enjoy being in the company of people, enjoy seeing people, talking to people, and most importantly listening to people. Management must get some degree of pleasure from a customer saying "This was a wonderful experience."

Excellent—Superior or eminently good
Customer—one who is willing to exchange cash for a product or service
Service—the work performed by one that serves

Excellent customer service is something everyone in the restaurant business hears every day. It seems that every customer-oriented company in the world says that excellent customer service is either part of their mission statement or vision, yet so few achieve it. Why is that?

First, explore exactly what excellent customer service is. From the separate definitions above it can be defined as *serving one in a superior manner*. But, superior to whom? The answer is superior to the competition. Every time a new restaurant opens and delivers a level of service above what is expected, the standards bar and the stakes have been raised. What was done 5 short years ago that was viewed as excellent customer service is simply what is expected today. The customer is more demanding because customers have had a different or higher level of service elsewhere. To make an impact, the dining experience must be made memorable.

Customers, through experience and exposure to the myriad restaurants available, have developed certain expectations dependent on the type of restaurant they are visiting. Service in a fast food restaurant is not the same that is expected in a slightly more expensive, sit-down casual dining restaurant. A manager walking the floor in a fast food restaurant to check on the quality of a customer's burger and fries is not common nor is it expected. But in a casual dining restaurant if the manager doesn't check on the satisfaction of the customer, it will affect the customer's perception, especially if there is a problem. Likewise, in a casual dining restaurant the customer doesn't expect a sommelier to recommend wine, uncork the bottle, and ensure that the wine is perfect before pouring a taste for the host of the table. However, in a fine dining establishment customers expect it to be done and done properly. Different levels of service are associated with different levels of dining. Along with that level of service comes the understanding that the higher level of service will cost more.

In a casual dining setting that expectation may be:

■ a friendly, welcoming greeting at the door;
■ a direct answer as to how long it will be before being seated;
■ a comfortable waiting area or enough room at the bar;
■ a timely, but not rushed, meal; and
■ a friendly server.

All of these seem reasonable. This is today's expectation. So do servers believe their job is done once the customer has paid the bill and left a nice gratuity? Let's hope not. This approach creates an upset server if the guests decide to remain and converse for an hour or two (this is referred to as camping).

The server might start complaining to the manager how the "campers" are taking up space and may make it obvious through body language, especially facial expressions that he or she is not pleased with the customers.

Excellent customer service must go beyond the meal itself. Customers are guests until such time they get in their car and head home. So, that might mean if it is raining, a staff member or manager walks the customer is walked to the car with an umbrella, or even gets the car for the customer. Many servers may shrug at this notion but if they do shrug, *they don't get it!* They are missing the point of excellent customer service. If someone is a guest in your home, you would make sure they make it to their car and get home safely. Why not in a restaurant?

Moments of Truth

Jan Carlzon[2] of Scandinavian Airlines wrote *Moments of Truth*. The main thrust of the book is that if a customer lodges a complaint, the person receiving that complaint is responsible to fix that problem, under any circumstance. Their job is not to go find the manager or pass the problem off to someone else. The customer is already upset. Why add stress to an already bad situation? If it affects the way people view the business, make them happy.

For many restaurant owners this "empowerment" of the staff is a difficult step. If an owner is willing to empower the staff to take care of the guest, the owner must understand that the staff will not automatically make the right decisions. However, instilling a passionate and caring attitude in the staff, sharing the vision, walking the walk, and properly teaching and developing the staff, an owner develops a staff where everyone eventually understands what it takes to deliver outstanding customer service.

Restaurant owners must view a **moment of truth** as any time that a customer can pass judgment on the business. The moments occur many times during the dining cycle: from the moment someone hears or reads about the restaurant, places an initial phone call to inquire about the restaurant to arrival and everything to their departure.

Moments of Truth in the Dining Cycle

Figure 9-1 depicts what is referred to as the dining cycle. In the following section, we cover the various elements.

SOMEONE HEARS ABOUT THE RESTAURANT People love to talk and will normally talk more about a bad experience or bad service than they talk about anything good that occurred. When your restaurant is discussed, what is it you want people to say? Well, that's an obvious answer. However, to get someone talking positively, the experience must be memorable and not just mediocre. If people dine out two to three times a week, they are not going to waste their time talking about each and every dinner, unless that time was memorable.

MOMENTS OF TRUTH
IN THE DINING EXPERIENCE

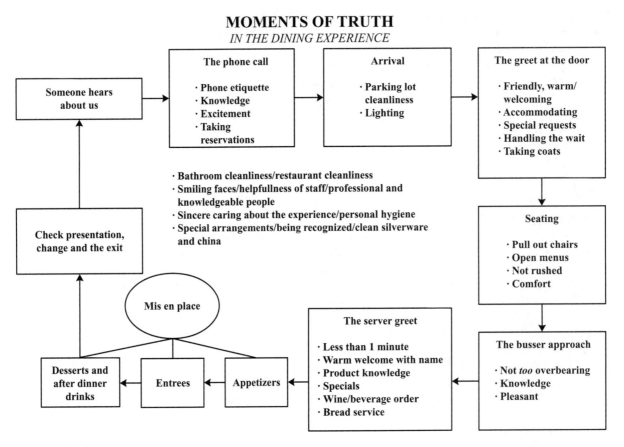

The phone call
· Phone etiquette
· Knowledge
· Excitement
· Taking reservations

Arrival
· Parking lot cleanliness
· Lighting

The greet at the door
· Friendly, warm/ welcoming
· Accommodating
· Special requests
· Handling the wait
· Taking coats

Someone hears about us

Seating
· Pull out chairs
· Open menus
· Not rushed
· Comfort

· Bathroom cleanliness/restaurant cleanliness
· Smiling faces/helpfullness of staff/professional and knowledgeable people
· Sincere caring about the experience/personal hygiene
· Special arrangements/being recognized/clean silverware and china

Check presentation, change and the exit

Mis en place

The server greet
· Less than 1 minute
· Warm welcome with name
· Product knowledge
· Specials
· Wine/beverage order
· Bread service

The busser approach
· Not *too* overbearing
· Knowledge
· Pleasant

Desserts and after dinner drinks

Entrees

Appetizers

FIGURE 9–1
Moments of Truth in the Dining Cycle.

So restaurant staff must do everything possible to ensure a great dining experience and get customers *"working for the restaurant"* by talking about their dining experience, which will drive customers into the restaurant. There are other ways to drive trial but none as effective as having someone talk about the restaurant in a positive manner. A newspaper ad can not convey the message as well as an individual hearing about a great dining experience.

THE PHONE CALL If a potential customer calls to inquire about the restaurant is the staff trained in **telephone etiquette**? Does the staff have the ability to answer questions, convey the passion in their voice, and take reservations? This responsibility rests with everyone who might answer the phone, not only the host staff.

Answering a telephone properly is just as important as greeting someone that enters through the front door. After all, the person on the other end of the phone is a potential customer. Use the following guidelines for telephone etiquette:

1. Answer the phone within three rings. The person on the other end might not be so patient.

2. Answer the phone with a smile. This smile comes across in the voice and the attitude.

3. Do not be rushed. This might come across as rude, and the potential customer might get the feeling that this call is an inconvenience to the restaurant.

4. Answer the phone with a pleasant "Good Morning, thank you for calling the Lakeside Restaurant, this is Joe, how may I help you?" This greeting accomplishes several objectives: the customer is being acknowledged that the call is important; the customer is being offered a name and are assistance. The phone should never be answered: "Hi, can you hold please?" That customer might be lost on the spot, or it could increase the customer's tension level on the first contact with the restaurant.

5. The person on the phone is important. However, so are the people in the restaurant so the employee on the phone should never turn his or her back on the people at the front door. Make eye contact with anyone entering the restaurant.

6. If telephone customers are put on hold, do not leave them on hold for any length of time because it can also be interpreted as rude or forgetful. Be aware of the person on hold. That phone call is the responsibility of the person who answered the call until the person that the call was intended for answers the phone.

7. If taking a message, make sure the person the message is for gets the message. Have a system in place for messages and copies are recommended.

ARRIVAL Any impression a potential customer has of the restaurant up to this point has been developed by hearing about the restaurant or what they perceived from the initial phone call. When guests arrive at the restaurant, they form their first physical impression of the place. The exterior of the building must be clean, well lit, and inviting. The restaurant is responsible for the exterior, even if the landlord owns the parking lot. Follow up on any repairs or lighting issues make sure they are done. Customers do not want to know it is the landlord's fault, they just want it to be clean and well lit.

THE GREET AT THE DOOR Finally, the customer has the opportunity to come face to face with a real live person. The greeting should be warm, friendly, and welcoming. Hopefully it is not the dreaded "Hi, two for dinner?" or "Smoking or nonsmoking." Wow! How more welcome can one feel? New restaurant owners and inexperienced managers have been known to say after interviewing a potential employee, "Well, I think this person can be good as a host but I don't think they are on the ball enough for a server position." So this manager wants them at the front door? The host or greeter is the first person customers see and talk to when they enter the restaurant. This impression must be positive. Hosts needs to be warm, smiling, intelligent, able to handle multiple tasks, accommodating, and quick on their feet. These qualities don't describe the person that is not smart enough "to serve the customers"—an employee should have to work up to this level.

Don't leave the first impression to chance. Ensure a high standard of quality for the host.

SEATING Showing the guests to their seats should not be a race for the host to get back to the front door. The time spent with the guest during the walk to the table, no matter how short of a time, is an opportunity to set the tone for the dining experience. Follow these simple steps:

1. Ask them for any seating preference. This question is not just to find out whether they want smoking, but whether they need a large table for meeting notes or a seat in a certain section. Do everything to accommodate each guest.
2. Try to engage the guest in some small talk.
3. Pull out chairs.
4. Wait for the guest to be seated and open menus. Never appear to be rushed.
5. Tell them the name of the server that will be taking care of them.
6. When leaving the table say "Enjoy your dinner, my name is Linda, if there is anything I can do for you, please let me know." They now have someone looking out for them.

THE BUS PERSON APPROACH Bus people are not servers, but they may come into contact with the guest before the server. This person must be pleasant and be capable of answering basic questions. This is a moment of truth that cannot be overlooked. The job of a bus person cannot be merely to clear dishes and pour water. He or she must possess some knowledge of the menu and understand his or her role. Conversely, an overbearing bus person can be a bother to the guest. Bus people should also be trained in sanitation because they handle plates, silverware, and glasses from many people.

THE SERVER GREET The guest will see the server as the person mainly responsible for the dining experience. The server will take the heat for any problems, whether the problem is related to service, kitchen, bartender, atmosphere, comfort level, or anything else that the guest does not like. The server must be up to this task. The server must be:

1. knowledgeable about the food, wines, and beverages—if the server can not answer simple questions about the menu or does not know what a Bombay martini, extra dry with a twist is, the guest satisfaction level begins to drop;

2. pleasant, smiling, and give the impression he or she enjoys what he or she is doing (if the server does not enjoy it, why are they serving guests?);

3. able to speak clearly and directly;

4. able to listen to guests and accommodate special requests; and

5. trained in the use of the POS equipment to ensure proper transfer of the order to the kitchen and save time at the POS machine.

SERVING FOOD AND DRINKS Timing is important during this phase of the service. Guests do not want to wait an extended period of time for drinks or food, and at the same time, they do not want to be rushed. Setting time standards for delivery of food and beverages, from the time they are ordered at the table is a good first step. For example:

6 to 8 minutes for appetizers;

10 to 12 minutes for entrees at lunch and 12 to 15 minutes for entrees at dinner; and

5 minutes for desserts.

These standards might fit well in a casual dining atmosphere where the guest has that expectation, but these time limits are a bit stringent for a fine dining restaurant. Table turns are more important for the casual dining segment, because price points are lower and a higher table turnover is needed to produce a profit.

A phrase to remember here is *mis en place*, which translates to "put in place." It is a term used often in the restaurant business and mostly in the kitchen. It is also interpreted freely to translate to, "If the customer doesn't need something in front of them, remove it. Extra glasses and silverware only take up space and clutter the table. If a customer does not want salad, remove the salad fork."

THE MANAGER MAKING THE ROUNDS During the dining experience, the guest should never have to wait to report a problem. Having someone of authority on the dining room floor at all times helps prevent such issues. A dining room manager needs to pay great attention to detail and be able to spot something out of place from across a room. The manager should be able to anticipate problems long before the guest even knows something is wrong.

A manager visiting each table and introducing him or herself to guests places the guests at ease. If a restaurant is operating on all cylinders, the number of pleasant table visits will far outweigh any problem visits.

CHECK PRESENTATION, CHANGE, AND THE EXIT Presenting the check should always be done in a neutral position, without assumption that any individual is paying the entire check, unless one of the guests directs the server otherwise. This is another point in the dining experience where people do not normally want to wait any longer than they have to. If the guests are finished with their meal, in the majority of cases they are ready to leave. Retrieve the check once the guest has paid it and do not, under any circumstance, use the phrase "do you need change?" Assume that change is needed and simply say "I'll be right back with your change." Allow the guest to say, "No thank you, we're all set."

Some customers want to sit and chat. This is normally a minority of guests, but a great dining experience may be lost if the guests feel they are being rushed to leave. Guests that just paid their bill will feel that they bought the table for as long as they want it. As long as the guest remains in the restaurant, they are still guests and should be tended to as if they have not yet paid the check.

As people leave the restaurant, they should feel like family. Say good night as they pass and the host should again check on the satisfaction of their dining experience.

Other moments of truth during the dining experience include, but are not limited to (because there are literally hundreds of these moments), the following:

1. bathroom cleanliness,
2. overall restaurant cleanliness,
3. employee personal hygiene,
4. being recognized,
5. special arrangements or accommodations,
6. clean silverware and glassware, and
7. sincere concern for the guest's experience.

Owning the Dining Experience

The previous topic dealt with moments of truth in the dining experience. The theory of **owning the dining experience**, when applied by the staff, creates a synergy with the moments of truth and creates a powerful standard of service. Owning the dining experience is a powerful concept. It is a simple statement meaning that everyone that comes into contact with the guest must take personal pride and *responsibility* to ensure a great dining experience.

A greeter or host—whichever name is preferred—is not a fixture by the front door charged with the responsibility of moving people to seats. It is the host's job to welcome the guest with open arms as if the entire staff has been waiting all day to serve them. The host must do this to each individual, consistently. With this first step, the host now owns this individual's dining experience. Ownership or caring for that person does not go away when the host seats the guest and returns to the front door. The host's "majority" ownership of that experience is in force until the next person in the chain greets the guest. Therefore, the host

Real World Scenario

At one restaurant, a host was asked why a server did not greet a particular table. She responded, "That is not my job. My job is to keep the rotation correct." The host was not being rude, but was taught that getting people seated quickly and keeping the numbers of guests per server even was her job.

must follow up with the next person to ensure that the guest is greeted at the table.

The next person greeting the guest at the table might be a bus person to fill water glasses or it might be the server. Either way, the next person greeting the guest now *shares* ownership of that dining experience. The host is still not relieved of responsibility. They now simply own a "minor" share of the experience —the "majority" ownership has shifted. However, the responsibility of the guests' experience remains with everyone comes into contact with the guest, whether that contact is direct or indirect.

The bartender who makes the drink must be concerned that it is made to the customer's liking, the chef or cook who prepares the meal must be proud to personally serve it, the dishwasher who cleans the plates and silverware must feel good about making a contribution, the food runner who delivers the food must not leave before making sure the guests have everything they need to enjoy their meal, the manager on the floor who upholds the standards in the restaurant and visits the tables to get the guests' approval, and everybody else who plays a role shares ownership of the dining experience. When this is done passionately with sincere concern for each guest, the results are incredible.

What Does It Mean to Serve the Customer?

Today's world is full of frustration, concerns, and stress. The job of the hospitality business, by its nature, is to lift these concerns from the guests for the short period of time in which they visit the restaurant. If the restaurant staff cannot deliver this experience, the guest will find a restaurant with a staff that can. Anybody spending any time in this business knows that some customers come in as if they are carrying the weight of the world on their shoulders. In their minds, maybe they are. The guest cannot be judged or and no one can understand how they feel except for them. Conversely, hospitality managers and employees are told to "check personal problems at the door." This is asking a lot and, at times it is very difficult to do, but staff must find a way to do it.

There is an old saying, "the customer is always right." Sometimes it is hard to believe this, but what good does it do to treat the customer as if they are wrong? Can the guests be wrong? *Sure they can.* But, under all circumstances, the

Real World Scenario

At one restaurant, part of the training program was to teach the wait staff and bartenders to read the customer. From this reading, the team member would rate the guest on a scale of 1 to 5—a "1" being happy-go-lucky and in a very good mood, "3" being average, and "5" being in a bad mood. When entering the table number on the POS system, the team member would put a the mood rating before the table number. If the expediter or any kitchen staff saw a 4 or 5, the floor manager was alerted. Without being too overbearing, it became the responsibility of all staff who had contact with this person to do everything they could to improve the individual's mood. Drinks might be expedited, food may have received a higher priority, or the manager may have made it a point to visit the table and ensure that everything was perfect.

Once, the manager at this restaurant bought a drink for an individual and the customer asked what the drink was for. The server simply responded that the manager does this sometimes. The manager would pick a couple of random tables and buy them a drink or send out complimentary appetizers. The response was more than expected and the individual left in a great mood.

This program actually made the staff more aware of the guests, because they had to engage them in conversation. The experiment allowed the restaurant to better serve the customers. The restaurant wanted to touch an emotion in such a positive way that they made the experience—even a simple lunch—memorable.

guest should only have contact with staff who have the attitude that whatever is the problem, it will be fixed. Consistently unhappy customers are sometimes a problem and may disrupt the experience of other customers. Sometimes it is necessary to lose a customer to ensure the pleasurable experience of others.

Barriers

In any industry, barriers must be dealt with to ensure that the staff can do their jobs properly. The job of an owner or manager is to uphold the high standards of the restaurant. Analyze each of the following areas and make appropriate changes:

Poorly Trained Staff A poorly trained staff will do more damage to a restaurant and its reputation than anything else. A poorly trained staff drives away customers, resulting in slumping sales and higher costs because of mistakes. The *USA Today* survey referred to earlier clearly reinforces this notion. Eight of the top 10 complaints from customers dealt directly with wait staff. A training program that not only teaches the staff about the menu, drinks, and service standards, but also the vision and passion of the ownership is imperative.

Part of the problem in the lack of training is that most owners see training as an expense rather than an investment. This approach gets the restaurant caught up in a vicious cycle: an individual is hired but improperly trained to take care of the guests, guests are unhappy and decide not to comeback, and the server quits

Real World Scenario

At a chain restaurant in a major metropolitan area, a guest came in who immediately complained before taking a bite of his hamburger that it was not cooked enough. The server brought it back, and to the amazement of the manager and grill cook, the burger was not even bitten or cut into. A new burger was cooked and a manager visited the table. The man just yelled "get it right, that is all I want." He was very loud and startled half the dining room. Two days later he returned and the exact same scenario again took place. In speaking to the general manager from a nearby unit, the manager discovered that the same thing had happened there the previous week. Four other units in the area were alerted and, within the week, one of the units had a similar experience. It was the same guy doing the same thing. Like clockwork, he appeared in the first restaurant within a couple of days. The manager asked him to stop frequenting this restaurant only because his demands could not be met. The manager decided it was better to lose a customer to keep its other customers happy.

because this is all too frustrating. The cycle goes back to the first step: hire another employee. The restaurant loses customers and begins to hire the first employee that comes through the door with an application. Owners then see only the cost because they have made the decision not to "invest" in the staff.

But, there is hope if a commitment is made to get out of the cycle. Owners must ask themselves "how would life be better if the staff were trained well enough that guests compliment the restaurant on the level of service provided? How great would it be if a server has been around long enough to cross-train into the kitchen, write schedules, fill in on management floor shifts, take on some neighborhood marketing, and give the owner a weekend off?" It is possible if an upfront investment is made in the staff.

This barrier of untrained staff has its own barrier: *The need for someone that has the ability to actually do the training.* An owner might say, "I have the best server that ever worked for me currently on my staff." That fact does not automatically make the server a good trainer. A good trainer must posses other characteristics, such as patience, good communication skills, organizational skills, and the desire to train others. A trainer must share the responsibility for turnover.

SUBQUALITY PRODUCT Servers have an easy time selling high quality, tasty, and well-presented food. If the kitchen gives them the same dish with old ingredients prepared half-heartedly and slopped on the plate, they will not be able to sell it. It will not happen. Servers find it easy to sell a high quality product and will shy away from selling something that is not right. Servers should be trained to refuse a product from the kitchen if it is not prepared to the restaurant's specification. If servers screen meals, cooks become aware that subpar quality will not be tolerated. In some restaurant an expediter also handles the food, which means three people look at the product before it goes to the table: the line cook, the expediter,

Real World Scenario

Once, an employee told a new manager at the restaurant that he was the lead trainer in the restaurant and had probably trained more than 100 servers in the past year. The server was very proud of this fact, but, unfortunately, the new manager was not impressed. He wondered where all the trained servers were. He told the trainer that he would be more impressed if the trainer had only trained 10 people and he could speak to eight or nine of these employees.

and the server. No matter the number, nothing should be so automatic that the server picks up the food and walks to the table. Everyone's job in the restaurant is to protect the guest. The guest must be protected from poor service, poor food, and an unclean facility.

LACK OF PROPER SUPPLIES Providing the staff with the necessary supplies is one of the ways to ensure that customers, both internal and external, are being taken care of. The owner's contribution to the process, as stated earlier, is to take care of the internal customer, which includes having enough forks, enough plates, or the proper amount of linens for each shift. Running out of tea bags or take-out containers may seem like a small thing, but the guest needs these items and the server is the one that has to face the guest.

FLAWED SYSTEMS Systems, rules, and regulations are necessary evils. Having systems such as opening side work, running side work, closing side work, and a system to handle customer complaints need to be in place. But when a system or rule gets in the way of delivering excellent customer service, the rule needs to be changed. When service standards are set, they in turn set an expectation for the staff to meet this standard. If cumbersome systems present obstacles, that standard is out of reach. For instance, if a guest has a problem with his dining experience, the server should be able to make a decision on what needs to be done to satisfy that customer. If the system is such that the server has to run through a flow chart to figure out what she is *allowed* to do, the owner is failing in his contribution to the process and actually hindering the staff from meeting the standard. The staff members need to understand that giving away the house for a dinner that is 5 minutes late is unnecessary and actually bad business. But, if the customer is upset for any reason, the employee should be allowed to evaluate the situation and make it right. Involved or cumbersome systems take away from spontaneity and sincerity. Systems must be easy to understand, easy to execute, and easy to follow up.

INDIVIDUALISM The word *teamwork* is not new to the restaurant business. It is mandatory that everyone work together for the good of the customer. Remember the phrase "if you're not serving the customer, you'd better be serving someone that is." What one individual does or does not do affects the ability of the team to take care of the guest. For example, if one staff member shows up late for his shift with disregard for the team member that has been there all day and shows no remorse for it, it causes friction between staff. If someone takes the last cup of coffee and does not start a fresh pot, that impedes the next person from serving coffee. Employees are sometimes too fast to say "it's not my job" or "why should I help him, he never helps anyone." First, get them to quit whining. Second, make it clear that everything is everyone's job. One person's primary job might be to serve customers in one section, but that person's secondary job includes everyone else in the building and helping with whatever they need.

If employees enjoy their jobs and their coworkers, work is not a struggle and can even be pleasant. This will show in attitude and reflect in the excellent customer service the guest receives.

UNDERSTAFFED Not having enough staff to do the job adds stress to the staff members that are working. The flow of business volume should dictate the scheduling and should ensure proper staffing levels. If the staffing levels are not right, the staff will become frustrated and the restaurant will have unnecessary turnover.

Customer Problems

No one is perfect. If management believes that neither managers nor the staff will ever make mistakes—no matter how slight the mistake may be—and the restaurant will meet all standards 100 percent of the time, management needs to *wake up*! How management and staff react to problems is the true test. There are choices to be made when something goes wrong. One option is to look the other way in hopes that the problem will go away. The other choice is to attack the problem head on and fix it and then go back and fix the cause of the problem.

By looking the other way, the customer goes away, but the cause of the problem does not. Some of the best customers are people that had a problem of some sort during their initial visit. When made aware of a problem, the manager has an opportunity to:

1. speak to someone "one-on-one" and find out what the problem is;
2. fix the problem immediately;
3. do what it takes to get them to return; and
4. fix the cause of the problem to prevent further issues in the future.

   There is a choice!

Empowerment

Empowerment is one of those business "buzz words." Managers jump on the empowerment bandwagon, telling their staff that they are empowered. But, most people do not understand what the word *empowerment* means. The concept seems to be an avenue for managers to believe they are building employee loyalty by allowing employees to make decisions. **Empowerment** is allowing the staff to make decisions necessary to take care of the guests without the manager's faulting the employees for their actions. Empowerment takes training employees and developing their understanding of the bigger picture.

Sincerity

To be sincere is defined as being genuine or honest. Everything the staff does must be done with a sincere concern for the customer. If the staff member is putting on an act, the customer may feel the lack of sincerity. From the moment customers walk in the door, they should get a genuine feeling of "I am going to be taken care of." Everyone must do specific things to create this feeling:

1.   make all customers feel welcome;
2.   smile;
3.   talk to people;
4.   never turn one's back to a customer;
5.   look straight into the customer's eyes; and
6.   be honest.

It is not a comforting feeling when to walk into a place of business and get the feeling that you are a bother to the employees there. This happens in restaurants. Servers gather close to the entrance to talk about nothing, or the host is on the telephone making plans for after work as a guest walks in the door. The host, of course, not wanting to be rude, turns her back on the customer to quickly finish the conversation as she says, "I have to go someone just came in, call me later." As the customer thinks, "Oh, sorry for bothering you, I would like to *spend my money here*!" Right from the start, the customer feels unwelcome.

It takes fewer muscles to smile than it does to frown. Upon entering a restaurant, if everyone is smiling and appears to enjoy what they are doing, the customer feels that and feels better.

People love to be heard. They do not seem to enjoy listening as much, but they like to be heard. People in the restaurant business need to listen because of this reason. The more customers talk and the more the staff listens, the more attached the customer gets to the restaurant.

Developing Customer Stories

Hearing stories of outstanding customer service is great, but having your staff create stories of their own is an incredible feeling. Only a staff that has a passion for customer service can create these stories. This cannot be done by a flow chart that specifically dictates to the staff "do X if Y happens." Combining the passion that the staff has with the belief that they must make each visit for each customer memorable, customer service stories will almost create themselves.

Here are some true stories created by people with a true passion for serving the customer:

■ You can't come to me, I'll come to you

The owner of a very popular restaurant has not seen one of his most loyal customers in 2 weeks. He makes some inquiries to find out why and discovers that the gentleman is getting over a pretty bad flu. He contacts the man and finds out that this loyal customer was about to make a reservation for the following night but does not know whether he feels up to venturing out in the cold. Not to worry. Dinner, including appetizer, entrée, dessert, and a bottle of wine are sent to the customer's home the next night, along with a personal waiter. This story must have been told by the customer a couple of hundred times.

■ A customer tears a tie on a splintered table

One day, while working the floor, a manager sees a man checking out his tie and then rubbing his hand over the table. The manager approaches to discover that the table is splintered and the tie has a noticeable pull in the front of it. The manager apologizes for the tear, goes to petty cash, pulls out $30, and hands it to the customer to purchase a new tie. The customer said that the same thing happened one other time, and the manager of that restaurant had him buy a new tie and bring in the receipt. The manager that just handed the money over said, "The damage is our fault, why should I inconvenience you to replace something we did?" The manager said that customer was in three times a week after that and always with clients.

■ We gave you the wrong order, why should you come back?

A customer placed a large to-go order from a restaurant. The restaurant packed half of the order improperly. When the customer called the restaurant to inform the manager, the manager asked for the address, repacked the proper order, added some dessert, and drove the order to the house.

■ The unexpected snowstorm

On a busy Friday night, snow started falling about 12 hours before the all-knowing weatherman said it would. Guests started to panic a little. The staff told the guests not to worry and to enjoy their dinners. The staff informed each guest when they felt they were 5 minutes from leaving the restaurant that they would start the guests' cars and clean them off. They started an impromptu valet service and had the cars warmed up and at the front door when people were ready to leave. The servers also gave them a complimentary dessert card for their next visit when they would have the time to enjoy their wonderful dessert menu. The manager said the response from that single action was incredible and he wished it would snow like that a couple of times during the course of the winter.

■ The lost coat at the coat check

Most restaurants have a sign by their coat check that states, "We are not responsible for lost articles." Does this include when the person at the coat check is negligent and gives away the wrong coat? This happened at one restaurant, and when it was brought to the manager's attention, the manager told the guest to go out and replace the coat and send the bill to the restaurant. The guest received a check in the mail within 3 days.

■ The flat tire

A customer leaving the restaurant went to her car to find the tire was flat. She was in a hurry for a meeting and returned to the restaurant to call the American Automobile Association (AAA) to change it. The manager said AAA would take some time to arrive, so the manager changed the tire.

Situations such as the ones above may not present themselves every day, but by adopting the attitude that "customers are my responsibility until they leave my parking lot," each employee begins to find ways to create stories of outstanding customer service.

■ CHAPTER REVIEW

Delivering excellent customer service is a constant challenge to an ever-changing public opinion on what the phrase means. Owners, managers, and all employees must focus on each and every customer on each and every visit. Treat customers as you would treat customers in your own home. Accept problems as opportunities—opportunities to show customers their experience does matter and to locate and repair problems in your service, atmosphere, or the quality of food and beverages.

■ KEY TERMS

empowerment   owning the dining experience
internal customer   passion
moments of truth   telephone etiquette

■ REVIEW QUESTIONS

1. Define passion.

2. Explain a moment of truth.

3. Give at least 10 examples of moments of truth during the dining experience.

4. Define "owning the dining experience."

Notes

1. *USA Today*, February 1997, Jerry Shriver.
2. Jan Carlzon, 1989.

CHAPTER 10

Human Resource Management

After reviewing this chapter, you will:

- Lead people in addition to managing the business;
- Manage time and become more productive;
- Motivate employees and managers to reach their peak performance; and
- Retain staff through increasing morale.

Human resource management is a key component of operating a successful restaurant because it deals with the most important part of the restaurant success equation: its people. Whereas managing cost areas, maintaining the physical plant, and controlling quality can be easily learned, becoming a true leader is a never-ending learning process.

Defining Human Resources

The human resource (HR) departments in corporate America have evolved over time from an office responsible for interviewing, hiring, and placing people in open positions in the company, assigning pay scales, and handling benefits into the HR departments of today, which are responsible for much more. Human resource management involves locating, hiring, training, developing, and retaining quality people. This is a vital part of being successful.

Small, independent businesses do not have the funds, manpower, or the need for a separate person or department handling HR needs. Therefore, the restaurant owner adds another role to his or her busy life: that of the HR professional.

The physical structure, atmosphere, and menu at a restaurant can be the very best but, as has been referenced throughout this book, to produce a quality menu and deliver outstanding service, it takes *people*! Not just anyone, but caring, passionate people that share the owner's vision. Once quality candidates have been hired, their knowledge and talents must be developed so they stay employed and help build a great restaurant.

The book *The Art of Managing People*[1] gives an example of leadership and the skills necessary to become an effective leader: a bicycle. The example starts with the frame. The three parts of the frame are technical aspects, people, and leadership. Refer to Figure 10–1.

The people are what comprise the business. These people include customers, employees, salespeople, and delivery people. Successful restaurateurs learn how to deal with, in a positive manner, people at all levels.

The other two aspects—technical and leadership—require a strong leader to bring all other skills together to make the operations successful. For example, continuing the bicycle metaphor, the pedals represent the two areas that drive any business: sales and costs. Refer to Figure 10–2.

The rear wheel of the bicycle is, of course, what gives it power. When the rider pedals the bike, the rear wheel is put in motion and propels the bike forward. This is analogous to the technical skills of a job—the managerial aspects that include the ability to perform specific work-related tasks such as serving and preparing food, conducting inventories, writing schedules, ordering product, and all other tasks. Refer to Figure 10–3.

The front wheel steers the bike to a specific destination. Refer to Figure 10–4. Without this front wheel, the bike is headed for disaster unless the path is a straight line- and, in business, the path is rarely a straight line. The leader directs the front wheel by steering the team toward a goal and fulfilling a vision. Therefore, the leader performs both of these roles: power the bike (technical knowledge) and steer it in a specific direction (vision and strategy). Figure 10–5 depicts a full bicycle ready to be powered toward a goal and directed by strong leadership.

FIGURE 10–1

Bicycle Frame.

Reprinted with permission of Simon & Schuster Adult Publishing Group, from THE ART OF MANAGING PEOPLE by Phillip L. Hunsaker and Anthony J. Alessandra. Copyright © 1980 by Phillip J. Hunsaker and Anthony J. Alessandra.

FIGURE 10–2

Bicycle Frame with Pedals as Sales and Cost.

Reprinted with permission of Simon & Schuster Adult Publishing Group, from THE ART OF MANAGING PEOPLE by Phillip L. Hunsaker and Anthony J. Alessandra. Copyright © 1980 by Phillip J. Hunsaker and Anthony J. Alessandra.

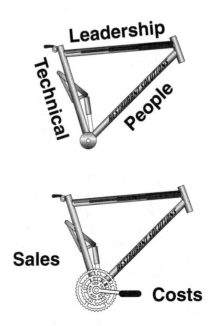

FIGURE 10–3

Bicycle Frame with Rear Wheel (The Technical Knowledge).

Reprinted with permission of Simon & Schuster Adult Publishing Group, from THE ART OF MANAGING PEOPLE by Phillip L. Hunsaker and Anthony J. Alessandra. Copyright © 1980 by Phillip J. Hunsaker and Anthony J. Alessandra.

Manager Skills and Duties

The skills involved in dealing with people or the HR aspects of the business include:

- efficient time management,
- leadership and communication,
- interviewing, hiring, and retaining quality people,
- conflict management, and
- coaching and counseling.

These elements are what HR management is all about. Without these skills, all the culinary and technical knowledge of running a business is worthless.

Efficient Time Management

Many books have been written and many seminars have been developed on the subject of time management. The objectives of most of these books and seminars are to teach people how to control the time that they have to complete their daily and weekly objectives in support of overall goals by planning the task, assigning priority codes, delegating tasks that can be delegated, and checking off the tasks as they are completed. All books and seminars offer instructions on how to be

FIGURE 10–4

Bicycle Frame with Front Wheel (Leadership) and Rear Wheel (Technical).

Reprinted with permission of Simon & Schuster Adult Publishing Group, from THE ART OF MANAGING PEOPLE by Phillip L. Hunsaker and Anthony J. Alessandra. Copyright © 1980 by Phillip J. Hunsaker and Anthony J. Alessandra.

FIGURE 10–5

Complete Bicycle.

Reprinted with permission of Simon & Schuster Adult Publishing Group, from THE ART OF MANAGING PEOPLE by Phillip L. Hunsaker and Anthony J. Alessandra. Copyright © 1980 by Phillip J. Hunsaker and Anthony J. Alessandra.

more productive. The basic principles and guidelines for managing time in the restaurant business are the same, but the restaurant manager's daily responsibilities and tasks are unique.

Time management involves learning to be more productive. One of the ways to become more productive in the long term is to *"Teach someone something everyday!"* In the restaurant business this can be:

1. how to write a schedule,
2. how to place a produce order,
3. how to check in deliveries,
4. how to present a pre-meal talk,
5. how to conduct an inventory, and
6. how to conduct a proper interview.

Many operators believe that it is easier to just do it, as that will save time.

However, consider this: if every day staff members learn something they did not know, soon the restaurant will have an entire staff of people that can effectively run the business. The owner or manager can then confidently delegate the technical tasks and concentrate his or her efforts on leading the team.

A typical day of a restaurant manager may go something like this:

1. enter the building and check quality of the close from the previous night;
2. check the books and the paperwork from the previous day and complete any reports for tracking purposes;
3. read the nightly log to find out that one of the fryers will not stay on;
4. call the repair company;
5. check in the produce order that has arrived at the back door before the kitchen manager arrived;
6. put the order away;

7. check the roster for the day;

8. make a bank run to deposit the previous day's receipts;

9. return from the bank to find that one of the day servers will not make it to work;

10. cover the shift;

11. complete a line check before opening because the kitchen is a little behind on the prep and needs help;

12. conduct a pre-meal meeting with the staff to review daily specials, check uniforms and appearance, offer tips on salesmanship, and get the staff motivated for the day;

13. run the shift and talk to customers and operate as the floor general;

14. correct a problem with one of the lunches sent out;

15. visit the table to take care of the guest;

16. start staff cuts and check out the staff;

17. conduct a one-on-one with one of the team members;

18. count the day bank and enter the daily invoices;

19. sit down to eat lunch at 3:00 and work on a marketing idea;

20. take a half a dozen phone calls during this time;

21. get the next shift set up and attend the nightly pre-meal, and

22. get the next shift going and head home after a 12-hour shift.

But there is still more to do. That marketing idea the manager has been working on still lingers. A new training class starts tomorrow and time is tight. And, it all needs to be done all over again tomorrow.

To learn to manage time under these circumstances is a bit different than what corporate America experiences in the 9-to-5 world. In the restaurant business, everything appears to be a priority. Leaving tasks undone until tomorrow when tomorrow brings the same obstacles accomplishes nothing.

When a manager learns to control time, the manager will:

■ be more effective as a leader, because there will be more time to spend developing and guiding the staff;

■ be more at ease, because the "too much to do syndrome" will be removed;

■ be more rested and attack each day with more stamina; and

■ have a more fulfilled personal life.

It takes a tremendous commitment to accomplish time management in the restaurant industry. The skills will not be mastered in one reading or after a couple of days of implementing change. Mastering the skills to manage time takes patience, dedication, and time. But once these skills have been mastered, the results make the effort worthwhile.

Goals

To maximize effectiveness and productivity, the restaurant manager must set goals. If an individual works in an industry or a job that is not appealing, that individual may struggle to wake up and face each day, and success is probably out of reach. Personal goals must contain objectives that personally support personal wants, desires, and needs. These values have to be the starting point. It would be a waste of time to set professional goals and learn the needed professional technical skills, if those goals did not correspond with personal desires.

Personal, long-term goals are the building blocks for everything else the restaurant professional decides to do. A good starting point is to set a 5-year plan based on personal desires. Goals in the business world will then be directed by personal goals. Goals should always follow the **SMART**[2] (Specific, Measurable, Action-Oriented, Realistic, Timely) rule, as discussed below.

SPECIFIC Goals must be specific. Ambiguous goals are open for interpretation and a person can easily be diverted from these goals with some slight setback or change of plan. Solid, specific goals keep the focus on the final outcome. From here, the smaller intermediate goals can be developed that help support the overall goal.

MEASURABLE It is hard to know if a goal has been met or even to determine whether the path to the goal is correct unless the results can be measured along the way. For example, the goal to reduce employee turnover to 80 percent annually requires a formula that calculates that percentage and a benchmark from the current year. The formula must be understood and used to set the base percentage and measure the results.

ACTION-ORIENTED All goals have to have an action associated with them. The action dictates the specific steps to be taken to make the goal a reality. Using the goal to reduce turnover 80 percent, specific steps might include:

1. developing a labor plan to determine the exact number of staff it will take to operate the restaurant efficiently;
2. conduct training classes for managers to improve interviewing skills and techniques that will allow for better hiring; and
3. conduct exit interviews to find out why people are leaving.

REALISTIC Any goal must be realistic or it will deter a person from trying because unattainable goals only demotivate. If the present turnover rate exceeds 200 percent, then a decrease to 80 percent in one year might be unrealistic. However, if the goal covered 24 or 30 months or included incremental goals of 160 percent in 3 months and 130 percent on 6 months, it would increase chances of reaching the goal.

Timely Goals need a time frame in which to be met. If a goal is set without a deadline, events will occur randomly. There is no incentive to make any necessary adjustments to drive the goal home.

Any goal that is set will not be achieved through luck.

Personal Goals

Personal goals are the road map that point to where an individual wants to be at some point in the future.

Answer the following questions for setting personal goals:

If you could look into the future, say 5 years from now, what is it that you would like to be doing?

Would you be doing the same job with the same company?

Would your personal life be the same?

Would you be living in the same place?

Would your income be much different?

Would you have any children?

These are only examples of the questions that can be asked. Begin to ask personal questions and do not hold back. Shape a future through these very personal questions. Once these questions are answered, short-term and intermediate goals that support these long-term goals can be developed. Any short-term or intermediate goals that do not support the more important longer range goals:

1. move the long-term goal further out of reach,

2. can place the goal-setter on a different path, and

3. waste time.

The restaurant business is very time-consuming, and achieving success at any cost, including sacrificing a personal life, will only hinder long-term success. Planning and setting personal goals is necessary for long-term self-fulfillment.

So how does one effectively use time? There are options:

- use a day planner,
- write everything down,
- be a teacher,
- delegate,
- learn to say *no*,
- plan personal time,
- don't automatically complete easy tasks,
- deal with procrastination, and
- conduct effective meetings.

Start Using a Planner

The purpose of a day planner is for more than just writing down tasks or priorities of the day. A planner is a tool to assist in organizing a busy life and to help achieve long-term goals.

Day planners are available in a wide variety of sizes and styles. Find one that is right for you. Important features of a day planner are that it is user-friendly and makes sense for the individual using it, not the salesperson behind the counter. Becoming a slave to the tools and systems that are designed to help people gain control over their time will have a negative impact, as that system will cease to be utilized.

In addition to a planner, index cards or a small planner should be carried at all times just to keep notes. These notes and reminders can be pulled out at the end of the day and used to complete pressing tasks or to fill in the planner and schedule for the coming days or weeks.

Write Everything Down

Don't try to remember the many details and disturbances that happen during the course of a day. Take the time to make simple notes.

Be a Teacher

Teaching is a great way to gain control of time. If you take the time every day to teach something you know, eventually you will have an entire staff capable of performing technical tasks. Once you teach someone, that person then has the ability to teach someone else, opening the individual to more learning. You, as the leader, then have time to concentrate on leading versus managing.

Delegate

Look over the goals and tasks and to determine which ones can be delegated. Delegating is not simply passing responsibility on to someone else or giving away tasks that seem to be bothersome. Delegating tasks is a way to increase personal productivity and the productivity of the team. But delegation has some steps involved that, in the beginning, will probably take more time, because delegating takes an investment in time and effort.

Write down all of the **areas of responsibility** in a restaurant. A sample form can be found in the appendix section of this book. Define specifically what each responsibility entails. For instance, if someone is responsible for payroll, it includes:

■ having all employees' paperwork (e.g., W-4, I-9) filled out completely,

■ entering employee information into the computer properly so they can clock in and clock out,

- reviewing daily entries for proper clock-in and clock-out times,
- filling out payroll worksheets with weekly times,
- faxing paperwork to the payroll company,
- receiving and checking transmitted payroll to compare to what was originally sent to ensure that there are no mistakes,
- signing checks for distribution, and
- dealing with any payroll issues an employee might have.

If the payroll responsibility is delegated, the person taking on the responsibility now has an understanding of what is expected of him or her. Two major benefits of delegating are that the manager becomes more productive by being able to spend time on other goals and the person accepting the role learns another facet of the business. However, do not delegate by saying, "Here are the instructions, just follow them, and everything will be fine." Leaders have a responsibility to teach individuals exactly what needs to be done.

Delegating is more than just assigning tasks and responsibilities. The time invested at the beginning of the process will be paid back many times over when several people in the building can complete multiple tasks.

Learn to Say No

Learning to say no does not mean that every time someone asks for a moment of time, the automatic answer is "no." There are times when saying no is appropriate, such as when an employee asks for 5 minutes of a manager's time when he or she is facing 10 pressing matters. Giving 5 minutes at that time may be more damaging than saying no and scheduling time later in the day when a manager can focus completely on the individual and his or her problem. Managers lose credibility by giving staff members only half of their focus.

Plan Personal Time

Planning personal time is not selfish. It provides time to recharge and is necessary to be successful. Personal time might include going out to dinner at a different restaurant, going to the gym, or simply reading a book. Do not live to work.

Don't Automatically Complete Easy Tasks

Each day, the easy tasks on the day planner should not be attacked first. If something is going to be time consuming and a high priority, do it first when interruptions might be at a low point.

Deal with Procrastination

Procrastination is a characteristic of and major fault of unproductive and inefficient people. However, an individual with goals will get things done.

Remember the old saying, "Don't put off until tomorrow what you can do today." Tomorrow is a different day and can bring many more hurdles getting in the way of accomplishing goals.

Conduct Effective Meetings

Meetings can be unbelievable time wasters. Meetings need to have a specific purpose and goals and should not be used to present new ideas for debate. Meetings should be used to present new ideas, debate previously presented ideas, and accomplish specific goals. A meeting should have a specific start time and end time. Start meetings on time no matter what happens or who is present. By starting on time, the manager sends a clear message that the meeting is important and so is everyone's time that has been invited to participate and that no individual's time holds more importance than the next person's.

Have an agenda. If time permits, have the agenda distributed to all attendees of the meeting beforehand so that participants can prepare questions or concerns prior to the meeting.

The agenda should include a time line set for each agenda. If 10 minutes is allotted for a topic, it should receive only 10 minutes. If the topic warrants more than that, ask everyone to think about the subject and call a meeting for that specific purpose, following the same guidelines outlined above.

Leadership and Communication Skills

Communication and leadership are presented together because of their large interdependency. Neither of these concepts is *mutually exclusive,* which means they are independent of each other. Leaders do not exist at any level unless they can communicate a clear vision and specific goals. Good communicators are often viewed as good leaders.

Leadership is managing people in such a way that everyone in the group shares the leader's vision, looks to the leader for direction, believes in the leader's decisions, and has a personal trust in the leader. Leadership is action-oriented and is not just a word or a position and does not automatically come with a title.

The leadership role differs from the manager's role. Managers that are not viewed as leaders accomplish goals by strong-arming the results. "It's my way or the highway" would be the motto of such a manager. Results that are accomplished in this manner with strong-armed tactics are short-lived victories. These results cannot withstand the test of time. The person that manages in this archaic way is given the title of "boss." Employees work for this boss simply because that boss is in charge and signs the paycheck. However, employees do not usually respect this individual. The minute the boss is not looking over the employees' shoulders, the employees will do only the bare minimum or do things their way. On the other hand, leaders set a vision and goals, which encourages the team to reach the stated goals.

In the restaurant business, more than one person is usually responsible for the restaurant operations. Although each of these individuals carries the title of manager, usually one stands out as the leader. This is the person that everyone goes to for answers. This is the person whose shifts operate with fewer problems than other shifts and things seem to run more efficiently. This is the person that even the public views as the "person in charge." This person is not necessarily the owner or the general manager, which can cause animosity and deter the restaurant from being successful.

The following pages review leadership and communication and how to develop the skills necessary to be a leader and a great communicator.

Not everyone can be a leader. One must have the desire to lead people through the ups and downs in the good times and the tough times.
A leader assumes the responsibility for the successes and is accountable for the failures.
Leading people is much different and more difficult than managing objects and numbers, because objects need a manager but people need a leader.

It is impossible for one person to be everywhere. Owners cannot spend 7 days a week, 24 hours a day in the restaurant. One person cannot serve every guest personally and prepare all the food. Therefore, there must be a team of dedicated people, with the same passion to take care of the guest. This is where strong leadership skills come into play.

Being a leader does not just happen. An owner or manager does not receive respect from individuals simply because of a title. Respect is earned through the words they speak and, more importantly, through the actions they take to stay true to those words.

People that work for someone with a title of "manager" set out on their daily journey to accomplish the minimum it takes to get the job done. There is no extra effort and no desire to excel. The person that works for a manager puts on a show and the minute the manager is out of sight, the individual stops trying. On the other hand, when someone works for an individual they respect and believe in, it is easy to accomplish what is expected because no one wants to disappoint the leader.

When an individual joins a team, that person must accept his or her role as designated by the team. Along with accepting this role, he or she accepts certain responsibilities and becomes accountable to both the leader and the rest of team.

A leader can rally the troops to conquer new goals and reach new heights. In his seminars and books, Dennis Waitley talks about how people rally around a winner. People seek out winners and want to be part of that person's team. This person is seen as a true leader. People want to be part of a winning team and know that it takes a strong leader to create that winning team.

Real World Scenario

A server at a very popular restaurant consistently outshined all other staff members. His uniform was always perfect, his attitude was always upbeat, and his check average was always higher than everyone else's. The GM was very impressed with this individual's performance and asked him to take a more active role in the unit and possibly work toward a management position. The server agreed and the GM placed the individual in a training role.

The individual struggled as a trainer and his personal performance began to falter. He was no longer the upbeat, positive individual. The GM removed him from the position and, within a short period, he was back to his original attitude and performance.

The GM inquired into this change and found that the individual, while a great performer, struggled with being in a position of authority. He did not have the communication skills or the patience or the desire to train. He took the role because he did not want to disappoint the GM.

For years, the premise was that a good leader had followers. These followers believed in the person and saw this individual as a winner. This premise has changed over the years. Some now view true leadership as an individual that develops other leaders. This view of leadership offers another perspective as to the real goal of a leader. If a leader views his or her role as being one who has to create other leaders, ego is removed from the mix and the leader starts to concentrate on understanding people.

One of the leader's goals should be to recognize the talent and dedication of the team and then develop the potential of each team member in his or her own right. Not everyone wants to lead—some people are quite happy taking direction, fulfilling one role, and working for the betterment of the team. There is nothing wrong with that, and, by forcing people to take on a leadership role with which they are uncomfortable is damaging to the individual and the team itself.

Walk the Walk and Talk the Talk

"Your actions speak so loudly I can't hear what you are saying." This phrase is heard often from people that work for someone who tells them one thing and does another. Leading by example in the hospitality industry is a must if employees are to perform to the restaurant's standards. If the manager preaches delivering excellent customer service but is indifferent to guests, the staff will ignore the preaching and see only a hypocrite. Credibility with staff can be severely damaged in this way. The leader is the standard setter. This is the person the staff will seek out to teach them what should be done.

A leader needs to be sincere. If a leader expects someone to act in a particular way, the leader must lead by example. By being sincere, a leader gains credibility every day. In his book *The 7 Habits of Highly Successful People*, Steven Covey writes about a "credit bank account." This credit bank account is what accumulates when people simply do the right things and others believe they can count on those individuals to be honest and to do what they promised. When things do not go right, as sometimes happens, it is not seen as an empty promise or same old operating procedure, because everyone knows that the behavior is contrary to how the individual normally performs. When it is needed, the credit bank account goes a long way.

Individuals on a team look at their leader and expect certain traits:

POSITIVE ATTITUDE If a leader wants people around them to have a positive attitude, the leader must consistently portray a positive attitude. "Every dark cloud has a silver lining" may be a bit much, but a leader may use the word *opportunity* in place of the word *problem*. This is sometimes hard to do, as Murphy's Law was probably written by someone in the restaurant business. Consider the following example: It is 1 hour before dinner on a Friday night and the power goes out. The GM learns that a transformer two blocks away was hit by a truck and that power will be out for about 3 hours. This is a difficult predicament to be in, but it provides an opportunity to say "Wow! This is great chance to look at the positives." But the fact remains that power will be out and there is nothing that can be done about it.

Leaders recognize that certain events can be controlled and certain events cannot. So, there two choices: (1) get emotional and start screaming about how much money will be lost in sales and product, or (2) accept the fact that power will be down and look for ways to keep the staff and guests calm. In dealing with the situation constructively, the leader:

a. becomes compassionate, understanding that the front of the house staff is losing tips and the kitchen staff may lose hours by being sent home;

b. finds ways to console the guests so they do not place blame on the restaurant, because the restaurant has no control over the transformer; and

c. look into the cost-effectiveness of a generator.

If the leader loses his or her temper, the staff will do the same and the guests will feel the tension.

HIGH LEVEL OF ENERGY People want their leader to be energetic and enthusiastic. When the leader smiles and walks with a sense of purpose, everyone around seems to follow. If the leader is lethargic, with shoulders slumped and moves as if it is a chore to be in the building, then no one wants to follow.

HIGH PERSONAL STANDARDS A leader must have high standards of excellence in both their personal life and their business life, because one feeds on the other. No one can hide his or her true behavior for long. Putting on a show for the staff will not win them over. People that work in the restaurant industry work too closely together for too many hours not to see the real person.

HONESTY Hidden agendas only prevent an organization from reaching its goals. They cloud the vision. Honesty in all communication is critical.

COOL UNDER PRESSURE If a leader loses his or her temper in the heat of the battle, then he or she will lose the respect of the team. When the shift gets hectic, members of team will start to look around, searching for the person "in charge." If no one is there to direct their efforts, the staff may get nervous. By remaining calm, the positive attitude of the leader shines through and the staff will trust the leader to make everything right.

How a leader reacts to the failures, problems, and roadblocks as well as to the successes will have a tremendous impact on the long-term, overall success of the team. If all of the day-to-day issues wear the leader down, keeping the team focused and moving forward in a positive manner will be difficult. For any leader, setbacks and failures will happen, but how the leader responds will determine his or her overall effectiveness and true ability to lead.

Individual and Group Motivation

As stated previously, a leader must get the best out of each individual, because each individual has something different to offer the team. In turn, all team members must understand their role and what they are expected to contribute. To get the most out of the team, a leader must:

1. have a vision that is shared with all members of the team;
2. set team goals;
3. work with individuals to set personal goals;
4. motivate individuals by discussing individual goals privately and praising individuals publicly for their contribution to the team; and
5. motivate the group by discussing group goals publicly and celebrating the team's small victories.

Set a Vision for the Team

In the realms of management many terms are tossed around: empowerment, mission statement, culture, and vision. Of these and all the other management phrases, the one that embodies the reason for existence is the vision of the leadership. The vision is what binds the team together. The vision answers the questions "What is this all about?" and "Why are we putting in these extra hours?" Having a vision of what the restaurant is about and the reason it exists answers these questions and explains why the management and staff work as hard as they do. Vision gives everything purpose.

The vision and the mission statement are separate entities. The mission statement is a summation of what the restaurant is striving to be. The vision is a conviction of why. The mission statement describes the standard that will govern the restaurant.

Examples:

VISION The vision is that this is the restaurant that everyone in the market will speak positively about and that other restaurant owners will look to and try to emulate. This restaurant is to be recognized as the gold standard.

MISSION STATEMENT The restaurant's mission is to be the best casual dining restaurant in the region, offering the freshest, highest-quality food combined with first-rate service in a clean, comfortable, and inviting atmosphere. The restaurant will deliver all of these things at a great value.

The owner normally develops the vision, the dream of what he or she wants to create, and the passion he or she wants to share. Through sharing the vision, to the leader gets other people caught up in the dream.

The following visions are from two different people and explain why they opened their respective restaurants. Read the two visions and then answer the questions that follow:

1. I dream of owning a restaurant where people love to come, enjoy a wonderful dining experience, share conversation, and just have fun: where everyone feels welcome and no one feels like an outsider. This includes staff as well as customers. As the saying goes, "step inside, for there are no strangers here, only friends you haven't met yet."

2. I always wanted to own my own restaurant. After years of working for someone else, I want to work for myself. I know I can be successful.

Who will have the successful restaurant?

Which restaurant do you think you will feel more comfortable dining in or having a cocktail?

The vision must create a picture and generate some inner excitement. Other people must get wrapped up in the owner's dream. The dreamer sets he vision but it is shared enthusiastically by all.

Everyone in the organization—owner, management, and staff—develops the mission statement. By so doing, all staff are involved in setting the standards that will govern their actions and "buys into" the mission. These standards are what the public will see and what the public will use to identify the restaurant. It will be more difficult for managers or staff to defend inappropriate action outside the boundaries of the mission statement if they helped to develop it. During this process, the individuals with a real interest in developing the mission statement will stand out.

Inaction to what has been written in the mission statement is self-defeating. The leader cannot let this happen. The mission statement must be a collaboration of the entire team if it is to have a positive effect on the way a manager goes about his or her daily business. This process should be moderated but not run by one person. Questions should be posed that get the team thinking. These questions should be started with what, how, and who (the why question is answered in the vision). Closed-ended questions that are answered with yes or no give no insight or commitment.

Rules of Leadership

Several rules need to be followed to be a great leader:

1. Always counsel in private.
2. Always praise publicly.
3. Find the right problem before looking for solutions.
4. Work to change behavior, not personality.
5. Develop listening skills.
6. Follow the Golden Rule.
7. Never make promises.
8. Coach individuals to self-empowering goals.
9. Get on the team's level to move the pile.
10. Celebrate the small victories.

Always Counsel in Private When a leader is trying to motivate an individual or has a problem with an individual, the leader should discuss the situation only with that person and in a private setting. The situation is between the leader and the individual and nobody else should be or needs to be involved unless there is a legal issue, such as harassment. Once a private conversation is held, it should be kept that way. When presenting a problem to an individual, the leader must be honest even if the person might take offense. The leader must present the situation or potential problem and allow the team member to respond. The leader must always listen and allow for the individual's side of the story without prejudice.

When counseling an individual, both the leader and the individual must leave the room with an understanding of the specific behavior that is expected and what the time line is for improvement. The leader encourages the person and follow up on the conversation. This follow-up will show that the leader is there to support the person to reach the agreed on goal.

Always Praise Publicly If an individual or the group has done something that should be recognized, do it in public and do it loudly. Let everyone know about the accomplishment. This accomplishes several objectives:

1. it gets the individual or group feeling good about themselves because they are seeing results;
2. the team recognizes that this accomplishment is important and the leadership is aware of their efforts; and
3. it gets the team to try even harder.

When praising an accomplishment or achievement, never forget anyone.

Find the Right Problem Before Looking for Solutions The problem that is present on the surface may only be a symptom of the problem. For example, if a restaurant is not producing a profit, an operator may look for ways to cut costs versus finding ways to increase sales. These cost-cutting methods may include reducing hours, cutting the purchasing of supplies, and even revamping the menu. If these measures do not cure the problems, morale issues may occur. If a team works hard at something only to find that they worked at the wrong problem, the team is discouraged and it may cost the leader credibility. The team trusted the leader and put heart and soul into fixing the problem only to find their efforts were meaningless.

WORK TO CHANGE BEHAVIOR, NOT PERSONALITY Something that a leader must understand is that everyone is different. People respond differently to situations, are motivated differently, and have different desires and goals. If everyone is treated the same and expectations are the same for each individual, it will be very difficult to lead the group. Although the group may have group goals, each individual within that group has personal goals and contributes on a different level to the overall success of the group. Look around at the team. Different behavior styles and the way people respond differently to situations will be evident. A good leader understands these differences and searches to find what each person can contribute to the overall success of the team.

When dealing with an individual, it is important to understand how to deal with that person's behavior. Behavior is the way a person responds or reacts in a

Real World Scenario

A chain restaurant was growing quickly in the Washington, D.C., market. In one unit, sales were stagnant for 2 years, while others in the chain were growing at 7 to 9 percent. The team worked on service standards, sales contests, and training, but sales could not improve. The chain sent in a new GM and, during the first weekend in the unit, the kitchen ran out of the catch of the day by 7:00 P.M. on a Friday. When the kitchen manager was asked why they were out so early in the weekend, he reported that the previous GM wanted to run out of "all of the high-cost items" as early as possible so he would always meet his food cost objective, which was a good portion of his bonus. This meant that the restaurant would run out of steak and ribs early. The new GM made it clear to the kitchen manager that the restaurant should never run out of anything on the menu.

The problem of stagnant sales was nothing more than having the items that were on the menu available for the customer. The customer was not going to gamble on whether or not the most popular items on the menu would be available. For 2 years the staff members thought they were doing something wrong from the service side. The kitchen workers thought their food was of low quality. Most of the staff wanted more advertising. Everyone thought the concept was dead in the water. Turnover was out of control. The answer was simple once the right problem was attacked. This, combined with some other minor areas of focus, turned the unit around and it was soon on a double-digit sales increase that lasted 18 months.

given situation. Reaction is usually responsive and a product of one's personality, experiences, the situation itself, and the person's mood at the time. When trying to develop people, always work to change or improve their behavior and not their personality. If the effort is placed on improving or changing the behavior, the individual will understand that his or her behavior is inappropriate and the person is not being attacked. The response will be more positive and better suited to the standards and the goals of the organization. If the personality is attacked, it may demoralize the person. Always search to find the good in the person. Communicate to the person that a particular behavior is getting in the way of his or her success.

Develop Listening Skills Listening will be covered in more detail in the communication portion of this chapter. It is an extremely important attribute for any leader, one most leaders must learn.

The Golden Rule The Golden Rule simply states that you should treat others as you would want to be treated. No matter how someone is motivated, they should not be treated any differently than anyone else.

Never Make Promises One of the ways a leader gains respect is to build a trust bond between themselves and the individuals of the team. *Unless the leader can control the outcome of a situation 100 percent, the leader can only lose by making a promise.* If a promise is made to someone and then that promise cannot be delivered, credibility and respect will be lost.

Credibility gains momentum by saying, "I'll do my best to deliver, then actually set out to deliver above what the individual expects." The old saying of "underpromise and overdeliver" works wonders.

Coach Individuals Toward Self-Empowering Goals If a leader sets goals for employees, the goals become the leader's goals, not the employee's. It is more important to get people to believe in the vision and the goals of the team. Once an individual "buys into" and "believes in" the vision, the belief in the team goals naturally follows. Through this process, team members can evaluate where they stand and develop personal goals for self-improvement.

The leader's role in this process is to be open, honest, supportive, and to coach the individual toward goals that are SMART. Plan with the individual a specific time to sit down and evaluate progress and redirect, if necessary, his or her focus and efforts.

Get on the Team's Level to Move the Pile If a manager expects the team to respond to a title, that manager is not a leader. Instead of bringing the team up to the standard, the leader must recognize the level of where the team is at that particular point in time. This can be called *the level of expectation*. If the team presently performs at a certain level, that is the best that can be expected right now. Get on the team's level. Instead of having team members play catch up to the expectation, personally bring them to new heights. An improvement of 1 percent per day in the performance of the team is a 50 percent improvement in just 50 days.

There is an old story of a French general that said, "I need to find out where my troops are headed so I can get in front and lead them there." This is not leadership.

Tip: The fastest way to get a team moving in the right direction is for the leader to get certain individuals on his or her side and believing in him or her and his or her vision. As people move to the leader's "side of the fence," they will have certain influences and slowly bring their followers with them. Target people that can help move the masses.

CELEBRATE THE SMALL VICTORIES It is important for people to see the fruits of their efforts. If the goals that are set will take a long time or more effort than the reward is worth, people will get discouraged and the energy level will dissipate. Set smaller goals that contribute to larger goals. And, when these goals are reached, let it be known and let it be known loudly.

COMMUNICATION One of the attributes a leader must have is the ability to communicate effectively. This communication includes speaking, writing,

---

Real World Scenario

A restaurant opened doing approximately $80,000 per week. However, each month saw a drop in sales numbers. In 8 months, the restaurant was on its third GM, second chef, and seventh or eighth assistant manager. The present executive chef had only been in the unit for 6 weeks when the new GM arrived. In that 6 weeks, the chef had been beaten up so badly that his attitude was negative. The GM knew that he first had to reach the chef to be successful. It was not easy, but the chef saw the GM listening, implementing standards, holding people accountable for these standards, and that the GM was not going to give up. As the communication lines opened up, and the chef started to believe in the GM, the reaction of his kitchen team started to turn positive. The employees that refused to jump the fence to his side started to bring a negative feel to the kitchen. They were quickly weeded out. These same steps had to be taken in the front of the house. The GM set out to really get to know the service, host, and bar staff. It was important to get to know their frustrations and slowly weed out the problems together. The GM stayed in the unit for 14 months and, at the end of this period, turnover was under 100 percent annualized and sales went from $32,000 per week to over $60,000 per week and continued to rise after the GM moved on. In addition, the sous chef was promoted to executive chef in another unit of the chain, and in a short time the two assistant managers were promoted to general managers.

and—as referenced earlier—listening. Every day of a restaurateur's professional career, he or she will need to communicate with other managers, employees, purveyors, and customers. Sometimes the communication will be pleasant, such as employee or management promotions, or outstanding service provided by a staff member. Other times, the communication will not be so pleasant, such as disciplining an employee, calling the produce distributor to find out why half the order is missing from the truck, or apologizing to a customer for their less-than-perfect dining experience.

What is communication? When two people are together they communicate. Even when nothing is being said, communication can be taking place. Communication is not only *what* is being said but *how* it is being said and to whom it is being said.

There are two parts to communication:

1. verbal

2. nonverbal.

The first skill of a good communicator is listening, not speaking. Listening is more difficult because people want to be heard. From infancy, people are encouraged to make speaking sounds. However, through the early years, the encouragement becomes "speak only when spoken to." Parents and teachers have a much more difficult time getting children to listen versus speaking. Human nature is to speak first and listen second.

Watch how people respond when someone is speaking. Very often, the listener has a tendency to speak prior to the speaker finishing his or her thought. Effective leaders and great communicators first listen, process what is being said and how it is being said, and then respond. Some people have a hard time focusing on a thought for a long period of time and have to respond because they don't have the patience or discipline to listen.

Speaking is the second part of the communication equation. When someone wants to convey a message, they put the thought into words and then say what they want to say. If someone cannot convey his or her inner thoughts, no one will know that individual's needs.

Because speaking is much more natural for people than the *art of listening*, miscommunication is usually more common than clear, precise communication. In the beginning of the communication process between two people, one individual becomes a speaker and the other a listener, then the roles are reversed and the process continues. As the communication process develops, each individual becomes more interested in holding on to the speaking part of the process. In so doing, each individual's attention to the listening process becomes less and less. People will only retain 50 percent of what they hear and this percentage diminishes over a short period of time. That is when the phrase "I thought you said. . ." is heard. Watch people's eyes as someone speaks to them. Are they looking into the eyes of the speaker or somewhere else? Listening skills are not easily learned.

Nonverbal expression is body language and facial expressions including eye movement, voice inflection, tone, and volume. Unless the speaker is an accomplished poker player, his or her body, eyes, hands, and face will all convey a message of their own. This body language can sometimes be heard more clearly than what is being spoken by the sender.

Example: A server, Mary, shows up for the shift 30 minutes late. She rushes in quickly past the hostess on the way to the ladies room to get dressed for the night. Her hair is partly wet and uncombed as if she had just gotten out of the shower. On her way to get dressed, she runs into the manager, who looks at her with a scowl and says in a low, unassuming voice, "You're 45 minutes late and that is unacceptable." Knowing she was 30 minutes late and not 45 minutes late, she is about to make her case known when she thinks better of it. The manager keeps his cool and tells her to hurry up, get dressed, come back and find him, and he'll give her the specials. Then, she needs to get her section in order before she can take a table.

Mary scrambles to get ready and is shaking. She finds the manager, who seems to be juggling a half a dozen things. He looks up, sees Mary, quickly checks his watch, reads over the nightly specials, tells her to get her section squared away, and finishes with, "We'll talk later."

Answer the following questions:

How effective is Mary going to be during the shift?

Did the manager handle this appropriately?

What could the manager have done differently?

Let's explore the same situation, handled differently and communicated in a different way.

Mary shows up 30 minutes late for work and looking as if she had just woken up, took a shower, and headed for work. The manager sees her scramble in and asks if everything is all right. Mary says everything is fine now, but it has just been a terrible day. The manager tells Mary to relax, take a deep breath, and go get ready for the shift. Mary, feeling a little more relaxed, gets ready and returns to the manager for the daily specials. He reviews them, again asks if everything is all right, and explains that he got her section ready to go. She thanks him and goes on her way to take care of customers.

Now answer the same questions as asked previously.

The manager might have been no less upset in the second scenario but knew that the way he communicated his feelings would affect the way Mary performed on the shift and how the guests were to be treated. At the end of the shift, the manager can sit down and discuss the tardiness. The manager earns some respect and credibility, the customers are taken care of, and Mary was still counseled about not having called when she was late, and was told that such behavior cannot be tolerated. He never attacked Mary as a person, only the behavior that is not acceptable.

Listening is not just hearing, but truly understanding someone when they speak. Leaders need to search for understanding, because many employees will only speak what is on the surface. In the book *Communicating at Work*,[3] authors Tony Alessandra and Phil Hunsaker describe listening as hard work. Their research shows that an active listener registers increased blood pressure, a higher pulse rate, and more perspiration. It means that true listening takes concentration and work. To listen to what is being said by another person, people must accept that the person speaking has something to say that is important. To develop listening skills, managers must make a focused effort each and every time they enter into a conversation. If something is important to someone and the existing relationship with that person is a priority, whether on a business or a personal level, then active listening should be important.

These tips will help to develop personal listening skills. The following guidelines should be used when conducting a one-on-one counseling session with an employee:

1. Make sure there is enough time to concentrate on the individual. When conducting a one-on-one with a team member, it is important to give this individual total, undivided attention. If the present time is not right, do not get into the discussion.

2. When entering into the communication process, find a quiet, out-of-the-way place where disturbances such as the telephone or other members of the staff cannot or will not interrupt the communication process. Both parties should turn off beepers and cell phones. (The technology wave has brought rudeness to a whole new level.)

3. Make the person feel comfortable. Get a cup of coffee or other soft beverage.

4. Have a pad of paper available, but only write if necessary.

5. Start with, "What can I do for you?"

6. Then *be silent* and listen. Maintain eye contact with the employee; do not look out the window or at the dust on the ceiling vent. If the person rambles, stop the person and reiterate what has been said with, "Let me see if I'm following you. What I hear you saying is _____." This method allows you to get back on topic and ensure that both parties are on the same page.

7. When the person has finished, summarize the conversation. Then dig below the surface if there is an underlying issue. Ask open-ended questions such a why, when, and how. Be cautious not to ask questions in a way that may seem as if doubt is being placed on the individual.

8. Resolve the issue in a way with which both parties feel comfortable.

9. Then, follow up so the employee feels he or she really were heard.

If employees talk to a leader about an issue but feel like they were not truly heard, they will eventually return to the original behavior. Ineffective communication with the staff makes being an effective leader difficult.

People may not listen for a variety of reasons:

1. *Personal feelings.* The leader may have or at least be perceived to have certain negative feelings toward an individual. This emotion could inhibit the leader from hearing anything that person may have to say. If personal

dislike or lack of respect for an individual is allowed to prejudice clear judgment, it hinders the communication process. This problem goes both ways. Somebody that does not respect the leader may find it difficult to listen to what is being said. The leader must clear this roadblock if there is to be any effective communication up or down the ladder.

2. *Hidden agendas build mistrust.* Communication must be honest and open.

3. *Different priorities.* If people are working on different goals, they each may have a different set of priorities. This breakdown in communication happened somewhere during the goal setting. A leader, to be cohesive with the troops, needs to share a vision and work toward the same goals or a communication breakdown will occur, because what the speaker talks about is not important to the receiver.

4. *Other pressing issues.* Pressing issues can make the mind drift to those issues and cause a loss of focus on the present situation. Consider the following example: A managers' meeting is called for Monday morning; however, the weekend was extremely busy, one cook did not show up, and two deliveries are coming in the back door. The chef will be more worried about the immediate tasks at hand than listening to anything that is being said at that meeting. Communicate when the audience can concentrate on the communication process.

5. *Poor delivery by the speaker.* If a speaker wants someone to listen to him or her, then the speaker should be excited about the topic.

6. *Negative emotion.* If a speaker says something that upsets the listening audience either from ignorance or misinformation, the listeners stop hearing what is being said. At a meeting with a restaurant chain's CEO, several of people in the audience were turned off by some of the statements the CEO made and, in turn, tuned out the balance of the message the CEO was trying to deliver. Here is what happened: this chain had three concepts and was about to open its fourth concept. The meeting was with the upper level management of one division of the multiconcept chain. The CEO was being questioned on the commitment to the future of the division. The managers wanted specifics from the CEO about plans for this concept. But he only talked about the senior concept, which he founded some 15 years earlier. He discussed how great that concept was and how the concept was holding up the rest of the company. The managers' interest did not lie with the senior concept, but with the concept they operated, because that is where they had put their hard work and that was the concept on which their futures relied.

THE AUDIENCE When speaking to a person or a group of people, it helps to know the audience. Speaking to a group of investors would require different content than if the talk was geared to the service staff, even if the talk was on the same subject. For instance, if the content of the talk was about increasing sales during the next quarter, the talk with investors might include:

1. previous quarter results,
2. comparison of results to previous year results,
3. sales trends,
4. specific goals,
5. marketing plans, or
6. training and development plans for the staff.

The investors are looking for facts, plans and enthusiasm. In speaking with the service staff, the talk may include:

1. sales objectives in dollars and percentages,
2. what the sales increase will do for them (the "**what's in it for me**" syndrome—WIFM),
3. marketing initiatives and the staff involvement in those initiatives, or
4. sales classes, concentration on salesmanship at pre-meal meetings, and contests with incentives.

The staff wants motivation and wants to know what they will get out of it if they are willing to put in this extra effort. If the talk geared for the staff carries the same content as the talk for the investors, the staff may not pay attention or understand the direction of the talk. They want to make money.

Once the audience is identified, it becomes easier to formulate thoughts into words. When speaking to an individual or a group avoid.

1. Using the phrase "in other words." If the other words better describe the thrust of what is being said, use those words first. However, sometimes what is said may not be understood by the entire audience or all of the audience. This is determined by eye contact. Merely ask "does the audience understand what I am saying?"
2. Using words that may require half the audience to pull out a dictionary. Use terms and phrases geared toward your audience.
3. Using the "um" and "ya know" phrases.
4. Speaking at a pace that allows people to drift or lose the train of thought. The human mind can process information much more quickly than it can be spoken.

Preventing Turnover

As referenced earlier in the book, finding, hiring, and retaining quality employees will remain a top priority for restaurants into the future. Many factors affect hiring issues. However, *having quality* employees is a must. The old saying "hire a duck, train a duck, and you end up with a trained duck" refers to the fact that only by starting with a quality candidate can the restaurant end up with a star. "Well, he's a body" and "I am short-staffed" is heard all too often in the restaurant business. Meeting the minimum requirements to hold a job does not mean the applicant is qualified to work in an industry that thrives on taking care of people.

As the labor pool of restaurant workers shrinks and more restaurants open, learning to keep employees is a critical to being successful. Every year, different figures are released concerning the cost of high turnover. This number is an educated guesstimate, as placing an exact figure on it is difficult. The reasons it is difficult to place an exact number include inexact estimates of the following factors:

1. the dollar amount it took to train the individual that left;
2. the mistakes they had made early on that cost in customer service, lost product, and improperly prepared food;
3. the cost of advertising for new help; and
4. the cost of training the new individual.

And the cycle continues. What can be done about it? Start at the beginning. See the following sections for more information.

LOCATING CANDIDATES Help wanted signs are almost a way of life at many restaurants. Placing an ad in the newspaper worked to some degree years ago. But one must really consider whether a newspaper ad will bring in the quality that is needed. One of the biggest truths facing a restaurant is that *quality candidates* are probably already working for the competition or in a different industry.

The attitude that restaurants must adopt is that everyone and anyone is a candidate and ways to find these candidates include:

1. go to any store where customers receive good customer service and you will locate a good candidate;
2. drive through a fast food restaurant, and note the person that takes the order and puts it together with a bright smile and good attitude, and you have located another candidate;
3. handing out business cards to friends and family members should be automatic—if someone you know comes into contact with someone that is a possible candidate, they should hand over the card;
4. customers in the restaurant could be potential employment candidates; and
5. current employees.

Most managers look at how to motivate and "pump up" their staff once they come to work. That is too late to discover whether the right staff has been hired. The wrong people might work there, and attempting to motivate the wrong people will only provide frustration.

Although experience in the kitchen is a plus, it is not always an asset when searching for front of the house staff such as greeters, servers, and bartenders. Kitchen staff can be trained and developed by working through positions such as dishwasher to light prep to cold side, sauté, and grill cook. When searching for front of the house staff, look for attitude, desire, and passion, which are more important than years of experience. Front of the house individuals need an outgoing personality, good communication skills, a sense of humor, and the ability to think on their feet. They do not need 3 years of experience. They may not have been trained properly by their previous employer and may bring bad habits with them that maybe hard to break.

APPLICATIONS An application is a formal request for employment. The application itself should only contain sufficient background information to permit the manager to make a preliminary evaluation and decide if further interviews should be arranged.

Applications cannot directly or inadvertently violate federal, state, or local statutes prohibiting various types of discrimination. Information requested on the application relating to membership in a union or reference to a specific race, color, nationality, or religion may be a basis for discrimination.

An application can tell a lot about a candidate and the application should be read before entering into an interview. Look on the application for danger signs referred to as **red flags** that might signify some problems, such as:

1. lack of attention to detail,

2. employment gaps,

3. length of times at jobs,

4. reasons for leaving jobs, and

5. whether the applicant will willingly allow a manager to contact references.

Lack of attention to detail is a critical deficiency in most restaurant positions. Servers, kitchen staff, and bartenders have to pay attention to many details in their daily tasks and, quite often, must do so under pressure. If the applicant cannot take the time to fill out an application correctly, will they be able to pay attention to the details of the job?

Employment gaps are a definite issue. If an applicant is willing to leave a job without gainful employment awaiting them, there is a definite problem that must be questioned. It can point to a lack of pride in an individual and he or she may just do the same again. For example, if a person leaves a job because he was not receiving enough hours, but is willing to go to zero hours, this is an indication of this person's thought processes. Or, if a person quit to spite her boss, but did herself more harm than what was done to the boss, how will that person perform in the future?

People that jump jobs often are a problem. The usual reason for job jumping is that the person did not get along with someone. If this is a pattern, the question must be asked, "Does the problem lie with the applicant or with the other people they left?" The entire restaurant staff must be able to get along with each other, because everyone will be working in close proximity and under pressure. If one person has a problem getting along with others, that person will have a negative effect on the rest of the staff.

Do not accept at face value the reason someone gives for leaving a job. Use open-ended questions to get the applicant to talk about the reasons. Clear up any issues immediately, not 3 months into the job.

Do reference checks. If an applicant does not know names and phone numbers at the time of filling out the application, ask the person to call back with the names and numbers. If the applicant cannot offer references, this signals a problem.

The Interview Scheduling interview times should be flexible. Flexibility ensures the good candidates *do not* get away and work for the competition. Some restaurants have a policy of interviewing only between certain hours. If there is a staffing problem, interviewing candidates should be a top priority and not be done only when it is convenient to the manager. If someone approaches a manager during the meal period and asks for an application, the response should be "Sure, let me get that for you." Before the person fills out the application, talk with them for just a minute. It should be evident within that minute whether this person is worth pursuing and interviewing formally.

Once candidates arrive for an interview, it is time for them to make a good impression. Allow them to do so. If the interviewer does all of the talking, it is difficult to discover anything about the individual. It is impossible to make a good, clear decision about people unless they are given the opportunity to talk about themselves, their goals, and their ambitions.

Effective interviewing is an art form that takes time to master. This skill is not inborn or immediately developed once someone possesses a title of owner or manager. However, most managers devote very little time the necessary skills to conduct effective interviews. Some people carry a card of questions to ask. This becomes more of a checklist and the manager becomes a slave to the card instead of focusing on the person. When conducting an interview, certain elements comprise the interview:

1. objective,
2. format, and
3. topics.

The objective is what the interviewer is trying to accomplish. Objectives include gathering information from the candidate on the ability to perform the job, the desire of the candidate to be employed by the restaurant and perform the necessary job, and for the interviewer to provide information on the job.

The format is how the interviewer enters into the interview process. Formats can be formal or informal, can focus on establishing rapport with the candidate, center on questions to ask the candidate, and involve listening to questions from the candidate and offering in-depth information about the restaurant.

Topics discussed during the interview should include previous work experience, education, personal goals, and the desire to work in the restaurant business.

At least two people should interview a potential candidate and try to schedule them on two separate days. This strategy provides for at least three benefits to the manager:

1. both interviewers get an immediate feel for the applicant's ability to arrive on time;
2. there are two perspectives on the applicant; and
3. the first manager, if a junior manager, can develop interview skills.

The first step in conducting an interview is to put the candidate at ease. Even very outgoing people can be intimidated in an unfamiliar setting. Building rapport with candidates is a key part of getting them to open up and talk freely.

The interview should be conducted in a quiet area where there will be no interruptions. Accepting phone calls or taking care of other issues while conducting an interview tells candidates that they are not that important. In a labor-intensive business, all candidates should be considered important.

The interviewer enters into an interview with certain goals:

1. to discover if the candidate has the ability to perform the technical aspects of the job;
2. to find out if the applicant has the educational background for the position;
3. to learn if the candidate has any relevant work experience for the position;
4. to get a feel for the commitment level the applicant has for long-term employment;
5. to see if the candidate will blend well with the culture that has been developed; and
6. to determine whether the applicant displays the necessary passion, personality, and attitude.

The applicant also has several objectives when entering into an interview:

1. to sell his or her ability to the interviewer;
2. to gather information about the job; and
3. to get a feel as to whether the chemistry fits between the applicant and the restaurant culture that has been developed.

There are many times when a candidate would fit the restaurant's needs and would probably desire long-term employment. However, because of a lack of interview skills, the candidate can be lost in the interview process if the interviewer decides they would not be a good fit. A typical interview might go as follows:

INTERVIEWER: "Good morning Jim, my name is Bill Thompson, I'm the general manager."

APPLICANT: "Good morning, Bill."

First, get the pleasantries aside and see if the applicant would like a cup of coffee or a soft beverage. Once the interviewer sits down with the applicant, the total focus and attention should be on the applicant. The interviewer should have previously read the application and the interviewer should have developed some specific questions to ask. The manager should not use the application as a crutch. Too often, managers hold an application and flip it back over and over as if they are going to find something on it that they did not already see. Interviewers should use the application as reference only and place their attention on the person and not the paper. Make the interviewee feel comfortable.

Look for information with open-ended questions. Open-ended questions are questions that cannot be answered with a simple "yes" or "no." Some explanation must accompany the answer.

INTERVIEWER: "So, Jim, what position are you looking for?"

APPLICANT: "I prefer the grill position, but I can perform other kitchen responsibilities such as pantry, prep, or sauté."

This immediately informs the interviewer that the person has at least been in a kitchen by the terminology he used.

Follow-up questions might be:

INTERVIEWER: "When did you start working in the restaurant business?"

"What was your first job in the business?"

"Did you work in any other business prior to the restaurant business?"

"Where have you most recently worked?"

At this point, the interviewer is searching for applicant's ability to perform the job. Certain positions might be trainable and a novice can come in and learn the position. However, in a grill position, some level of experience is most likely desirable. Once it has been determined that the applicant has the skills necessary to perform the job, it is time to find out about the person. The best way to do this is divert the "business" talk to something else. This is simply to build a rapport with the candidate.

INTERVIEWER: "What do you do when you are not working?"

Here the interviewer is looking for something of interest that might help the interviewer and candidate make a connection. Whether that connection is sports, a school they attended, hobbies, or anything that may be of interest to the candidate and any member of the team. Friendships that are developed are a great way to keep staff. Keep up with the small talk for a couple of minutes and then return to the business topics.

Determine whether the applicant has a steady work history, usually leaving one job to go to a better, higher-paying position.

Follow-up questions to support this:

Interviewer: "Where are you working now?"

"Why are you looking to leave?"

"How long did you work there?"

"If you don't find something else, will you remain at that job?"

"When I call for references what will I be told about your work history and you as a person?"

"How well do you get along with other people?"

"Have you ever had a problem with another employee, customer, or manager? Please explain."

"What are your personal goals? Where do you see yourself 5 years from now?"

This information will give some background of the applicant's personality and integrity. If an answer is unclear, rephrase the question to make sure there is clear communication. Offer the applicant some information on the job duties and some history about the restaurant. Talk about the goals and philosophies of the restaurant. Then, ask if the candidate would like to ask any questions.

If an applicant is applying for a technically skilled position in the kitchen, walk him or her through the kitchen and introduce the person to the staff. See how the applicant responds to the staff. Also, see if the applicant knows his or her way around the kitchen and whether he or she was able to sell his or her knowledge.

One important part of the interview is to make sure that the applicant fits the needs of the restaurant. If the need is for a weekend grill cook and the applicant needs every other Saturday off, there is no match. Likewise, if a server comes to you and needs to make $500 per week in tips but the top three performers only average $400 per week, the server's employment will be short-lived.

When the interview is complete, tell the applicant whether or not there is a fit. If there is, inform the applicant that references will be checked. Give a specific start date. Never let an applicant hang on whether or not they will have a job. Be honest and upfront with applicants. If there is not a fit, let them know that.

Once the decision has been made that the individual will be an asset to the team, it is time to reiterate the expectations, standards, and the level of commitment it will take to be a successful part of the team. Assume nothing. An employee should never be able to say, "I didn't know." Inform new team members that the restaurant is about to make an investment in them by taking the time to develop their skills for the job they were hired. Although servers and bartenders will be concerned about the lack of tips for the training period, they need to understand that the investment that is being made is costly and that while they are training they are not producing revenue for the restaurant.

One important aspect of hiring quality candidates is that quality breeds quality. When a restaurant has quality, professional people working for them, quality, professional people will knock on the door for a job.

Always contact references. Problems can be avoided by checking references. A reference check gives some indications about the candidate. If the reference gives a glowing review, odds are the candidate is a good hire. If the reference says nothing or "what would you like to know?" this could be an issue. References do not want to give negative references, so they will not be liable, so they say nothing. A reference that speaks positively does so because they believe it or they want the candidate to find another job. There are numerous stories of people checking references and finding out that the person they are interviewing is wanted by the police. There are also stories of no checks being done and the employer later learning that a person is a criminal when the individual commits a crime at work.

There are many reasons to hire or not to hire someone. Do not get caught up in the an applicant's level of experience unless the position requires a certain amount of experience. Look for personality, maturity, ability to learn, attitude, and professionalism.

Some danger signs revealed in the interview process include:

1. applicants who can not give good reasons for leaving their last job;
2. applicants that do not want references to be checked;
3. applicant that are willing to accept much less than they are making now;
4. applicants that have domestic problems—*do not* delve into this—just know that it can be a problem;
5. too many jobs in the past few years; or
6. large gaps in employment history.

Another issue managers encounter is when a present employee knows the applicant and has something to say. Unless this person can be completely trusted, do not automatically reject the applicant. At times it is just a personal issue.

LEGAL REQUIREMENTS There are legal ramifications in questions asked in the interview process as well as reasons for not hiring. These are some of the questions you may not ask in pre-employment interviews. Please review this with an attorney, as an attorney may insist on more stringent interviewing.

1. date of birth or age
2. birthplace
3. birthplace of relatives
4. applicant's religious denomination or affiliation
5. attendance of religious services
6. questions indicating race, color, or reference to complexion of skin
7. requiring a photo
8. date of citizenship
9. date of arrival in the United States.

INTERVIEWING AND ADA GUIDELINES

1. Make sure the interview spot is accessible.

2. If you are in doubt as to whether a person with a disability needs help, ask, "May I be of assistance?"

3. Establish a relaxed atmosphere with the applicant (small talk).

4. Describe in detail the critical and essential functions of the job, never indicating whether the applicant is capable or not to perform these functions.

5. If the applicant has a disability that is known or visible to the employer, the employer may ask how the applicant can perform the function. There may be a need for reasonable accommodation. If reasonable accommodation is deemed necessary, check with an attorney.

Orientation

When an employee arrives at a new job, anxiety is common. A new place, new people and new things to learn all contribute to this anxiety. New employee orientation has several objectives:

1. to place the individual at ease and get them feeling comfortable in the new surroundings,

2. to introduce the person to the staff and management,

3. to set expectations for the upcoming weeks,

4. to review the restaurant's goals,

5. to instill the standards that make the restaurant a success, and

6. to set a training program and guidelines.

Training and Development

Now that an applicant has been hired, learn what you can about that person: their desires, their goals, and their motivations. By understanding each individual on a personal level, you can help your individual staff members find personal job satisfaction. As the new employee becomes more comfortable in the position and around the other team members, it is less likely that they will leave for unknown territory. Never lose that personal touch. Say hello in the morning and good-bye at night. Say "thank you" for a great job each day. Show appreciation to your staff.

Once a candidate has been hired, there must be a training period. This training period is for the new member of the team to learn the technical part of his job and to become comfortable with the restaurant and the other staff members. This training program should be well documented and be a priority of the new member, management, and the rest of the staff.

If the training program for a server is 2 weeks long, let the employee know that it will be 2 full weeks of training regardless of experience level. If the training period is by-passed, the restaurant standard is being lowered. Sometimes, kitchen staff members are not trained properly because they are paid more money and drive up the labor cost. The kitchen staff needs to be developed and requires the same investment as the front of the house staff.

During the training program, make sure that the new employees understand that their level of commitment to the program will set the stage for their future success. It is also a good idea to let them know that feedback and input on the training program is welcome. This helps to constantly improve the training and allows the new employee to feel like part of the team. But, do not give this feedback loop "lip service." Show sincere interest in their input.

The training program needs to include verbal and written testing, as well as role-playing.

Retention

It is tough to retain a quality staff. Business is directly affected by the quality and stability of the entire staff, from dishwasher to manager. Everyone counts.

Every person has a different motivation to stay in any situation, including a job. Is it money? Is it stability or a comfort zone? Is it scheduling flexibility? Is it social interaction? Or, is it a combination of several? Know the answer to this question for each employee.

Each individual should have goals. If a server is not performing to the standards set, find out what can be done to help that individual. If the manager simply starts putting a server on the slower shifts, this demotivates the individual and the performance will suffer even more until the person eventually work his or her way out the door. Then, the cycle will start all over again. The skill that it takes to develop an individual is known as **coaching**. Simply writing off these individuals does not solve the problem. Once someone is hired, there is a commitment made between two parties. Hold up your end.

Exit Interviews

Exit interviews are used to find out why people are leaving employment. Conducting these interviews should be standard operating procedure. Some employees might not want to discuss it. In such a case, there should be a form for these employees to fill out that will give an idea of why they are leaving.

Why do you care about people that are leaving? Because you just might find a pattern of reasons people are leaving that can be easily fixed once it is identified. People leave for many reasons, and many of those reasons make perfect sense. However, if you are losing people because they do not feel that they are being taken care of, the exit interview will tell you this.

You do not win with high turnover.

Conflict Management

Conflict management entails dealing with any conflict that may arise between any two individuals or groups of people and finding a positive outcome for all parties involved. When working with people, conflict will inevitably arise. Conflict can occur among guests, employees, guests and employees, and management and any possible combination. Recognizing the conflict early is critical to eliminating future issues.

One of the worst things a leader can do when a conflict arises is to bury his or her head and hope the problem goes away. The problem will not evaporate. It will only fester and become worse. One of the main points about "managing" conflict is that the leader cannot automatically take sides. Listen, listen, and listen some more to both sides. Do not make assumptions.

Here is an example from the bar manager point of view: A server is promoted to bartender because of personality and work ethic. After initial training, the new bartender is given a test that every bartender receives, but fails it. The bar manager talks to the bartender and makes a game plan to help her get better. The bartender does not get better and personal conflicts flare up between the bar manager and bartender. The bartender still serves tables as her main job. Whenever she is waiting tables, she is very demanding on the bar manager. The new bartender approaches a manager and tells her side of the story. The manager has to approach the bar manager in a nonthreatening way and ask what the situation is. There are a couple of pitfalls in this scenario. First, if the manager and the bar manager have a good relationship, the conversation might be almost joking and half-hearted. This must be avoided. The restaurant manager is responsible both for individual employees and, legally, to investigate any issues. The manager must investigate sincerely and not take the situation lightly.

Never, under any circumstance, should a manager allow any conflict—no matter how small or insignificant it may seem to go unchecked. It might be extremely significant to someone else. Document all conversations and any witness statements. If the conflict is of a serious nature, such as harassment, the situation needs to be followed up until all parties are satisfied that it has been dealt with appropriately.

If someone files a harassment charge, *do not* automatically discipline the accused without investigation. Do take the charge seriously and investigate quickly and methodically. Consult an attorney for advice as soon as possible. This is serious and can cost dearly.

Always be swift in action, fair in decisions, and face problems head on!

Coaching and Counseling

Upholding standards in the restaurant business is critical to the success of a restaurant. Holding all employees to these standards is also critical. If an employee does something outside of an acceptable level of these standards, the manager must counsel the employee.

Counseling someone is a learned art and often very difficult. It is not a "parent to child" talk. Use the following strategies:

1. enforce the standard across the board, never showing favoritism to anyone,

2. counsel in a private area—never discuss employee issues in front of anyone else,

3. present the violation and allow the employee to explain from his or her perspective,

4. attack the behavior and never the individual,

5. document the conversation and enter it into the employee file, and

6. leave the table with a clear understanding of what is expected and write specific goals to change the behavior.

Before terminating an employee, management must be sure to document everything and make sure the employee understands that termination is possible if the behavior is not changed. Any termination or discipline should be clearly documented to show a progression of counseling that did not result in improved performance by the employee.

Performance Appraisals

Performance appraisals give feedback to managers and employees on their performance as measured against:

1. the standards of the restaurant,

2. goals for the individual, and

3. previous appraisals.

The frequency of appraisals is a personal choice, but should occur at least twice a year, especially if there is a pay raise connected with the evaluation. Team members may be evaluated more often than management, such as quarterly, because the more feedback they receive, the more likely they are to perform to the standard.

During any appraisal, no one should be shocked at the performance evaluation. If an employee is shocked, something went wrong during the day-to-day running of the business. The formal appraisal should not take the place of every-day communication. Management must be straightforward and not wait until appraisal time to give employees honest feedback on performance.

A great opportunity to give constant feedback is an informal one-on-one. This is simply a 5-minute discussion about performance, strengths, and weaknesses.

Never criticize someone in front of others, and never praise behind closed doors.

Performance appraisals are not necessarily observations about past performance, but rather discussions on how to affect future behavior. Always evaluate what you are expecting from an individual. Employee appraisals would include:

- teamwork,
- reliability,
- professionalism,
- salesmanship,
- position knowledge,
- appearance,
- attitude, and
- guest concern.

Manager appraisals include:

- professionalism;
- leadership;
- hiring;
- training and development;
- communication skills;
- problem solving;
- guest focus;
- standards, and
- financial understanding and planning.

You get what you reward.

One-on-One Appraisals

The chapter earlier discussed the informal on-on-one. A formal one-on-one is somewhat different. It should be done with three or four employees a week. This way, there is constant improvement in performance and morale.

A one-on-one is simple and should consist of the following:

1. set aside about 20 minutes;
2. allow the employee to analyze his or her performance;
3. give your analysis of the individual's performance;
4. compare performance against the standard—never compare the individual's performance against the performance of another;

5. give specifics from notes you have kept;

6. infuse some small talk just to find out about the individual: spouse's name, children's names, classes they take, goals, aspirations, and so on;

7. ascertain how the employee's working relationship is with fellow employees; and

8. conclude with an understanding of what is expected and some small goals for the individual—the should tell you what his or her goals are.

It is always good to end a one-on-one by saying, "thank you for your time," and something like, "I am glad you are part of the team." This will go further than anything else you can say or do!

Documentation

Management should keep records on all interactions with employees. Once a potential applicant fills out an application and hands it over to a manager, the restaurant assumes the responsibility to track that application. If an applicant does not qualify for any job on the restaurant, the application should be kept on file with a note attached as to why this individual does not qualify. As a good practice, do not write directly on the application.

If the applicant is hired, there is specific information needed for that employee, including a W-4, an I-9, the application, and anything the employee is asked to sign in reference to their job (i.e., an employee signing a form stating that they received the employee guide). This is important for future reference.

Any appraisals or coaching sessions that are conducted should be entered into the employee's file. This is especially critical if there are performance issues with the employee.

Any documentation, including communication logs, should also be kept. Never write negative comments about an employee and never use foul language when writing in these logs.

■ CHAPTER REVIEW

Many businesspeople spend years learning their craft but little time to learn about how to handle their most important asset—*people*. Success is rarely achieved if a business owner does not interact well with people. It is critical to understand that good people skills are required in the restaurant business. A restaurant owner depends on high quality people to:

1. cook the food,

2. serve the drinks, and

3. interact with other team members.

That same business owner must be able to recognize and develop the necessary skills of the staff in order to be successful.

■ KEY TERMS

areas of responsibility

coaching

conflict management

counseling

mission statement

performance appraisals

red flags

SMART

time management

■ REVIEW QUESTIONS

1. Explain the bicycle theory.

2. Why could it be argued that making promises is a mistake?

3. Explain SMART Goals.

4. List five questions that can not be asked on an application.

5. What does management gain by conducting exit interviews?

Notes

1. Anthony Alessandra and Phillip Hunsaker, *The Art of Managing People*, Simon & Schuster, Adult Publishing Group, 1986.

2. Hyrum W. Smith, *SMART Goals—The 10 Natural Laws of Successful Time Management* – © 1994 Warner Books.

3. Tony Alessandra and Phil Hunsaker, *Communicating at Work*, Fireside Books, Simon and Schuster, 1993.

Conclusion

All the previous chapters are designed to give you a solid foundation for building a rewarding and successful career in the restaurant business, whether as an owner or manager. We covered a variety of related topics, but no book in the world can give you all the knowledge or experience you need to be successful. Learning by doing and observing is the key to success.

If you are not making any mistakes, you are not doing anything.

Learn from mistakes, make decisions, and watch out for the comfort of your guests. After all, they are the reason we are in business. They count!

SUCCESS IS IN THE CLIMB; WHEN YOU THINK YOU'VE REACHED THE TOP, LOOK UP BEYOND THE NEXT HORIZON. THERE IS MORE TO CONQUER.

So never be complacent because good is not good enough.

Industry Support

A tremendous amount of support is available to restaurateurs. Local, state, and national chapters of the restaurant association are the first step. The members' knowledge is extensive. The National Restaurant Association publishes a weekly trade magazine that covers many topics and trends. The NRA also has products available that will assist owners operate more efficiently. Once you are a member, you may receive discounts on many of the products and publications.

Many local restaurants work together to drive business into their areas. *Good operators work with each other versus trying to beat each other*. There will be many times your neighbor will borrow product from you and vice versa.

Join the professional associations, become active in local chapters, and the restaurant business will be more enjoyable. Some of the associations include:

National Licensed Beverage Association

National Restaurant Association

Dietary Managers Association

American Hotel & Motel Association

The Internet

Restaurant owners use the Internet for several reasons. The most obvious is the development of a web page where customers can view exciting new menu items, milestones, awards received, online discounts for regular customers, and even offer feedback to the restaurant. But the Internet offers much more than simply posting a web page.

The Internet is a tool for doing market analysis, researching recipes, keeping up with hot trends in business, and accessing other web pages designed to help restaurants.

There are training seminars, forums, books, manuals, and contacts through the Internet. Access to the Internet is almost imperative in today's world. If needed, take a class to learn how to use such a powerful tool.

Employee Manual

An employee manual is used to set the standards of the restaurant. Do not over-burden the staff or management with a cumbersome document. Several points need to be addressed upfront with the staff for execution and guest satisfaction purposes as well as legal protection for the owners. The following pages contain generic documents that can be used as a base for developing a restaurant-specific employee manual.

Each of the following areas must be addressed when developing an employee manual. These areas include the standards and how the standards will be enforced:

Dress Code

Makeup

Jewelry

Hair

Smoking Regulations

Payday

Schedule—Posted Where and When

Shift Changes

Define Covering a Shift

Define On-Time for Work

Disciplinary Action

Sexual Harassment

Vacations

Calling in Sick

Welcome

In joining the _____ team, you are joining a team of people dedicated to delivering the highest standards in dining in the region and we are committed to delivering a great dining experience to every guest that comes into our restaurant.

You were selected to join this team because we believe you are mature and possess these same high standards. You will become a very important part of the team, as each team member is critical to the success of the restaurant. Our commitment is to deliver a great dining experience in our food, beverages, atmosphere, and service. We can only do that through hiring the best people.

We want all guests to enjoy their time with us as just a guest in our own home would. That responsibility lies with each individual and as part of the team. You as a member of that team must make that personal commitment.

This manual is intended to outline policies, procedures, and operational philosophies of _____. Through this manual, we hope to convey as much information as possible, to help set a pleasant, fun, mutually profitable, and safe work atmosphere as well as create a great restaurant.

Please read this manual carefully and refer to it often. It will assist you in being successful with us.

It is our belief to deliver great customer service you must understand what *great customer service* is. Also, you must be able to identify *bad* customer service. In so doing, you can make the necessary compensation and adjustment, to make a positive situation out of a bad situation, as well as learn from the experience.

A Great Dining Experience

A *great dining experience* does not start, nor does it end, with serving high quality food. The food is definitely an integral part of what we deliver, but there is so much more to delivering a great dining experience. Food happens to be, along with beverages, the product that you can see, touch, and taste. Service is a bit more abstract. You can't put your arms around service. Yet it is vital that we deliver *outstanding* service to each and every guest, each and every time. Remember, we are only as good as our last guest says we are.

Good service is done through care and passion,

Bad service happens all by itself.

There are several components that we must have to be successful:

- Quality Food—It's a must. The highest quality ingredients, proper preparation, and appealing plate presentation allow us to deliver great food.
- Atmosphere—People must feel comfortable when dining or enjoying a drink. Comfortable dining is where the person in jeans can sit next to and talk to the person in a suit. All guests are *welcome* and we need to make them feel that way.
- Service—Caring service where each member of the team takes personal ownership in the dining experience.

- Value—Competition for the dining dollar gets tougher and tougher each day. We need to deliver all of the above in such a way that when guests leave our establishment, they feel they received a good value for their hard earned dollar. That will ensure our long-term success.

- A Team—The only thing people can do on their own is fail. It takes a team to be successful.

Equal Employment Opportunity

_____ is committed to recruit, hire, train, and promote employees without discrimination to age, sex, race, national origin, disability, veteran status, or sexual orientation. This policy extends to all aspects of employment including salary, promotions, job assignments, and discipline. _____ maintains an open door policy whereby any member of management is available to discuss any problems or issues that may arise from neglect of this policy. If the manager does not satisfactorily handle the issue, it should be brought to the attention of another manager.

Guest Relations

It is our goal to have each and every guest not only return but also to tell others about our restaurant. It is critical to our success that we make each guest feel important and we will take good care of the guest while they are here with us. We must add to their relaxation and help them get away from the frustrations of every day. This means that every one of us, from the cook to the dishwasher and the host to the manager, takes ownership of the guest's experience. We want to know our guests and we want them to get to know us.

Grooming

Proper, professional grooming standards are very important in the restaurant business. All employees are expected to maintain good personal hygiene, which includes being bathed, teeth brushed, and deodorant applied. In addition, if you are dealing directly with guests, you must adhere to the following:

- hair must be clean and pulled back so as not to cover the face;
- mustaches and beards must be neat and trimmed or you must be clean-shaven; partial beards or beards in the process of growing are not permitted;
- no face rings besides earrings are permitted;

- excessive jewelry is not permitted—this is at the discretion of management because health risks are involved;

- fingernails must be trimmed and cleaned—no chipped or outrageous color polish may be used; excessively long nails are not permitted due to health reasons; and

- chewing gum is not allowed on the floor or behind the bar.

Employee Meals

In order for the staff to become more familiar with the food, the ingredients, and the presentation (all of which will help the staff sell the food, therefore enhancing the guest's dining experience), employee meals are offered at discounted prices. Employees are offered a 25 percent discount on working days. A 15 percent discount is offered on nonworking days and can include friends and family once a month. Fully compensated meals are offered for employees working doubles or the closing shift.

Employees as Guests

We want everyone to be proud of where they work and enjoy our food and atmosphere. You are welcome to do so, but please remember that we are in business and may not be able to accommodate you during busy times. Please understand and work with us on this.

An employee is not allowed to sit at the bar at any time.

Performance-Based Employment

_____ is a performance-based company. This means that performance of your job will determine shifts, promotions, and pay incentives. Seniority will not determine any of these.

Attendance

We hire each individual to fill a mutual need. If your availability changes from the initial availability given to us, and your performance meets our standards, we will do everything possible to continue to fulfill your scheduling needs. It may, however, not be possible to fulfill your needs 100 percent if our needs do not coincide.

Because we did hire you and schedule you accordingly, it is imperative that each individual shows up at the scheduled time and fulfills his or her responsibilities. If you do not do this, you will put a strain on the rest of your team and impede us from reaching our goal of delivering our standard of guest satisfaction. Repeated offenses will result in disciplinary action up to and including termination.

■ scheduled time means you must be here at that time;

■ if you call to inform us you will be late, you will receive a 10-minute grace period;

■ you are responsible for covering your shift if you will not be able to work;

■ request time off is simply that—a request. We will do everything possible to honor your request, provided we are given sufficient notice; and

■ if you are to be absent, you need to call and speak only to a manager—do not leave a message with another employee.

Smoking Policy

_____ will only allow smoking with the permission of a manager and never inside the building. Smoking is a privilege and must be viewed that way. The guest must come first always. Smoking will take place only in designated locations. Hands must be washed immediately after smoking and a breath mint used.

Misconduct, Discipline, and Terminations

_____ will achieve our stated success only through presenting a professional image and each person conducting themselves in a mature manner. In order to do that, it becomes necessary to ensure that the policies and procedures are followed. It is unfortunate that when mature people take on a responsibility, it becomes necessary to enforce policy through disciplinary action. However, it is also human nature to make mistakes. We will also handle each disciplinary action on a case-by-case basis, taking into account the severity of the infraction, the length of service from the employee, and the past record of the employee. We will discipline in a progressive counseling way, but some infractions may result in immediate termination. Otherwise, our discipline procedure will be:

verbal warning

written warning

final written warning

termination

The following are some of the behaviors that are unacceptable and will result in disciplinary action up to and including termination:

- verbal or physical misconduct toward supervisors, employees, guests, or anyone you come into contact with during working hours;
- knowingly serving alcoholic beverages to someone under the legal drinking age;
- fighting or unsafe horseplay;
- dishonest acts such as theft, falsification of records, or misuse of company supplies—theft may result in criminal prosecution;
- insubordination;
- violation of any company policy as outlined in this guide; and
- unsatisfactory job performance.

Alcohol, Drug Abuse

It is completely inappropriate for an employee to arrive at work under the influence of or in the possession of alcohol or drugs. It does not make for a safe and fun workplace atmosphere. Any violation of this policy will result in termination.

Again, we welcome you to the _____ family and hope that you enjoy your work here. We also hope that you contribute to the fun, excitement, and energy that are generated here.

Remember, if we don't take care of the guest, someone else will.

Job Descriptions

Job descriptions should be used for three main reasons:

1. legal protection for you;
2. allows you to set and maintain a standard; and
3. employees know their exact responsibilities.

    Again, these job descriptions are meant to be used guidelines:

    General Manager

    Assistant Manager

    Executive Chef/Kitchen Manager

    Sous Chef

    Bar Manager

    Bartender

    Host/Hostess

    Server

    Bus Person

    Food Runner

    Line Cook

    Prep Cook

    Dishwasher

General Manager

Job Description

The general manager (GM) is directly responsible for the proper operation of all departments. This includes meeting our high standard on quality, operating a clean and safe environment, while achieving sales and budget cost goals.

The GM has overall authority for the day-to-day operations of the business following the standards of _____.

Specific Duties and Responsibilities

Leadership—The GM is directly responsible for creating a fun, clean, upbeat, and productive work environment. Projection of a positive can-do attitude is required at all times. The GM is responsible for development of the staff in all aspects of the operation including but not limited to specific job duties, customer awareness and service, and sanitation standards.

Personnel—Responsible for recruiting, hiring, training, developing, and scheduling a quality staff, which will ensure quality food being served in a timely manner to our guests.

Recruiting and hiring responsibilities include the following:

■ establish and maintain appropriate staffing levels and keep informed to any changes that may impact staffing needs (including special functions, holidays, and a staff member who may change availability or leave the employment of the restaurant);

■ ensure all employees' personnel files are complete and up to date in accordance with any state or federal laws;

■ keep turnover to the minimum so as not to have a negative impact on customer service or labor cost; and

■ conduct exit interviews to determine any trends that might be costing turnover among the ranks.

Training and development responsibilities include the following:

■ establish a training program where all employees are trained thoroughly in their respective positions prior to be allowed to operate solo;

■ establish a training program to ensure all employees are educated in the use of all equipment; and

■ establish a cleaning program all employees are familiar with and use proper sanitation procedures.

Administration responsibilities include the following:

■ complete quarterly review of all staff; and

■ maintain accurate paperwork for employee file including termination, counseling, disciplinary documentation, accidents, injuries, and so on.

Purchasing—The GM will be responsible for the purchasing of product and supplies to properly operate the restaurant. Each department will order as necessary but the GM will be accountable for the expense.

Financial and Profitability—The GM is responsible for working with the ownership to maximize sales and profits through menu design and management of food and labor costs. The GM is expected to work with the ownership in analyzing food cost, kitchen labor cost, occupancy, and supply cost as it affects the business. From this analysis the GM is expected to develop and implement a game plan to control future cost issues. The GM will be responsible to produce a complete and accurate physical food inventory on at least a weekly basis or as deemed necessary by ownership.

Quality Assurance and Sanitation—The GM must ensure strict adherence to the restaurants standard for quality of food to include:

■ freshness;

■ proper handling and storage;

■ proper use of cooking techniques;

■ proper and sanitary cooling techniques;

■ taste;

■ portion size; and

■ presentation.

Additionally, the GM must maintain high standards in all areas of safety, security and sanitation. All preventive maintenance, cleaning, and repairs are scheduled in a timely manner. All health department regulations are enforced on a daily basis.

Qualification standards include:

■ able to train and develop a large staff;

■ able to stand for a 8 to 10 hour shift;

■ possess strong leadership and team building skills;

■ 2 years of management experience;

■ 5 years of food service experience; and

■ exhibits excellent cooking and culinary technical skills.

Executive Chef

Job Description

The chef is directly responsible for the operation of the kitchen. This includes meeting our high standard on quality, operating a clean and safe environment, while achieving cost goals. The chef works as an integral part of the management team and works to build sales and guest satisfaction to help grow the business.

Specific Duties and Responsibilities

Menu Development—The chef will be responsible for developing a menu, which satisfies the restaurant market needs, recipes for the menu items, gross profit, and profit margin and plate presentations. The menu will be changed and updated as necessary. Special menus for private parties, special dinners such as wine dinners, and daily specials will be developed as necessary in a timely fashion.

Leadership—The chef is directly responsible for creating a fun, clean, upbeat and productive kitchen environment. Projection of a positive can-do attitude is required at all times. The chef is responsible for development of the kitchen staff in all aspects of kitchen operation including but not limited to culinary knowledge, safety and sanitation, proper equipment operation, and guest awareness.

The chef will also take the lead role in developing the menu knowledge of the entire staff and management team.

Personnel—Responsible for recruiting, hiring, training, and scheduling a quality kitchen staff, to ensure quality food being served in a timely manner to our guests.

Recruiting and hiring responsibilities include the following:

■ establish and maintain appropriate staffing levels and keep informed to any changes that may impact staffing needs (including special functions, holidays, and a staff member who may change availability or leave the employment of the restaurant);

■ ensure all kitchen employees' personnel files are complete and up to date in accordance with any state or federal laws;

■ keep turnover in the kitchen to the minimum so as not to have a negative impact on customer service or labor cost; and

■ conduct exit interviews to determine any trends that might be causing turnover among the ranks.

Training and development responsibilities include the following:

■ establish a training program where all employees are trained thoroughly in their respective positions prior to be allowed to operate solo;

■ establish a training program to ensure all employees are educated in the use of all equipment including proper knife techniques and equipment operation including cleaning and maintenance; and

■ establish a cleaning program all employees are familiar with and use proper sanitation procedures.

Administration responsibilities include the following:

■ complete biyearly review of all kitchen staff; and

■ maintain accurate paperwork for employee file including termination, counseling, disciplinary documentation, accidents, injuries, etc.

Purchasing—The chef will be responsible for the purchase of food items including seafood, dairy, produce, meats, poultry, and all other dry and frozen goods. The chef will also be responsible for placing orders through our main supplier for any other area of the restaurant that might need food supplies such fruit and dry goods for the bar.

Financial and Profitability—The chef is responsible for working with the management team to maximize sales and profits through menu design and management of food and labor costs. The chef is expected to work with the management in analyzing food cost, kitchen labor cost and supply cost as it affects the kitchen. From this analysis the chef is expected to develop and implement a game plan to control future cost issues. The chef will be responsible to produce a complete and accurate physical food inventory on a monthly basis or as deemed necessary by management due to high cost areas.

Quality Assurance and Sanitation—The chef must ensure strict adherence to the restaurants standard for quality of food to include:

- freshness;
- proper handling and storage;
- proper use of cooking techniques;
- proper and sanitary cooling techniques;
- taste;
- portion size; and
- presentation.

Additionally, the chef must maintain high standards in all areas of safety, security, and sanitation. All preventive maintenance, cleaning, and repairs are scheduled in a timely manner. All health department regulations are enforced on a daily basis.

Qualification standards include:

- able to train and develop a large staff;
- able to stand for a 10- to 14-hour shift;
- experienced in high-volume food sales;
- possess strong leadership and team building skills;
- 3 years of management experience;
- 7 years of food service experience; and
- exhibits superb cooking and culinary technical skills.

Sous Chef

Job Description

The sous chef is directly responsible to the executive chef for the operation of the kitchen during his or her shift and in the absence of the executive chef. This includes meeting our high standard on quality, operating a clean and safe environment, while achieving cost goals. The sous chef works as an integral part of the management team and works to build sales and guest satisfaction to help grow the business.

The sous chef position is recognized as a stepping stone to the executive chef position and the expectations are not the same for a sous chef as an executive chef but always upholding the standard is expected.

Specific Duties and Responsibilities

Menu Development—The sous chef will be responsible for assisting in developing a menu that satisfies the restaurant market needs, recipes for the menu items, gross profit and profit margin, and plate presentations. The menu will be changed and updated as necessary. Special menus for private parties, special dinners such as wine dinners, and daily specials will be developed as necessary in a timely fashion.

Leadership—The sous chef is always expected to project a positive can-do attitude. The sous chef is responsible for assisting the chef in the development of the kitchen staff in all aspects of kitchen operation including but not limited to culinary knowledge, safety and sanitation, proper equipment operation, and guest awareness.

The sous chef will also assist the executive chef in developing the knowledge of the entire staff in reference to the menu.

Personnel—Responsible for recruiting, hiring, training, and scheduling a quality kitchen staff, to ensure quality food being served in a timely manner to our guests.

Recruiting and hiring responsibilities include assisting the executive chef in the following:

■ establish and maintain appropriate staffing levels and keep informed to any changes that may impact staffing needs (including special functions, holidays, and a staff member who may change availability or leave the employment of the restaurant);

■ ensure all kitchen employees' personnel files are complete and up to date in accordance with any state or federal laws;

■ keep turnover in the kitchen to the minimum so as not to have a negative impact on customer service or labor cost; and

■ conduct exit interviews to determine any trends that might be costing turnover among the ranks.

Training and Development responsibilities include assisting the executive chef in:

■ establishing a training program where all employees are trained thoroughly in their respective positions prior to be allowed to operate solo;

■ establishing a training program to ensure all employees are educated in the use of all equipment including proper knife techniques and equipment operation including cleaning and maintenance; and

■ establishing a cleaning program all employees are familiar with and use proper sanitation procedures

Administration duties include assisting the executive chef in:
■ completing biyearly review of all kitchen staff

■ maintaining accurate paperwork for employee file including termination, counseling, disciplinary documentation, accidents, injuries, etc.

Purchasing—The sous chef, in the absence of the executive chef or by direction of the executive chef, will be responsible for the purchase of food items including seafood, dairy, produce, meats, poultry, and all other dry and frozen goods. This includes placing orders through our main supplier for any other area of the restaurant that might need food supplies such fruit and dry goods for the bar.

Financial and Profitability—The sous chef is expected to work with the executive chef and the management team in analyzing food cost, kitchen labor cost, and supply cost as they affect the kitchen. From this analysis the sous chef is expected to develop and implement a game plan to control future cost issues. The sous chef will be responsible to produce a complete and accurate physical food inventory on at least a monthly basis or as deemed necessary by management due to high cost areas.

Quality Assurance and Sanitation—The sous chef must ensure strict adherence to the restaurants standard for quality of food to include:

- freshness;
- proper handling and storage;
- proper use of cooking techniques;
- proper and sanitary cooling techniques;
- taste;
- portion size; and
- presentation.

Additionally, the sous chef must maintain high standards in all areas of safety, security, and sanitation. All preventive maintenance, cleaning, and repairs are scheduled in a timely manner. All health department regulations are enforced on a daily basis.

Qualification standards include:

- able to train and develop a large staff;
- able to stand for a 10- to 14-hour shift;
- experienced in high-volume food sales;
- possess the aptitude to develop strong leadership and team building skills;
- 3 years of food service experience; and
- exhibits superb cooking and culinary technical skills.

Assistant Manager

Job Description

An assistant manager is directly responsible to the GM for the proper operation of all departments when the GM is not on site. This includes meeting our high standard on quality, operating a clean and safe environment, while achieving sales and budget cost goals. An assistant manager has overall authority for the day to day operations of the business in the absence of the GM.

Specific Duties and Responsibilities

Leadership—An assistant manager is directly responsible for creating a fun, clean, upbeat, and productive work environment. Projection of a positive can-do attitude is required at all times. An assistant manager is responsible for development of the staff in all aspects of the operation including but not limited to specific job duties, customer awareness and service, and sanitation standards.

Personnel—Responsible for recruiting, hiring, training, developing, and scheduling a quality staff, which will ensure quality food being served in a timely manner to our guests.

Delegated Roles—An assistant manager may also be assigned specific roles by the GM for which the assistant will be held accountable. These roles may include sanitation management, staff training, or payroll.

Recruiting and hiring responsibilities include the following:

■ establish and maintain appropriate staffing levels and keep informed to any changes that may impact staffing needs (including special functions, holidays, and a staff member who may change availability or leave the employment of the restaurant);

■ ensure all employees' personnel files are complete and up to date in accordance with any state or federal laws;

■ keep turnover to the minimum so as not to have a negative impact on customer service or labor cost; and

■ conduct exit interviews to determine any trends that might be costing turnover among the ranks.

Training and development responsibilities include the following:

■ establish a training program where all employees are trained thoroughly in their respective positions prior to be allowed to operate solo;

■ establish a training program to insure all employees are educated in the use of all equipment; and

■ establish a cleaning program all employees are familiar with and utilize proper sanitation procedures.

Administration responsibilities include the following:

■ complete quarterly review of all staff;

■ maintain accurate paperwork for employee file including termination, counseling, disciplinary documentation, accidents, injuries, etc.

Financial and Profitability—An assistant manager is responsible to control costs is any area the GM has assigned to that manager. The assistant will be held 100 percent accountable for the costs in that area

Quality Assurance and Sanitation—The assistant manager must ensure strict adherence to the restaurants standard for quality of food to include:

- freshness;
- proper handling and storage;
- proper use of cooking techniques;
- proper and sanitary cooling techniques;
- taste;
- portion size; and
- presentation.

Additionally, the assistant must maintain high standards in all areas of safety, security, and sanitation. All preventive maintenance, cleaning, and repairs are scheduled in a timely manner. All health department regulations are enforced on a daily basis.

Qualification standards include:

- able to train and develop a large staff;
- able to stand for a 8- to 10-hour shift;
- possess strong leadership and team building skills;
- 3 years of food service experience; and
- exhibits some cooking and culinary technical skills.

Bar Manager

Job Description

The bar manager is responsible for maintaining a professional, clean, and inviting bar and pub atmosphere. The bar manager will have overall responsibility to the GM for proper operation of the bar and the performance of the bar staff.

Essential functions include:

- maintain proper inventories for wine, liquor, beer, and supplies to include but not limited to fruits, garnishes, glassware, and any supplies needed to properly operate the bar.
- perform a minimum of one bar inventory per month;
- interview, train, and hire bar staff;

- develop and maintain cleaning lists and responsible for bar cleanliness;
- help promote the bar business;
- schedule bartenders for shifts including banquets;
- responsible for costs in the bar area;
- take an active role as part of the management team; and
- write and perform bartender evaluations.
- be 100 percent responsible for the operation of the bar as part of the overall experience.

Qualification standards include:

- read, write, and understand English;
- ability to hire, train, and develop a bar team;
- working knowledge of accounting procedures;
- at least 3 years bartending experience;
- recommended by the GM; and
- professional, upbeat attitude at all times.

Bartender

Job Description

A bartender is responsible for delivering 100 percent guest satisfaction to both the guests at the bar and the guests being served by the service staff. The bartender must be knowledgeable, proficient, communicate well, clean, and at all times professional. The bartender has several areas of accountability. First, each guest must be dealt with in a professional manner and our standards of excellence must always be upheld. The bartender is responsible for all cash received over the bar and liquor, beer, wine, and supply costs. The bartender must remember at all times that he or she is not in business for him or herself but an integral part of the restaurant.

Essential functions include:

- provide maximum level of service to the restaurant standard;
- follow service delivery guidelines as outlined in the bar training manual;
- knowledgeable about our food menu, beer, liquors, and wines;
- offer food to all bar guests;
- prepare drinks in accordance with restaurant standards;
- provide prompt, efficient, and courteous service to the service staff;

- check ID of all patrons under the age of 25 and be able to assist service staff in determining the same;
- stock and maintain the bar in accordance with guidelines and ensure the following shift is set up prior to leaving;
- uphold all cash handling procedures and be responsible for the cash drawers and gift certificates; and
- clean and maintain bar areas at all times.

  Qualification standards include:

- read, write, understand, and speak English;
- able to stand for a 10-hour shift;
- able to lift, bend, and stoop;
- consistent cash handling skills;
- able to work independently;
- able to work as part of a team for the good of the guest; and
- able to work in a fast-paced, high-pressure environment and continue to smile.

Host/Hostess

Job Description

The host or hostess is responsible for greeting our guests with a friendly and courteous manner, and has responsibility for maintaining a smooth flow of our dining room. The host and hostess is responsible for dealing with guests in a professional, courteous manner. All decisions must be based first on what is good for the guest without hurting other employees or the physical plant.

Essential functions include:

- greet and seat guests;
- answer the telephone and handle calls;
- take preferred seating and confirm party reservations;
- assist service, bar, and busser staff;
- maintain front door so it is inviting to our guests;
- maintain all menus;
- communicate with staff regarding special needs of guests;
- complete side work; and
- complete additional projects at the discretion of management.

Qualification Standards

> read, understand, and speak English;
>
> able to stand for an 8 hour shift;
>
> able to work independently and make decisions when necessary; and
>
> able to contribute to the team for the benefit of the guest.

Server

Job Description

A server is responsible for delivering 100 percent guest satisfaction to our guests at all times. A server must understand that everyone in the restaurant is our guest and their guest and not just the people at their table. A server must be knowledgeable and comfortable talking about our food, beer, wine, and liquor. The server is directly responsible to deliver the guest a great dining experience. They must own the dining experience and understand that we build our business one guest at a time.

Essential functions include:

- provide maximum level of service to the standard;
- follow service delivery guidelines as outlined in the server manual;
- be knowledgeable about our food menu, beer, liquors, and wines;
- use sales techniques to enhance the guest dining experience;
- provide prompt, efficient, and courteous service to our guests;
- check ID of all patrons under the age of 25 that order alcoholic drinks;
- stock and maintain their tables and area of side work as designated by the shift captain; and
- uphold all cash handling procedures and be responsible for cash, gift certificates, credit card receipts, promotional, and voided checks.

Qualification standards include:

- read, write, understand, and speak English;
- able to stand for a 10-hour shift;
- able to lift, bend and stoop;
- consistent cash handling skills;
- able to work independently;
- able to work as part of a team for the good of the guest; and
- able to work in a fast-paced, high-pressure environment and continue to smile.

Busser

Job Description

The busser is responsible for clearing and cleaning tables after guests have left, so we can seat new guests in a timely manner.

Essential functions include:

■ stock and maintain side stations with all necessary supplies;

■ clear, wipe, and clean tables quickly, without disturbing surrounding tables;

■ reset table to _____ standards;

■ clean condiments, seats, and table tents as needed;

■ maintain clean floors in the dining room and surrounding areas; and

■ check and maintain restrooms every half hour.

Qualification standards include:

■ frequent bending, stooping, and lifting;

■ carry up to 50 pounds of glassware and plateware;

■ able to communicate with staff and management the needs of customers and tables that are open and ready for seating;

■ able to interact with guests in a professional, pleasant manner, understanding that while not directly serving the guest, their needs must be fulfilled;

■ always have an upbeat and positive attitude;

■ always have a clean professional appearance; and

■ no experience required.

Food Runner

Job Description

The food runner is responsible for delivering food, hot foot hot and cold food cold, to our guests and responding to their needs for anything that will make their dining experience more enjoyable.

Essential functions include:

■ stock and maintain designated side stations with all necessary supplies;

■ deliver food to guests using the pivot point system;

■ respond to the needs of the guests and any requests they may have for any item that will enhance their dining experience;

■ communicate with the service staff concerning the needs of their guests; and

- maintain table when delivering food so unnecessary plateware, silverware, and glassware are cleared.

Qualification standards include:

- be able to read, speak, and understand English;
- frequent bending, stooping, and lifting;
- carry up to 50 pounds of glassware and plateware;
- able to communicate with staff and management as to customer's needs;
- able to interact with guests in a professional, pleasant manner, understanding that while not directly serving the guest, their needs must be fulfilled;
- always have an upbeat and positive attitude;
- always have a clean professional appearance; and
- no experience required.

Line Cook

Job Description

The line cook prepares food to order according to our standards of recipe, quality, and timing. In preparing food, all sanitation, cleanliness, and safety standards are to be maintained. Additional accountabilities include any guidelines the chef may require to properly serve our guests.

Essential functions include:

- set up, maintain, restock, clean, and organize work area;
- prepare food according to our procedures and standards within allowable time lines;
- responds positively to any guest's special request;
- safely operates all equipment; and
- practices proper and safe food handling, storage, receiving, and rotating stock,

Qualification standards include:

- lifts and carries sacks, boxes, and product of up to 50 pounds from floor to above waist level;
- stands and walks during 8- to 10-hour shift;
- hazards include but are not limited to cuts, burns, slips, trips, and falls;
- performs job at continually high pace, under pressure, while maintaining quality standards;
- reads and understands English;

- interacts verbally with other line positions;
- works closely with other staff members, usually in confined areas;
- flexible in performing other related tasks as designated by management;
- meets all restaurant standards for safe food handling;
- must be able to reach, bend, stoop, and wipe;
- must have experience and knowledge of kitchen equipment, including but not limited to: knives, slicer, salamander, stove, oven, mixer, and fryer; and
- requires experience by:

  ___Fryer   ___Sauté   ___Pantry   ___Broiler   ___Expo

Prep Cook

Job Description

The prep cook prepares food in accordance with _____ standard recipes. Maintains assigned par levels of food items while keeping the kitchen and all work areas clean and organized. Prepare food items to recipe with regards to quality, consistency and time standards, thus creating satisfied guests and help to build sales. The management team may assign additional accountabilities.

Essential functions include:

- uses knives correctly and safely;
- completes assigned tasks within the allowable time standard;
- follows all recipes and procedures;
- cleans and maintains work space;
- follows sanitation and safety standards;
- safely operates and maintains cleanliness of equipment;
- receives, stores, and rotates food items; and
- performs other assigned duties from the management.

Qualification standards include:

- reads and understands English;
- lifts up to 55 pounds and carry short distances;
- hazards include, but are not limited to cuts, burns, trips, slips, and falls;
- stands and walks during 8- to 10-hour shift;
- able to work closely with other staffs, at a consistently fast pace while performing a variety of "time constraint" tasks;
- must reach, bend, stoop, and wipe; and
- previous experience required.

Dishwasher

Job Description

The dishwasher is responsible to maintain kitchen dish area and equipment in a clean and orderly condition, while ensuring all plateware, glassware, silverware, and cooking utensils are clean for use by the staff and guests and cleaning of the restaurant as determined by the management team. This cleaning will include but not be limited to the kitchen, guest areas, and restrooms. Ensures that dishware, glassware, utensils, and so on are consistently clean; dish machine is working properly and chemicals are correct; kitchen work areas are clean and safe. Additional accountabilities include cleaning and responsibility list as determined by the management team.

Essential functions include:

- scrapes food from dirty dishes and places them in dish racks, washes all utensils, glassware, and dishware;
- washes pots, pans, and other cooking equipment by hand;
- sorts and removes trash to dumpster;
- sorts and stocks clean glassware, utensils, and dishware;
- changes dish machine chemicals and water frequently; and
- clean a variety of work and dining areas as directed.

Qualification standards include:

- able to stand for 8- to 10-hour shift;
- frequent bending, stooping, lifting, and reaching;
- frequently works in a hot, damp, and small workspace;
- lifts and carries racks of up to 45 pounds, up to 80 times per shift; reaching and placing these on high shelves;
- works mostly indoors but will spend part of the shift working outdoors on trash runs and general exterior cleaning—cleaning includes any cleaning duties assigned by management including restrooms, hallways, and basement areas;
- hazards include but are not limited to cuts, burns, slips and falls, back injuries;
- able to communicate with staff regarding needs for utensils, plateware, and so on;
- flexible in performing other related tasks as designated by the manager; and
- no experience required.

Training Guides

Each position in the restaurant, from manager to dishwasher, must have a training guide. The training guide should be used to make sure that any person filling any position comprehends the standards. In order to do this, it is important to have the standards on paper. The following guides will give you an idea of the type and amount of training each position should receive. There is nothing more important that an owner or manager can do than train their employees. The employees are the ones that are interfacing with guests, the end user of your product. It is guests that votes to spend their money in your establishment. Your salespeople must be trained how to deliver that service.

Orientation

On the first working day for all employee or manager, they must adapt to a new environment, new people, and a change of routine. This will naturally be accompanied by nervous energy and anxiety. This anxiety will make it difficult to learn and absorb information. Therefore, all employees and managers should be required to attend an orientation. The main goal of orientation is to get the new team member to become comfortable with the people and the surroundings. This comfort level will help the new member learn the standards and their specific role more quickly.

Orientation should include the following:

Welcome to the team

Fill out all paperwork

- I-9 forms complete
- W-4 forms
- State tax forms
- Liquor liability form
- Issue guidebook and signed receipt

- Schedule availability sheet complete—should coincide with application
- Employee data sheet complete

Tour the restaurant

Discuss proper uniform

Brief history of the restaurant

Management team

Discuss teamwork and attitude

Review employee guidebook—policies and procedures

Review upcoming training schedule and put it in writing

Training will include a food running shift and host training

Place new employee in computer and show employees how to clock in and out

Where schedules are posted and how to request a day off

Busser Training

Introduction

The bus person holds an important position in delivering outstanding guest satisfaction. The bus person actually has several areas of opportunities to make or break the dining experience. These opportunities are what we refer to as "moments of truth."[1] Examples of these moments are:

- cleanliness of the table;
- cleanliness and availability of the condiments;
- crumbs or debris around and under the table;
- cleanliness of the table tents; and
- ceats and chairs being clean and free of debris.

The bus person will also have a direct impact on how fast we can reseat a table if one guest leaves and another guest needs to be seated. This is critical to the long-term success of the restaurant. If we can keep a wait to a minimum, then people are more likely to frequent our establishment. If we extend the wait, then people are more likely to look elsewhere.

The busser needs to work hand in hand with the wait staff as well as the host staff—assisting where needed and communicating constantly with both the host and wait staff.

The following training outline will detail the training necessary to properly perform your job.

Day One

- Attend a pre-meal
- Review table numbers
- Learn the chemicals used and why
- Proper bussing techniques

1. clearing dishes and where to place tray (bus tubs are not allowed)
2. wiping properly and using clean towels
3. checking under the table and all condiments
4. resetting the table properly
5. communicating with the host team
6. proper stacking of plateware—remember the dishwasher is part of your team and help them by properly stacking plateware and silverware
7. where to place bar glasses
8. changing out bar bus tubs
9. interaction with the guest—minimal, but they may ask you questions— be ready to properly respond

You will be working with another busser. This will allow you to get your steps down. If you have any questions feel free to ask. We are here to help. Tip out from servers and bartenders will depend on how quickly you turn their tables, as well as how well you clean their tables. After the shift, the manager will evaluate you.

Food Runner Training

Introduction

The food runner is an important part of delivering a great dining experience to a guest. There are times when a food runner will make or break the dining experience through their moments of truth. A moment of truth is any time when the guest can form an opinion about our restaurant. This can be positive or negative. Examples of these moments for the food runner are:

- delivery of food to the right person;
- making sure that all extra silverware and condiments are delivered with the food;
- asks if the guest needs anything else and then responds to it;
- proper communication with the servers; and
- the food runner must be knowledgeable about our food, beer, wine, and liquor so you can properly respond to the guest needs.

You must also remember that you are dealing directly with the guest and must be able to communicate their needs immediately to their server or personally be able to respond to their needs.

Day One

- Food class part one
- Liquor, beer, and wine training
- Attend a pre-meal
- Review table numbers
- Pivot point system
- Proper placement of food on tables and how to clear unnecessary plateware, silverware, and glassware
- Where to put cleared items
- Opening, running, and closing side work
- How to plate a service tray and carry it

Day Two

- Review day one including food
- Food class part two
- Liquor, beer, and wine basics
- Attend pre-meal
- Observe a server picking up food from the kitchen, tray placement, and delivery of food for first part of shift

After this day you will be tested on the food, wine, liquor, and beer. We are here to assist you, so if there are ever any questions, feel free to ask.

Server

Introduction

A server is the individual that has the most impact on the dining experience. The server is the individual that owns the majority of the interaction with the guest. Therefore, servers must be taught the standards of the restaurant and understand the impact they will have. The training program can not be minimized to account for previous experience. Each server must comply with the standards set by the restaurant and the restaurant should not settle to comply with the standards set by the server.

Day One

____Review any questions from orientation especially on policies and procedures

____Review clocking in and out procedures on POS

____Tour the restaurant and review table numbers

____Introduction of food menu Part I

____Review dining room service

- Table set up
- Pivot point system
- Reading a check from the kitchen
- Approaching a table
- Importance of check back
- Consolidation of steps
- Check presentation—express lunch/making change/not making the guest feel rushed)
- Hello/goodbye policy
- Smoking and nonsmoking section—how to work a smoking section.
- Can you get my waiter? How to handle this.
- Lost and found
- Restroom checks—why we do it and how to do it.
- Guest right of way
- Applications and interview times—we always talk to a potential applicant
- Dining cycle

Table Approach and Greet

Offer your name and let the guests know that you are there to ensure a great dining experience

Suggestive Selling

1. Beer, liquor, wine
2. Appetizers
3. Entrees
4. Add-ons
5. Desserts

Timeliness of Delivery

1. Drinks—2 to 3 minutes (frozen drinks, stouts, cask, and samplers will take a little longer)

2. Appetizers—6 to 8 minutes

3. Lunch entrees—10 to 12 minutes*

4. Dinner entrees—12 to 15 minutes*

5. Desserts—5 minutes

*Allow ample time for salads, soups, and appetizers.

Do not make the guest feel rushed! Check back for satisfaction 2 to 3 minutes after each course is served. Tasks include:

■ pre-bussing—if the guest does not need it, clear it from the table;

■ proper stacking procedure in the dish room—it is important to understand the tough job the dish people have and to help them out to better serve the guest; and

■ Check presentation and making change—do not use the terminology, "Do you need change?" Assume they automatically do and say, "I'll be right back with your change. Let the guest say, "It is all set."

Follow a trainer for the shift. This is the first day of hands-on training for the new team member. The trainee should always remain by the side of the trainer and not become a gopher for the trainer, nor should the trainee be pulled away to do anything else by another server or manager. Review in depth all of the above.

Day Two

_____Answer any questions from previous training class

_____Food review Part II

_____POS operation—use POS training synopsis

1. _____How to start a check

2. _____How to add on to a check

3. _____How to split a check

4. _____Credit cards, gift certificates, comps, voids (know the differences between comps and voids)

5. _____Review all pages, modifiers, abbreviations, and hot keys

_____Attend a pre-meal if one is given while you are in the building

_____Scheduled host shift to understand the flow of the restaurant

■ Seating guide and wait sheet

■ Preferred seating

- Telephone etiquette
- Intercom procedures
- Station charts and seating rotation
- Kids and how to handle
- Menu counts
- Stocking the host stand

Day Three

____Food quiz Part I (score of 85 or better is required to complete the day)

____Attend a pre-meal

____Bar training with wines and liquors and what we carry

- Basic drinks
- Wine service—offering, opening, and pouring
- How to garnish drinks
- Be positive and pleasant while waiting for drinks
- Carding the guest—third-party liability
- Questions to ask for martinis, margaritas, manhattans
- Spindling tickets

____Follow trainer

Day Four

____Food Quiz Part II

____Review previous day training

____Checking your station for proper setup before the shift begins

____Review opening, running, and closing side work and where they are posted

____Change bank

____Review steps of service and the time standards

____Review bread service

____Review cash out

____What we mean by reaching the WOW

____Serving the internal guest

____Remember, as you work the floor, we are a team and must work that way. The host, the server, the bartender, manager, cook, and dishwasher are all here for one purpose, *to take care of the guest!*

____Follow trainer

Day Five

_____Practice on POS using POS scenario sheet

_____Attend a pre-meal

_____Review table approach—actually greet guests during the meal service with trainer observing

_____Take orders and place in POS

_____Run food/Do side work/Clear plates and so on

_____Get checked out by shift captain

_____Sit down and review progress with manager

Day Six

_____Attend a pre-meal

_____Review any questions you may have with the trainer and be ready to take the final exam

_____Run shift solo with minimal assistance from the trainer—trainer will evaluate your performance and report to the manager. This is still a training shift. These tables belong to the trainer.

_____Take final exam—will include food, beer, wine, liquor, steps of service, policies and procedures, and general questions on the restaurant. *You must receive a score of 90 percent or better to be complete with training.*

Server Training Checklist:

Follow: _____Initial

Follow: _____Initial

Follow: _____Initial

Be Shadowed: _____Initial

Host Shift: _____Initial

Food Runner Shift: _____Initial

Food Quiz 1 Score_____

Food Quiz 2 Score_____

Beer Quiz Score_____

Wine and Liquor Quiz Score_____

POS Quiz Score

Final Score_____

Host

Introduction

The host presents the first moment of truth for guests. Host responsibilities include knowing the phone system, knowing the menu, seating guests, and ensuring each guest has a memorable visit.

Day One

The checklist

The phone system

Table numbers

Food class Part I

Retail responsibilities

Acknowledging a regular guest

■ Review the host manual and what the host position means to the restaurant.

■ First thing you do after clocking in is to go through the checklist to ensure the host area is set for the day.

■ It is important to know the proper operation of the telephone system. This includes the intercom as well as placing people on hold. Never let anyone sit on hold for a long period of time. In most cases, 30 seconds is the maximum but never allow them to sit for more than a minute. You own the phone call until such time that the caller has been taken care of.

Day Two

Review day one and answer any questions

Food class Part II

Host stand—observe the host positions and spend 30 minutes with each position Greeter, Seater, and Point

1. Greeter—When we run full staff, as we most likely will do on busy nights, there are three positions. The first position is the greeter. This is the individual that greets the guest. The responsibility here is to make sure the guest feels welcome and invited. Smile, open the door, and greet with a friendly, warm smile. You take their name and place it on the wait list, following the procedures outlined in the host manual. Make sure they hear you when telling them of the wait time. Give them a beeper and take the time to write down all the pertinent information.

2. Seater—The seater has the responsibility to walk a guest to the table and getting them comfortably seated. Sometimes a guest may request a certain seat. Always accommodate them and never say NO to a guest. If this action conflicts with the "Double Seating" procedure, just do it, inform the manager and the server. Also, it is okay to tell the guest that the server just started another table and it might be a few minutes before their server comes over to them. You informed them, now as a team we can beat that expectation.

3. Point—This is the individual running the wait. They take the sheets from the greeter and have the responsibility of ensuring people are seated in time.

As you can see, communication among these three is vital to properly running a wait and ensuring that our guests have an enjoyable experience. Communication is also important from the host staff to the server, manager, and chef.

Menu counts keep the kitchen informed of how many menus are out and what to expect. This is important early on a shift and late on a shift. Once on a wait it really does not matter how many menus are out.

Day Three

Beer, liquor, and wine class
Spend the rest of the shift at the door, answering phones and taking care of guests

Day Four

Take all tests—Host, food, general information test.

Kitchen Training

One of the places where restaurants fail to spend time training is the kitchen. The reason for this is usually cost. Sometimes it is due to tight labor markets where the cook is hired the day before the cook is needed for a busy weekend. This is a huge mistake and should be avoided under any and all circumstances. If cook are allowed to work their positions solo the first night at the job, you will probably be looking for a new cook by the end of the weekend. No one can be expected to walk into a new kitchen and deliver.

The cook also has never been introduced to your systems, your standards, and your plate presentation, and you can not possibly hold this person accountable because he or she will have no idea what to expect. Take the time and train them properly. Do not allow anyone to work in your restaurant his or her first weekend with you. Allow them enough time to get familiar with your systems and your expectations. Take the time up front to teach them.

Day One

Food class

Cheat sheet for stations

Sanitation and its importance

Position set up

Specs and recipe book

Observe the person working your position

Break down station and clean up

Day Two

Set up station with minimal help

Run position with assistance and ask questions

Break down station

Review day with chef or sous chef

Day Three

Set up station

Work station on own

Break down

Take the food test

Review test and work with chef or souse chef

The first days should be the slower days so kitchen help can get their steps down. The second week should be basically the same and staff should be up to speed by the second weekend.

Bar Training

Training a bartender is quite a bit different than training a server, host, or cook. Many of your staff will work toward being a bartender and you will usually have a waiting list of people. Remember that the best server does not make the best bartender. Good bartenders are very hard to find. If you happen to find a personality that you believe would make a good bartender, then you must give them the skills necessary to be successful. The following bar training manual should give some insight as to what is expected from a bartender.

As far as standard pours and drink recipes, those are specific standards you must set. However, there are several good guidebooks in the market such as Mr. Boston Bartending guide. Usually, a good bartender or bar manager can recommend what is normal for your area. Once you set the standard, all bartenders should use the same standard.

Bartending

The Basics

Bartending is a unique business and profession unto itself. A bartender is "on stage" at all times. Unlike the server, the bartender has no place to hide. The bartender is constantly being watched. A bartender must be multitalented and multitask-oriented. He or she must be able to speak to one guest about sports, another about current events, make change for a twenty, take a drink order from one guest, describe the daily specials, and make drinks at the service bar, all at the same time.

The stress level can overwhelm the average person if not properly prepared. "Properly prepared" does not mean knowing liquors and drinks. Of course, this is a big part of being successful. Knowing the drinks, while maintaining calm under pressure, while holding conversation and keep smiling, is the key to a successful bartender.

The bar, especially in a brew house, is a major source of income for the restaurant as well as a focal point for the guest. Bartenders must understand the relationship between themselves and the restaurant. There is a balance between building a good business and doing what's positive for the business, and being out for oneself. Working for themselves and advancing their own income, without regard to the overall success of the restaurant, is not acceptable under any circumstance.

A bartender must be a salesperson and tour guide. Most people that sit at the bar are looking for social interaction as well as a good cocktail, glass of wine, or beer. Many people will eat at the bar. They are also looking for that social interaction. Guide them through the experience and you will succeed in creating a great atmosphere and a great business.

Remember, when the doors open, it's show time.

Criteria to Be the Ultimate Bartender

The characteristics of a great bartender follow:

- good sense of humor;
- great personality;
- conversationalist;
- ability to make great drinks;
- sense of urgency;
- attention to detail;
- knowledgeable in many areas;
- confident;
- ability to prioritize and consolidate; and
- always smiling.

Always give guests 100 percent attention. Going to the corner to complete the daily crossword puzzle is not being a good bartender. Be aware of your guests and focus on delivering a great experience to each and every one of them:

- make eye contact;
- remember to always smile; and
- maintain enthusiasm.

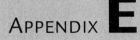
Forms and Checklists

Many forms and checklists can be used in the course of day-to-day operations. These forms can become cumbersome and time-consuming. They are not meant to be that way. Forms and checklists should be tools to assist in managing the business more effectively, not to consume time so managers can prove they are performing their job duties. If checklists and forms become the business, stop and evaluate what is being done. Adjust the following forms to specific need and only use those that are necessary.

CASH HANDLING

I understand that during the course of my shift I will be collecting cash and credit card receipts from guests. I also

understand that I will be responsible for this cash, credit card receipts, Gift Certificates redeemed and promotional

certificates and all other tender used in lieu of cash.

Mishandling of any of the above could result in disciplinary action up to and including termination.

Signature_____   Date_____

FIGURE A—1
Cash Handling

DAILY ROSTER
Manager

AM
Servers:

1. _____
2. _____
3. _____
4. _____
5. _____
6. _____
7. _____
8. _____
9. _____
10. _____
11. _____
12. _____

Host:

1. _____
2. _____
3. _____

Bar:

1. _____
2. _____
3. _____

Busser:

1. _____
2. _____

Runner:

1. _____
2. _____

FIGURE A—2

Daily Roster

INTERVIEW FORM

DATE_____

NAME_____

POSITION_____

FIRST CONTACT_____

SECOND INTERVIEW_____

FIRST INTERVIEW

1. Introduction
2. Explain screening process…2 interviews plus references
3. Small talk to put applicant at east
4. How did you hear about us?
5. Position desired
6. Days and shifts available
7. Number of shifts expected
8. Rate of pay or weekly money requirements
9. Is there any transportation problem getting to work?
10. Can we check references and what do they say about you?
11. We may have to do training on days that you have other obligations. For initial training purposes, are you willing to rearrange your schedule to get through the training?

SECOND INTERVIEW

1. Why are you interested in a job with us?
2. What do you enjoy most about working in a restaurant?
3. When you're not working, what do you enjoy doing?
4. Tell me about a tough situation you had to handle at work.
5. What does it take to be a good (Position)?
6. What do you like or dislike about your previous job?
7. Probe any questions that may arise from the application such as employment gaps, reasons for leaving the jobs, movement down when leaving.
8. Will you have any problem with not being able to smoke at work?

Explain training and how important it is to the restaurant. Let them know we take it very seriously and the purpose is to se the individual up for success.

Notes

FIGURE A—3

Interview Form

Reference Check

Employee_____   Date_____

Name of Reference 1_____	
Phone Number_____	
Is candidate eligible for re-hire? Yes [_____] No [_____]	
Was candidate dependable and team oriented? Yes [_____] No [_____]	
Would you recommend this candidate for employment? Yes [_____] No [_____]	
Manager_____ Date_____	

Name of Reference 2_____	
Phone Number_____	
Is candidate eligible for re-hire? Yes [_____] No [_____]	
Was candidate dependable and team oriented? Yes [_____] No [_____]	
Would you recommend this candidate for employment? Yes [_____] No [_____]	
Manager_____ Date_____	

Name of Reference 3_____	
Phone Number_____	
Is candidate eligible for re-hire? Yes [_____] No [_____]	
Was candidate dependable and team oriented? Yes [_____] No [_____]	
Would you recommend this candidate for employment? Yes [_____] No [_____]	
Manager_____ Date_____	

FIGURE A—4
References Check

AREA	Responsible	Second	Notes
Kitchen			
Hiring			
Training			
Ordering			
Cleanliness			
Inventory			
Food Cost			
Scheduling			
Bar			
Hiring			
Training			
Ordering			
Cleanliness			
Inventory			
Scheduling			
Health Inspections			
Banquets			
FOH			
Hiring			
Training			
Supplies			
Cleanliness			
Scheduling			
Administration			
Employee Documentation			
Payroll			
Banking & Bills			
Marketing			

FIGURE A—5
Areas of Accountability

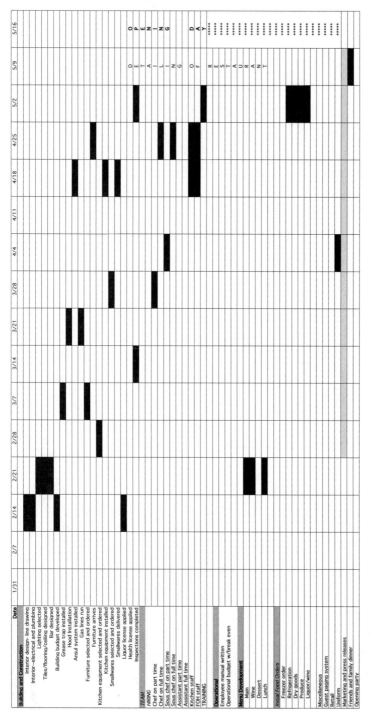

FIGURE A—6
Operational Timeline

Item	Size/Style	Brand	Price	Quantity	Extended Price	Book and Page
Flatware						
Teaspoon						
Iced tea spoon						
Bouillon sppon						
Dinner fork						
Knife						
Steak knife						
China						
Large rounds plain white						
Large pasta plain white						
Small rounds						
Bread and butter						
Large platter						
Tea–coffee cup						
Bouillon cup						
Oil and vinegar cruets						
Ramekins 2 ounce						
Tea pots						
Tabletop						
Salt and pepper						
Sugar caddy						
Ashtrays--Glass (simple pattern)						
Pepper mills						
Glassware						
Pitcher						
Sampler/Sidewater						
Martini						
Red wine						
White wine						
Champagne flute						
Rocks						
Highball						
Brandy						

FIGURE A—7—1
Inventory Checklist

Item								
Beer Pilsner								
Beer English Pub 16 ounce								
Pint glass								
Irish coffee								
Pots Pans and Utensils								
Steam pan full 2"								
Full 4"								
Full 6"								
1/2 size 4"								
1/2 size 6"								
2/3 size 6"								
1/3 size 2"								
1/3 size 4"								
1/3 size 6"								
1/4 size 4"								
1/6 size 4"								
1/6 size 6"								
Adapter bars (Might be with unit)								
Lid full size								
Lid half size								
Lid 1/3 size								
Lid 1/6 size								
Mixing bowls 8 qt								
13 qt								
30 qt								
Heavy-duty stock pot 60 qt with spicket								
Pasta warmer								
Sauce pot 3 3/4 qt								
Sauce pot 5 1/2 qt								
Fry pans 10"								
Bake pans								
Brazierre								
Measure alum 1 cup								
Measure alum 1 qt								
Measure 2 qt								
Measure 4 qt								
Dredges								
Loaf pans								
Saute pan steel								
Rolling pin								

FIGURE A–7–2
Inventory Checklist

Ice scoops					
Ingredient scoops					
Pastry bags					
Pastry brushes					
Pastry tips					
Dough scraper					
Cooks fork 22"					
Pastry spatula					
Cutting boards					
Solid spoons 15"					
Solid spoons 11"					
Slotted spoons 15"					
Slotted spoons 11"					
Ladles short handle 2"					
Ladles 1 ounce					
Ladles 3 ounce					
Ladles 4 ounce					
Ladles 6 ounce					
Ladles 8 ounce					
Skimmer					
Tongs spring 12"					
Grill brush					
Scoops #10					
Scoops #8					
Utility carts					
Whip, French					
Whip, piano					
Measuring cups sets					
Measuring spoons					
Tomato corer					
Pound scale					
Ounce scale					
China cap fine					
Can opener					
Mandoline					
Thermometer, pocket					
Wine bucket					
Pie pans					
Fry skimmer					
Grease filter holder					
Grease filters					

FIGURE A—7—3
Inventory Checklist

Perforated spatula							
Cambro Storage Bins							
Full size							
Half size							
1/3 size							
1/4 size							
Cam square food containers 22 qt							
18 qt							
12 qt							
8 qt							
6 qt							
4 qt							
2 qt							
Drip pan inserts							
Round storage container 22 qt							
18 qt							
12 qt							
8 qt							
6 qt							
4 qt							
2 qt							
Sizzle platters							
Spatulas red handle (heat protected)							
Dish room							
Bus pans							
Silver cylinder							
Silver baskets							
Dish rack dolly							
Dish rack peg							
Dish rack open							
Dish rack glass							
Dish rack cups							
Garbage cans full size							
Slim jims							
Server tray stands							
Server tray large							
Server tray medium							

FIGURE A—7—4
Inventory Checklist

Item					
Server tray small					
Server tray cocktail					
Miscellaneous					
Mop bucket					
Mop handle					
Mop head					
Wringer					
Wet floor signs bilingual					
High chair					
Booster seats					
Bissels					
Vacuum					
Ticket spindles					
Floor squeegee					
Squeegee for dish rack					
Brooms					
Dust pans					
First aid kit					
Diaper changing tables					
Ketchup marrier					
Bar Supplies					
Ice scoop					
Liquor pour spouts					
Store and pours					
Fruit trays					
Wine openers					
Mixing glasses with strainer					
Sip stix					
Swords					
Bar cutting board					
Salt rimmer					
Muddler					
Bar glass washer					
Bar spoon					
Bar mats					

FIGURE A–7–5
Inventory Checklist

Paper Supplies					
Cocktail napkins					
Dinner napkins					
Paper roll towel brown					
Toilet paper					
Straws					
POS paper					
Trash bags					
Toothpicks					
Day dots and dispenser					
Kitchen Paper					
Foil					
Film Wrap					

FIGURE A—7—6

Inventory Checklist

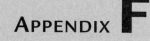

Pre-Meal Topics

Pre-meal is a set time, say 20 minutes before a shift, where the entire team gets together to discuss the day. Pre-meals should include:

1. daily specials
2. points of focus for the shift, that is, teamwork, placing orders properly, pre-bussing, and so on;
3. public praising of any team member that has done something above and beyond;
4. introduction of new team members; and
5. contests.

Pre-meals should be upbeat, fun, and educational. If it is raining, do not go to pre-meal and say, "Oh well, it will probably be slow because of the rain." The staff will walk away wondering why they're working if it is going to be so slow. Be upbeat and motivational. This is a great time to check for proper uniform and grooming standards. Also, the manager should not do all the talking. Let the staff get involved.

Topics:

1. proper plate presentation;
2. menu review;
3. salesmanship;
4. consolidation of steps;
5. service stories from your restaurant or another;
6. wine review and proper wine pouring techniques;
7. safety and security;
8. liquors and drinks;
9. communication between kitchen, service, bar, host, and management;
10. reading the guest;
11. how to learn and remember names (fun contest here);

12. sanitation;

13. teamwork;

14. upcoming charity events and why we should be involved;

15. delivering great service and how to recognize poor service; and

16. looking through the eyes of the guest.

This list will just get you started. Discuss any area of service or food that an employee has to know. The main point of delivering a great pre-meal is to plan it, be enthusiastic about it, and make it a priority.

Recommended Reading

Clement Ojugo, *Practical Food and Beverage Cost Control*. Copyright © 1999 Thomson Delmar Learning ISBN 0-7668-0038-5.

Jim Sullivan and Phil "Zoom" Roberts, *Service That Sells*. Copyright ©1991, 1995 by Pencom International ISBN 1-879239-00-0.

Kenneth Blanchard, PhD; Donald Carew, PhD; Eunice Parisi-Carew, EdD. *The One Minute Manager Builds High Performing Teams*. Copyright © 1990 by Blanchard Family Partnership, Donald Carew, and Eunice Parisi-Carew ISBN 0-688-10972-1.

Mary L. Tanke, *Human Resource Management for the Hospitality Industry*. Copyright © 2001 Delmar a division of Thomson Learning, Inc. ISBN 0-8273-7321-X.

Philip Hunsaker and Anthony J. Alessandra, *The Art of Managing People*. Copyright © 1980 by Philip Hunsaker and Anthony J. Alessandra ISBN 0-671-62825-9.

Stephen R. Covey, *The Seven Habits of Highly Effective People*. Copyright © 1989 by Stephen R. Covey ISBN 0743269519.

Stephen R. Covey, *Principle-Centered Leadership*. Copyright ©1990, 1991 by Stephen R. Covey ISBN 0-671-74910-2.

T. Scott Gross, *Positively Outrageous Service*. Copyright © 1991 T. Scott Gross ISBN 0-942361-40-7.

Glossary

86 A term used in the restaurant industry meaning "out of a specific product". For example, "86 salmon" would indicate to the staff that the restaurant is out of salmon. *Fun Note:* There are several rumors as to the origin of this term. The most common is that a restaurant, years ago, would allow employees to have a shot of 86 proof whiskey when they were cut for the day. The employee would tell the bartender they were 86'd and then have his shot of whiskey.

A

accounting period The period of time, such as monthly or quarterly, that business owners use to account for and analyze their business. This analysis is often used to compare same period sales from a previous year, purchases against budget, etc.

accrual method of accounting The bookkeeping technique that realizes sales and expenses immediately when incurred, not when money changes hands. Many businesses have lines of credit and may not pay for inventory or services for 14, 21 or even 30 days after receiving goods or services.

Americans with Disabilities Act (ADA) The Americans with Disabilities Act (ADA) prohibits discrimination on the basis of disability in employment, state and local government, public accommodations, commercial facilities, transportation and telecommunications. To be protected by the ADA, one must have a disability or have a relationship or association with an individual with a disability. An individual with a disability is defined by the ADA as a person who has a physical or mental impairment that substantially limits one or more major life activities, a person who has a history or record of such an impairment, or a person who is perceived by others as having such an impairment.

areas of responsibility A list of duties to be performed.

assets Cash, marketable securities, property or any item of monetary value.

B

bacteria Bacteria are the foremost concern for food service operators because most cases of food-borne illness are bacteria-related and include Escherichia coli (e. coli), Salmonellosis (Salmonella), Shigellosis, Campylobacter and Botulism. Bacteria are living organisms that absorb nutrients through their cell walls.

balance sheet A spreadsheet accounting for all assets and liabilities of a company. The difference is known as "equity".

base price method A method of assigning a price to a menu item. Once the price is assigned, the menu developer backs into an acceptable food cost objective. The set price may be competition or market driven.

boxing A way of highlighting an offering by placing it in a box on the menu. These items are frequently a high profitability item or a signature dish of the restaurant. Boxing is used sparingly to draw the eye of the reader to that part of the menu.

branding Building a name and image for a product or service that becomes clearly identifiable in the marketplace.

break even analysis An analysis conducted to determine the break even point of a business

break even point The point at which enough revenue is generated to satisfy all expenses, but no net profit is realized.

building line drawing An initial drawing of the building, showing the layout of walls, restrooms, equipment, etc.

building permit A permit issued by the local building department that grants approval for construction.

C

C corporation The most common form of corporation, the C Corporation is not limited in the number of shareholders it can have. This type of corporation will also pay taxes on any profit that may be realized and may distribute the profit to the shareholders who will then be liable for their portion of the profit. (Note: At the time of this writing this "double taxation" was under review by the United States Congress.)

Center for Disease Control (CDC) The government agency that investigates outbreaks of food-borne illness, studies the causes and control of disease, and publishes statistical data.

certificate of occupancy (CO) Issued by the local building department, the CO allows for public assembly in a building. The CO is usually not issued until all of the associated departments (electrical, plumbing) have inspected work completed under their control.

change order Issued once the work has started, a change order is either work that was not foreseen or a change that owner would like to make once work in underway.

check average The median dollar amount spent per customer during a given meal period. A dinner check average is expected to be more than a lunch check average.

coaching and counseling The role of a manager to help team members perform their jobs more effectively.

competition pricing Setting a price similar to other restaurants in the market.

concept The theme that defines how the market views the restaurant (steakhouse, seafood, Italian). The concept will define the direction of the menu as well as influence the décor package and menu price points.

conflict management To address any conflict between individuals or groups, and find a positive outcome for all parties involved.

construction manager The individual hired to oversee the construction and supervise the contractors. The construction manager might not actually perform any of the work, but has overall authority to complete the project.

cost of capital The cost (interest, fees, etc.) associated with the capital needed to operate a business. Business owners must consider such things as interest charged for a loan or return expected for a sale in stock. Investors may be willing to invest a substantial sum of capital, but expect a higher return for their risk, whereas a bank may charge a lower rate but require more collateral for that loan.

cost of goods sold (COGS) The total of any costs associated with producing an item and selling it to the customer. This is used to analyze management's ability to control inventory.

customer feedback Constructive criticism, support, or general opinions from restaurant patrons. Customer feedback is either offered freely or solicited by management to help develop the menu offerings or pricing structure.

customer sensitivity The attitude management and staff take in understanding and responding to customer needs.

D

---

declining budget A system used to control operational expenses. In the beginning of the accounting period, a dollar amount or percentage of sales is assigned to each category. At the end of each week within that accounting period, the cost of each line item is entered displaying the balance left to be spent for that accounting period.

demographic Statistical information about a certain population.

dog A menu item with low unit sales and low gross profit

E

empowerment The understanding instilled in employees that they can take any reasonable action to ensure the positive dining experience of a customer.

F

federal employment identification number Issued by the Social Security Administration, and is the equivalent of a personal social security card, this number is mandatory with very few exceptions to conduct business in the United States.

feedback loop The cycle of information from customer to decision makers.

first right of refusal The right of a lessee to be given the opportunity to purchase a property or a building if the landlord decides to sell that property.

fixed cost A known expense that is constant and can be expressed in dollar terms.

focus group A small group of people representing a cross-section of the population brought together to provide feedback on a specific subject.

Food and Drug Administration The FDA is the central federal agency charged with ensuring the health and safety of the public through food, drug and cosmetic manufacturing and sales. The FDA, in addressing food and food safety, is mainly concerned with setting and enforcing standards at the source of production including livestock, produce, seafood and dairy, manufacturing, and packaging and distribution.

food-borne illness A illness that is contracted by ingesting spoiled or tainted food.

food cost objective The desired food cost for the restaurant. This number is a management tool to control food cost and should not hold more importance than profit contribution.

G

general contractor (GC) An individual or company that oversees the construction of a project. The GC will perform some or all of the necessary work, or may hire subcontractors that specialize in specific fields such as plumbing or electrical work.

geographic market area The acceptable distance to a restaurant that people would travel to dine at that restaurant.

grandfather clause An exemption allowing operations to continue under previous laws. For example, when building laws or codes change, some buildings cannot meet these new codes without financial hardship. Local authorities may set a grandfather clause in the new code allowing existing operations to continue under the old code.

gross profit Profit after the cost of goods sold has been subtracted from sales.

H

---

hazard analysis critical control point This system of food inspection was first developed for NASA to insure the astronauts were receiving safe food on their trips to space. The system follows food from the raw state to the prepared state when it is served to the customer. There are critical points during the process where the food is most susceptible to bacteria and other germs. These critical times are known as Critical Control Points.

health permit A health permit is issued by the local health agency stating that a food service operation may operate in the designated location.

heating, ventilation and air conditioning (HVAC) The systems, including duct work, that heat and cool the restaurant.

I

---

internal customer Any employee of the restaurant. Staff members should treat each other with the same consideration with which they treat paying customers.

inventory turnover The value of the inventory divided by the cost of the inventory. This helps management to understand how tightly inventory is being controlled. A low turnover, depending on the type of restaurant, could indicate too much inventory, which means capital is being tied up unnecessarily.

L

---

liabilities Debts owed by a company.

limited liability company (LLC) A hybrid of a sole proprietorship and a corporation. Unlike a corporation, there is no issuance of stock, which would limit transferability. However, an LLC has "pass-through" taxation, similar to a sole-proprietorship or partnership, and there are no ownership restrictions.

liquor license A license issued by the state or local governing board allowing alcoholic beverages to be sold.

local planning board Most municipalities have planning boards that set zoning regulations. These boards have the authority to grant variances that allow businesses to operate outside of the guidelines that have been set.

M

market research The process of learning what drives a particular market.

market saturation The condition occurring when the number of restaurants open in a particular area exceeds the market's ability to support them.

market segment A subsection of the target market with specific purchasing needs.

mark-up pricing A basic method of menu item pricing that divides the raw food cost by the food cost objective.

marrying down To transfer product to the smallest possible container.

menu engineering The layout and organization of a menu designed to influence customer purchasing decisions and maximize profitability.

menu price A calculation that divides the raw food cost by the desired food cost percentage. (Raw food cost = $4.50. Desired food cost percentage = 30%. Menu Price = $4.50/30% or $15.00.)

mission statement The stated purpose of the restaurant.

moments of truth Any moment when a customer may form an opinion regarding the restaurant (e.g. when greeted at the entrance or when reviewing the menu).

N

National Sanitation Foundation (NSF) The NSF sets standards for equipment manufacturers.

O

owning the dining experience A philosophy that every employee who has contact with a customer can positively impact his or her dining experience.

P

par level Determined by usage demands, the inventory of a product that should always be on hand.

parasite An organism that lives in, with, or on another organism.

partnership A business owned and operated by two or more individuals sharing responsibility.

passion An intense desire for or devotion to some activity, object, or idea.

performance appraisals Periodic performance reviews given to managers and employees to help increase effectiveness in the restaurant and aid in the development process.

pH level The level of acidity in food. The lower the pH level, the higher the acidity, which helps prevent the spread of bacteria.

plowhorse A menu item with high unit sales and low gross profit

point of sale The point at which an entry is made

price/value perception The perception by the customer that they are receiving value for the price they are paying.

profit and loss statement (P&L) The most widely used financial statement that indicates sales, costs and whether a profit or loss is being generated. When compared to the budget, management may be able to locate problems in the operation

profit contribution The difference, expressed in dollars, between sale price and cost, contributing directly to gross profit.

pro forma A future projection of what a business will generate in sales, expenses, and profit.

punch list A list of items that need to be finished by the contractor before his work is considered complete.

puzzle A menu item with low unit sales but high gross profit

Q

---

quick ratio The quick ratio is a snapshot comparison of liquid assets such as cash and marketable securities to liabilities. In the quick ratio, assets such as furniture, fixtures and equipment are removed from the equation to give a better picture of solvency. (Cash, marketable securities, and accounts receivable divided by current liabilities)

R

---

raw item usage This refers to how often raw ingredient is used in menu items. When the same raw ingredient is utilized in several menu items, the potential for spoilage is reduced.

repurchase intent The intent of a satisfied customer to purchase a specific menu item on a subsequent visit.

return on investment The rate of return an investor will expect when they invest in a business. The return on investment must be worth the level of risk involved.

road setback The minimum distance between a building and the road.

round table Similar to a focus group, a group of people brought together to discuss a particular subject offering management insight.

S

S corporation A corporation licensed through the Secretary of State for an individual or group of individuals to conduct business in that state. Stockholders in an S corporation are liable for taxes for their portion of stock ownership, whether or not that profit is actually distributed to them.

sales and use tax license Issued by the state, this license allows for sales tax to be collected.

sales mix A chart of how many of each menu item is sold.

sanitation management program A program set up by management to teach, plan, implement and control sanitation standards.

seat turnover A calculation (total customers divided by the total number of available seats) indicating how often a customer fills a seat during a particular meal period.

server station Located at specific areas throughout the restaurant, a server station is designed to help service staff better serve customers. A server station may contain silverware, coffee and tea, soft beverages, linens or napkins, condiments and any other item that the customer may require.

Serv-Safe A program developed by the National Restaurant Association that teaches food service safety.

signature items Specialty or unique menu offerings designed to build a restaurant's reputation.

sole proprietorship A business owned and operated by a single person.

standard operating procedure Acceptable staff actions and behavior in the completion of various tasks.

star A menu item that has high unit sales and high gross profit

strategic business unit (SBU) A revenue generator within the restaurant.

T

target market The specific segment of the population making similar purchasing decisions (grouped by age, income, gender, geographic location, or any other defining criteria) to which a business is designed to appeal.

time management The process of becoming more effective and productive through a detailed planning process.

truth in menu The concept that no menu item should be portrayed inaccurately, intentionally misleading the buying public (e.g. an item should not be labeled "homemade" if that item was purchased pre-made).

turnkey A business that is purchased, turned over to a new owner, and ready for immediate operation.

U

United States Department of Agriculture (USDA) In dealing with the nation's food supply, the USDA is responsible for the inspection and grading of meats, meat products, poultry, dairy products, eggs and egg products, and fruits and vegetables shipped across state boundaries.

use of funds and investment A detailed description stating how invested or borrowed funds will be used.

V

variable cost A cost that is directly affected by the volume of business, usually expressed as a percentage of sales.

variance A waiver of a certain zone or building use requirement.

virus The smallest living organism known, viruses attack living cells, reproduce in those cells and then explode, releasing the virus to attack more cells. They do not reproduce in food, but merely use the food to transmit the virus.

vision An idea of how an owner sees a restaurant operating and becoming successful.

volatility of cost The price fluctuations inherent with certain products, occurring outside the control of producers. For example, seafood may have a high volatility of cost due to fishing restrictions or inclement weather. Restaurant owners should take this variability into account prior to setting menu prices.

W

word-of-mouth advertising The expectation that customers, having dined at a restaurant, will share their experiences with other potential customers. This is the most effective form of advertising since no cost is involved.

workers compensation An insurance policy paid by an employer to cover lost wages for employees that are injured on the job. The rate for this insurance varies and can increase if claims against an employer are particularly high.

working capital The difference between current assets and current liabilities.

Z

zoning laws Laws written by local authorities dictating acceptable uses for certain land or geographic locations under their jurisdiction.

Index

Note: Page numbers in *italics* indicate material in figures.